THE WRITER'S TOOLBOX
Buying and Using a Computer
For the Literary Life

JANET RUHL

PRENTICE HALL, Englewood Cliffs, New Jersey 07632

Library of Congress Cataloging-in-Publication Data

RUHL, JANET
　The writer's toolbox : buying and using a computer for the
literary life / Janet Ruhl.
　　p.　　cm.
　ISBN 0-13-969429-3
　1. Authorship—Data processing.　2. Computers—Purchasing.
　I. Title.
　PN171.D37R8　1990
　808'.02'0285—dc20　　　　　　　　　　　　　89-48635
　　　　　　　　　　　　　　　　　　　　　　　　CIP

Editorial/production supervision
　and interior design: **BARBARA MARTTINE**
Cover design: **KAREN STEPHENS**
Manufacturing buyer: **RAY SINTEL**

 Published byPrentice-Hall, Inc.
A Division of Simon & Schuster
Englewood Cliffs, New Jersey 07632

The publisher offers discounts on this book when ordered
in bulk quantities. For more information, write:

　　Special Sales/College Marketing
　　Prentice Hall
　　College Technical and Reference Division
　　Englewood Cliffs, NJ 07632

Printed in the United States of America

10　9　8　7　6　5　4　3　2　1

ISBN　0-13-969429-3

PRENTICE-HALL INTERNATIONAL (UK) LIMITED, *London*
PRENTICE-HALL OF AUSTRALIA PTY. LIMITED, *Sydney*
PRENTICE-HALL CANADA INC. *Toronto*
PRENTICE-HALL HISPANOAMERICANA, S.A., *Mexico*
PRENTICE-HALL OF INDIA PRIVATE LIMITED, *New Delhi*
PRENTICE-HALL OF JAPAN, INC., *Tokyo*
SIMON & SCHUSTER ASIA PTE. LTD., *Singapore*
EDITORA PRENTICE-HALL DO BRASIL, LTDA., *Rio de Janerio*

Dedication

To Joanna, who, by learning how to read, brought back for me the glory of it all.

What is written without effort
is in general read without pleasure.

Samuel Johnson 1709-1784

CONTENTS

PREFACE   xi

ACKNOWLEDGMENTS   xv

PART I:
Thinking about Computers

1   **THE MUSE AND THE MOUSE:**
Do You Need the New Computer Tools?   **1**

The real cost of computerization. Will your computer be a tool or a toy? Worthless reasons for buying a computer. Justifications that make sense for the writer.

2   **THE TOOLS IN THE WRITER'S TOOLBOX**
AND WHAT THEY DO   **23**

What is a computer tool? Tools to produce and format manuscripts. Tools to organize your thoughts. Tools to organize information. Tools to organize yourself. Tools to get and share information. Tools to produce publications. Tools to manage your computer.

3 WILL USING A COMPUTER CHANGE YOU?   58

*Why you probably think you ought to hate computers.
Computers and faceless bureaucracy. The real issues
involved in opting for computer mode.*

PART II:
Tooling Up: Putting Together the Writer's Toolbox

4 PRIMING THE WETWARE:
Getting the Education You Need to Begin   72

*Filling the emptiness between your ears before attacking
the space on your desk.*

5 COMPUTER SCIENCE 101:
Everything You Need to Know to Keep
from Making a Perfect Fool of Yourself
with a Computer   80

*Why the confusion: some thoughts on computer jargon.
What computers do and how they really do it. An overview
of computer hardware and software. How computer logic
works. What is a computer program.*

6 THINKING ABOUT HARDWARE   108

*A brief history of hardware. The "Great Laws
of Hardware". The Good-Enough computer. Choosing
a computer family.*

7 CONFIGURING YOUR SYSTEM   128

*Choosing the processor. Memory. The BIOS. Disks
and Diskettes. Monitors. Keyboards. Do-It-yourself hardware
configurations. Aftermarket boards. Ensuring that your
system can grow.*

8 PRINTERS, MODEMS AND EXTRAS   149

*You're only as good as your printer. Types of printers. Modems.
Mice or is it "Mouses?" Other bells and whistles. Portable
computers. Accessories.*

9   WHERE AND HOW TO BUY HARDWARE   **167**

Do you want used equipment? Dealing with computer stores. The trouble with department stores. Mail order. Where to get up-to-date information. Why service and support should be the tie breaker.

10   CHOOSING YOUR WORD PROCESSOR   **183**

The sane approach to acquiring software. Building a cheap but useful software collection with disposable software. What should be in your starter set. Choosing a word processor. The most vital features of your word processor. Features that all "real" word processors have. Vital features for writers. Word processor features that are useful for writers. Features that are frills for the writer.

11   ACQUIRING MORE SOFTWARE TOOLS   **207**

How to select tools to organize your thoughts. How to select tools to organize other kinds of information. How to select tools to organize yourself. How to select tools to get information. Preparing now for Desktop Publishing later. The utilities you should own.

12   HOW AND WHERE TO BUY SOFTWARE   **228**

How important is support? Why is software so expensive? How to buy safely with mail order. The software alternative: almost free software. Viruses. How to find help choosing software.

PART III:
Using Your Tools

13   USING YOUR SOFTWARE TOOLS   **244**

Getting your bearings with the manual. Installing your program. Mastering your software and keeping it fun at the same time. How to tell when you're not a beginner anymore.

14   WHEN THINGS GO WRONG   **255**

Developing a troubleshooting mentality. The Troubleshooting Cookbook. When a program that used to work stops working.

When your program tells you something is wrong. If you can't get a brand new program to work. Problems that look like your hardware is broken when it really isn't. Signs that you do have a hardware problem. People to call for help and how to call them.

15 BACKUPS:
The Single Most Important Chapter
in this Book   **282**

Living each day as if it were your system's last. Why data gets destroyed. Types of backup for hard disk systems. Backups for the floppy disk systems. Scheduling backups. Rotating backups. Your computer fire drill.

A. SOFTWARE MENTIONED
IN THIS BOOK   **292**

B. HARDWARE BUYING CHECKLIST   **298**

C. COMPUTER COMPETENCE CHECKLIST   **301**

D. LIST OF COMPUTER USERS GROUPS IN THE
U. S. AND CANADA   **303**

E. GLOSSARY   **312**

INDEX   **319**

PREFACE

Do you, the writer, need a computer? What's involved in getting one and is it worth the hassle? Will your computer be more than merely a fancy typewriter? Can you buy a computer without impoverishing yourself or getting ripped off? And, once you've taken the big step of bringing a computer home, how do you get it—and keep it—running, without experiencing the hair-tearing frustration and work-destroying accidents so many new computer users have to go through?

This book attempts to answer all these questions and more.

It is written for real writers, people whose writing goes beyond generating one page memos: for creative writers, freelancers, journalists, students, researchers, and academics. It is written for writers just beginning to think about buying computers, for writers who already own computers but would like to make better use of what they have, and for writers who have become comfortable using computers at work but don't know enough about the systems they have been using to duplicate them at home.

This book is also meant for the many writers whose initial experiences with computers have been less than delightful, who have found out the hard way that they need some outside help to deal effectively with the confusing error messages, frozen keyboards, balky printers, and the other disturbances which more often than not are the computer neophyte's fate. This book gives the information they need to make their encounters with the computer pleasant and productive.

My qualifications for being the Dante who leads you through the computer inferno are these: I myself am both a writer and a professional computer programmer. I was a writer before I was a programmer. As a writer I sold works of historical biography and social commentary to mass circulation magazines, did academic research and a book-length masters thesis in the field of 19th century cultural history, and worked on several novels before a series of random events led me to learn programming. During this first phase of my writing career I loathed computers. My only contact with them was when they screwed up my bank statements. I assumed that computers were the province of dull technocrats: plaid-shirted, crew-cutted engineers, whose qualification for doing computer work was that they were good at math. Faced with a choice of learning a simple computer language or French for my graduate school exams, I dug out my fifteen-year-old high school textbooks and swotted the French.

Well, I've never gotten much beyond doing arithmetic on my fingers, but since then, driven by the need to make a living, I've learned enough about designing, coding and testing computer systems to have been able to make a decent living doing it for almost a decade. I was hired as a programmer by IBM in 1980. There I worked as part of a team developing a complex piece of computer software known as PROFS. This was one of the first computer tools designed both to handle word processing and to go beyond word processing to computerize other needs of knowledge workers. After several years with IBM I went on to work on my own as a highly-paid computer consultant.

As I've pursued my career in computers I've continued to write too. My first book, *The Programmer's Survival Guide*, sold well and was widely reviewed in the computer press. I've also written a series of monthly columns for *Computerworld*, the computer industry trade magazine, and I've sold feature articles to many other mainstream computer magazines. In the course of doing this writing I moved from working on large multimillion dollar industrial computers owned by multinational companies to working on my own computer setup, which I bought, software and all, for under $2,000.

Given that I've seen computers both as an insider and as an outsider, as a humanities-oriented writer and a technically sophisticated programmer, this book has a perspective different from that of other books that offer to introduce you to computers.

In my years as a programmer I came to realize that working with computers has precious little to do with math and a lot to do with understanding how people work and think. I also realized that the skills characterizing people who worked well with computers were the same skills that made for good writers and researchers: the ability to think logically, the ability to understand interrelationships in complex systems, and the ability to manage a lot of text. Working extensively with text-oriented software I've come to love what computers can do. I've come to perceive computers not as mathematical engines but as thought extension tools that are potentially far more and useful to the creative thinker—and writer—than to the bureaucrats and businesspeople who monopolized them in their early years.

My purpose here is to show you how to use a computer to its fullest to help with your work as a writer and thinker.

Right now you may have trouble seeing yourself as a person comfortable with technology. You may have had bad experiences with books that assume that if you are using a computer for writing you are either a business executive, a clerk, or a technician, or you may have encountered books that treated you like an imbecile, explaining what little subject matter they covered at the fifth grade reading level.

This book is different: written for writers, not typists, it respects your intelligence, provides you with the information you need to get going, and most of all, gets you—the writer—excited about what working with a computer can do for you.

The emphasis throughout is on giving you enough information so that you understand what is going on with your computer and are able to make reasoned decisions for yourself. Rather than tell you what computer hardware to buy or what word processor is best, this book attempts to give you the information and insight needed to make the decision that will be right for you.

This book is different too because it takes you beyond the familiar territory of word processing. As a writer your primary task is thinking, not typing. Therefore this book covers not just how the computer can set your margins and number your pages but how it can help organize your thoughts and bring order to the raw material you work with.

This book is divided into three main sections. The first section is designed to answer the question, "Do you really need a computer?" It attempts to give you a realistic idea of what owning a computer can and cannot do for you as a writer. It covers both the benefits of using a computer and the problems caused by bringing a computer into your life and work. It looks specifically at what a computer can bring to the many tasks that make up the writer's day and makes it clear that buying a computer is by no means for everyone, perhaps not even for you.

The second part of this book leads you through the confusing and expensive process of putting together a computer system. Its goal is to give you enough technical information so that you can understand what you are buying. It seeks to ensure that you understand what hardware and software you need. It shows you where to go for the latest up-to-date information about what is currently on the market. It prepares you to be able to resist high pressure sales tactics. It shows you how to find the best places to buy hardware and software. And last, but not least, it encourages you to explore the wealth of useful free and almost-free software available for your computer.

The third and last section of this book is perhaps the most valuable. It teaches you how to become comfortable using your new computer system. You will learn how to install and master your new software. You will learn who to turn to for help and how to approach them. And, unlike most other introductory books this one includes instructions on how to do your own troubleshooting. It provides detailed discussions of what to do when things go wrong. It teaches you how to tell the difference between a truly broken computer and problems caused by misunderstood software. Best of all, this book alerts you to the simple backup strategies that can prevent 99% of all computer disasters that afflict both new and seasoned computer users.

No book can make you an overnight computer expert, but this book was written to give you the guidance you need to begin the process of becoming a competent computer user and to encourage you to believe that the skills you already have as a writer are just the skills you need to master the new technology.

Good luck!

ACKNOWLEDGMENTS

I'd like to thank all the many computer consultants active on the Compu-Serve CONSULT forum who are always ready to answer my questions on any conceivable subject. In particular, I'd like to thank the following consultants for sharing with me their experiences working with new computer users and the perils their clients have encountered: Theresa W. Carey, Frank M. Cook, John Cornicello, Joan Friedman, Paul Graf, Stan Dvoskin, Peter Jagielski, Jim Kyle, David Moskowitz, Stuart M. Mulne, David Ramsey, Rob Sacks, Ellen Sander, Guy Scharf, Martin Schiff, and Conrad Smith. My apologies to anyone I've left out.

I'd also like to thank the members of the two computer users groups I have been active in, especially Richard Dill and Bob Zurek of Hartford, Connecticut's Hart /PC, and Mike Walker and Mort Sternheim of the Pioneer Valley PC Users Group in Amherst, Massachusetts. Special thanks are due to Denis C. Lozen for sharing with me his list of users groups.

This book would not have become a reality if it hadn't been for the advocacy of my original editor, Ed Moura, the support of my new editor, Paul Becker, and the work of production editor, Barbara Marttine. I was greatly aided too by Ed Yourdon, who encouraged me to write it and forced me to take seriously the claims of the Macintosh computer.

All errors, of course, are attributable only to myself.

1

THE MUSE
AND THE MOUSE:
Do You Need
the New Computer Tools?

Man is a tool-using animal...Without tools he is nothing, with tools he is all.

Thomas Carlyle, 1795-1881
Sartor Resartus

Shakespeare and Jane Austen managed to get along just fine without a computer, but the chances are, if you're a writer today, you are beginning to think you need one.

The reason is simple. Using a computer lets you get your hands on something that writers, unlike other craftspeople, never had before: tools. Julius Caesar and Charles Dickens did their writing using almost identical technology. Even for twentieth-century writers the lone improvement made to writing by the advent of the machine age was the invention of the typewriter, and its contribution to the writing process was only to speed it up a bit and make handwriting more legible.

Yet suddenly, within less than 10 years, a whole generation of technology went from birth to maturity—a technology that gives you, the writer, powerful new tools. Undoubtedly you have heard about the word processors that eliminate the physical drudgery of preparing and revising manuscripts. But the word processor is only part of the tool kit that the computer makes available to the writer. Beyond the word processor is a whole constellation of other tools: tools to help you arrange thoughts, tools to manipulate random bits of information, and tools to help you do research. The purpose of these tools is to make it easier to get control of the writer's raw material, the very facts and ideas that the writer transforms into written work.

There is no question that these tools are effective. There is no question that these tools are alluring. But these tools, with all their power, will only be worthwhile to you, personally, regardless of their potential, if you are ready for them—and not everyone is.

In spite of the representations of the world's best-paid sales force, getting involved with computers, even with all the recent advances, still requires a major investment on the part of the beginner: an investment both of cash and of effort.

I'm a believer. I've used a computer long enough that taking it away from me would leave me bereft. But I was a writer long before I was a computer user. I wrote, and sold my writings, long before I discovered these powerful new tools. And because of this I know that no one *needs* to use a computer to be a writer. And I've seen the downside of computer use too: the people who buy computer systems without understanding the magnitude of what they are getting into, who use them a little, run into trouble, and, feeling like idiots, put them away in the basement wishing they had never begun.

The key to being happy with a computer is to get a clear and realistic idea of what it can do for you, and a clear and realistic idea of what you will have to do for it, before you start the tooling-up process. Your involvement with the computer should resemble a courtship. Instead, for all too many new computer users, the relationship ends up being a lot more like an arranged marriage, with the computer salesperson playing the role of marriage broker and the face of the beloved revealed only after the point of no return.

The goal of this book is to give you the information you need to make an informed choice. And having a real choice means starting at the very beginning and asking whether, in fact, you really need a computer at all.

THE REAL COST OF COMPUTERIZATION

Computers Are Not Priced for the Starving Artist (Yet)

If you have just sold the movie rights to your novel, or if writing is something you do after you finish your day's work as a well-paid employee of Megacorp, you can probably skip this section. But if you are trying to make a living as a professional writer and going through what most writers go through—by which I mean that writing brings you deep personal satisfaction and tiny checks at irregular intervals—you are going to have to face the fact that the cost of a computer system will be a large expense when offset against your income from writing.

We all know that the cost of computer hardware has dropped at a phenomenal rate since the days when a computer as powerful as a pocket calculator cost several million dollars. But computers still cost enough so that they are not in the same category as food processors or popcorn poppers, items you can buy and forget. They are not even in the same range as microwaves and VCRs.

In 1989, while you could get a computer for less, the going rate for the hardware setup that included what you need to do serious work hovered around $1,500. And this amount covered only the machine, not the software tools you needed in addition to the machine.

If you can spend this amount without being overwhelmed by the kind of anxiety that will make you spend each session with your computer in a nerve-racking argument with yourself about whether buying it was the right thing to have done, you've passed the first hurdle. If not, the very good news is that there is absolutely nothing wrong with postponing the decision to computerize. In fact, there are a lot of good reasons to postpone buying a computer, even if you are dying for one right now.

Learning to Use a Computer Takes Time

Why is that? Because the really big investment that you must make in a computer is not the cash. It's the time and effort you will need to spend in order to figure out how to use it.

The dirty little secret that computer dealers don't want you to know is that computers do require a major effort on your part. While there have been attempts to market computers as if they were just another consumer item, these efforts by and large have failed, and the bulk of all computers sold today are bought by businesspeople who are able to pay—lavishly—for the help and hand-holding that new computer users require to help them master their new machines. The home market is opening up only very slowly and is confined in large part to people who have already gone through computer boot camp at work.

Computer manufacturers yearn to crack the home market. As a result you will see a lot of advertising promising that you can use such-and-such a system as soon as the incision from your lobotomy heals. And you can. But not to do the kind of things that computers are worth buying for.

The price for falling for this line of advertising is steep: You will be stuck using whatever kludgey software the computer company or the computer store got cheap. You will pay a lot of additional cash for things that you wouldn't need if you knew the slightest bit about what you were doing. But, worst of all, you will be left confused, scared, and helpless the first time something unexpected happens with your system—which usually occurs within fifteen minutes of your turning on the machine for the first time.

Working with a computer does not have to be painful. This book is based on the deep conviction that intelligent devotees of the humanities who flunked "Physics for Poets" are perfectly capable, indeed well suited, to mastering what must be learned to bend the computer to their will. But the reality is that doing this is going to require some mental effort, some study, and some time.

If you can accept this and have room in your life to spend a few months learning what the computer is about and going through the breaking-in process involved in using a computer, then the true cost of a computer is within your reach.

WILL YOUR COMPUTER BE A TOOL OR A TOY?

But even if you can afford a computer, in terms of both cash and effort, bringing a computer into your life makes sense only if it is a tool you need. A tool implies a job to be done and your ultimate satisfaction with a computer will depend on whether the jobs you need done are those the computer can simplify. What we are going to do next is try to sort out what a computer could do for you and at the same time clear up some of the misconceptions about what computers are good for.

The Key Is Quantity

Computers are good in situations where you have a lot of similar things to manage. This is because the real power of the computer only emerges when you have more stuff to deal with than you can count on your fingers or list on a notepad.

Writers do have lots of a lot of things: words, ideas, and even, sometimes, facts. This makes them among the few groups in the population who have a real need for computers. Among businesspeople who are the computer's biggest fans, word processing is universally considered to be one of the prime justifications for buying a computer, and the top word-processing programs are perennial best sellers. But you are a writer, not someone whose job is to produce a ceaseless torrent of memos and business letters. This means you still need to give some thought to whether using a computer for word processing is truly a reasonable justification for you.

Whether it is or not depends, to a great extent, on how many words you push around in the course of a week or month. If your writing is confined to the occasional thousand-word piece, you may very well not need a computer at all. This is not to say that writing even a page isn't easier with a word processor than without one, because it is. But if you write 30 or 40 pages a year you don't need a word processor in any real sense of the word "need," and having one will not make a significant difference in your writing.

Using a computer for word processing starts making sense when you are cranking out hundreds of pages or more a year. When writing begins to feel like typing. When you have to pay for secretarial help to prepare manuscripts.

When you are dealing in this kind of volume, the word processor opens up a whole new way of working which eliminates a lot of typing and makes it much easier to rework, restructure, and revise your work. If you are already dealing with thousands and thousands of words, buying a computer will be worth every penny.

But this is where you must be honest with yourself. Are you already turning out thousands of words or just wishing, with some emotion, that you were? Are you thinking of buying a computer with the hope that it will suddenly give you the power to be a better and more prolific writer? If so, there is a real chance that instead of doing this the computer will merely introduce another layer of confusion into your life, make it even harder to work, and in the end become a very expensive reminder that you had hoped someday to begin to write.

To a large extent the quantity test applies to all uses of the computer described in this book. The computer is a great tool for organizing facts, both those that must fit in structures and the more fuzzily-related ones. But if the only facts you need to organize can be stored in your desktop phone book, on a few note cards, or in your head, while a computer can make them easier to manage you don't *need* a computer to do this.

There is nothing wrong with buying a computer as a toy. In fact, buying a computer as a toy may be a great way to prepare yourself for the day when you actually need to use one as a tool. The pressure is much lower when you are not trying to deal both with deadlines and a confusing new technology. But it is a good idea to make sure you are clear on the difference between the computer that you will use as a tool and the computer you will experiment with as a toy.

COMMON AND FAIRLY WORTHLESS REASONS FOR BUYING A COMPUTER

The literature of computer puffery is full of embarrassing lists of reasons for bringing a computer into your home, penned by enthusiastic and copy-hungry journalists swayed by computer company publicists. Most of these reasons are rotten. There do happen to be some excellent reasons for buying a computer and we will get to them later in this chapter, but first let's dispose of some of the more worthless arguments you are likely to have heard for buying a computer.

Managing Finances

One of the most frequent justifications you will hear for buying a personal computer is that it is a wonderful tool for managing your finances. Is this false? No, it's quite true that a computer is unrivaled in the area of financial management. The problem is that most of us rarely have finances complex enough to make using a computer to manage them worthwhile.

If your finances boil down to balancing your checkbook and keeping some kind of fuzzy hold on your credit card balance, then the work involved in doing it on a computer is more trouble than it is worth. To computerize your finances effectively you will have to type in information about every check that you write and every charge that you make—after you have bought checkbook management software and figured out how to use it. Since most of your checks are probably written at places like K-Mart and the grocery store, having a computer that is capable of printing out beautiful checks is a total waste. And, if in the midst of using your financial management software you type in a single wrong digit, your monthly statements won't match your records and you will still have the same checkbook management problems you had before you bought the computer. For most of us the information produced by computerized financial management can more easily and cheaply be obtained using a calculator, pencil, and paper.

The computer will not be much help to you in managing your investments either, unless you have a large number of stocks and bonds and are a devotee of some form of chartism—the pseudoscience of predicting stock movements from past stock activity. You can get stock price quotes on-line, for a hefty price, but this is hardly worth thousands to you if you are tracking only one or two stocks. If your interest in stocks is limited to looking up a mutual fund in the newspaper once a day, then the computer is even less likely to be of use here.

What about managing the business side of your writing? If you manage your writing as a small business and track your income and expenses for income tax purposes, then a computer is nice to have around. There are several different kinds of software that you can choose from to track expenses or even, for that matter, to do your taxes, but again this will be of use only *if* you are religious about recording all appropriate tax-related information correctly in the appropriate place on the computer in a timely fashion.

Again, the key is volume. Tracking your business expenses, in and of itself, is a primary justification for investing in a computer only if you are successful enough as a writer that your business is very active and involves a great number of expenses and income items—more than you can comfortably manage with a single-entry bookkeeping system. When considering the effort and expense of a computer system this use is really only a nice extra.

Managing Home Information

Other commonly touted uses for computers in the home are cataloging your stereo collection and keeping track of recipes. But here, again, the amount of work involved is more than all but the most fanatic would be willing to put in. Do you really want to have to type in all your favorite recipes just so you can go to the computer, wait for the system to boot up, search for some collections of ingredients, print them out, and return to cooking?

Maintaining electronic phone books and calendars is another very common reason given for using a computer. If you already have a computer that you can justify for other reasons, having a system pop up your daily calendar, ring an alarm when it is time to remember something special, or find you the phone number of an editor is very nice. But if this is all you are doing with your computer then it probably falls into the category of conspicuous consumption.[1]

Giving Your Kids a Boost

A few years ago it was fashionable among those attempting to peddle home computers to Joe Sixpack to suggest that children not provided with computers would fall hopelessly behind in life. Fortunately Texas Instruments, whose TV ads were the most obnoxious proponents of this philosophy, failed miserably in the home computer market and discontinued their home computer product (suggesting that executives provided with computers can also fail miserably at life). Since then this particular claim has been advanced more quietly.

But it is still advanced. Forget it. Using a computer will not make your kids, or anyone else's kids, smarter. School is about mastering basic reading, writing, and thinking skills. You need to have already developed these skills before you can use a computer as anything more than a fancy, interactive TV. In fact, there is a good chance that if your kids start using a computer to play the video games that are sold in every mall it will seriously undermine their school work. Video games, particularly the

---

[1]Of course, if you incline toward conspicuous consumption, dropping your bucks on a nicely configured PC is a lot more interesting and mentally challenging than spending it on a Rolex watch or a mink! And if you have the PC around, you might be surprised at the useful things you end up doing with it!

better ones, are considered by many child psychologists to be addictive, and some observers are claiming that the arcade types of games can raise aggression levels, decrease attention span, and incline children toward violence. Even if your child is not blasting aliens out of the sky or wasting commando troops but just uses the computer as a word-processing tool, you must question how beneficial it is to use a spell checker on homework in place of looking things up in the dictionary and learning, in that admittedly miserable process, how to spell the core words that make up civilized English. Word processors are not available for college entrance writing samples, nor for that matter, college essay tests.

Computers are thought-extension tools, and the key to getting value out of their use is to have thoughts complex enough that such a tool can help. Children who have mastered the fundamentals of reading, writing, and thinking things through are ready to use a computer as a tool, and it will be useful to them precisely to the degree that they are sophisticated enough to *need* tools. If your child falls into this category, then having a computer around might be nice, and he or she may surprise you with the creative use they make of it. But this makes the computer a reward for already having learned what is needed to get ahead in life, not an aid to learning it.

Finally, there is no question that using a computer can help little children learn to read. But while computer reading programs may teach so-called "reading skills" such as letter and word recognition, there is serious question whether reading "skills" learned playing computer games, and reinforced by singing and dancing sprites rather than by the fruits of real reading itself, will encourage children to develop the basic reading skill: the desire to read books. Sadly, it may work against it.

Also, before adding your kids into your list of justifications, consider whether you really want to have to fight with whining children or sullen adolescents for time on your own computer, since it's guaranteed that once you do get one and get comfortable with it, every member of the family will come up with something that has to be done on the machine every night!

JUSTIFICATIONS THAT DO MAKE SENSE
FOR THE WRITER

So much for the junk, now let's get to the good stuff. What real justification can the writer find for investing in a computer system? Can the computer help the writer do useful and truly important things that would be difficult or impossible to do without it? What can the writer with a computer really expect to do?

Turn Out Decent-looking Manuscripts
Without Paying a Typist

If you have been paying typists to produce your manuscripts but are capable of typing yourself, then you may be able to justify a computer on this count alone. Manuscript typists usually charge a dollar or two a page. If your manuscript goes through more than one cycle of professional typing then the cost of the system may come in around the cost of typing a single book.

Most writers buy computers to simplify the mechanics of producing a large manuscript. However, while you will be able to replace the typist eventually, you will do so only after learning many things that the typist already knows and after wrestling with a lot of computer lore that you emphatically do not know now. If you are working on a book-length manuscript that needs to be in final form in the very near future, taking the money you were going to use for the typist and spending it on a computer and word-processing software and attempting to turn out a professional-looking manuscript yourself might be enough to put you in an asylum.

There is a simple equation that expresses the process involved:

Computer + Word Processor + Reams of Paper +
6 times the amount of time you planned to spend =
One Professional- Looking Manuscript

If you bear this in mind and give yourself a lot of leisure in which to master your system, then a computer with word-processing software *can do* a lot of things to make your manuscript look nice. The word processor lets you type in words and then effortlessly erase the ones you don't want. You can move a word, sentence, paragraph, or even pages of what you have typed to anywhere in the manuscript, leaving no trace behind. You can pick up pieces of one manuscript and stick them in the middle of another manuscript. And you can quickly find a word or words you are looking for using just a few keystrokes.

Besides letting you effortlessly change the text you type in, the word processor also helps you with the mechanics of making your document look right. Your lines automatically format in the correct number of characters per line and lines per page. You can get page numbers printed where they belong automatically, and you can even, in many word processors, automatically generate a properly laid-out table of contents or an index. You can check your work for misspellings and even get suggestions for the correct spelling of the word you were trying for. You can get the software to put a line at the top or bottom of the page with the name of the manuscript or any other text you want to appear on each page. You can make sure all your chapter headings and subheadings share a common format.

This may not sound like much in cold print, but once you get used to it on the computer you will, like thousands before you, quickly discover the flexibility that using such a tool gives to your writing, and soon find it very hard to work any other way. Being able to use such a word processor is the leading reason given by all computer users—in business or not—for having a computer.

WHAT ABOUT WORD PROCESSING MACHINES? But of course, you don't need to buy a computer to use a word processor. There are electronic type-writer-like word processor machines available now that provide many word-processing functions. These machines feature screens and may even use diskettes like computers do. Couldn't such a machine give you what you need?

To some extent, yes. Such a machine is a great advance over a standard typewriter. If such machines were priced at under $200 they might be a good compromise for the technology-hungry starving artist. Unfortunately, they cost enough so that if you buy one you will probably feel that you have to use it for a few years before you can justify spending even more on a true computer, so it is worth taking the time to look at the limitations of such word processor machines.

A major limitation is that such machines are not capable of handling manuscripts consisting of more than a fairly limited number of pages. They are designed for business correspondence: letters and memos. This means that you won't be able to take advantage of the many book-length-manuscript-oriented features that are available with computer-based word processors.

Such machines come with one set of functions built in and don't let you upgrade to a more powerful set after you become adept. In contrast, a single "real" computer can run any of a vast selection of word processors, meaning that as you become more sophisticated you can use more and more powerful tools and never outgrow your machine, as is all too easy to do with the limited word processor machines.

Finally, a word processing machine can do just one thing, word process-ing, while a computer can do anything you can find software for. With a word processing machine you can't take advantage of any of the rest of the tools discussed in the rest of this book. With the price difference between a word-processing machine and a bottom-of-the-line, but expandable, computer being just a couple hundred dollars, it makes a lot more sense to buy a real computer, rather than a glorified typewriter.

Cut the Time It Takes Your Publisher to Produce Your Book

You, the author, can help reduce the time it takes to get your manuscript published when you submit your manuscript in electronically readable form. This is particularly true if you write books. When you have a book manuscript accepted for publication it can take a year or more until the book comes out. A major reason for this painful delay is that after your manuscript is copyedited it has to be retyped for entry into the typesetting system that prepares the camera-ready copy.

If you can send your manuscript to the publisher in a computer-readable form, the lengthy and, for the publisher, expensive retyping step can be eliminated. As a result, your book may take much less time to produce.

While this is of the greatest benefit when your subject matter is current, even if you are writing what is intended to be timeless literature it is a lot more satisfying to see your book come out quickly.[2]

However you should be aware that if you take this route you may be increasing your own workload enormously, since it will be *your* job to put the copyeditor's changes, entered on a printout of your manuscript, into the computer file form of the manuscript when you accept them.

Effortlessly Put Together Outlines Good Enough to Sell Your Work

Simplifying manuscript production is useful, but for most writers the hard part is getting to the point where they have a manuscript that someone wants to produce. Getting their ideas into a clear and understandable form that can be sold to an editor is the challenge faced by most free-lancers and book writers. In fact, even when you aren't trying to present your ideas to someone else, it is still a real challenge to organize your thoughts in the early and often most difficult part of a writing project.

Most of us learned to work with outlines in school, but when using paper and pen, or a typewriter, the outline is at best a cumbersome way of summarizing the ideas that you have already come up with rather than an effective thinking tool. If you want to expand an outline written with pencil and paper, revising it and moving things around in it becomes too much work. Since many publishers want to see an outline as part of a proposal, writers do put them together, but it is not a pleasant job. Often the detailed outline is prepared at the end of the writing process as a selling tool, not at the beginning as an aid in the writing process itself.

This is where the computer offers a truly new and highly useful tool to the writer, a tool not available in the traditional environment.

---

[2]Actually the technology is readily available now that would allow your publisher to run a scanner over your typed manuscript pages and convert them into computer readable form. However don't hold your breath waiting for the publisher to do this, since most publishers tend to be conservative where technology is concerned and most are still slapping themselves on the back congratulating themselves for using computer input at all. It will probably take some time for all but the most forward looking publishers to start using this technology.

Computer-based outlining software allows you to put ideas down randomly, and then lets you connect them to each other in whatever way you choose. Outlining software enables you to move pieces of an outline around with just a few keystrokes preserving the relationship of outline items to each other or changing them as you wish.

And this is only the beginning. With these new, thought- sculpturing tools you can create different views of your outline with a single keystroke. For example, you can look at a version of the outline that includes only chapter heading and subheadings to get a bird's-eye view of the work, and then with just a few keystrokes you can look at a paragraph-level outline that lets you look at the relationships of individual topics.

Because you are able to work so fluidly with an outliner, you may find that you spend your time moving ideas around in outline form, instead of cutting and pasting your drafts. Extremely detailed outlines are easy to work with on the computer. In fact, you may entirely eliminate a couple of drafts from the writing process because the outline software lets you go deeply enough into your ideas during the planning stage so you can see that the sequence of ideas you originally came up with does not flow quite the way you had intended, or that there are structural problems in your very detailed outline that you would usually begin to see only after writing the first draft.

The outline created by quality outlining software is more than adequate to submit to an editor, and is often enough to sell an article or book idea, particularly since you can easily provide an editor with both high-level and detailed outlines giving different views of the same work.

Do Research in On-line Databases

You are probably aware of the many on-line databases that can be accessed from a computer using a regular phone line. Examples of these services are Dow Jones, for financial data; DIALOG, which claims to be the world's largest on-line research database indexing over 300 different periodicals and reports; PAPERCHASE, a medical database that indexes medical journal articles; and IQUEST, a census information database. There are many more. You usually get access to these services by subscribing to an on-line service like CompuServe, DELPHI, or GEnie, and then paying a surcharge or a cost per search for the use of the specialized database itself.

If you are a nonfiction writer who writes about topics where information is available on-line, being able to access one of these services might be a powerful justification for owning your own system.

However, you should be aware that searching on-line can be very expensive and makes sense only if it enables you to cut the hours you would have spent using your usual research techniques or if it provides access to information you could not get at all through other methods. Here the key is probably to try before you buy. If you have never used on-line databases and find the concept appealing, you can probably find a college or city public library that will do such searches for you for a slight fee above the on-line service charge. The library should also have lists of available databases and descriptions of what information they have available. You might be surprised to find that the information you were hoping to search for isn't accessible, or that what you receive could be gotten in a quick trip to the library and a scan of the periodicals index. Find out what the charge per search is too. Because these databases are usually used by businesspeople, their pricing structure may be prohibitively high. Rates of $10 a search or $25 an hour are not unusual.

Analyze Statistical Information and Share Mainframe Data

If you write academic papers you may be able to do any statistical work that is necessary on your own computer. In fact, if statistics are an important part of what you do this may in itself justify having a computer.

This is particularly true for those, like social scientists, whose statistical work uses standard routines and who can therefore choose from cheap, easily available statistics packages to get the job done. However, if you have been relying on an academic mainframe to do statistical work for you, you probably ought to try to get some statistical software from a colleague and test it on either their machine or a rental machine to make sure that the work you are doing can be handled by a PC class machine in the price range you are considering. Many statistical applications can be, but if you are doing state-of-the-art number crunching, you may find your machine tied up for hours slogging through the calculations that an academic machine could accomplish much faster.

If your work is dependent on using computer programs and files on a large mainframe computer, transferring the programs to your own system may be a Herculean undertaking, depending on what language your program is written in and what software environment it assumes. If you are sophisticated enough to be writing your own programs in FORTRAN on a mainframe, mastering your PC should be relatively simple (but still, sad to say, not painless). But transferring programs from one family of computers to another is generally a complex undertaking. Don't blithely assume that because you are buying a computer you can replace another computer your work is dependent on.

Again, if your data requires tremendous amounts of data entry that you can have done at no expense at a university, moving the whole operation to your own computer may only make your personal workload a whole lot heavier. You may be able to download the data you have already entered on the mainframe into files on your own system, but then again you may not. Mainframes store and process data in a multifarious number of ways, some of which are a lot easier for a PC to deal with than others. You will have to achieve a pretty sophisticated level of technical knowledge or have a very good friend at the university data center if you intend to try to use data that is currently stored on a mainframe.

At this, the planning stage, the main thing is to be aware that statistical work and work with mainframe data can be done, but that you can make no assumptions about how easy it will be to do until you do a lot more research. Each situation is different too. Assuming that you can do what the guy down the hall did to his data with his PC may lead to real disappointment.

Create Your Own Illustrations

One nasty discovery that many writers make after they have a book accepted for publication is that the publisher charges them for the cost of producing illustrations, deducting the expense from the author's royalty. The same is true of complex tables and graphs.

Computer software can make it a lot easier to produce illustrations, tables, and graphs, particularly those involving line illustrations, and can thus save you money. A great number of software products exist to produce graphs and charts of all kinds, most of them oriented toward the kinds of charts that businesspeople like to present in slide shows. Other programs allow you to create drawings either by using a collection of supplied graphics images or by creating your own. By hooking a piece of equipment called a scanner into your system it is even possible to take line drawings and halftone photos that exist on paper and convert them into computer-readable form, which you can then modify on the computer using specialized graphics editing programs.

The only caveat here is that the quality of your final illustration is almost completely a function of the sophistication of your printer, and unfortunately, a printer good enough for all your other needs as a writer may still not produce graphics output that your publisher will accept as camera ready, necessitating a further step in the production process and resulting in your having to pay for the illustration after all. In the attempt to produce your own illustrations you may also discover that your publisher has complex standards for how diagrams and charts should appear and considers your attempts woefully inadequate. For example, problems may arise with the shape of your arrowheads on flowcharts, the thickness of lines in charts, or the typefaces and sizes you have chosen. You will also find that the look of computer-generated halftone images in most cases is not up to the quality you would get from the publisher's art department.

If the problem is the quality of your printer you may be able to use a higher quality one if you know people who have better printers, if one is available where you or your spouse works, or if your local print shop has one installed as part of a desktop publishing service, as many are starting to do. In this case you may be able to use illustrations you created on your own system to produce camera-ready output printed on a borrowed or hired system. However, if the problem is more stylistic, then you will have to continue to depend on the publisher's staff or invest some time in studying how to produce professional-looking graphics.

Self-Publish

If you are interested in self-publishing, this may be the most exciting of all writer-oriented uses of the personal computer. Most self-publishing is done by offset printing from plates made from camera-ready copy. Desktop publishing computer software allows you to do the typesetting and layout on your computer so that you produce camera-ready copy, including graphics, without an intermediary.

But before you get too excited about desktop publishing, you must realize that it is one of the more difficult computer uses to master, and, even worse, unfortunately, the one computer application that you can't do effectively with the kind of relatively cheap equipment that it makes sense for the beginning computer user to buy.

All the other writer's tools that we discuss in this book can be run on a system priced under $2,000, using software that is cheap enough that if you hate it you can throw it away. But desktop publishing requires that you buy a high-quality laser printer filled with expensive type fonts and connect it to a computer that is at the middle or high end of the range for speed, which means an expensive machine. To top it off, for truly professional-looking desktop publishing you need to buy and master software packages that cost over $500 apiece. The experts at *PC Magazine* estimated at the end of 1988 that the very cheapest setup that would let you produce professional-looking desktop publishing output would run around $5,000 and that a truly decent system would cost several thousand dollars more. This is not the sort of thing you should plunge into until you know what you are doing.

If you build the kind of introductory setup described in this book, and master the kinds of software described here—which, though selected for beginners, is by no means simple-minded or second rate—in a year or two you may very well be technically sophisticated enough to be able to get started in self-publishing and to know what hardware and software you must buy to do it. At that point the availability of this technology means that you can truly be a publisher yourself, producing professional-looking books, not only for yourself but for others.

But to attempt to do this as a new recruit would be idiocy.

Although you should probably not plan to make this your central use of the computer at the very beginning, if you get the hang of using software and are interested in publishing for a specialized group, or plan to market your own books through mail order, desktop publishing might be a totally empowering tool.

Create Newsletters and Fanzines

The limitations we just mentioned apply only when you intend to produce typeset-quality output. Even without the top-of-the-line desktop publishing software, owning a cheap computer and some cheaper software *will* enable you to produce attractive, readable newsletters and the labels you need to send them out. (Sad to say, it won't help with the steadily increasing cost of mailing them.) Newsletters are the poor man's magazines, and having a computer makes producing them a lot easier.

The term "desktop publishing" has been hijacked and forced to mean "producing printed material that looks expensive." But you can do plenty of real publishing from your desktop if you are not hung up on making your output look as if it were produced by an expensive typesetter. And you don't need special software packages to do it either; you can have access to all the mechanical help you need just by using one of the several commonly available word processors that include some desktop publishing features.

All these word processors allow you to make your text flow into columns like a newspaper and let you use whatever typefaces (fonts) your printer is capable of for laying out headlines and subheadings. You can lay out blank space for illustrations you paste in later or, if you have illustrations created on the computer, a word processor like WordPerfect or MicrosoftWord can even print them out as part of the page. If funky communication rather than a corporate image is what you are going for, the inexpensive computer tools described here will put you in business.

But again, if you already produce such a newsletter and use a typist or outside help of some kind, don't plan to meet a Monday deadline with a machine you bring home the previous Friday. Mastering the subtleties needed to produce a newsletter on a computer, like everything else, takes time.

Incorporate Non-Roman Alphabets in Your Documents

If your writing is primarily scholarly writing in which you need to cite Russian, Hebrew, or Greek phrases, or use any of a great number of other non-Roman alphabets, you will find that there are specialty word processors available that can both display these alphabets on the screen and print them. These programs are available for the garden-variety computers you buy at your neighborhood computer store, although using them in the mode where you can see the foreign letters displaying on the screen may require buying some additional but easily available hardware.

Promote Your Work

While many of the business-oriented functions that tend to dominate the world of computer applications have little appeal to the writer, who, for example, is unlikely to waste time producing pie charts illustrating "Chapters Finished" or "Monthly Prose Production," one business-oriented function *is* of enormous use in making the writer's most unpleasant task easier—the ability to generate form letters custom tailored to the recipient.

Almost any word processor you buy will allow you to generate 15 copies of a cover letter for an article, automatically addressing each one to a different editor and inserting one paragraph into each one that is unique and points out how your work is suited for that publication's specific market. You end up with what looks like a customized letter. But it is really created by a "junk mail" routine, the same kind of routine that is responsible for sending you notification that you may have won big money in a magazine wholesaler's lottery. Although you use junk mail technology, your letter emerges looking identical to a customized letter, and only you know how many other editors got the same paragraphs.[3]

Since attempting to get published usually involves sending manuscripts out to dozens of potential publishers, automating this function is very useful.

Once you have a published work out in the marketplace the computer makes the ongoing task of publicity a lot easier too because you can store different paragraphs puffing your work on-line and assemble customized fact sheets or publicity releases tailored to the specific person you are trying to impress with your work.

Produce Professional-Looking Lecture Aids

If you lecture in public, modestly priced software lets you produce respectable lecture aids, such as overhead projector foils or simple charts and graphs. Certainly you don't *need* a computer to do this, but it's a nice side benefit to be able to do so, and the work you produce will have just that much more of the professional edge to it so that you appear to be an old hand at this sort of thing, even if this is your first public talk.

---

[3]Unless, as all too often happens, you put the wrong letter in the wrong envelope, but this is not the computer's fault.

Automate Teaching Responsibilities

If, besides writing, you also teach, there are further helpful tasks your computer can do for you. Software designed for teachers includes grade-recording programs and grade analysis programs, multiple-choice exam generators, lesson plan tracking systems, and even programs that let you design your own Computer-Aided Instruction flows.[4]

Make Electronic Contacts

Earlier we talked about on-line databases and the communications services that provide them. If you have a computer capable of going on-line you will find open to you the intriguing world of computer bulletin boards. Computer bulletin boards are, simply speaking, computers that store messages and other things and that run a special bulletin board program all the time. You can call these computers up over the phone line and read the stuff that is stored on them. They are operated by all kinds of people who have in common a love of communication with strangers. There are hundreds of these around the country and around the world.

When you call a computer bulletin board you can read messages left by other callers, leave messages yourself, whether addressed to specific people or to anyone, or you can get copies of computer programs stored in a program library on the computer. Some computer bulletin boards are part of bulletin board networks such as FIDONet. The way that these networks work is that each board's operator sends messages out nightly to another board on the network and receives new messages from yet another board, so that the system is like an enormous chain and messages from one board eventually reach all the others.

This means a message you leave on one board can be bumped around the country to all the other boards on the network. If you are trying to reach people with a specific interest that is not very widespread, messages on computer bulletin board systems may get you in touch with people all over the country who share your interest. You might also be able to find people to interview on obscure topics or people who can answer questions for you.

Besides these bulletin boards there are the megaboards operated by commercial communications services, one of the best known of which is CompuServe. These services, which we will look at in more detail in Chapter 2, allow you to post messages in special interest areas that may be read by literally thousands of people, a certain number of whom are sure to respond, beginning what can become months of on-line correspondence.

---

[4]Designing Computer-Aided Education scripts will be useful, however, only if the computers at school use the same operating system as the one you own. What an operating system is we will get to later in Chapter 5.

When you are plugging a book, these boards and commercial communications services may be of enormous help in locating people willing to review your book. If you are having trouble getting attention in the more obvious media, bulletin boards and on-line services may be a way to reach out to people who you otherwise couldn't get to, particularly if your work would be of interest to the kinds of people who tend to be what some call "Modem Junkies."[5] While hard-core computer enthusiasts and businesspeople make up the majority of those who use these services now, other groups are starting to use them too, people with interests ranging from maintaining food banks for the homeless to collecting rare tropical fish.

You might even let readers sample your work by putting excerpts in a file on a bulletin board or on-line service. These excerpts can then be "downloaded," or copied onto their own computers by people that call in. Some authors have put whole books out in such on-line files for people to read for free, asking for a contribution from readers who like their work. Science fiction writers and computer writers are heavily represented right now on-line, but as more people acquire computers and on-line capability, the general audience for all kinds of writing will grow.

Because you communicate on bulletin boards via the written word, this kind of interaction is particularly rewarding for writers, who so often send their writing out into a silent, unresponsive world. Messages you write and post on an electronic bulletin board often generate a rash of responses, also written, and can lead to phone calls, visits, and real friendships.

Indulge Other Creative Outlets

Writers are, by definition, creators, and many do not limit their creative outlets to the written word alone, but are involved in music or fine arts too. Therefore, before leaving our discussion of justifications for buying a computer system we should take a brief look at some creative functions that the computer can perform, other than its writing-related ones.

Perhaps the most powerful creative outlet your computer can open up is in the field of music. If you already own an electronic keyboard or a synthesizer that is MIDI compatible,[6] with the addition of some easy-to-install hardware you can turn your computer into a full-screen digital sequencer capable of representing hundreds of different tracks of music and editing every single feature of every single note you have played on your keyboard. If you have several MIDI-compatible musical instru-

[5]A modem is the piece of equipment that allows your computer to talk on the phone.

[6]MIDI stands for Music Interchange Digital Interface. All electronic instruments that are MIDI compatible can be hooked up to each other. They can also be hooked up and controlled by computer programs running on computers that are equipped with some hardware features that make them, too, MIDI compatible.

ments you can control them all simultaneously with these programs. You can also create and load voices into many MIDI-equipped tone generators. What this means is that with only a very limited ability to play music on a keyboard you can compose and play back sophisticated or even symphonic electronic music, the quality of which is limited only by your musical hardware and, of course, your musical intelligence.

There are many drawing programs available for computers. There are also many serious artists experimenting with computer-generated art. If you enjoy fooling around with software and are artistically inclined you can fill up many hours with this kind of thing. Perhaps the most fun and challenging visual arts computer applications that you can easily work on at home without very expensive equipment are animation programs that can take an original drawing and create "slide shows" or even animated sequences.

Deal with Creative Drought

Now to the darker and less comfortable moments of the writer's day. Not every day is there something to call to an editor's attention. There are long, dank, doubt-filled periods during which many of us feel that we have said all we could ever possibly have to say, or times when the sound of our own voice echoing off the paper is as irritating as the spiel of a telemarketer trying to sell us investment planning.

Most writers have to deal with such periods, except for those lucky and irritating exceptions prone to boasting in magazines that they never experience writer's block at all. How the writer deals with these periods is an idiosyncratic matter, and what works for one person makes another feel worse. So it would be misleading to suggest that use of a computer can magically lead the way back to the internal voice.

But the computer, in its incarnation as a writer's toolbox, does at least provide a new entry in the venerable list of cures for writer's block. You no longer need envy musicians who when they run dry of creative ideas, can still play exercises and keep their fingers on the keyboard, working away, feeling as if they are doing something musical, even when blocked.

The computer allows the writer, in his or her more empty days, to do something akin to playing scales: play with fritterware. *Fritterware* is a word coined by computer columnist Steven Manes to describe programs that have so many features that the user is tempted to fiddle with them endlessly, playing with all their capabilities, rather than doing real work. A typical fritter, for example, would be attempting to get an article to print out in three columns with hanging indents, and three different sizes of headlines when you know perfectly well that all you need is an 8 1/2"-x-11" piece of paper with the copy typed neatly double spaced!

Several of the tools that writers use, particularly the more powerful word processors, fall into the fritterware category. The writer who comes up blank no longer has to stare at a blank piece of paper. He or she can sit down in front of the keyboard, turn the power on, and putter around, playing with manuscripts, seeing how a different style sheet would affect the way they look, attempting to output a single graph exactly right, or just cleaning up old files and neatening things up in the electronic libraries.

Not only that, but there are vast libraries of programs, termed *public domain* software or *shareware* (discussed in more detail in Chapter 12), of which the salient thing you need to know now is that they are free or almost free if you want to try them out. Using these programs, which can be found on bulletin boards and elsewhere, the writer can while away many a pleasant afternoon trying out new programs to control the printer, drawing pictures on the screen, or even annihilating alien space invaders. Since some of these programs are distributed with rudimentary instructions on how to use them and require some ingenuity to get working, getting into frittering can become almost a full-time job in itself.

Days can go by this way with the writer busily working at the keyboard and not forced to deal with feelings of brainlessness. In fact, as the writer's computer expertise grows and he is able to pull off fancier and fancier stunts on the system, a new source of pride and feelings of accomplishment emerges. "This stuff is tricky, but I made it work," crows the writer, instead of, as in the old days, staring at a blank piece of paper and feeling worthless until driven to drink.

If computer frittering can break the cycle of panic that writer's block brings on, it can become a very positive way of dealing with the empty-brain syndrome. And when inspiration returns, the writer is right there, at the keyboard, ready to work, perhaps even with a better organized work environment and a few more tools, just like the musician who has finished his finger exercise and is ready to begin.

This is not, of course, for everyone. Some people hate learning complex software, are perfectly happy having mastered the rudiments of a single program that lets them type in their text, move it around, and print it. They have no interest in ever learning another one. Some people can begin playing computer games when blocked, and end up feeling like addicts, having deepened a sense of self-revulsion by having wasted so much time on nothing.

IT'S UP TO YOU

You may need no more justification for buying a computer system than the thought that it looks like it would be fun to own one. If it doesn't turn out to be what you were expecting, who cares—you can sell it or keep it around for the kids.

Or you may agonize for months over the decision to get one, telling yourself that you will feel justified in buying one when you finish the first draft of the novel or when you get a contract with a publisher, or when you sell three freelance articles that actually result in checks.

It's up to you. If nothing you've read so far sounds tempting, maybe it's time to put this book down, sit down at your typewriter (or notebook), and get back to work! If you change your mind next year you will probably be able to buy a much nicer system for the money that it takes to get a starter system now. That's how computer prices have traditionally worked. But if your interest has been piqued, let's go deeper. We've looked at the broadest level of what computer tools can do for the writer. Now it's time to look more closely at the many tools available in the electronic toolbox, so that you can get an even better idea of what these tools could do for you.

2

THE TOOLS
IN THE WRITER'S
TOOLBOX,
AND WHAT THEY DO

There will be little drudgery in this better ordered world. Natural power harnessed in machines will be the general drudge.

H. G. Wells, 1866-1946
Outline of History

Chapter 1 looked at the work you do as a writer and asked how computer tools could help you do this work. It looked at these tools and their functions in a very broad and general way, as its purpose was just to give you some idea of the tasks a computer could help you with. Chapter 2 looks at these computer tools again but in greater detail, so you can get a clearer idea of what the individual computer tools do and what is involved in using them.

The discussion here is, of necessity, more detailed. If you have been seriously flirting with the idea of getting a computer, then you may be very interested in this information. Although you've heard repeated claims about the power of the computer, the vagueness of those claims may have left you with no idea of what, really, the computer will do for you. This chapter attempts to make such computer encomiums more concrete, to help you make up your mind about whether you really want to go through the effort required to get your own computer.

If, on the other hand, your interest right now is more broad than deep, and you are not ready to consider computer tools in this kind of detail, feel free to skim the following descriptions and move on quickly to the next chapters.

WHAT IS A TOOL?

We have been throwing the term computer around very loosely, using it to refer to the metal and plastic box with a keyboard and a screen that sits on your desk, as well as the functions that box performs. This is really sloppy. So before we go on to look in more detail at computer tools we need to get a little more understanding of what computer tools really are.

When computers emerged into the popular consciousness, back in the days when we used to watch breathless TV specials about "Our Friend, the Atom," they were portrayed as "thinking machines." Society has become far less credulous about the glories of nuclear energy, but the idea of the computer as a mysterious thinking machine still lingers on, to the point where the majority of the population believes that computers, like living things, can actually get sick—by catching a virus.

This is reflected in how we talk about computers. People say the computer "knows" what typeface to use for business letters or that it "talks" to other computers on the phone. But, in reality, computers do no such thing.

The computer, as a machine, has no inherent "intelligence"—artificial or otherwise. The only inherent ability that computers have is the ability to run a computer program—a piece of software—a process not all that different from the way that a stereo plays a record. Without a program to "play," a computer can do nothing.

What Is a Program?

A computer program itself is nothing more than a long series of instructions that the computer executes, one after the other, which tell it in painful detail exactly what to do. And by saying that the program tells a computer what to do we do not mean that the program says "look for misspelled words" or "calculate the volume of a cube."

Instead, every impressive function that the computer performs is really carried out by being broken into thousands or even millions of very small, extremely generic, simple-minded instructions. These instructions are so simple and generic that the individual instructions used to find a misspelled word are the exact same ones used to find the volume of a cube or, for that matter, to do anything else that computers do. What differentiates the program that checks your spelling from the one that computes the orbit of the space shuttle is mainly the *sequence* in which the program gives the computer these generic instructions.

Computers can only do exactly what they are told to do by the sequences of instructions embodied in programs. So the designers of a program must think, beforehand, of every single event that could possibly come up during the use of their program. If something occurs that was not checked for and provided for in the program that the computer is running, the computer will be oblivious. It will keep doing whatever it is told, no matter how stupid, until it gets so tangled up that it can't find the next thing it is supposed to do, at which point it will stall and perhaps beep at you. That most programs do work most of the time is a tribute to the creative and imaginative gifts of their designers.

What makes these computers look smart in spite of performing what are in effect fairly simple-minded activities, is the speed at which they execute the instructions that make up a program. Zillions of simple generic instructions can be performed one after the other in a second or two, and the results can be pretty impressive.

What Is in a Software Package?

So much for what a program is to the machine. What does a program look like to you?

When you buy a computer program it generally comes to you re-corded on a diskette, the computer disk that most of us are familiar with. These diskettes are made out of exactly the same material as recording tapes: a Mylar plastic base and a metallic oxide coating that is able to retain a magnetic charge. What is recorded on these disks as a pattern of magnetized and nonmagnetized spots, is a "machine language" version of the program that the programmer wrote.[1] The program itself is often only one part of what is recorded on the disk. The disk most likely also stores in magnetic form information that the program uses for reference.

A word processing program, for example, may come to you in a package with 10 disks, but only a small part of those disks may actually contain the program. Because the word processor is designed to function with every printer ever manufactured anywhere on the earth, and because almost every one of these printers does something different from all the rest, the word processing program probably has reference files containing information that the word processor uses to communicate with any printer a buyer could conceivably hook up to his computer, even though you, personally, only need the information for one.

One disk in the package probably includes a spelling dictionary and another a thesaurus, both probably stored in a "compacted" form in which a special space-saving code has been used in place of the usual electronic form in order to save room. Another disk probably includes a program that "installs" the word processor—that is, picks out the pieces of control information you will need for your system and copies what is needed to the disk or diskette you will be using to store the working copy of the software.

---

[1]He did not, however, write it in "machine language" but in a human-readable, letter-based language. He then ran a computer program which translated it into the computer-readable form.

Some software packages are really clusters of programs with a master program that "calls" the subsidiary ones to perform specific functions, for example your word processor might have a separate printing program that it uses when you are ready to print a manuscript and that translates it into a form that your printer understands.

Some software tools, no matter how fancy their packaging, consist of only a single computer program, and may fill up only a small portion of the diskette. Others are like the word processor we just described and include many programs and masses of control and reference information. Some packages that you can buy at a software store actually are a whole set of different software tools performing loosely related functions. Some tools require very particular hardware configurations, others work on a broader set of machines, although as we will see when we look at software more deeply in Chapter 5, all programs are designed in such a way that they can run only on a single family of machines. For instance, a diskette containing a program packaged in a box that says "Apple IIe Version" would never run on an IBM PC.

You will learn a lot more about software later in this book, but for now you merely need to realize that when you talk about a computer tool, you are really talking about computer software—programs and their related bits and pieces—that you buy and run in your computer.

Now it's time to look at the tools you would use to accomplish the functions described in the previous chapter. You will see the broad range of tools available and learn about some of the issues involved in using them. In each section you will see, identified by name, products that fall into the group under discussion. These names are mentioned to familiarize you with popular products and to point you toward some programs worth investigating. However, the inclusion or omission of a product in these pages in no way implies that it is better or worse than other competing programs. I have used many of these programs but, as it is not possible to test all of them, I have relied on product reviews to supplement my knowledge. For a list of all products mentioned in these pages, including the companies that sell them, turn to Appendix A.

TOOLS TO PRODUCE AND FORMAT MANUSCRIPTS

Word Processors

Word processing is probably the computer application you are the most familiar with as a writer. It has a long and venerable history measured in technological time, meaning it goes back some 20 years.

Developed originally to produce customized form letters, the earliest word processors did nothing more than record what the typist typed onto magnetic tape or cards, which could then be "played" back. These protoword processors then typed the recorded words out to paper, perhaps stopping at specially coded spots in a letter to allow the typist to type in the nonform parts of the letter, such as the address.

These early systems were followed by systems that not only recorded what the typist typed—on computer disks by now—but also displayed it on a screen where it could be more easily revised. These word processors allowed the operator to type a document and save it, to move chunks of text around, to erase chunks of text, and to search for words in the text. They could also handle basic formatting operations, such as setting margins, centering text, and numbering pages, but not much more.

The spell checker, developed at the end of the 1970s, was the first really impressive addition to the word processor's repertoire and when first demonstrated it seemed almost magical. This new tool not only showed you which words were spelled wrong but came back and *suggested the right spelling!*

By the time the spell checker was developed, most word-processing software ran on either special stand-alone minicomputers or large industrial-strength mainframe computers where hundreds of users used the same computer at the same time, working at individual terminals. Because of the high cost of such systems word processors continued to be the province of junk-mail generating business users and could be afforded by only the wealthiest or most successful of writers. A handful of hardware vendors like IBM, Wang, and

TABLE 2.1   Tools to Produce and Format Manuscripts

Word Processors	Specialty Word Processors	Word Processor Accessories
Create, modify, format, and print text Number pages, set margins, manage typefaces Check spelling See Table 10.1 for features	Work with non-Roman alphabets Format equations	Stand-alone spell checkers Stand-alone thesauri Envelope addressers
Grammar Checkers	Graphics Software	Scanners and Software
Analyze syntax and flag errors Flag over-used phrases Rate readability Find typos that are correctly spelled	Create charts and graphs Draw and paint images that can be further manipulated by software	Read in printed text and translate to computer readable form Bring in illustrations in form that graphics software can work with

Lanier, controlled the word processing market and the only software available was what these vendors supplied with their machines.

But things were never the same after the personal computer revolution of the early 1980s. This revolution brought computers capable of running word-processing software into the price range of a much broader range of buyers. Though the first home computer and PC word-processing programs were not much to brag about compared to what was available on the stand-alone minicomputers, the sheer size of the market for word-processing software that could run on cheap machines stimulated an explosion of competition among word processor developers, which eventually led to the availability of first-class word-processing software for affordable personal computers.

As a result, there is now a dazzling array of software products calling themselves word processors, which run on the kind of cheap computer you can probably afford. *PC Magazine's* annual word-processing issue in 1988 reviewed some 55 word processors designed for IBM PCs and compatible computers, admitting that this was by no means all of the ones available. Software reviewer Dan Shafer, writing in *MacUser* in November of 1988, was able to profile no less than seven major Macintosh word processors powerful enough to serve the needs of professional writers.

Some of these word processors still provide only the more basic abilities to set margins, type in some text, change it and save it, and maybe move text around. But others can do tricks like automatically creating a table of contents from your paragraph and chapter headings, generating an automatic index and printing it at the end of your document, and even saving your document automatically while you are staring into space thinking, in case you should trip over your power cord and unplug the unit while overwhelmed by a great idea.

Some of these word processors communicate with you through easy-to-understand menus—lists of things that the software can do that appear on the screen in little boxes overlaying your manuscript. Other word processors make you memorize bizarre combinations of keystrokes, so that you may find yourself scratching your head and wondering does hitting the keys marked "Ctrl" and "F6" copy the sentence you just marked to a new page or does it erase it for good?

Some come with "tutorials." These are computer programs that teach you how to use the word processor, walking you through the functions like an instructor in a class and letting you execute examples. Others display so-called "context- sensitive help screens" that show you the appropriate explanation relating to what is in front of you on the screen at the time. Many, unfortunately, do neither.

Some word processors let you work on several different writing projects at once, switching from one to the other by hitting the appropriate key. Others allow you to work on only one. Almost all the word processors available now include some kind of spell checker. Some include a thesaurus, so that you can look up a synonym for a word you want to use. Some let you build footnotes and some let you control how and where these footnotes appear. Many have functions that simplify creating tables of data. Some create standardized headings and captions and even let you refer to a figure with a "floating reference" that always prints the right figure number and page number when you refer to a figure in your text, no matter how much you fiddle with the manuscript or how many additional figures you add. Some include a legal or medical dictionary for the spell checker, some even create a legal table of authorities.

Most word processors let you create junk mail by combining a canned letter with a mailing list. Some have special routines to create mailing labels from a mailing list. And, if all this is not enough, lately the trend has been toward adding fancy "desktop publishing" features, such as the ability to format your text into several columns per page, and to use the bewildering capabilities of laser printers to produce the kinds of typefaces and sizes that were only available from typesetters a few years ago.

All in all, it is exhausting just to contemplate the features that are available, and this list by no means includes all of them.[2]

To make it more confusing, if you go out to buy one of these the salesman is quite likely to end up trying to sell you something called integrated software. Integrated software refers to a single software package that includes, in one box, a set of programs that provide one program from each of the most popular families of computer programs, designed in such a way that you can easily use the data generated by one program in another. Since word processing is the number-one reason people use computers, all integrated software includes a word processor. The rest of the programs making up the integrated package are usually a database program and a spreadsheet, both of which are discussed later in this chapter.

Some hardware vendors, such as Leading Edge, Vendex, and Tandy, whose sales efforts target the "home" computer market rather than just the office market, even throw in a free word processor with the machine, although the quality of these varies widely.

Faced with this kind of complexity in the marketplace and with almost endless choices, most people ignore it. The sales figures show a few word processors way ahead of the others in terms of sales, and most people seem to jump on the bandwagon and buy one of these.

In the IBM world the "biggies" in terms of sales are WordPerfect, Microsoft Word, MultiMate, PC-Write, DisplayWrite, PFS:Professional Write, and Wordstar, although of course, the sales figures change constantly. WordPerfect appears to be the all-time winner by everyone's

---

[2]Chapter 10 provides a more in-depth look at the features available with various word processors.

count, and is likely to be what the salesperson recommends if you ask for one. If you are looking for word processors to run on the Macintosh family of computers you can get a version of WordPerfect here too, but many writers who work on the Mac prefer Microsoft Word, a program which was originally designed for the Macintosh and thus, some people claim, takes full advantage of its unique graphic interface. Other Macintosh word processors of interest to writers are Write Now (a descendant of Macintosh's original MacWrite program) and FullWrite Professional.

However if you hang around with publishing snobs they are likely to argue that all of the above programs pale to insignificance before XyWrite III Plus, which such snobs will claim is what "real" writers use. XyWrite is the word processor used on several magazines (including *PC Magazine* itself) and by Time/Life Books. If even XyWrite III isn't enough for you, consider Nota Bene, a XyWrite-like word processor chosen by *PC Magazine* as one of its picks for best word processor in 1988. Designed with the needs of academic researchers in mind, it comes with a built-in note management system, allows cross-references, and even gives you the ability to reformat your footnotes and regenerate your bibiliography as needed to fit the idiosyncratic stylistic requirements of any one of a long list of academic journals. If that isn't enough it also gives you the ability to work interchangeably in Hebrew, Russian, and Greek.

After you buy one of these word processors, and bury yourself in the books necessary for mastering it, you may visit a friend someday and be blown away by an "ease-of-use" word processor like Symantec's Q&A Word, a PC program that doesn't have as many features as some of the leaders but is so well designed that you can teach yourself how to use it almost entirely from the help screens. Unfortunately, a lot of these ease-of-use oriented word processors have been designed with the ease of the business memo scribbler in mind and unfortunately lack some features that are vital for any writer who works on longer documents.

Beyond these, there is a new kind of word processor emerging: the chameleon. Because there are enough users who have been working with particular programs for years and are "set in their ways," companies looking to market a new product to these people have started to realize that they are going to be able to sell their new product to users of other software only if that new product lets the user use his old keystroke patterns. Sprint, one of these chameleon programs, unlike most programs lets you choose what you would like the program to look like, in terms of what keys do what and what screens you see. The program comes with "user interfaces" that use menus and keystrokes that mimic a number of popular word processors like Word-Perfect or Microsoft Word, in case you are already used to using one of these, or you can design your own interface. Or, if you are new to word processing in general and have no ingrained preferences, you can use Sprint's own interface, which comes in two versions—a simple and an advanced model.

Specialty Word Processors

If your writing is scientific in nature and you regularly work with mathematical formulas, specialized symbols, and the Greek alphabet, you may be interested in a more specialized group of word processors designed specifically for the especially tricky formatting requirements and the alphabet changes that scientific writing requires. *PC Magazine* found no less than 12 of these specialized word processors to review in 1988. Yet other word processors allow you to prepare text in alternative alphabets, such as Hebrew with its right-to- left character movement, Tamil, Greek, Parsi, or Viet. In some cases these require that you install specific pieces of hardware to handle the screen display. In others, only the software itself is needed.

However if you choose to use these specialized features, your choices of word processor and of the features that come along with the package may be more limited than if you are able to use one that doesn't provide these specialty features. Undoubtedly as the competition between the market leaders continues, they will begin integrating these specialty features into their products too.

WYSIWYG

In reading descriptions of word processors you will often see the word WYSIWYG used. This word, pronounced "wizzy-wig" is an acronym that stands for "what you see is what you get." When applied to a word processor it means that the way that your text appears on the screen is exactly the way it will appear on the page. This is by no means the case with all word processors and there is some difference of opinion among people who use word processors about how important it is to have your word processor be WYSIWYG. Many word processors will display a double-spaced manuscript on the screen so that it looks single spaced. Others will display codes and other odd letter combinations on the screen when you select a particular fancy function, such as creating a footnote or changing type fonts. This probably is not an important issue for you unless you intend to use your word processor not only to create manuscripts but also to do layout and paste-up—desktop publishing—or if your manuscripts routinely include a lot of tables, lists, or other complicated paraphernalia making it useful for you to be able, as you create them, to see them exactly as they will print on the page so you can be sure that your output will look right.

Word Processor Accessory Software

If the word processor you buy doesn't have certain features, you can buy separate accessory programs that may help. Programs independent of the word processors can be bought that check the spelling of your prose, give you thesaurus look-ups, fancify your printout with nice fonts, address your envelopes, or build an index. These programs may run side by side with your word processor and "pop up" at a key stroke when you need them, or they may run as a separate step that you run after you have created your draft with the word processor and saved it.

Style Analyzers

Buoyed by the success of spell checkers, software developers have gone one step further and come up with programs that purport to improve your grammar, style, and readability. If the word "readability" makes you cringe, as it does me, then you might be tempted to go on to the next section. That might be a mistake. While these programs cannot provide the level of grammatical or stylistic help that the professional writer gets from a copy editor, they can come in handy. The problem is that to get to the useful stuff you have to sit through a lot of embarrassingly stupid features designed for illiterate memo scribblers.

Programs like Rightwriter and Grammatik III ponder your prose and flag constructions as "redundant," "ambiguous," and "wordy." They offer "fog indexes" and "readability indexes" that can tell you, among other things, what grade level of education a reader needs to understand your phrases and how your effort compares in "readability" with the average insurance policy. Most of this is pretty worthless for the writer who has passed English Comp.

These grammar checkers work by applying sets of rules which, though good enough to trap a lot of simple grammar mistakes, still run into trouble with grammatically complex English sentences. At their worst they may issue error messages when a writer uses complex dependent clauses (the analyzer may get confused as to parts of speech when it encounters subordinate clauses and prepositional phrases), an adult vocabulary (the analyzer will flag these as too hard to understand) or, heaven forbid, the passive voice.

Still, there may be a place on your computer for one of these programs. The most compelling reason is this: the best analyzers, such as Grammatik III, are very good at eliminating hard-to-spot typos—the kinds of things that can slip past a spell checker because the misspelled word happens to be in the dictionary. Such programs are also useful in controlling a tendency toward run-on sentences and the overuse of certain words and phrases. And unless your writing really is flawless, they may actually be useful in eliminating bad grammar. If you are willing to sit while the program erroneously flags 50 correct constructions, you may hit pay dirt when the grammar checker finally unearths one dreadful, illiterate phrase that somehow crept in while you were thinking about something else.

Given the impressive improvement in these programs over the past few years, it is just possible that eventually one will emerge that can function without seeming to be quite so much the idiot savant.

Graphics/Chart-Making Programs and Drawing Programs

So much for your words. What about illustrations? To create illustrations you will need to get some kind of drawing or business graphics program. You may also need some additional hardware. If creating illustrations is your primary interest, you may want to seriously consider buying an Apple Macintosh computer as working with illustrations is that computer's forte.

Most of the PC word processors you encounter work in what is known as "character mode." Knowing that you are likely to display letters a lot on your computer screen, manufacturers build "character sets" into the screen and the printer. Thus when the program wants to display an "A" it just tells the screen hardware, "Give me an A" and up comes the "A" on the screen. The hardware doesn't have to waste time drawing the "A" dot by dot. But when you start messing around with pictures you have to change modes and go into something called "graphics" mode. Now, in order to put an image on the screen or paper, you have to tell the screen hardware or printer which dots you want turned on and which dots you want turned off to create the picture you want. Since there are hundreds of dots in each square inch, it takes a lot longer to fill in a screen.

The Macintosh, in contrast, is designed in such a way that it is always in this graphics mode.

Graphics programs are programs that allow you to work with items created in this graphics mode. They let you create and edit illustrations, whether they are drawings you made yourself or a "canned" image that came on a diskette in a "library" of images. Graphics programs store images by a definite format, and most graphics programs use one of a few popular graphics formats. If you are going to use images created with one piece of graphics software with the output of another program that uses graphics, such as a high-end word processor, it is extremely important that the graphics format used by your graphics software is understood by the second program.

Many of the PC graphics programs, like Harvard Graphics and Freelance are designed to allow you to create that most mind—numbing of art objects, the business presentation graphic, otherwise known as the pie chart and bar graph. Many of these programs contain built-in routines allowing you to perform all sorts of permutations and combinations on the basic pie chart or bar chart and to automate the creation procedure. These programs usually also have some facility that lets you put letters around your graphic—something on the order of "Sales in April" and "North Central Widget Production."

The graphics libraries you can buy also tend to have a business tinge to them, and include all the visual cliches you are used to seeing in the ads for local businesses in the neighborhood throwaway free paper: smiling salesmen, movie tickets, gleaming cars, diesel trucks, stars, and the rest of what used to be called "stock cuts."

Many of these programs have full-color capability and display nicely on the higher resolution screens—those that display denser concentrations of dots per inch. However, when printing you are limited by what is available in the way of color printers. The class act in printing right now is the laser printer which produces typeset-looking print and respectable graphics. But color laser printers cost anywhere from $12,000 to $25,000 each, putting them out of reach for almost everybody. The color printers that are affordable—which create the image by using multi-color typewriter-like ribbons—simply don't cut it as far as looking truly professional, that is, photographic. Ink jet printers are only slightly better. As a result, some graphics programs, rather than sending the image to your printer, create computer files that are intended to be sent as input to slide making systems at commercial slide preparation shops. This solution is called for only when fancy color is called for, such as for illustrations or really impressive business presentations.

There are software products that go beyond the packages that create pie charts and let you do much more with drawings, especially for the Macintosh. Drawing and painting programs include Cricket Draw, in versions for both the PC and the Macintosh; PC Paintbrush Plus for the PC; and MacPaint, Adobe Illustrator, Aldus Freehand, SuperPaint and Pixel Paint for the Macintosh; to name just a few.

And beyond these are even more complex programs, called CAD (computer-aided design) programs, developed to fill the needs of engineers, which allow a drawing to be rotated and otherwise manipulated. These programs vary in the depth to which they are tied to engineering or architectural thought-forms, and, unless you are a writer in an engineering-oriented field, you are unlikely to need to use one of these.

Once you have a graphics file containing a picture you would like to put in a manuscript there are several ways of getting it there. You can just print it and glue it into a blank space you left for it in your word processor manuscript, but no hard-core technophile would do this. They might use a program which electronically pastes the image into the word processor manuscript, if their word processor has the capacity to work with graphics images as an increasing number of word processors can. Some word processors are able to import graphics files without the use of any additional software and yet others are even able to display the graphic part of your manuscript on the screen. However, unless you have an expensive machine, this may work very slowly.

Other graphics-oriented programs include map making programs that come with libraries containing maps of the United States and the World, flowcharting programs which are designed to draw things like organizational charts and system flowcharts, animation programs, slide show programs, and programs to edit video and photograpic images.

Because of the popularity of combining graphics and text in a single document, developers of word processors are moving toward including graphics handling features. Some word processors allow you to look at your document before you print it in a special "preview" mode and can display your graphics images within the document at that time; others can't display it on the screen but can embed a graphics image in your document when printing it. If your word processor doesn't let you mix graphics with text, the very powerful desktop publishing programs do. However, working with most of these is not for beginners.

One reason you might want to have the ability to combine graphics and text is to be able to create a computer-generated letterhead that prints atop your computer-generated letters. You can use a drawing program to do this, or you can get cheap specialty programs, such as the PC program Letrhead, to do this. Whichever you use, the net effect is to enhance your professional image.

Scanners and Scanning Software

Scanning technology is the latest wrinkle in the graphics world. Scanners are machines (something like FAX machines) that hook into your computer and take whatever is on a page, whether it be text or pictures, and read it optically, converting it, if text, to character mode text or, if a picture, into graphics files that your computer can then process with software. Since it is an optical technology the scanner must use complicated routines to figure out what letters it is looking at, either by comparing the scanned image to stored images of various type fonts, or else by analyzing their shape. The resulting character mode text file created from the scanning process may not be 100 percent correct but if the scanned page was printed or typed in a commonly used typeface it may be as much as 95 percent or more accurate.

Line drawings, which don't have to be interpreted the way text does, scan well. Halftones tend to come out somewhat the way they look when you copy them on a copier. Scanners come in both hand-held and flat-bed (copier-like) forms. This technology, which is still very new, promises to be of great use for many writers as it matures. Using scanner technology, you can pick up any image and then fiddle with it via a graphics editor, as well as being able to virtually "inhale" any printed text from any source for future use. Already photographers are looking into the legal ramifications of what happens when a copyrighted picture is slurped into a computer file and then "edited" before being passed off as something new (and not, therefore, due for royalties).

For most writers the biggest limitation on using this technology is currently the cost[3] and the quality of the graphics images it creates, which is usually not quite good enough for book and magazine illustrations. However if you need to get a lot of printed information into a computer file quickly, and understand enough about your computer to know where this text should go and how you want it organized, the scanner is worth considering.

TOOLS TO ORGANIZE YOUR THOUGHTS

It is when you get beyond the word processor and beyond the tools that handle illustrations that things really start to get interesting, because it is here that you start to find the brain extension tools that allow you to go beyond organizing your text and to start organizing the inchoate ideas and random facts that are the raw material of your writing.

TABLE 2.2   Tools to Organize Your Thoughts

Outliners	Hypertext	Personal Information Managers
Create and modify outlines Brainstorm	Create networks of links between words and illustrations allowing the audience to follow its own path through a presentation	Collect and arrange various kinds of information Organize and prioritize ideas and tasks

Outliners

We mentioned outliners in Chapter 1 as being among the most exciting thought tools available on computers. PC-Outline, Think-Tank, MaxThink, More, MindWrite, Acta, and Grandview are good examples of such outlining tools. Outliners let you enter in outline elements and then effortlessly alter the way they relate to each other. Depending on the particular outliner you use, each of these outline elements might be a phrase or sentence or even 20 pages of text. To show you briefly how this plasticity lets you play with ideas and their relationship to each other, look at the example in Figure 2.1.

When using an outliner you begin by typing in a series of loosely connected thoughts as they emerge, not worrying about their relationship to each other for the time being:

[3]Although in 1988 you could buy a hand-held four-inch scanner for about $300 the image it stored was far below what a publisher would want for camera-ready copy.

A. Dinosaurs may have been brightly colored

B. They may have been warm blooded

C. They may be ancestors of the birds

D. Children love dinosaurs

E. Bigger than parents

F. Evidence of large stones in their gullets

G. How to determine how fast they moved

H. Look at foot prints

I. Scientists change their minds as more research accumulates

J. Older books say dinosaurs were slow-moving, cold-blooded reptiles

K. Pictures in old books always show gray or green dinosaurs

L. How to explain science to children

M. Dinosaurs a good example

N. How theories change

Figure 2.1: Initial Outline

At this point you have been brainstorming, getting the ideas out on the screen with very little structure imposed. By the way, I and J could easily be entered after you had entered the later entries in the list by simply moving the cursor, the line that points to where you are on the screen, to where you wanted to enter the new lines.

After you look at what you came up with, the outliner software makes it easy to arrange these listed items in logical relationships with each other using only a few keystrokes, thus rearranging the whole thing to look like Figure 2.2.

HOW TO EXPLAIN SCIENCE TO CHILDREN

A. Children love dinosaurs

   1. Bigger than parents

B. Dinosaurs a good example of what is a theory

   1. Scientists change their minds as more research accumulates

   2. Theories about dinosaurs have changed

      a) Older books say dinosaurs were slow-moving, cold-blooded reptiles

         1) Pictures in old books always show gray or green dinosaurs

      b) New theories about dinosaurs

         1) They may have been warm blooded

            a> How to determine how fast they moved?

               1> Look at foot prints

         2) They may be ancestors of the birds

            a> Evidence of large stones in their gullets

            b> Dinosaurs may have been brightly colored

Figure 2.2: The Outline Rearranged

```
HOW TO EXPLAIN SCIENCE TO CHILDREN

A. Children love dinosaurs
B. Dinosaurs a good example of what is a theory
   1. Scientists change their minds as more research accumulates
   2. Theories about dinosaurs have changed
```

Figure 2.3: The Outline with Only Major Headings Revealed

So far so good. Now we have a place to start, and if we don't like this arrangement it is simple to move any item around within the outline until we come up with a structure that satisfies. Up until now what we did could be done on paper, although it would take longer. But now we are going to do what we can only do with a computer. With a few more keystrokes we can make all of the lower level entries in the outline disappear instantaneously, which will make the outline look like Figure 2.3.

This lets you see your ideas at a high level to see if they are flowing in a logical manner. But all the lower levels remain in the outline, they are just not displayed. You can rearrange these high-level items knowing that the lower level stuff will be rearranged with them, maintaining their relationships. Or, with a few more keystrokes, back comes the full outline and you can suppress a lower level if you want.

This ability to get multiple views of an outline without destroying the original is a tremendous gift to the thinker. You can concentrate on a single section which you see in expanded form while displaying the rest of the outline at the high level only. You can rearrange your work at the chapter or section level or just move a paragraph. In this example we had only a few items to arrange. But the outliner makes it practical to put together 10- or 20-page outlines, allowing you in effect to start with an outline made up of single sentences and then expand each outline item into a paragraph. At any point you can use the outliner's ability to hide text and display only your topic sentences so you can see displayed on a single screen the flow of ideas in a chapter, or indeed, the shape of a whole book.

This kind of software is one of those things that you have to try using yourself before the true power of it hits you. It is probably not like anything you have ever used. And like the equally unexplainable mystical experience, those who try it and "see" it tend to become converts and enthusiasts, to the point where working without these tools leaves them feeling crippled.

Hypertext

Hypertext software is another kind of software that lets you link up your ideas in a free and creative manner, but hypertext dispenses with the rigid structure of an outline. Hypercard, a piece of software that comes free with Apple's Macintosh computers and Guide which is available for both the Macintosh and the PC are some examples of this kind of tool. MaxThink, for the PC, though an outliner also provides some hypertext features. While the product of the outliner is something that you can print out on paper, hypertext really only makes sense in the context of interactive computer screens.

What hypertext allows you to do is make some area on a screen a special "link" area where you can place your cursor or mouse pointer. Then when you press a key or click your mouse you are taken to a new screen that has some predefined relationship with the entry point. The link area can be a word or an image. You can link forward and backward or follow a chain of these links as far as you want to go. The information on each screen is related to the information on other screens by a matrix of relationships as complex as the designer of the hypertext "stack" wants it to be. For example, if you click on the word "cats" displayed on a hypertext screen you might find yourself whisked to another screen that displays a list of breeds, where each listed breed name is the entry point into a chain of screens that contains information about that breed, which screens are further cross-linked into a wide variety of subjects. Alternatively, selecting the word *cat* might result in the display of a picture of Fluffy. With the Mac's Hypercard there is a whole programming language available so that you can, if you are technically inclined, create whole software applications of your own.

This may be a little too vertiginous for most writers though, because, after all, hypertext is trying to break you out of a sequential, page-bound way of thinking, but as a writer you need to come back to a sequential mode or you aren't going to be able to write.

The primary use of hypertext right now seems to be preparing very spiffy business presentations that allow the target of the presentation (I hesitate to say reader because it is all so screen based) choose what he wants to learn more about following his own, not some author's, path.

Hypertext has been kicking around as an idea for a long time and when programs were introduced that enabled people to put together these hypertext applications, great things were predicted (including, of course, the total end of linear communication). While there are plenty of hypercard stacks available now for Macintosh users, linear thinking appears to be holding its own. However, depending on how your mind works, this might be an interesting way to arrange your thoughts in a multidimensional matrix so that you can jar your mind into seeing them in new relationships.

Personal Information Managers

The newest wrinkle in the thought-management department is software that automatically stuffs your random mental flotsam into predefined categories, giving it order and meaning that might have escaped you. A piece of software that can do this kind of thing is called (sometimes) a "personal information manager." Lotus' Agenda is the best known product in this niche. Symantec's Grandview, a piece of software that is primarily an outliner, also includes some of this kind of function. Other programs have elements of this too; Agenda and Grandview's success led to a rush among software companies to redefine other software tools, which used to be considered members of other tool families, as being just such personal information managers or PIMs.

The programs that fall into this category (or are jimmied into it) are very different from each other as far as what the actual items you sort into categories are and how they get sorted. The item may be a word or a 50 page document. In some software the sorting occurs the minute you type an item in, based on the words found in the item. In others you have to tell the software what category the item should be stashed under. Some programs keep track of every word making up the item, others just look at certain key words. Finally the programs vary in the degree to which you can rearrange the items you have in different patterns once they are entered in.

These programs can range from the confusing to the Byzantine as far as the difficulty of learning them goes, but there is no question that they are pointing the way to a new generation of extremely useful "thoughtware" a few years down the line, and for the thinker they are probably the most interesting software development yet. Such tools at their best allow you to store, contemplate, manipulate, and extract meaning from large amounts of very raw stuff—snippets of facts, quotations, statistics, hunches, newspaper clippings, phone conversations—the whole range of mental flotsam that through the alchemy of human thought turns into a cohesive work.

TOOLS TO ORGANIZE INFORMATION

The tools we just looked at were idea organizers. They worked with information, but it was loose, unstructured, random information: ideas and bits and pieces. While you have probably heard all your life that computers process "information" the ability to work with this kind of mental flotsam on a computer is very new. The information that traditional computer systems manage is very different from the stuff that floats through your mind. Traditional computer information management tools work with highly structured information. With these more traditional tools you must already know a lot about the items making up your information and their relationships with other information before you can use computer tools to work on them in any useful manner.

TABLE 2.3   Tools to Organize Information

Database	Random Database	Special Purpose Database	Spreadsheet
Maintain structured records in a rigid format Sort and arrange records Search for records by search criteria Generate automatic reports	Maintain unstructured data Index data and search using indexes Sometimes in notepad format	Database set up to manage one particular kind of data in one particular fashion. Examples include citation and bibliography systems and databases set up to track publications or business contacts.	Stores numerical data and formulas that operate on that data along with text in a grid

Databases

Using a database software package is one of the main reasons people buy computers, and some sort of database software usually comes as part of integrated software. It may even be thrown in free with the system. If you ask a salesman for a database package, he will probably bring out dBase, FoxBase, RBase, FileMaker Plus, or perhaps Paradox. These are among the more popular (and expensive) databases, although by no means the only ones. However, while these might be excellent choices for managing business information, they are much less satisfying for the kinds of information writers need to work with.

The reason is this. Business information systems are built around the need to track huge amounts of patterned information. For example, if a businessman is collecting information about his clients he would want to gather information about what their credit history is, what they like to order, what bills they have outstanding, and what payments they have made. This information will be useful to him both for day-to-day operations, such as billing and tracking expenses for taxes, as well as for getting a feeling of who is buying what to help in planning future inventories.

Because the businessman needs to collect exactly the same information for each client, the database he uses will probably add an entry, called a database record, every time a client puts in an order. Each record will contain the same kind of information: item ordered, price of item, number of items, date ordered, date delivered, payment received, and client account number.

After accumulating hundreds of order items the businessman can use routines that are part of the database software to generate reports that analyze and summarize his information. For example he may want a report of sales per item, which will list how many of each item were sold in the time period and the total sales for that item; or he may want a customer report, showing total sales to the customer broken down by item sold; or he may want a customer payment history. Producing this kind of report is the goal of traditional "data processing."

Traditional database software packages make collecting and summarizing this kind of information very easy. They excel in situations where things need to be counted, sorted, and tabulated and where clear hierarchical relationships exist between data elements.

But the key thing to note here is that although the businessman is managing a lot of information, it all fits the same very simple pattern. And pattern is what characterizes information stored on computer databases.

But this is probably very far from what you had in mind when you imagined tracking information! The information that you want to collect is not cut-and-dried repetitive items the way business information is; instead, it is made up of a whole lot of random and complex pieces whose relationship to each other probably will become clear to you only as you prepare to begin writing. If you were keeping a customer record database like the one described above, you would want to have some way of storing things like how the customer liked the product he bought, why he chose it, what his neighborhood might be like, what his family situation is, and how it is changing his buying patterns as well as a host of similar, nebulous, possibly important facts that taken together could be of great use. This kind of hard-to-quantify information is almost impossible to manage on a traditional database.

If you try to use such a business-oriented database for managing the stuff you used to keep on note cards that you shuffled around until they were organized or in notebooks filled with random observations, you will quickly see why trying to jimmy your kind of information into the rigid structure of a conventional database, though it can be done, is probably the worst way to go about managing it—possibly a total waste of time. Because you don't know how to lay out identical records for this kind of information, but the database software insists that you define the shape of your database records before it will store anything, you must know in advance what you need to keep and how large each item should be. If you ignore structure and just define the record as a big note card, the system will not be able to do much to it except print it out for you, wasting huge amounts of computer storage space in the process, since if you have told it to make each database record one-thousand characters long every time you enter a piece of information, even if it only takes up ten characters, the database will store one thousand, mostly blank, characters. This can fill up your computer disks pretty quickly.

Random Information Managers

The alternative to using these traditional databases is to use a different class of information managers sometimes called "random information processors." Examples of these are Ask Sam, IZE, Instant Recall, and Tornado Notes, although there are many more. This family of software shades into the family of personal information managers we discussed earlier in the section about tools that organize your thoughts.

Such random information databases each take a different approach to the problem of managing unstructured information, but what they have in common is that rather than trying to store your information in uniformly laid out records they store it more flexibly.

Some programs build complex indexes pointing to this information, allowing you to retrieve it in a variety of ways. These indexes may index every word or may ask you to suggest indexing key words. It varies with the program. But by using these indexes the software can quickly retrieve elements you stored that pertain to certain themes or topics and subtopics.

How well this will work for you has a lot to do with which program you use and exactly what you are trying to do with exactly what kind of information, which makes any broad generalizations about these tools impossible. However they are available and many people report finding them useful. It is probably a good idea to master simpler software, such as your word processor and an outliner, before attempting to move up to one of these.

Other programs take a "notepad" approach. These notepad programs allow you to store jottings in an electronic notepad that can be displayed right on top of some other program's screen. This means that if you get a great idea for an article on elephants while slogging away on another assignment in your word processor you can pop up your electronic notepad screen and write down the information in a note you label "elephants" and store it in a notepad named "article ideas". Later you may be able to print out these notes and you may be able to search all your notepads for the word "elephants" when you need to find this note later. Notepad management programs can become extremely complex and highly useful.

While the software described in the previous paragraphs was generic, there are also special purpose programs designed to organize very specific kinds of information that writers may need. Examples of such programs that can run on an IBM PC are a program called Biblio-File which manages citations or Reflist which creates reference lists for scientific and technical manuscripts. Another such program, Muses, is intended to keep track of a writer's articles and publishers. A similar program available for Macintosh users is Writer's Workshop, a specialty database which tracks manuscripts, income, and publishers. Other special-purpose database programs track contacts, which can be very useful for storing information about who you talked to at what magazine or publishing house, who you queried, and for what, and what follow-up is needed, when. Some of these programs will also generate mailing labels for you.

Having a well-designed program that already does exactly what you need without having to struggle with setting up a generic database system can be a great help. What is also nice is that these specialty programs are often very inexpensive shareware programs, programs you can freely copy and try out, paying for them only if you like them.[4]

Since so many different kinds of software can do duty in so many different kinds of work, and since, unfortunately, information stored by one database or random information manager is all too often inaccessible to your other software, figuring out what software to use for a given kind of information is often the biggest challenge you face when working with your computer.

```
  F10                                          Empty Cell
       A       B       C       D       E      F    G      H
  1                            TAXES for 1988
  2
  3 Employee Wages:
  4            Estimated      22500.00
  5
  6            TOTAL WAGES                    22500.00
  7
  8 Interest                                    150.00
  9 Dividends                                     0.00
 10 Royalties                  2550.00    [             ]
 11 Writing related expenses   1100.00
 12 Total business income                      1450.00
 13 TOTAL GROSS INCOME                        24100.00
 14
 15 Deductions
 16            Mortgage              3215.00
 17
 18            Tax      House    950.00
 19                     Car       54.78
 20
 21            Total Taxes        1004.78
                                                   mem=97K
 =Menu Options F1=Context Help F2=General Help F3=Edit F10=Recalc All
```

Figure 2.4: Tax Spreadsheet Displayed on Two Screens

[4]Shareware is explored in depth in Chapter 12.

Spreadsheets

The other major software product family that is commonly used to manage information is the spreadsheet. The spreadsheet was the first program designed specifically for the microcomputer, and it has become a major reason for the explosion of personal computer use by business. The best known spreadsheet programs are Lotus 1-2-3 in the PC world and Microsoft Excel available for both PCs and the Mac. These bestsellers are expensive, since their primary market is businesses for whom they are essential. Quattro and VP Planner for the PC and Multiplan and MacCalc for the Macintosh are less expensive spreadsheet programs, and there are shareware spreadsheets available for PCs too, most notably PC-Calc + from Buttonware, and Qubecalc.

Spreadsheets are often part of integrated packages (along with word processors and databases) and a "brand X" spreadsheet may be thrown in free when you buy a computer, so popular are these tools.

What do these spreadsheets do, and are they anything a writer needs

```
    F32                                              Function
          A       B       C       D       E       F       G       H
 22             Charity                 500.00
 23
 24 Total Deductions                            4719.78
 25
 26 GROSS minus Deductions                     19380.22
 27
 28 Exemptions                                  1950.00
 29
 30 TAXABLE INCOME                             17430.22
 31
 32 TAX on INCOME                             | 2614.53 |
 33
 34 Self Employment Tax
 35                                             188.50
 36 CREDITS
 37 Daycare Credit                                0.00
 38
 39 TAX DUE                                     2803.03
 40
 41
 42
    IF(F30>29750,(F30-29750)*.28+4462.50,.15*F30)        mem=97K
    Press Esc to exit.
```

Figure 2.4: Tax Spreadsheet Displayed on Two Screens (*cont'd.*)

to know about? Let's look at an example of a useful spreadsheet to illustrate their function.

Spreadsheets create a two dimensional grid (or table) of information. Each box on the grid can contain either some text, a number, or a formula. In our sample spreadsheet, created using Buttonware's PC-Calc + and shown in Figure 2.4, we have set up a spreadsheet that will estimate income tax. It closely resembles the 1040 form. The amount of estimated employee wages is stored and displayed in grid box D4 and the calculated tax displays in grid box F32. However this tax amount in F32 is calculated based on what we have entered in the other boxes. We didn't type in an amount here, instead what was entered in this box was a formula. On the second screen we have located our cursor on box F32 which causes the formula associated with that box to display on the bottom line of the screen. However what we will see on the spreadsheet itself (and a printed report) is the calculated value, not the formula.

The beauty of a spreadsheet is that once you have the correct formulas entered in you can change the numbers and the spreadsheet almost instantly recalculates all the formulas for you. So if you had set up a tax spreadsheet like the one in the example you could instantly see how your taxes due would change if you got paid a $20,000 advance this year, simply by typing in $20,000 on the box set up for royalties. This would cause all the formulas in the spreadsheet to be recalculated, including F12, Total Business Income, and F32, Tax on Income, and the screen (or a report generated by the spreadsheet) would display the new, higher tax.

As you can see, the formulas can be quite powerful. The formula displayed for F32 manages to express, in one line, the amount of tax due on taxable income no matter what amount it might be.

This is a terrific tool for any kind of accounting work such as doing taxes or tracking business expenses. However there is one major caveat. The formulas have to be correct. If your formulas are not correct, and it easy for this to happen, what you end up with is a very plausible-looking grid of wrong numbers and no way of knowing that what you have *is* wrong. This is particularly likely to happen because the spreadsheet usually displays only the numbers that result from applying the formulas you are using, not the formulas themselves, which are hidden.

There have been court cases where businesspeople sued spreadsheet manufacturers claiming that they used spreadsheets to calculate significant business items, such as project bids, but that the answers they came up with were wrong, causing their business to fail. These suits were lost since the software companies were able to argue that it wasn't their fault that the users used the wrong formulas. But it is all too easy to trust the numbers you see on the screen and forget that you left out some vital piece of information. For example if you use last year's spreadsheet to do this year's taxes you may forget that social security rates change, leading you to estimate your taxes incorrectly.

As a writer you probably will use spreadsheets in your writing only if you do a lot of mathematical or statistical work. Spreadsheets often include routines to generate business graphics (those pie charts and bar charts). If generating graphics would be your only use, you don't need a spreadsheet and might be better off with the graphics software we discussed earlier.

However using an inexpensive spreadsheet can be a great way to track your business expenses as they arise for later use in putting together your tax information, whether for yourself or an accountant.

TOOLS TO ORGANIZE YOURSELF

So much for tools to organize information. We turn now to a set of useful computer tools whose goal is to help you get through your day.

Desktop Utilities

Desktop utilities are another of those kinds of programs that you will not really get excited about until you get a chance to try one out. That is because they do things that you can only really appreciate once you have begun working in the computer environment. Popular Desk top utilities are Side Kick and Side Kick Plus, Lotus Metro, Homebase, and PC-Deskteam, the last two being shareware for the PC. The Macintosh computer environment integrates the concept of "desktop accessories" and some packages available for that environment are MockPackage+, Sidekick, DiskTop, and Top Desk.

Desktop programs are what is called TSR[5] or "pop-up" programs. Usually when you are in the middle of using a program you can't use a different program until you either end what you are doing in the first

TABLE 2.4   Tools to Organize Yourself

Notepads	Calendars	Phone Books	Text Search
Pop up when using other software Can be used for random information Sometimes combined with cut and paste software	Can be used for scheduling May have pop-up alarms that work when you are using other software	Can pop up and be used with other software May be able to dial phone if you have a modem	Allow you to find "lost" data anywhere on the system no matter what kind of software stored it

[5]TSR stands for terminate and stay resident which is what, in programming terms, these programs do to allow them to pop up.

program or until you use a special command that temporarily interrupts what you are doing in the first program and allows you to use the other program, which you must then end before returning to the first. This can be time consuming and break up the flow of your thought.

On the other hand, these desktop programs are programs that, once started up, run quietly beside the main program you are using, but can be called up with a special set of keystrokes right in the middle of what you are doing. When you are done with one of these programs for the moment, you hit some more keystrokes and it vanishes, but it keeps your place in it so that the next time you call it up you are exactly where you were when you used it before. This allows you to quickly flip back and forth between two programs without any waste of time.

Desktop utilities usually include several functions that are things you are likely to want to use when in the middle of using other software. They are called "desktop" utilities because most of these functions originally corresponded to things you would have had on your desk, like a calendar or a notepad. Usually these programs include routines to provide calendars, notepads, and calculators. In addition each company's program may have a few other features, like a phone dialer or a file manager.

The calendar part of one of these is just like a regular desk calendar except that you can set alarms on it so that while you are flailing away in your word processor, lost to the world, you don't have to worry about forgetting to call that editor at 11:10 after she is awake but before she goes to her three-martini lunch and is for all intents and purposes lost to you for the rest of the day. You set an alarm in the calendar and at the appropriate time no matter what program you are using the program will pop up and announce "Call Sue" with her phone number. Some calendars include "to-do" lists that you can roll forward from one day to another.

Desktop utilities also usually have the pop-up notepads which we discussed earlier in the section on random information databases. Some give you just one notepad that you can jot things on. Others are almost as complex as a database and let you keep an unlimited number of notepads going with sub-notepads on each one. These may include indexes to let you quickly find the note you are looking for.

Some let you design specialized notes like a preprinted form, so you can build a notepad full of "While You Were Out" phone slips or can use a searchable notepad as a telephone number database. A pop-up phone dialer is a related feature that comes with some desktop utility packages. It really is a database of phone numbers that you can pop up and search. Then, if you have a modem attached to your computer, you can have the modem actually dial the number before letting you use your phone to talk.

One last extremely useful desktop feature is what is called "cut and paste." After you have used your computer for a while you will end up with stuff stored all over the place under the control of different programs.

You will have pages of text typed into your word processor's files. You may have a database of publishers that lists addresses, editors' names, the magazines' requirements, what you have submitted to them, what you have had accepted, and what you have been paid, and you may have notepads or random information databases full of all sorts of random thoughts, facts, interesting ideas for follow-up, and so forth. Unfortunately, your word processor can't get at the information stored in your notepad, nor can it get to the publisher's address from your database.

It is ridiculous to end up jotting this information on a napkin (after backing out of your word processor and bringing up your database screen to find it) and then typing it into your word processor. But without cut and paste that is exactly what you may have to do!

Cut and paste pops up and solves this problem by being able to copy anything on your screen into a holding area and then writing it out on the screen later. So you can look at the database screen, pick up the address, go to your word processor and with a few keystrokes "paste" in the address in the proper place. The better cut-and-paste programs are not limited to a single item either, but can pick up a series of screens full of stuff and then dump them later in the order that you picked them up. This can allow you to transfer pages of typing from one incompatible program to the other.

Text Searchers

Another kind of program separate from the desktop programs that may be useful in organizing your work is a text search program, like ZyINDEX or the shareware programs Psearch and Fgrep. If you do end up accumulating lots and lots of text on your system, for example three drafts of a novel, a couple of short stories, and notebooks full of sketches and ideas, it may be hard to find out where you put what. Since all your information is stored by document name or in databases controlled by different programs, you can't just look through it easily the way you look through paper files. This means that it is possible to "lose" information in your system. True, your word processor will have a "search" command which can find text in a particular manuscript, but it is no use at all when you are looking for some information that could be stored anywhere on your computer by any of 10 different software packages.

Text search programs help you in this situation because they are able to look quickly through all the stuff on your computer (or a narrow selection, for example, all chapters of one book). Text search programs can look for specific words or for combinations of words. The "smarter" programs (smarter because the people who wrote them put in fancier logic), can look for the occurrence of one word or group of words followed by other words later in the same patch of text. This means that if you are working on a novel and know that you described George's pet dog somewhere but can't remember if it was a dachshund or a Labrador, you could search for the words "dog" and "George" occurring in the same paragraph in all your chapter files. If you don't find this combination in your chapters, you might want to look in the database of random thoughts that you built when scoping out the book. The same text search software can scoot through your database and your notebooks too, still looking for "George" in association with "dog." Obviously the more random information you have stored on your computer, the more useful this kind of program is.

TOOLS TO GET AND SHARE INFORMATION

For less than a hundred dollars you can add a piece of equipment to your computer that will let it use an ordinary phone line to call up computers anywhere in the world. The piece of equipment is called a modem and it allows you to do two things that may be very useful to you: It lets you call computer bulletin boards, and it lets you call commercial on-line services. Equipped with the right software, and a large-enough hard disk you can go one better—you can run your own bulletin board, and leave your computer at home to answer the phone as callers from all over call you and leave messages, read files, and send you new programs.

Accessing Bulletin Boards

If you want to call bulletin boards you will need some sort of communications program. Before you rush out to buy one of these be aware that many modems include this software in their price. There are also excellent communications programs available as shareware or in the public domain. These programs allow you to store phone numbers in a list with some sort of description and call them up. They usually keep a "log" of your session, so that you can look at what scrolled across your screen when you were communicating with another computer. They also have features that let you "download" and "upload" files, so that if a bulletin board has

TABLE 2.5 Tools to Get and Share Information

Communications Software	Special Communications Software	Bulletin Board Software
Call any on-line service or bulletin board Upload and download files Post or read messages	Automate calling of a single on-line service doing as much work off-line as possible	Turn your computer into a computer bulletin board

a collection of free programs you can have them sent to your computer disk over the phone line, or you can send something of your own, perhaps a set of short excerpts from your best writings, for other people to download.

If there is a computer users group in your local calling area they may well have a bulletin board that is a local call for you. Or you may find that a local hobbyist has one. Some bulletin boards are free, others request that you pay an annual fee to cover the operator's expenses.[6] Employment agencies sometimes run these too, although they currently tend to be for computer-related jobs only. Some companies selling specialized software (like MIDI music software for example) run bulletin boards that let you pick up public domain software and also advertise products they sell. If you want to find out where there are bulletin boards, listings are available on the on-line services described below.

Running a Bulletin Board

Why would you want to run a bulletin board? Because it's fun. If you are a compulsive communicator, having hundreds of people calling in and leaving messages that you can scan at your leisure may be utter heaven. But there are other reasons too. If you are involved in a special interest, a bulletin board can be a way of coordinating information. For example, antihunger groups have used bulletin boards to bring together restaurant owners or merchants with excess food that might otherwise be thrown away, and the shelters that can use it immediately. Your writing may be part of some larger effort and you could use a bulletin board as a focus and resource for all the people who are interested in the same topic.

Bulletin Board Software

While the general communications programs we mentioned earlier are able to receive calls from specific callers, you will need a special program to run a bulletin board because the software must automatically handle people who call. The software usually asks callers to identify themselves and verify that they are the person they say they are with a password. Then the software must offer the caller the choice of looking at messages, leaving messages, looking for files or uploading and downloading files, and last but not least, leaving messages for the system operator—SYSOP in communications slang—you.

---

[6]Bulletin board operators who request a fee are not trying merely to get rich off of you. Operating a bulletin board costs money. It causes a lot of wear and tear on the system and requires upgrades on hardware that can be expensive. There is also a lot of time involved in running one well, including checking the quality of uploaded files and communicating with users.

Believe it or not, if you use a PC you can get a version of this software completely free in a package called RBBS. In addition, you can join networks like FIDOnet, that are popular on college campuses.

On-line Service Software

Commercial on-line services are operations like CompuServe, BIX, GEnie, DELPHI, and Prodigy, which offer services similar to those found on a bulletin board to users nationwide, as well as access to large searchable databases. These services, since they are moneymaking operations, tend to have a lot of shopping services on them, which are probably not worth paying hefty on-line charges to use since they duplicate catalog shopping you can do for free. But there are interesting features on some of these services, including the major databases like Paperchase and IQUEST, and various news services.

These services are a valuable resource for all computer users. Once you have figured out how to use one of these services you can get in touch with people to help you with problems you run into with just about any piece of software you have inflicted upon yourself. The only problem, unfortunately, is that mastering the software needed to get to these services and figuring out how to use them takes some time, and time on these services is not cheap.

With some of these services you can use the same software you use for accessing bulletin boards. But others, such as Prodigy, require that you use a special vendor-supplied program. CompuServe can be accessed with either general purpose software or specialty software that streamlines the access process and makes it easier to use the forums and file libraries of the service cheaply.

TOOLS TO PRODUCE PUBLICATIONS

Desktop publishing is the term used to describe the production of camera-ready copy using desktop computers. While you will occasionally encounter chintzy programs that claim to let you do desktop publishing but really produce amateur looking output suitable only for "Roommate Wanted" posters on college bulletin boards, real desktop publishing requires powerful specialized software, super-fast computers and excruciatingly expensive complicated laser printers.

Unlike most printers, which print a line at a time (or a letter at a time), laser printers use a technology similar to that used in photocopiers to produce a page at a time. They have come down in price a lot over the last few years but still cost several thousand dollars by the time they are set up with all the things you need to have in order to do desktop publishing.

The dominant desktop publishing packages are Ventura Publisher (Xerox) and Aldus' PageMaker. These take the output of a word processing program, set it in type, and integrate this text with the graphics images you have stored on your computer. These programs allow you to specify typefaces and sizes, which are limited only by the capabilities of your printer, which may require you to have font software too. Desktop publishing programs let you put graphics (pictures) on your pages, move them around, snake text around them, and index your document. Desktop publishing programs operate in graphics rather than character mode, drawing the screen dot by dot, which means that their performance on a cheap system may be so slow as to cause pain.

However, the biggest problem with desktop publishing software is that to use it correctly and really turn out professional-looking copy you must have mastered two technologies: You must know something about how to do layout and you must know quite a lot about working with software and hardware. Lacking the knowledge of graphic design you are likely to turn out amateur desktop publishing efforts, which resemble those odd instruction booklets that come with products assembled in distant corners of the Third World. Things won't look right for reasons that are hard to figure out. Until you see the clumsy output of such desktop publishing you don't appreciate how much technique and artistry go into producing most of the printed pages that pass by your eye. If the typefaces and sizes are wrong, or the lines are too long, or if boxes have the wrong-size lines bounding them, in spite of your expensive software your effort will look crude.

But even more daunting is the amount you must master on the computer end to be able to use one of these setups. The problem here is that the hardware configuration required is so expensive that you really can't put it together and get it up and running right without professional help. If you are rich and can afford to pay a consultant $50/hr to set up your system and get you through your first project successfully this isn't a problem. But if you are a starving artist with hopes of becoming a small press you would be best advised to avoid attempting to use desktop software until you have mastered the computer basics and know what it is that you need to know.

Desktop publishing is alluring to the writer because the output looks so printed, and lord knows it is hard enough to get someone else—i.e. a publisher—to set your words in type. But the reality is that for most writers these desktop systems are really not necessary items. Their primary market is for small businesses who print out things like price catalogs and large companies that use them for throwaway intracompany newsletters. Indeed, if you have a publisher, you may discover that your publisher can't handle the output of these systems. If you are dealing with a magazine, for example, they may well use a mainframe-based ATEX system and require you to submit electronic materials in the simplest form possible, with all control codes stripped out, which means that you can't use desktop publishing software at all. And if you are working on a book for a publisher, the company probably has its own standards for typesetting and its own, much more powerful systems, so that your using such a desktop publishing package may only complicate the already complicated publishing process.

While desktop publishing software started out as a unique set of programs, the makers of word processors have been racing to add desktop publishing features to their word processing products. Microsoft Word and WordPerfect have full desktop publishing features integrated into their products, so if you have certain kinds of video displays you can get an effect similar to using one of the stand-alone desktop publishing packages with them. However, since these features are buried among all the hundreds of other features in the word processors there is a certain trade-off in design, and they may not be as easy to use as a program set up to do only the desktop publishing tasks.

Even a relatively cheap word processor like Borland's Sprint includes features that make it possible to do desktop publishing, and it is unlikely that any word processor that doesn't incorporate these features will survive in the intensely competitive word processor marketplace.

If you have one of these desktop-publishing-capable word processors and a cheap dot matrix printer you can fool around a bit and get a feel for desktop publishing without committing to the expensive hardware necessary to do a quality job. If you plan to do only one or two books a year, you might do a lot better, both in terms of cost and in terms of what your output looks like, by taking the manuscript created by your desktop-publishing-capable word processor to a print shop that specializes in desktop publishing. These offer top-of-the-line equipment (much better than what you could afford) and the services of trained graphic artists who can set up the pages using your word processor input.

TOOLS TO MANAGE YOUR COMPUTER

We have almost completed our quick look at the tools in the writer's toolbox. Only one set of tools remains, and these are not tools you go out and get because you are a writer. These are tools you go out and get because you own a computer. These tools are what you use to manage all the other stuff you have on your system. Such programs are called utilities.

TABLE 2.6   Tools to Manage the Computer

Shells	File Managers	Editors and Browsers	Disk Utilities
Simplify working with the operating system Provide menus Start programs	Move, copy, erase, and rename files Create, delete and rename subdirectories	Change the contents of system files Look at any file without being able to change it or inadvertently mess it up	Clean up organization of files on hard disk to improve performance Speed up performance Recover from disk formatting and accidental erasure

Utilities do things like back up your work—make copies that you can lock in the safe deposit vault in the bank in case your house burns down, or, more likely, that you can reload after you have accidentally erased your work by doing something stupid. Utilities let you look at what you have created on your computer and eliminate the junk that creeps in—fragments you abandoned months ago, backup copies that the software created and you forgot to erase, logs of on-line sessions on bulletin boards you no longer visit—stuff that seems trivial but which, as your disks begin to fill up, starts taking up more and more usable space.

Other utilities do things like speed up your disks. They can do this by reorganizing the way that data is physically written on the disks or by playing tricks in memory that let the system do less real reading from your disk, holding large chunks of your most commonly used stuff in the computer's memory where it can be accessed much more quickly than the stuff on the disks can be.

A whole other set of utilities serves the purpose of insulating you from the technical details of your computer environment by giving you sets of screens that let you invoke some of the more common functions that the computer could perform for you. These menu-making utilities are considered by some people to be the only sane way to use a computer. To others they are a time-consuming pain in the rear since they make you look at screen after screen when you can achieve the same effect by typing in a few words if you know what you are doing.

There are utilities to change the typeface on your printer, and utilities to print files out in fancy fonts on the cheapest kinds of dot matrix printers. There are utilities to compress files so that you can keep huge amounts of data in a smaller amount of disk space than you would otherwise need. There are utilities to print labels on your diskettes that list all the files on those diskettes and there are utilities to encrypt your files—put them into a code that only you can decipher with a special key.

One kind of program some people find useful is a print spooler. Many word processors assume that you have nothing better to do than to sit and wait while they print your document for you. Since it can take hours to print off several chapters using the nicest looking print on a cheap printer, this can mean that you are effectively robbed of your system in the meantime. Print spoolers are programs that let you send a long manuscript or several manuscripts to the printer while you continue to run other programs on your computer at the same time.

There are utilities that play tricks with your hardware: If you have a black and white screen there are utilities that may let you run programs that say "Color Graphics Required." There are utilities that change the functions of keys on your keyboard. There are utilities that test your hardware and report on whether it is getting ready to break down.

A very important subcategory of utilities works with your files. One type allows you to look at them and another type allows you to go in and change their contents. The programs that look at files are called "browse" utilities, the ones that let you change things are called editors.

A certain number of utilities will come, built in, with the computer you buy, or rather, with the operating system that you get with the computer. Which ones you will then need to acquire on your own depends a lot on what machine you bought and on how much you enjoy fooling around with this kind of stuff.

Many software companies sell sets of utilities, particularly for file management and for file backup. But before you rush out to buy any of these you should be aware that it is in the family of utility programs that you are most likely to find cheap or free software on bulletin boards or from the shareware services that are discussed later. This is because writing a utility is many programmers' favorite way to spend a rainy day, and distributing a popular utility, even if it brings in little money, does bring the programmer a certain kind of fame and immortality. Therefore, writing utilities and uploading them to bulletin boards is how many would-be programmers attempt to establish themselves, so there are literally hundreds of these available.

There is only one serious problem with utilities from your standpoint as an unsophisticated user: utilities are too powerful. Too many utilities let you fiddle around with things that you don't understand and some of them, unfortunately, let you mess things up so badly that you can render your system unusable. Anything that lets you make sweeping changes to your system may enable you to make mistakes on a similarly grand scale and wipe out weeks of work. If you are new to using a computer and have put "backing up the system" into the category of things you will do after you get comfortable with your word processor and figure out how to get your fancy new printer to work, fiddling with a powerful utility might lead you to do the kind of completely preventable damage that gives computers a bad name.

Chapter 14 discusses how to avoid these kinds of disaster situations by protecting your system with useful backups; you should make sure you have done this before you try any new utilities. And you should make a point of never using any utility whose function you don't really understand.

3

WILL USING A COMPUTER CHANGE YOU?

"The power of doing anything with quickness is always much prized by the possessor, and often without any attention to the imperfection of the performance."

Jane Austen, 1775-1817
Pride and Prejudice

WHY YOU PROBABLY THINK YOU OUGHT TO HATE COMPUTERS

An astonishing amount of drivel has been written about the impact of computers, both in the popular press and in so-called "serious" publications. Generally this material falls into two genres: worshipful futurism and skulking jeremiads.

The worshipful futurists gape in wonder at product demonstrations that their copy makes it clear they didn't understand. They make sweeping predictions of how within a generation the computer will eliminate all vestiges of our current civilization. Their visions are painfully ugly. They prophesy a world where there are no books but only on-line information retrieval, a telecommuting workplace where each worker is isolated in an "electronic cottage," and a shopper's "paradise" where electronic salespeople pitch schlock around the clock, wise to our electronic profiles. Finally they show us the bookless electronic classroom where computers have replaced kindly Miss Philby, the kindergarten teacher. It is not a pretty picture.

Probably in response to these pundits another group of pundits has emerged, exemplified by writers like Jeremy Rifkin,[1] who portray the computer as the vehicle of impersonal forces, controlled by "a new priestly class" of computer programmers, who are asocial, cold, godless, technocrats bent on the enslaving of the individual.

People who work with computers and experience both their power and their limitations tend to ignore this kind of writing or assign it to the same category as horror movies about computers that run wild and impregnate young women. Certainly anyone who has spent time with programmers has learned that, while there are a lot of unflattering adjectives you can rightfully use to describe them, "priestly" is not one of them. Anyone who is going to develop a program that real people are going to be able to use must understand a lot about how people think and work, and this means they have to be more than usually aware and sensitive to other people.

But the issue here is not the reality of what the computers and the people who run them are all about, it's how you may have already come to think about them. And the chances are very good that as a writer and therefore a reader, what you have read about computers has left you feeling that by deciding to get involved with computers you are somehow selling out.

If your image of yourself is built around the idea that you are an artist and therefore, by the sheer nature of your being, in essential conflict with the forces of corporate, industrial, life-deadening conformity, you may well have come to see the computer as being allied with the enemy in the struggle, a tool for enforcing conformity and for extending centralized control. To use a computer with this mind-set brings up emotional responses at the level below reason.

This requires some further thought.

Computers are tools. There is absolutely no question that they can be used effectively by bureaucracies to collect and monitor information about individuals and that this represents a threat to privacy. What thwarts this threat, more than any single factor, is the sheer inefficiency of bureaucracies staffed by lowly operatives whose only purpose is to make unpleasant the lives of their fellow men. As long as computer systems require great intelligence to design and implement—which is unlikely to change anytime soon no matter what you read in business magazines—the sheer incompetence of the people who work for the more nefarious bureaucracies makes it unlikely that the computer systems they might like to use to control and constrict will ever work properly!

[1]Jeremy Rifkin, *Time Wars* (New York: Henry Holt and Co., Inc., 1987). See in particular, p. 153.

But the real reason that computers are associated with such a negative antiindividualistic strain in our society and are identified so closely with faceless bureaucracy is only that for the first generation of their existence they were so expensive that only faceless bureaucrats who were part of enormous, wealthy organizations could afford to own or use them.

THE SCRIBES IN THE TEMPLE—COMPUTERS AND BUREAUCRACY

Few of us remember that writing itself was the sole preserve of a real priestly class for thousands of years. In Sumeria where writing first developed, as in Egypt and many other early societies, learning to write was a major part of the education of the priestly class, which is why a portion of that priestly class were called "scribes." In such societies just mastering the mechanics of writing set you apart from the proles. And this wasn't the case just thousands of years ago. Just six hundred years ago you could beat a murder rap anywhere in Europe if you were a Clerk, that is, a cleric or churchman. How did you prove that you were one of these priviledged individuals? By proving you could read and write.

In such times books were prohibitively expensive and could be owned only by institutions or members of the ruling class. And where writing was limited to a small percentage of the general population the subject matter of writing was extremely limited too. Religious subjects got a lot of ink—not surprising when writing was limited to a priestly class. But one other subject dominated writing from the days of Cretan Linear A to the eleventh-century Domesday book of Norman England: detailed accounting records used for tax collecting. Many of the ancient written records we have list the names of taxpayers and what they owed the temple or the king.

There is little doubt that in those pre-Gutenberg days a lot of smart, tough peasants felt that something about reading and writing turned a man into a snobbish, peasant-crushing prig, intent on squeezing the last penny out of the poor. It is also just as likely that creative bards of such times, making a clear distinction between themselves as artists and the denizens of the regimented tax-collecting priesthood, considered the ability to memorize thousands of verses in meter the mark of the truly free creative artist and had only contempt for those chicken tracks in the clay.

This situation changed only when access to written materials was widely available to all classes in society and this only occurred after the invention of the printing press.

Well, computer history moves a lot faster. The first computers emerged during World War II and at that time and for the next 25 years they were very much the province of a highly select, and therefore mysterious and, yes, priestly, class. And yes, the tax collectors and others of their ilk, most notoriously banks and insurance companies, were the first to use computers in their first nonreligious uses.[2]

But the last few years have seen the price of computer technology drop to where computers—real ones capable of sophisticated work—have become affordable even for artists. There is nothing faceless, oppressive, and limiting about computer technology per se, only about the kinds of people who monopolized its use when it was prohibitively expensive. And that time is past. The technology that you (or anyone else) can buy today for under $2,000 is better than anything the bureaucrats had to work with until very recently, and is so mind-blowingly powerful that the only real limit on its use is that most of us don't have thoughts complex enough to need its power!

Therefore the decision to take advantage of computer tools can be a decision to strengthen the individual and, therefore, to strike a blow against the grim, faceless, bureaucratic priesthood that technophobes fear. The more that truly creative, intelligent, thinking people have access to this technology the more they can put it to work doing the important things that it is good at. And the things computers are good at range from providing a bridge to the world for the physically handicapped, to allowing worldwide communications with strangers via bulletin boards about things that the corporate power structure and the media outlets they own don't want you to learn.[3] This is a lot better than letting computer technology be wasted by the jerks whose idea of exciting ways to use technology is to design nuclear weapons or to target your zip code for a shampoo mailing.

THE REAL ISSUES INVOLVED IN OPTING
FOR COMPUTER MODE

So much for getting over feelings that somehow using a computer associates you with the wrong sort of folks. But there are issues that you should devote some attention to before you leap into wholehearted acceptance of these new tools.

Computers fit into your mind the way that a tool fits into your hand. They are mind extenders in the same way that the written word is. But if you use them extensively, which is how you will use them once you

[2]Since the first uses of the computer were military and the cynic could argue that "defense" is our national religion, religion being defined as that which is most central to existence and therefore soaks up the most resources.

[3]For example, on CompuServe recently, computer writers, breaking through the writer's traditional isolation, have been able to find out from each other which are the best publishers to work with and what rates they should be getting, without having to pay agents to get this important hidden information.

discover their power, there is no question that you will have to become aware of and come to terms with their nature.

What are the real issues involved in computer use? How will using a computer really change you? The rest of this book concentrates to a large extent on the many positive contributions that using computer tools can bring to your work as a writer. Here we are going to look closely at some of the less positive aspects of computer use.

Getting Hooked

For a thinking person the computer represents the most seductive toy imaginable. Not at first. At first a computer is usually frustrating, frightening, maddening, and at times utterly incomprehensible. But, assuming you are able to read and persevere through some of the world's dullest written material, and that you are willing to hunt up people to answer the questions you come up with that the instruction books don't make clear, and that you give the whole procedure some time, the computer begins to make sense.

It makes sense and then it goes beyond just making sense, and you discover that you are in a world where if you do things "right" you get what you want. That may not sound like much, but no other complex environment on earth acts that way. Everywhere else you can do things right till you are blue in the face and most of the time the outcome is a tossup, where luck, chance, and fate seem to play as much a part as anything else.

Not with a computer. Once you understand a computer it has to do exactly what you tell it. And you can tell it extremely complex things, and watch it doing what you told it to do. It becomes an intricate game, this commanding and watching the result. Of course, if you forget to tell it what you want right down to the last detail you may get some peculiar results. These are also the result of its doing what you told it to do, and point out how hard it is to know what you really want.

The computer with its maddening refusal to respond to any but the commands it has been programmed to respect and its enormous but often uncontrollable power is much like Rumpelstiltskin, the surly troll of fairy-tale fame who spun flax into gold for the beleaguered princess but in return claimed her firstborn child. Rumpelstiltskin, like the computer, could be mastered only by those who could guess his secret name, an almost impossible process. But oh, once mastered, the thrill of having Rumpelstiltskin in chains!

When the learning period is over you may begin to find that much of your creative energy is going not into your former outlets but into thinking of complex effects that you can get your computer to achieve for you. You will begin to find that the experience of having this wonderful environment responding to your imagination and doing the things you think up for it becomes mentally addictive. And note the use of the word environment, because when you become comfortable with the computer it is as an environment that it appears to you, not as a machine.

Computer programmers experience this all the time at work. Many programmers I've known expressed a real fear about bringing a computer into their homes because they suspected that they would then never leave its side. The intensity of the mental game that you can become involved in once you become comfortable in the computer environment is indescribable: Not as media reports of teens who talk only computer language suggest, because the computer lets you escape into a cold machinelike world where you are escaping from people, but because a computer lets you think in such complexly interconnected and fundamentally creative ways.

Needless to say, I am not suggesting that a few weeks with a word processor will turn you into a zombie. It won't. It may take years for you to get comfortable enough with it to even see the horizon of the creative place in the computer environment. But see it you will. That is when you begin to understand how your software works, what it looks at in making decisions, how software logic functions, and how you yourself can begin to take shortcuts because you understand these things. Then you begin to use your software in creative ways that it was not necessarily designed for. All this leads you into wanting to do and learn more.

Once you get that far the truly impressive thing is how easy it all is. Programming is not some abstruse subject requiring mathematical and engineering ability. Colleges have thrown a lot of courses into the curricula of computer science departments that do require these abilities. But this is more a political move that ensures that only a small number of people get through those programs than a reflection of what you really need to know to master computers. The ability to program is known to be a knack very closely allied mentally to the ability to learn languages or improvise music. It can be tested for by using the same kinds of analogy testing that you find on tests of verbal ability. So the truth is that it is a knack likely to be found among the talents of the creative, word-loving writer.

So there is a small but real possibility that by getting involved with a computer you are opening up a lot more involvement than you had intended, that you will become attracted and even addicted to its powers, its responses, and its use.

How Computer Use Can Change Your Method of Writing

There are other concerns. Writing on a computer is not like writing on paper, and there are subtle changes in your writing method that may creep up on you and cause you trouble. Whether or not this becomes the case has a lot to do with what your current writing method is. If your words come out right the first time, then moving to a computer will have a minimal impact on your style, but if you write incrementally, approaching your final text through a series of drafts, each one a closer approximation toward what you are getting at, then using a computer will give you new temptations to deal with.

These new temptations arise from the fact that once you get your word processor up and running, your text is so temptingly revisable. All you have to do is bring the system up, call up your file, and then you can move this paragraph from here to there, change this word, add that sentence, and embroider on your first draft until it is completely unrecognizable.

There are two things, then, that are not going to happen here that used to happen. First of all, you are not going to have to start typing the whole thing from scratch when going into a revision, the way you used to have to do with a typed draft. This means that you may not get into the forward momentum that so often results in a revision that is inspiringly different from the copy you started with because of flights of ideas that seemed to pop out of nowhere when all you intended to do was tighten up the prose.

You may read the above and reply that you realize how important it is to work through several drafts and that you will simply print the early draft out and erase it off the computer. Don't count on it. Erasing something you have written on the computer is right up there with turning off a life support system hooked up to a loved one. You will find you just can't bring yourself to do it. At best you may be able to convince yourself to copy your draft to a diskette to be stored in a box, which you will keep for the rest of your life. At worst you will keep your draft and every other thing you ever write right there on your hard disk until you completely fill it up.[4] The temptation to keep working with what you already have typed in on a computer, rather than starting over and doing it right, is almost irresistible.

The second thing that happens is that, unlike what happens when you make minor revisions on typescript, the crossed-out words and inserted sentences you add when you revise with a word processor become seamlessly one with the original text and you have no record of your revisions. This can be a problem if you are prone to go in and ruin good stuff with too many fussy changes. If you do this on paper you usually notice how bad the revisions are the next time you look at the manuscript. But with computer emendations, the original version is gone. You can, if you are extremely disciplined, make intermediate copies of your work, but you have no easy way to compare the old and the new, and few people even bother to do this.

---

[4]And, if you should actually bring yourself to erase something, you are guaranteed to need it a few days later.

So a single afternoon of uninspired word swapping can end up ruining a work, and you may not even realize it because you don't have the "before" version left with the revisions scrawled all over it as a road map to what you have done.

Given that this is a problem it is only fair to mention that while using a computer may cut down the number of drafts you are tempted to write, using the outlining software we discussed earlier may eliminate some of the *need* for extensive redrafting. If you can train yourself to work in the outliner when in your planning stage you may be able to end up with 20 or 30 pages of highly detailed outline where you clearly see the relationship of each paragraph or section to the next, rather than having to flounder through writing a hundred pages of poorly sequenced paragraphs, which will require extensive rewriting, merely to get your ideas out to where you can see them.

Working with a word processor makes it all too easy to get hung up at the word level. Since it is possible to move everything so easily and since the on-line thesaurus waits to prompt you anytime you are at a loss for words, you may end up working obsessively on a few paragraphs at the beginning of a work. As you word them and reword them you may fail to ever break out of warm-up mode into the inspired, flowing, middle stage of creativity.

Without a computer you may have been used to just sitting down and writing, typing away, knowing that you would probably throw the first two pages out, once you broke through to what you were trying to say. With the word processor you may end up belaboring those first two pages until you forget entirely what they were supposed to lead to.

And even when you have written something terrific, the facility with which you can revise on the word processor can lead you to keep working on your prose until it is overworked. It is just so easy to make changes. Nothing corresponding to a heavily inked- up paper full of crossings out and caretted sentences remains to show you how much revising you have done.

But none of this may be a problem to you at all. To what extent the ease with which you can make revisions will be a problem and to what extent it is a benefit is a subjective thing, and has a lot to do with your style as a writer. Interviewed in *Writer's Digest*, Ann Rice described the freedom of revision that the computer gives as what lets it become "the pure poetic tool it is capable of being," and exulted "The computer really enables you to get *exactly* what you want to get. There's really no physical barrier anymore between you and your vision."[5]

Losing Contact with Your Back Pages

Another problem with using a word processor emerges as you become more comfortable with it. At first you will undoubtedly print out every

---

[5] Stanley Walter, "Ann Rice," *Writers Digest*, Nov., 1988, p. 42.

page just as soon as you have entered it in, to see what it looks like on the printer. The printer's output is what you think of when you think of writing, after having spent all those years with your typewriter, and the screen never really looks the same.

But after a few months, if not sooner, you will become confident that what you are typing into the computer is getting in there properly, and you will begin to be appalled at the reams, and I mean literally reams, of paper that you are burning through printing out your work. The reason for this is partly that cheap printers tend to spew out blank but unusable sheets of paper every time you want to look at what you just printed. Every time you print a single page on many printers you have to spit out an empty page to tear off the printout. This leads to an awful lot of wasted paper. But the main reason for wasted paper is not this. The main cause of wasted paper is that every time you print out your manuscript, you will invariably see something that needs to be changed. If it were typed you would just do it in pen. But the computer makes it so easy to correct the typo, or rephrase a paragraph, or change the spelling on a word or even the type style or margins, and then print it out looking *perfect* that you invariably do it, and end up printing an article or chapter not once but three or four times, if not more, until it is utterly, unquestionably, flawless. Somehow scribbling in a correction in pen on a printed-out manuscript seems ridiculous when you have access to the word processor's power. The upshot of this is that you will begin buying paper by the box and astound yourself by how fast it disappears.

Eventually, when you come to feel comfortable with your software you will compensate for this tendency to chew up paper by printing things out only when they approach their utterly final stage, and here is where the new problems emerge.

Once your scribbles are stored in electronic rather than paper form you will find that you are much less likely to go through them. You can't sit down on a rainy day and just leaf through your old stuff the way you used to, appreciating your own efforts and being amazed at how good so much of what you threw away is. Instead you end up with diskettes full of files, each identified only by a file name, whose contents you forget. While you can use your word processor to load them in and look at them, doing so is a lot more work than leafing through old paper files. The experience of this computer browsing is not much fun. It is not something to do snuggled in your favorite chair on a rainy day, and so the chances are that you won't do it.

Screen Scrunch

Finally there is the issue of working with the screen. Programmers have found that no matter how many years they work on computer terminals, reading a program on the screen is simply not the same as reading the printed paper version. You miss things.

Why that is is not clear, but there is no question that it is true. And you will find it to be true too when you complete printing out a 60-page story only to discover that somehow egregious errors have crept into each page: sentences with missing words, glaring typos, poor sentence flow; somehow they don't leap out of the brightly lit screen at you the way they do off of a printed page. And the spell checker won't save you either, as your printed page can still contain typos—they just happen to be words that are found in the dictionary.

This is why most people who use computers a lot, no matter how enthusiastically, tend to be the least likely to look forward to a bookless future in which computers have replaced paper entirely. Reading a screen is always, unlike reading paper, hard work. Perhaps advances in screen technology will change this, but for the time being you probably should resign yourself to dealing with it.

The Fritter Factor

As we discussed in an earlier section, having a computer to futz with can be one way of dealing with writer's block. By giving the writer the equivalent of finger exercises, the computer may give you something to keep you in your study and at your desk until you are ready for productive work. But it doesn't take genius to see that having your computer there, full of things to fiddle with, can also lead to wasting the time you had intended to give to creative work by frittering with endless text formatting, making your letters to the electric company perfect, and graphing your checking account balance.

So productive can you feel while involved in frittering that you may not realize for a long time that you have effectively stopped working. Whether or not you are prone toward this kind of behavior is something only you can gauge but it is something that you will have to stay alert to once you have become comfortable with your computer.

Getting Hung Up in the Mechanics

One problem you may have working on a computer, at least for the first few months, is that you will not be able to give yourself up completely to the creative task because there is simply so much to learn and remember about the mechanics of using the new hardware and software. This is to be expected, and it does lessen after a certain amount of time, but if you bought your computer expecting to get the benefit of your new tools immediately, you may end up feeling ambivalent if not downright hostile after your first few days. Having to stop what you are doing to look up one thing after another in the manual just to get a typed page out may be so frustrating or so anxiety provoking that it short circuits your creativity. If you are not a good typist, your frustration may be even worse, because added to all the text you have to type are a whole lot of other keystroke combinations too.

Reading this book should at least keep you from unrealistic expectations when you begin using the computer and should protect you from situations where you end up feeling frightened, helpless, or stupid, feelings which are the most likely to sour your relationship with a computer for the long term and put a crimp in your creativity too. If you remember nothing else after reading this book, you will remember that you have to allow for a learning period when getting involved with a computer, and that you have to expect that your creativity will be fettered for a time while you figure out how to use your new tools. However, this is a short-term problem, and most people find that the technical details of using these tools gradually, like learning to type on a keyboard, become second nature and fade out of their consciousness while they are working.

Health Concerns

Whether or not computers cause health problems is a hotly debated subject and one you should consider before bringing one into your life.

The issue has been raised in the workplace by unions concerned about CRT operators whose jobs involve typing at computer terminals all day long, entering customer addresses and accounting information for huge industrial systems.[6] These operators were the first large group of workers whose work involved spending many hours a day in front of computer screens, and over the last decade a lot of anecdotal evidence (that is, evidence that scares the bejeezus out of the public but is not entirely convincing to scientists) has accumulated to the effect that prolonged peering into a computer screen can be harmful to your vision, your fertility, and possibly your sanity.

The most commonly reported complaints are stress-related problems: backaches, nervousness, and headaches. To some degree these problems are caused by the mind-deadening nature of what most CRT operators have to do, which is to type things like insurance policy records all day. The usual suggestion for helping these problems is that the operator take a break every hour. But then again, these problems also stem from prolonged staring at one small area that typifies working on a computer, and therefore are of interest to the writer.

---

[6]CRTs are cathode ray tubes. This is a term used to describe the TV-like screens found both in computer terminals attached to large systems and in PC monitors. They are also called VDTs, short for video display terminal.

Other health problems stem directly from the nature of the display itself. A computer screen, like a television image, is made by an electron beam that constantly refreshes the screen image as it scans across the screen from top to bottom at a rate that is too fast to be consciously perceived. This constant rewriting of the screen causes a subliminal flicker which you don't notice but which does effect your eyes. Eyestrain is a definite risk.

Many computer users also find that peering at a computer screen for long periods of time seems to cause focusing problems, particularly for people thirty years old or older. After five or six hours of working on a manuscript on a computer you may well discover that your eyes feel like they have been pulled out of their sockets and twisted around, and that reading a book is almost impossible. The American Optometric Association in its booklet "VDT User's Guide to Better Vision," claims that these vision problems are not serious and can be treated with—surprise—frequent visits to the optometrist! Optometrists also say that the focusing problems that afflict so many older computer users are merely a by-product of the general stiffening of the focusing muscles which everyone experiences as they age and that the strain you experience staring at a computer won't actually damage your eyes, though it is annoying. For those who wear glasses, they suggest you may need a different prescription to work comfortably with a computer screen since the distance at which you read the screen is not the distance you probably read books at. Some people find eye exercises useful for counteracting this kind of strain.

Staring fixedly at a screen, besides causing eyestrain, also leads to the development of a wry-neck and other painful musculoskeletal imbalances. To counter this the experts suggest that you make a conscious effort to look around from time to time and that you take a 15 minute break once every hour from your computer-based work. Unfortunately, given the orphic haze into which the creative writer may descend and lose all awareness of time, this may not be a realistic solution. I don't want to set an alarm clock to interrupt my writing every hour!

Another reason given for eye problems is improper lighting and glare in the computer work area. The American Optometric Association suggests that you keep your computer screen away from a window and use shades or curtains to block out bright sunlight which could reflect off the screen. When you buy a screen keep these guidelines in mind and look for one that has a glare-reducing surface and can be swiveled or tilted both to minimize glare and change the angle of your neck as you peer at it.

The most controversial claims that computers cause health problems relate to the broad spectrum of nonionizing electro-magnetic radiation that the monitors give off. While this radiation, which is also emitted by your TV, has been certified as safe in several studies, the unions who represent CRT operators continue to demand further study. Most worrying is the possible effect of this radiation on your cells and on your potential offspring. Unions have demanded investigation of ominous "clusters" of higher-than-expected numbers of miscarriages and birth defects among groups of CRT operators, the most recent of which occured in the offices of the newspaper, *USA Today.*

For years industry spokesmen rushed to pooh pooh these scattered claims, and employers posted xeroxed rebuttals of CRT-induced problems on the bulletin boards of offices where CRT operators and programmers worked on these terminals. Then a 1988 study of 1,583 pregnant women run by the Kaiser Permanente Medical Group found that the rate of miscarriages among women who sat in front of computer terminals more than 20 hours a week was twice that of women who did not. However, because the study was based on questioning participants after the fact and thus was dependent on the respondent's memories rather than direct observation, there is still some question as to whether its results are entirely valid. Some people argue that people whose pregnancies had negative outcomes might exaggerate their memories of their computer use after the fact as a way of seeking an explanation for what happened. Nevertheless, there is enough data to make you give the issue serious consideration.

Finally, as if all this weren't depressing enough, doctors who study occupational medicine have noticed an epidemic of cases of "repetitive motion syndrome" or "carpal tunnel syndrome" among office workers who use computers intensively. These terms describe an excruciating inflammation of the nerves of the hand brought about through performing the same motions over and over—in short, by pounding endlessly on a computer keyboard. The computer, these doctors claim, has made typing more dangerous because typing on a computer, unlike typing on a traditional typewriter, is not broken up by pauses to change paper or move the paper forward. Hours of unrelieved pounding on delicate hand structures not designed for this sort of thing can lead to tinglings and shooting pains in the hands, which, if ignored, can lead in time to irreversible nerve damage and incapacitating pain that cripples the sufferer, in the worst case making it impossible to ever use a keyboard again!

Some solutions to this problem suggested by experts in "ergonomics," the science of designing for the workplace, include obtaining "properly" designed keyboards, using special rests for the wrists to keep the hands at a less stressful angle, and, once again warning computer users to take an hourly break from computer-based work.

All these issues are widely discussed in the media and are of grave concern to the business community, if for no other reason than that if they turn out to be true every employer in America will be facing some serious law suits. They should concern you but not necessarily keep you from using a computer. If you have to cut down your exposure to the kind of radiation monitors put out, trashing your color TV would probably be as good a place to start as refusing to use a computer. You can be alert to muscle aches and other signs of physical stress when using a computer and take steps to prevent such stress. And you should discuss any persistent problems with a knowledgeable doctor if you can't eliminate them yourself. Certainly, when considering a computer it would be a good idea to go to the library and read up on the latest research before committing yourself wholeheartedly to the new technology.

4

PRIMING THE WETWARE:
Getting the Education You Need to Begin

I only took the regular courses...the different branches of Arithmetic—Ambition, Distraction, Uglification and Derision.

Lewis Carroll, 1832-1898
Alice's Adventures in Wonderland

We've looked at what the new technology can do for you, the writer. We've looked at some of the reasons you might or might not want to try it. Now it's time to get serious and figure out how to go about putting this stuff together.

You could, of course, go down to your local computer store—be it Radio Shack, Sears, or Joe's Byte Shop—explain your needs, and ask the salesperson what he or she would recommend that you buy. But frankly, doing this is right up there with asking a used car dealer to recommend a likely vehicle. You might end up with a terrific system that includes all the hardware and software you need. But the chances of this happening are not very high. Most likely you will get whatever the store management is pushing that week, whether because of dealer incentives, inventory needs, or the personal biases of the store owner. If you are obviously at sea and clearly not part of a large company whose continued business is important to the store, you may well end up with soon-to-be discontinued models, obsolete configurations, and older, less feature-filled versions of the software you wanted. Even if this doesn't happen, you may end up being sold a system that would be great if you were running a small manufacturing company but not so great for the impoverished, but creative, artist.

This isn't just a subjective opinion either. The Better Business Bureau has noted that the number of computer-related complaints has increased greatly over the last few years, and the cutthroat competition between computer manufacturers, software companies, and computer retailers is only likely to make this trend worse.

What then are you to do?

FILLING THE EMPTINESS BETWEEN YOUR EARS BEFORE ATTACKING THE SPACE ON YOUR DESK

Traditional guides start out by showing you how to buy hardware and then moving on to software. But this ignores the most important "ware" you need to acquire: "wetware." Wetware, to borrow a common science-fiction writer's term, is the stuff between your ears.

Before you are ready to go out and buy anything, you need to acquire a small but powerful set of concepts, just enough to keep you from falling into the traps that wait for those who don't know what it is that they don't know.

This may sound daunting, but it should not really be. There are more resources—good ones—available to help you pick up the knowledge you need about computers than you would find in almost any other area. And as a writer, a person who is comfortable with the written word, you already have the most important skill necessary to learn and to enjoy learning the subject matter involved. The tales of misery you hear from people stymied by computers are less a reflection of the difficulty of learning about computers than of most people's inability to learn anything at all once they are out of school in our painfully word-blind society.

If you have been in a bookstore or a magazine stand lately you cannot have helped but notice how many publications are devoted to computers and computer-related subjects. Many chain bookstores that are otherwise filled almost entirely with TV star biographies and diet books have shelf after shelf filled with well-written computer books at every level of technical expertise. This reflects the simple fact that computer users are readers—one of the only groups of readers left. People involved with computers tend to be people who not only can read but enjoy doing so. To keep up with the huge amount of ever-changing technical information concerning computers, serious computer people have to read, because a large proportion of the information they need to know about computers is only found in print.

Books: Great, but Not When You Start Out

Having extolled the tremendous print resources available to help you learn about computers, we are going to tell you to ignore them for now—except, of course, for this book! The reason is that none of them will do you much good, or for that matter make much sense to you, until you have a chance to use a computer yourself.

The problem with reading a book about computing before you have had a chance to work on a computer, is that you are in a situation much like that of a prepubescent teenager handed one of those "Everything Teens Need to know about Sex" books. What you read simply isn't real to you. You won't know what the books are talking about, really, until you try it yourself. And if you try it without some guidance from those more experienced than yourself you are likely to end up in one of those "someday we'll look back on this and it will all be funny" tragicomedies.

Books don't help much until you get the feel of what computer use is like. But there is a further problem. Unfortunately, most of the books you will find on the computer shelves are product- oriented books that assume you have already decided to buy one or another kind of computer and load into it particular software products. These books also assume that you understand some things you don't know yet. Later, after you get some guided hands-on experience, these books can be life savers—even highly experienced computer owners buy them— but for most people it is almost impossible to get started learning computers with the help of books alone.

Therefore, if the temptation to buy a computer has not gone away after you take a long restful nap, the absolutely first thing you should do is to get your hands on a computer long enough to get a feel for what a computer is like, in a setting where someone who understands that computer can hold your hand.

Where do you get this kind of exposure? Many computer stores offer classes, but the catch here is that you only get to take them after you have bought the system they foist on you. Clearly this is not the way to go.

Hands-on Courses

Your best bet if you live in an urban area of any size is the local community college or any university extension service: in other words, adult education departments. Introductory computer courses have been big moneymakers for these schools, so you may find that there are several flavors of introductory courses to choose from in your region. If you are paying for these courses yourself, avoid for-profit schools as well as seminars given by consultants. The same courses given by these kinds of groups will cost a lot more and not necessarily teach you more. For the information you need you don't need gold-plated instructors or industry mavens, just someone who has used a personal computer for a few years, can explain what he knows, and enjoys helping beginners as they make the classic mistakes over and over again.

If you can't find community college courses, you might be able to find something at the local high school. Don't turn up your nose at these classes either. You really do need a very introductory course. Failing that, if you have a "day job" you might be able to finagle yourself into getting sent, at company expense, to an introduction-to-computers course intended for managers. To get this to happen you will have to demonstrate to your boss how using a computer could make you a more valuable employee.

What you probably don't want to get involved in is the introduction-to-computer courses given for credit at a college or university, not because this kind of course is not filled with useful information, but because such courses are usually part of a rigorous program designed to flunk out would-be programmers. As a result they can be extremely difficult and may focus on topics related to computer programming that will contribute little to help you master your own computer.

Once you have found some courses, you need to screen the course descriptions to locate the ones that are the best for your purposes.

What you want is a class where you will get both lectures from an instructor and a chance to sit at a computer and try things out, with the instructor present. The course you are looking for probably features a course description that touts it as a chance to "meet the computer." Hopefully it allows you to sample different kinds of software as well as giving you an introduction to working in a common computer environment like DOS or the Macintosh environment.

Avoid courses that focus on BASIC programming. BASIC is a computer language that many schools use in their introduction to computer programming classes. Later on, when you have more experience, you may find one of these courses interesting, but learning to program is not what you need right now. Also avoid product-specific courses— courses on "Using dBase" or "Mastering Lotus 1-2-3," for example—unless you know enough about the product the course is built around to have a serious interest in learning it. If there is a word processing class available you might find this a good way to start, as long as it doesn't assume as a prerequisite that you are already familiar with computers, but be aware that the word processors taught are often not the ones you would choose as a writer, often they are those that are more suitable for secretarial work and memo production. Nevertheless, before buying a system yourself it is a very good idea to get a chance to get the feel of word processing, even with a word processor you don't plan to buy.

The classes you actually find listed in your adult education catalog usually reflect several things: the hardware the college got talked into buying, the subjects that the college's staff feel comfortable with, the products that are the best sellers in your area, and lastly, the needs of local employers, since employers often subsidize community college courses if they think their employees would benefit from them. If possible, try to talk to the instructor before signing up for the course to determine whether you will be getting a chance to sit at a computer, not just to listen to lectures.

Although you will learn a lot working on any small computer, ideally you should look for courses that use the hardware and software that you are most likely to end up buying, and right now at least that means that you want to avoid the elementary-school-oriented Apple II systems and the game-oriented Commodores that often seem to be standard equipment in educational institutions. These computers were purchased by school systems by the hundreds during the home computer frenzy of the early 1980s when parents were sold the idea that if their children didn't get a chance to become "computer literate" in school they would end up sweeping floors. These computers are nowhere near as powerful as the IBM PC-style computers and the Apple Macintosh computers—which are not at all the same as the Apple IIs used in many schools—which are the computers most commonly used by writers and other professionals. You are interested in PC-class computers so you should avoid classes build around the more powerful DEC and Unix-based computers that you sometimes will find in colleges. These are wonderful computers but are much more powerful than the systems you can buy and they use entirely different software.

If you have a choice try to take a course where you will have an IBM compatible or a Macintosh personal computer to bang away on, and where you will learn the fundamental concepts of computer use.

Computer Users Groups: Your Best Resource

If you live anywhere near a large city or near a university, you may very well have another great resource available: a computer users group. Computer users groups are nonprofit organizations whose aim is to bring together people who share an interest in computers. These groups usually coalesce around specific machines, so that you will find a PC users group focusing on IBM PCs and compatibles, a Mac Users group, a Commodore users group and so forth. Usually the group meets once a month and features a speaker of interest to the whole group. But the real value of a users group is its Special Interest Groups or SIGs. SIGs give people with a common interest in certain topics a chance to get together on a regular basis and focus on these topics. What makes this a resource for you, as a beginner, is that most users groups sponsor "New User" SIGs whose entire purpose is to answer the questions and address the concerns of people like you.

Usually New User SIGs are led by people who are very experienced in using computers, who can answer the more common kinds of questions that new users have and can, in addition, direct you to other members of the organization who might have the specialized information that you need. For example, you might be put in touch with other writers, or people who use computers for sophisticated business writing.

The membership of users groups tends to be diverse. You will find some people who make their living working with computers, a lot of people who use them to support their own home-based businesses, students, hobbyist fanatics, and people like yourself who are looking for help getting oriented.

Computer users groups are the place to find answers to questions like: What local stores have the best reputations—or the worst, where are good courses available, does product X you have read so much about let you put footnotes at the end of the book or must you always print them at the foot of the page, has anyone tried putting board "Z" in a such and such computer, has anyone ever had trouble ordering from XYZ mail-order company.

You can also get suggestions from user group members about what magazines and books would be best for you to start out with.

Some users groups offer discounts to members on items like paper and diskettes. Some have arrangements with reputable mail order merchants for discounts. Most have a newsletter. But the other two most useful services that many perform are, first, to maintain libraries of "try-before-you-buy" shareware and free public domain software which they sell cheaply, for maybe $6.00 a disk, and, second, to maintain bulletin boards where members can send messages to each other and where you can find a nice selection of free programs to download. As we will discuss later, these programs can form the nucleus of a very useful, cheap system that is particularly appealing if you are short on cash.

Some computer users groups like The Boston Computer Society are huge, internationally known organizations and their meetings are announced in the media. Others are smaller groups that meet on college campuses or perhaps at the local library, and may be harder to locate. Appendix D gives a list of some users groups around the United States and Canada. You can also find users groups listed in the back of *Computer Shopper*, a magazine. However, many excellent and active users groups never seem to make it to any public listing. If you are having trouble locating the nearest computer users group you might try calling local computer stores and asking if they know of any such groups. If that doesn't turn one up don't give up. Try calling the local newspaper and asking them if they are aware of any, or calling the computer science department at a nearby college and asking a staff member if they know of any such groups. There may be several users groups in your community, for example a PC users group oriented to IBM PCs and compatibles and a separate Mac users Group.

If You Use a Computer at Your Job

If you have come into contact with a computer at work or school you may be very tempted simply to buy one like it, since it is what you are familiar with. This is not a bad idea—after all, your employer can afford to pay experts to evaluate technology and recommend the best systems available. But, by the same token, the system at work may have been chosen as the best system by criteria far different than the ones you might apply. Or it might have been bought years ago and there may now be better systems available.

If you are already familiar with using the work computer and its software, the temptation is very great to assume that you have already gotten past the stage where you need to prime the "wetware." You probably know how to turn the machine on, call up the word processor, and get to work and this may have convinced you that you know all you need to know.

But if you make this assumption you might be making a big mistake, because the chances are that your employer has only taught you the absolute minimum amount necessary to get you going, and it is likely that someone else at work has been doing a lot of useful things to the system you use to get it to where you can use it so effortlessly—things you are going to have to do yourself when you get your own.

You also may end up buying a system like your employer's and miss out on competing products that you might like a lot better.

At a minimum, try to find out exactly what your work computer really is. This means looking beyond the brand name or the model number. You may discover, for example, that it has been enhanced with expensive add-in boards and additional memory in order to be able to do some of the functions it performs. It may also turn out that some of what it is doing, it can do because it is attached to a mainframe system with expensive network software that will be out of your range. Finally, figure out what products are installed on it by talking to the person whose responsibility it is to keep it up and running at work. This person, by the way, if you can identify him or her, may be able to tell you how you could improve on the work system on your own, or might be able to suggest software alternatives to you that are less expensive than what your company uses.

Nimble Fingers Make Fast Work: Keyboard Skill

How well you can type will make a tremendous difference in how you feel about your computer. Here again is a topic no one is trumpeting to the press because the last thing that the people selling $10,000 work stations to executives want to call attention to is that being able to type is essential to using them! As everyone in the business world knows typing is something that low-status females do at receptionist desks, not something that anyone with pretensions to the executive suite would be caught dead doing. Even replacing the word "typing" with the word "keyboarding" hasn't removed the onus.

Using a "mouse" is one way of avoiding typing and it is very popular with executives. The mouse is a "pointing device" that you slide around the desktop controling a little arrow that moves around the screen. You use this pointing device to point to pictures that stand for the things you want to do on the computer and then push a button on the mouse to cause the computer to take some action.

But get yourself together, man—you're supposed to be a writer, and writers can't be too proud to type! Typing speed is not per se a necessity for using a computer. But if you are planning to write books you will be doing a lot of typing anyway, and most word processors have some very useful features that are easiest to use if you know touch typing, so that you can hop around your manuscript with a keystroke here or there, and quickly call up the word processor's many features. If you have been relying on the hunt-and-peck technique, this might be the time to sharpen up your typing skills by taking a touch-typing course or after you get your computer, by buying one of the software typing tutorials that lead you through the same exercises a teacher would.

Working in a word processor with hunt-and-peck typing is almost like forgetting to put on your glasses before looking through a powerful telescope!

5

COMPUTER SCIENCE 101:
Everything You Need to Know to Keep from Making a Perfect Fool of Yourself with a Computer

Good too, Logic, of course; in itself, but not in fine weather.

Arthur Hugh Clough, 1819-1861
The Bothie of Tober-naVuolich

Fundamental to your being comfortable with a computer is developing an outlook that assumes the computer is something that you will be able to understand and master. Probably the biggest obstacle you face in doing this is not the computer itself, which is fundamentally a very reasonable and understandable object, but the thought forms that surround it in our society.

Because computers are machines full of electronic components, most people assume that you need a certain amount of mechanical and engineering know-how to use them.

This is simply not true. You do need a lot of engineering skill to *design* a computer, but you don't need any engineering knowledge to use one. And using a computer—as opposed to building one—takes in everything from printing out a one-page memo to writing your own programs to designing your own database.

But aren't computers "scientific"? Isn't "Computer Science" a branch of mathematics, calling for the kind of mind that enjoys calculus and did better than a C- in "Physics for Poets"?

Surprisingly, no. There is nothing scientific, mathematical, or unbearably technically complex that you need to learn in order to be the undisputed master of a computer system. Thousands of people make their living today as computer programmers, coaxing corporate computers to perform all kinds of shenanigans, none of whom could ever explain to you what is really going on inside those machines from an engineering point of view.

What those programmers and the millions of other people all around the world who have mastered computers *do* know is the structure and function of what, for lack of a better term, I will call the Computer Archetype. This computer archetype is a mental construct that simply but adequately describes what goes on in the hardware of an ideal computer. The architecture of this ideal computer is really all you need to understand to be able to reason your way toward the rest of what you need to know.

The computer archetype is, above all, simple. It expresses the common features of all computers without reference to the differences that divide them. There are great differences between different computers, which the experienced computer expert comes to know—a myriad of trivial details which must be learned if you want to use these computers—but the differences are differences of dialect between different computers, they are not fundamental differences in design. The key to understanding computers is mastering something very much like the computer as Platonic ideal.

Once this pure form is held in the mind it is a lot easier to learn the details that separate one computer system from the next. Just as when you have studied one Romance language, like French or Spanish, you have encountered most of the grammatical concepts necessary to learn another, which simplifies learning the second even though you must master the new language's syntactic quirks and its vocabulary.[1]

And the best part of this is that once the writer has fixed the archetype in mind, when he finally gets to the level where he must begin to pay attention to the differences where he must learn the "vocabulary" of computers, it is here, surprisingly, that he begins to find himself at home. Because the writer who enters this world quickly begins to see that the key to the world of the computer is words, his oldest and dearest friends.

Once you have mastered the very basic set of concepts that describe what goes on in the hardware part of a machine, the rest of what you must learn is software. And what you must master to use software is the proper way of using special words, powerful words, words that function in the computer like the magic words of fairy tales.[2]

No matter how wise you are in electronics or the rest, failure to remember the correct invocation with which to call a certain function leaves your computer as obdurate as Rumpelstiltskin, and, like Rumpelstiltskin,

---

[1]Fortunately, computers and computer "languages" are much more similar to each other than human languages are.

[2]"Magic words" play such a large part in using computers that it is not all that surprising to find out that young students of computers tend to spend their spare moments in fantasy role-playing games in which they become magic word-wielding lords and wizards.

your computer can resist you until, at last, you call it by its correct name and it must bend and whimper at your feet to do your bidding.

WHY THE CONFUSION? SOME THOUGHTS ON COMPUTER JARGON

If computers are so easy to understand, why do they have such a reputation for being unfathomable? One problem is computer jargon. Jargon is something people steeped in the humanities have come to loathe, and for good reason. Jargon—a term that derives from the Old French word for the chattering of birds—is the term used to describe new words coined by practitioners of a specialized discipline. Most jargon that we encounter was designed to make simple things sound more important than they are or to confer importance on the jargon's user by making it sound as if the field he works in abounds in difficult mysteries.

Medical jargon, for example, replaces the word "headache" with the jargon term "cephalgia" without, in the process, adding any new meaning to the word. The purpose of such jargon is only to make it hard or impossible for the person who is not an insider to understand what is being said. Social workers began talking about "attention deficit disorder" when too many parents started understanding and using the word "hyperactivity." Again the jargon term here contributes no really new meaning. And everyone knows and loathes the jargon-laden doublespeak used by the government and the military.

This use of jargon is infuriating and takes us all back to that time in our childhoods when grown-ups spelled out things they did not want us to understand or even said them in a foreign language. But unlike the jargon found in the social sciences and elsewhere, the jargon that computers have spawned wasn't invented to confuse you and or render you inferior. The jargon used in computers is made up of new words that are necessary because these new words, or new uses of words, are needed to describe some truly new things.

A sure sign that computer jargon serves a real purpose is the way the words sound. Unlike the jargon in other fields which tends to use ponderous Greco-Roman multisyllabic constructions to denote things that could be described with existing short Anglo- Saxon words, the new computer words themselves are sharp, short, and to the point. Where obfuscatory jargon always replaces a terse understandable word with a longer construction, computer words are usually as brief as possible. This explains the tendency of computer people to use acronyms. These short new words are useful ways of expressing many new concepts which, without acronyms, would have to be described in much longer constructions. But they can constitute a steep barrier for the neophyte who wants to learn about computers.

They are a barrier, not because these terms are hard to understand, but because people who are familiar with these terms forget that others are not and tend to litter their explanations with them. Not only that, but many words when used in reference to computers have special meanings that are not their usual meanings in spoken English. This can lead to the neophyte's assuming that he knows what a word means when in fact it has additional and important computer overtones that he is missing.

None of the jargon words or computer concepts that you need to learn to be comfortable with computers are particularly mentally taxing. But you will have to accept that all too often a person who is supposed to be introducing you to these concepts himself has so totally absorbed computer jargon and the underlying concepts that describe the computer environment that he forgets that he didn't start out by knowing this stuff and he forgets what it took to get to where he knew it.

Unfortunately, when confronted with a computer expert who is making no sense while explaining some computer feature, most people, particularly those from a nontechnical background, assume it is they who are at fault, not the expert, and that this stuff is unbearably hard to understand.

But take my word for it, once you have learned the basic terms you need to know and absorbed the fundamental concepts yourself, you will be guilty of the same fault, using terms that befuddle the uninitiated and mystify the friends you try to excite about some new feature of your computer.

With that in mind, the discussion that follows will paint for you the broad outlines of the "Ideal Computer" and introduce you to some of the technical terms which you must understand to be able to make the informed choices involved in buying and setting up a computer system. In short, what follows is intended to "prime the wetware."

If you already are familiar with computer concepts you can probably skip this section. But a certain amount of caution is advised in assessing how much you really do know. Many of us have seen so much about computers in popular magazines and on TV that we feel as if we are well versed in computer lore. More of us use computers at work and as a result feel comfortable with them. But you may find that there are some holes in your understanding that will show up when confronted by the acid test—buying and attempting to use real hardware and software based on the suspicion that it will do the job you need to get done. Obviously this is not the place for misplaced pride.

So unless you already are writing your own computer programs and batch files, or are the local WordPerfect jockey, stick around and examine the components of a model computer, and in the process prepare yourself to get to work.

THE COMPUTER IS A CLUSTER OF COMPONENTS

When you think of a computer you probably picture a screen, a keyboard, and, if you are a bit more sophisticated, a little box with a slot for diskettes. Maybe, if you are older, you picture tape drives, the things that look like old-fashioned tape recorders, which have had an honored place as illustrations of things computer-oriented, even though for more than a decade computers have used them only for storing backup copies of old files.

What you are thinking about, in a vague kind of way, is hardware. Your computer is not a single machine. It is, instead, a colony of hardware devices, a cluster of separate machines connected to each other the same way that the parts of a component stereo are.

The key thing to bear in mind when thinking about hardware, is that you don't have to understand very much about it. It is doing fascinating things at the molecular level and you can read about them in engineering texts, but all that is irrelevant to you when you want to use it. All that you need to know about this computer hardware is what you know about your stereo: what each piece does.

You probably have no idea how your stereo receiver picks up radio stations, but you know that it does, and you know how to get a stronger signal. Probably too, after having used your receiver for a while, you know what features you would like your next receiver to have, such as push-button station selection. This is the level at which you will come to know computer components.

Our first task then will be to get clear on what it is that computers really do. Because most of what we read about computers is about what computer programs do, rather than what computers as machines do, we think of computers as being very powerful and complex machines and imagine that they perform a lot of very different functions. After all, they manage to send us our bills, tell city traffic lights when to turn on and off, plot satellite trajectories, and, last but not least, format our manuscripts. They must therefore be pretty awesome critters.

But the awesomeness of computers lies not in the vast number of things that they can do. Instead, as we will see, the really impressive thing about computers is that they manage to do so many different complex operations simply by combining in radically ingenious ways the very small number of operations that they actually can perform.

At the highest level we can break down the work that computers perform into three basic functions. They take stuff in, which is what we call **input,** they fool around with it, which is what we call **processing,** and they give us back the result, called **output.** These three functions and these three alone can be used to describe every single computer application known to man!

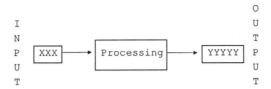

Figure 5.1: What Computers Do: At The Simplest Level

Every component of the computer performs one of these functions. Armed only with this knowledge, we can already describe the function of several of the components of the computer. A keyboard for example, is an input device. Its job is to do nothing more than get stuff into the computer: letters and numbers and function keys whose precise meaning varies with what program we are using. A screen on the other hand is an output device. When stuff hits the screen it stops and goes no further. The computer writes information on the screen and then waits for us to input something else at the keyboard.

We have two pieces of the equation now, the input and output part, but what does the processing?

The Processor and Memory

The processing is done in a **central processing unit** (CPU), which, in personal computers, is usually embodied in a single silicon chip possibly aided by some helper processing units on other chips. These **processors,** as they are called, live in the system unit—the boxy part of a computer, where they are usually clipped or soldered onto what is known as the **motherboard,** the large sheet covered with electronic gadgetry that fills the bottom of the system unit. The processor is the heart of the computer but it doesn't stand alone. Associated with the processor, and probably near it on the motherboard, you will find the computer's main memory, sometimes called RAM, short for **random access memory.**[3]

The processor and main memory work together to provide the third function the computer performs: processing. Here is a simplified version of how this works.

The processor is what textbooks that insult your intelligence call the computer's "brain." This is very misleading because nothing remotely like thinking is going on in any processor anywhere. While processors are extremely fast, they are in no way smart. If you look at

---

[3]Sometimes a processor or memory may be on what are called **cards** rather than on the motherboard, but the function is identical. Cards are little boards that plug in and effectively become extensions of the motherboard.

TABLE 5.1 Hardware Components and Their Functions

DEVICE	TYPE	FUNCTION
Keyboard	Input	Sends characters to processor
Monitor	Output	Displays characters and graphics pixels
CPU	Processing	Reads in bytes containing program instructions and data from memory Adds bytes Compares bytes Writes bytes back to memory Branches to new program instructions
Memory	Storage	Holds bytes that the processor works on Holds program instruction bytes Transfers bytes at high speed to processor
Disk Drive	Input/Output	Writes bytes sent from memory onto a disk Reads bytes from a disk and sends them to memory
Diskette	Storage	Removable permanent storage device Stores data organized in files Contains an index of its files called a directory
Hard Disk	Storage	Fixed permanent storage device Stores data organized in files Contains index to files, called a directory made up of tree-structured subdirectories
Port	Connector	Transfers data bytes to other devices Serial ports send data in a single stream down a single wire Parallel ports send data in a set of streams sent down several wires simultaneously
Slot	Connector	Allows a device on a card to be plugged directly into the motherboard Motherboard bus must match card

what they really do your first response might be amazement at how simple their functions are. The processor certainly does nothing that in any way faintly resembles thinking.

The processor can do very simple arithmetic but nothing very fancy, and in fact the computer can only "count" to two. And while a processor can add and subtract it can't even multiply without the help of a program.

The thing that processors *can do,* which sets them off from other machines, is look at two items—never more—and decide, using fancy electronic circuitry, if those items are the same, or if one is arithmetically larger or smaller than the other!

What else can a processor do? To understand some of its other functions we need to look at the second part of the processor/memory team we mentioned. We noted that the processor can work on only two items at a time, but it needs to work on millions of these items one after the other to pull off the fancy feats it does. So when an item is not in the processor being compared or added it has to be kept somewhere, and that place is the computer's main memory. Memory is a special holding zone for items the computer is going to process, and, most important, main memory is the only place where the processor can actually find these items. If an item is not in memory, the processor doesn't know about it and can't fiddle with it.

Everything the processor processes has to be stored in memory while the computer is working with it. One of the processor's most important talents is that it can take an item that came into it from one place in its memory and copy it to another place in memory. The ability to move things around in memory doesn't sound like much but it is the key to most of what computers can do. Where an item happens to be stored in memory can be assigned a human-understandable meaning. Portions of memory can become the matrix holding the pages of a book. Other portions can be set up as tables of values, while still other portions can be designed as switches and holding areas. Because the processor can manipulate memory, memory becomes the stage on which programs can work out their logic.

The processor's last and most important talent is that it can *change* the items it processes and store them back in memory with different values.

Computers Don't Store Information, They Store Bytes

But, hey, let's back up, what *are* these information items we're talking about?

Well, they really are not at all like what you or I think of when we think of information, or even of data. They are not facts. They are not equations. They are not complex relationships between logical elements. No, they are nothing more than the settings of eight little on-and-off switches! When the processor changes an information item, what the processor really is doing to this "information" is turning switches on and off.

You've heard about these switches, they're called **bits.** Eight of them together make a **byte,** and these bytes are the basic unit of information. Since groups of bytes—sets of eight little switches—are all that the computer can process or store, anything that you want to store into the computer has to be transformed into a series or group of these switch settings.

Fortunately, this is not hard. Just as Morse code is able to express all the letters and numbers with combinations of dots and dashes, computers use codes that are made up of the possible on- or-off switch settings of our eight little on-and-off switches. For the letters of the alphabet we use a code that assigns a unique pattern of the eight switches with some on and some off for each letter, so that we can feed the processor a capital letter A in the form of eight switches set "off off on off, off off off on." To keep ourselves sane we write this by writing a zero for a switch that is off and a one for a switch that is on, thus: 0010 0001. The letter B can be coded in bytes as 0010 0010.[4]

By the way, this particular code, which is used to store the alphabet and other printable characters on PC-type computers, is called the ASCII code. There is an ASCII code value for all the letters, upper and lower case, and numbers, as well as some extra codes that have special meanings to the computer, which are called special characters and which, when sent to the screen, cause it to display hearts, smiley faces, and other junk.[5] Once a letter of the alphabet is stored in memory in this coded form, the processor can look at it and determine if it is an "A" or not by asking if the switches are set to 0010 0001 in that byte.

So when you come right down to it, what the processor can really do is add, compare, and copy whatever can be reduced to little groups of eight on and off switches, as well as flicking these switches on and off at will.

What Software Does to Hardware

Hang on, we're almost through the hard part. We have only one more challenging concept to cover, and that is the one that explains how the processor's pathetic little repertoire of behaviors is able to put men on the moon (or women for that matter).

Think, for a minute, of how we get a machine to do something. Sometimes we have knobs or buttons that correspond to the functions the machine can perform. Hit the brights switch on your car and on come the bright headlights. Hit the accelerator and more gas goes into the carburetor. Press a button on your television control and the channel advances one. Press another button and your toast pops out.

But our processor doesn't have any buttons! We don't have an add button or a copy button or a compare button on our processor. How does the processor get its instructions?

This is the truly brilliant part. We mentioned that the information on which the processor works comes into the processor in small chunks from memory, is processed, and then is put back in memory. But what

---

[4]To further keep from going nuts, computer people use a shorthand to communicate these strings of 0s and 1s. To understand this shorthand you need to understand a little about nondecimal number systems, which I am not going to attempt to explain in a footnote. However what it boils down to is that there are 16 possible settings of four switches and each of these possible switch settings can be represented by a single base-sixteen number. We write these numbers by using the number sequence: 1, 2, 3, 4, 5, 6, 7, 8, 9, A, B, C, D, E, F, 0. The base-sixteen number system is also called the **hexadecimal** number system. You may see these "hex values" mentioned in manuals. You don't really need to understand this now.

[5]You usually see these when something has gone wrong and the computer has sent the wrong things to the screen.

controls the process is this: some of the bytes that come into the processor from memory are the very instructions that tell the processor what to do with the rest of the bytes that are floating through it!

Some of the bytes that the processor receives hold codes that activate the processor's routines. These instruction bytes are the buttons that get the processor adding, comparing, moving, and changing!

The whole process starts out with the processor getting one of these instruction bytes from memory. The instruction tells it what to do (add, compare, copy, turn a switch on or off) and what particular bytes of data, stored in memory, to do it to. Then it gets the bytes of data that the instruction applies to. Once the operation is complete the processor expects to get another instruction byte, and in fact, will treat whatever comes in from memory as an instruction byte. Then, again, it gets the bytes that the new instruction applies to, does what the instruction says it should do to them, and continues doing this for some million instructions or so until it runs out of instructions.

The series of instruction bytes that tell the processor what to do to what data bytes is what we call a computer **program, or software.** *It* is what pushes the buttons on the processor, and it is by putting together lengthy and complex sequences of instruction bytes—sequences that get the processor comparing, moving, changing, and turning bits on and off for the thousands of bytes stored in memory— that computer programmers manage to get the computer to do all the nifty things it does.

The program, then, is a string of bytes. Believe it or not, if you look at them, they look just like the bytes that store characters, in fact if you use a browse program to look at a file containing a computer program you will see a bunch of letters and special characters scattered around in it. That is because the program is a string of instruction bytes and some of these instruction bytes are identical to the codes for letters and special characters. The only thing that makes them instructions rather than data, is the *time* in the instruction byte/data bytes cycle that the processor receives them.[6]

PROGRAMMING LOGIC. But how can a program that simply tells the processor to add, compare, and copy bytes, end up accomplishing so many different and powerful functions? The answer to this is found in the elegance and power of programming logic.

[6]This, by the way explains why if your program is screwed up you can bring your computer to a screeching halt. Usually what has happened is that the processor has gotten a piece of data when it is expecting an instruction and is trying to perform the operation which that piece of data codes for when it is an instruction. Since the data in reality is probably a piece of your short story or some such thing it tells the computer to do something that leaves it utterly confused and unable to proceed.

Programming logic shapes the sequence of instructions that are sent to the processor and assigns complex human-understandable meanings to simple byte switches and blocks of memory that allow them to symbolize complex entities.

A program can assign the value "line number" to a few bytes in memory and then query, as part of a routine to print a manuscript, whether "line number" is greater than 26. Then, based on the result of the comparison, it can branch to a routine that makes the printer skip to a new page and print the page number on top of the page or not.

The computer can add items. So your program can add 1 to the byte that symbolizes "line number" every time it goes through the sequence of instructions that send a line to the printer.

Programs can set switches on or off. This can be used to save useful information that the program will need to know later on in its processing. So the program might set aside a bit switch to which it assigns the arbitrary meaning "All lines printed." By setting the switch on, the program can save the information that all lines *have* been printed. Thus by testing the on-or-off status of that single bit, the program can determine if it has finished printing all the lines making up your manuscript and take action based on that information.

Finally, and most powerfully, programming logic lets you take various paths through the program based on what switch settings and counter values you find. Your program can say: IF the all-lines-printed-switch is equal to "ON" then go to the end-of-printing-clean-up-routine ELSE IF the all-lines-printed-switch is equal to "OFF" then go to the beginning of the print-a-new-line routine.

This last feature, the ability to go somewhere else in the program, allows the programmer to construct a loop. A program loop is a series of instructions where the program branches back to the same instruction over and over again, but in such a way that the repeated instructions operate on a different piece of data on each pass. For example, a single loop containing a few instructions could be used to print thousands of lines of text. All the program must do is add 1 to the line number of the line to be printed before repeating the loop again.

This is powerful magic.

Using the processor's ability to compare things and set switches, combined with this ability to branch and loop, combined with the human ability to assign meaning to patterns—in this case, bytes in the computer's memory—programmers have developed techniques for breaking any task down into simple sequential steps.

It is not our goal to teach you how to program, but it does help to have some sense of how programs are constructed if you want to use them comfortably and be able to deal with them when they misbehave. You can get a feel for the flavor of programming logic with the following simple analogy.

A SAMPLE PROGRAM. If you were to send a spouse to the store to buy a can of peas you would probably tell him (or her): go to the store and see if they have any canned peas in the canned vegetable section that don't cost more than a dollar. Then, if they do, buy them.

But if you wanted to accomplish this kind of operation using programming logic, you would have to build your logic to look something like what you see in Figure 5.2.

```
This program is started by giving the computer this command:
                    PEAS StoreName
```

```
The Program:
```

```
GO TO the store named "StoreName"
OPEN door
    Set the current aisle number to 1
A: WALK down aisle with the current aisle number
        IF the sign on the aisle says "Vegetables"
        SET the more-cans switch to "on"
        PICK up a can
        B:   IF the more-cans switch is "off" leave the store
            IF the can says "peas"
                LOOK at the price
                IF the price is greater than $1.00
                    GET the next can
                    IF there are no more cans
                        SET  the more-cans switch to "off"
                    GO to B:
                ELSE   [to get here the price must have been
                        less than or equal to $1.00]
                    TAKE the can to the checkout
                    PAY for the can
                    OPEN the door
                    LEAVE the store.
            ELSE
                IF the can doesn't say "peas"
                    GET the next can
                    IF there are no more cans
                        SET the more-cans switch to "off"
                    GO to B:
        ELSE [it is not the vegetable aisle],
            ADD 1 to the current aisle number
            GO TO A:
```

Figure 5.2: The Peas Buying Program

This sample program gives you both an idea of how computer programs are designed and some hint of why you encounter the kinds of problems with programs that you do.

This program tries to find your can of peas by looking at every can on every shelf in the store, one after the other. This would be a ridiculously slow way for a person to go about solving the problem in real life, but since the computer does millions of operations a second it can get away with this kind of approach in handling bytes, even if it has to look at thousands of bytes to find the one it is looking for.

Notice that the program compares the sign on the aisle to the word "Vegetables." If your spouse followed this program exactly the way that a computer would but the sign on the aisle said "Produce" you would never get your peas. In fact you would never see your spouse again. The program would just have him endlessly going from aisle to aisle looking for the word "Vegetables" until he ran out of aisles. At that point the program does not tell him what to do next and he would most likely hit the wall. The only way to get out of the store in this program is to find the "Vegetables" aisle.

This is a bug. There is nothing wrong with the computer here—your spouse—just with the program logic. This is just like a real computer bug.[7] The programmer didn't allow for all the things that could happen and as a result, when the program was run, his logic failed.

The solution to this problem might include adding a test for the word "Produce" after the test for the word "Vegetables." But a good programmer would also put in some logic that would count up how many aisles had been inspected and include instructions to leave the store after a reasonable number of aisles—perhaps 99—had been examined. Of course, if you then moved this program over to a Sunbelt Superstore where everything from automotive supplies to pets is sold under one roof and which had more than 99 aisles this program logic would fail again!

This example is simple and farfetched, but it demonstrates very realistically what a computer program is all about. Programs are controlled by switches that can be inspected at different points in the flow of instructions. Programs are built around "loops" where the logic circles back to the same place but because counters are incremented—the aisle number and the can number are each larger by one every time you go through the same logic—the program is processing different data, in this case, a different aisle or can.

You might notice that the program is careful to remember to open the door when entering or leaving the store. If this step is left out the hardware will crash: the shopper will smash into the door. When a program is executing, *nothing* can be taken for granted. Every single thing must be spelled out in the program because the computer can do only exactly what it is told.

---

[7]Although the very first computer "bug" was a moth that was found in an early tube-built computer by pioneer programmer Dr. Grace Hopper.

The program in our example is invoked—started—by giving the computer a command, "PEAS," followed by a word that gives the program a vital piece of information without which it cannot be executed correctly. This word, in the example the name of the store, is called a **parameter.** If it is not supplied to the program, the program will again crash—another bug—since the computer will have no idea of what store to go to when the program begins and so will not be able to get past the first sentence.

Good programming technique would supply a **default** value for the parameter. This means that the program would assume you meant Shop Rite unless you gave it the name of another store when you invoked it. Or the program might have a routine to stop and ask the person who invoked it—you—to tell it which store it should go to. Or it might just give you a message to inform you that your syntax is incorrect and end.

You can already see why seemingly "magic" words have so much power over your computer and its software. When you invoke a program and neglect to give it the parameters it needs, what happens is a function of how good the programmers were who wrote your program. You may get defaults the programmers put in, or you may see a message that tells you that you invoked the program improperly but neglects to tell you what the correct parameters are that should accompany the command. Or you might get no response at all.

And perhaps you can see why a single mistyped letter in a command will cause it to fail too: the words you enter must match every bit of the corresponding word in the computer program or the program won't find a match and as a result won't be able to take action.

Even the much-hyped artificial intelligence programs are really just very complicated logic patterns that try to provide for all the things that a person could respond to a program, given what we know about people. Such artificial intelligence programs are very complex and have logic built in to store the responses that the program generates and the more successful paths through the logic which have been taken in earlier runs. But underlying these artificial intelligence programs are still programs like our sample above and they too depend on the same looping and comparing, as all other programs do.

The Operating System

The program, then—the string of instructions fed into the processor of our computer—is what makes the whole thing go. A processor without a program is dead. From the time you turn on your computer until you turn it off (or crash it), your processor is processing a single continuous stream of instructions and data.

How does this jibe with the fact that you think you are running a series of different programs: your word processor, the outliner, your database program and so forth?

What is really going on is this: Your computer has a "master program" which loads when you start up the computer. This master program is the *operating system*. The master program includes the routines that do many of the common functions that all programs must perform, functions like writing a screen, reading and writing files, and sending characters to an external device like a printer.

Remember how programs have the ability to branch, to go to a new place in the flow of instructions? The operating system, which is itself a program, is able to copy into memory the program you want to run, bringing it in from the disk file in which it is stored. Its own logic then branches to the instructions in this new program, so it then has control of the computer. These "guest" programs branch back to the operating system occasionally when they want a function performed that the operating system handles, like reading a file. When this guest program is done it branches back to the operating system, which then takes back control of the computer. In computer terms when one program branches to another it is said to **call** the other program.

Because these guest programs—the application programs that are the reason you want the computer in the first place—work so closely with the operating system, it is only possible to use software that was specifically designed to run under your operating system. This makes the choice of what operating system you will use very important, since it will limit your choice of software to the programs available for that operating system. Note, by the way, that the actual hardware you buy may be able to run more than one operating system, although for various reasons it may run only one of them fast enough to be of much use to you.

DOS is the operating system usually used on IBM PCs and compatibles. OS/2 is another one that runs on this family of computers, as is PC-MOS. Other operating systems used in small computers are versions of UNIX and CP/M. The operating system that comes with the Macintosh is called its System Software, and is probably the least intrusive of the operating systems you will encounter, its Mac Interface having been designed to take most of the pain out of working with an operating system. Some computer games operate like operating systems and have to load in when the system **boots,** the time when the computer is first turned on.[8]

---

[8]When you first turn the computer on what happens is this: The computer contains a chip that has a small program on it which contains the routines necessary for the computer to read in the rest of the operating system, which resides in files on your disk, and then branch to the main part of the operating system. This process is called **booting,** an allusion to the processs of pulling yourself up with your own bootstraps.

Clearly the operating system is a very significant feature of your computer. Without it installed you can't run any other program! Unfortunately some PC vendors are not above advertising cheap systems whose price is low because, among other things, the operating system is not included. Whatever else you may do without in your system, an operating system is required!

Besides comprising the master program, which effectively runs your computer for you, the operating system usually comes with a couple of handy programs that are utilities, just like the ones we mentioned earlier in our discussion of tools. These utility programs are called **system commands** and are listed in the operating system manual. They do things like copy files or display the list of files on a disk known as a directory. These system commands are just programs, just like any others you might code up or buy in the store, but their quality ranges from the useful to the abysmal. Often you will see utilities that replace or supplement the operating system commands advertised for sale.

A useful function that some operating systems provide is the ability to create **batch files** or other kinds of automated procedures. These procedures make it easier to use your system by letting you "batch" together commands and programs you frequently use. Thus, if you find yourself typing in the same series of commands over and over, you can type them into a special type of file. Then the system will know that when you type in the name of the batch file it should execute all the commands listed in the file one after the other automatically. This feature is very useful for PCs equipped with DOS. If you have one, take the time to master it. It will let you build everything from backup procedures to envelope-addressing routines.

We have looked at our input devices, our output devices, and our processor now, and have begun to understand the computer a little better. Perhaps too, we have gotten a little bit of a feeling for what a program is and what it does in our computer. Now it's time to look at where our computer data spends its time when it is not in the computer's main memory. It's time to talk a bit about storage devices.

Storage Devices

You can have a "real" computer with just an input device, a processor, and an output device. A lot of sleazy merchants sold just that kind of configuration to the unwary back in the early 1980s at the height of the home computer craze. But such a computer is not a very useful object because it is missing a very significant piece.

If you remember, it was mentioned earlier that the processor can "see" only items that are stored in the computer's main memory. This main memory, because it works so closely with the processor, must be able to operate at a speed close to the speed the processor is working at—millions of instructions per second—so that when the processor is ready for its next byte it doesn't have to wile away precious cycles waiting for memory to respond. To achieve this kind of speed, memory is also made out of computer chips, called memory chips, each one of which can store thousands of bytes in a single chunk of silicon and can quickly send any of these bytes to the processor. You can see the chips, encapsulated in plastic, lined up in rows inside your system unit box, usually on the motherboard. This memory storage is measured in bytes or a multiple of bytes because, as we have seen bytes are the basic unit processors work on. (Just remember that one letter of the alphabet can be stored in one byte.) Today's PCs usually come with at least 512K or 640K bytes of this kind of chip-based memory.[9] Many desktop computers can now be configured (set up with) four, five, or even eight million bytes of main storage.[10] However, there is one problem with this chip-based memory associated with the processor—it loses the switch settings it is holding whenever you turn off the electric power supplying it. What it stores is not stored permanently. So it is not a very good place to store anything you want to keep around for more than a very short time, particularly if you are prone to tripping over power cords.

But even if you never turned off your system, memory would still not be a good place to store things for another reason. Each program that you run needs to use a big chunk of that memory to work out its own logic. Not only that, but since the only place that the processor can "see" bytes is in memory, the bytes making up the program itself that you want to run must also be loaded into memory before you can run it. This means that anytime you start up a new program you effectively wipe out the values that used to be stored in the piece of memory that contains the bytes making up the new program, as well as the bytes that the program manipulates as it works out its logic.

Clearly you need some way to store programs and data that are not currently being processed in such a way that they won't get destroyed every time you turn off your machine or change from one program to the next, and in such a way that you can easily load them back into memory when you want to use them again. And this leads us to another class of very important devices: the permanent storage devices, including computer disks and diskettes.

Disks and Diskettes

Disks and diskettes are able to store bytes of information, just like memory does, but they are able to retain their switch settings—the bytes of information—even without power, just like cassette tape and videotape do. Therefore these storage devices are where computer programs must

---

[9] A K is the power of 2 that is closest to 1,000, which happens to be 1,024.

[10] Sizes over 999K are counted in "Megs" which is short for megabytes where "mega" represents the power of 2 closest to a million, which is 1,048,576.

put anything, be it programs or data, that they want to keep for longer than the length of one session on the computer. And, because storage would be useless if the data stored couldn't get in and out of memory, such storage devices serve as both input and output devices.

When a program wants to store something, it writes the bytes that comprise that something (be it a program or some data) on a disk. Then when the computer wants to work on something or run a program, it reads that data or program off a disk into its memory, which, as we mentioned, is the only place that a processor can work on information.

Technically speaking, there are really two parts to what I have been calling a disk. There is the machinery that reads and writes the information, which is called the disk drive, and the actual disk itself which holds the information. This may be removable, like the floppy disks you are probably familiar with, or the actual disk may be hermetically sealed inside the drive itself, as it is in the kind of disk drive called a "fixed" or "hard" disk. A floppy disk consists of a single disk "platter" made out of plastic, which is encased in a protective envelope, made out of paper or plastic.[11] A hard disk contains a stack of metal disk platters one on top of the other, sealed in an airtight container.

Diskettes store the magnetically coded bytes on the same kind of material that recording tape is made out of: a magnetic metallic coating. Hard disks use a metal plate as the base for the recording surface while diskettes use Mylar, but both use the same kind of magnetic coating to store the bits and bytes that make up the data. These bits and bytes are stored as a pattern of magnetized particles in this coating, and are read and written by a recording head.

The bits and bytes are stored in a pattern of concentric circles; each circle is called a track. Disk drives spin like phonograph records when in use. The diskette drive spins only when you give it a command to read and write a diskette. The hard disk spins the whole time the computer is on. While the disk is spinning the read/write heads move in and out from the edge to the center of the disks in order to locate the track that holds the data.

An important part of any disk drive from your standpoint as a user is the little light on its case, which is usually on the front of the computer. When the computer reads or writes data from or to a disk, which is called "accessing the disk," this light lights up. Whenever you are saving data,

---

[11]The protective paper envelope of the diskette which you should never disturb is not to be confused with the diskette "sleeve," the paper envelope that slips on and off the diskette. The protective envelope won't come off the diskette unless you tear it. The sleeve *must* be removed before you put the diskette in the diskette drive. You should avoid touching the brown Mylar surface of the diskette, but you shouldn't worry too much otherwise about harming a diskette. If you don't crunch them, chew them or expose them to powerful magnets, diskettes are pretty tough.

that is, copying a file to a disk, the light on the disk that should receive the data will light up. If you don't see this happening then you are probably not saving your data![12]

Computer operating systems are often not as bright about dealing with disks as you would like. If the program you are using tries to read a file on a diskette drive that has no diskette in it, the light will go on in that diskette drive and the computer will just sit, looking broken, until a predetermined amount of time has gone by during which the attempt to read has "timed out." At this time you will usually get a message which may or may not explain the problem.

Even if you have put a diskette in the drive you may still get a scary-looking error message when you try to read or write to it if the diskette is brand new and you have not prepared it prior to using it by subjecting it to a process known as **formatting.**

FORMATTING DISKS. Before a disk drive can write on a disk the disk must be divided into areas called sectors and have some other areas defined on it. Formatting involves writing information about these sectors on the diskette itself, setting up control areas on the diskette, and testing the entire surface of the diskette for areas that are defective and marking them as unusable so that data loss doesn't occur in those areas. The reason that the diskette manufacturer doesn't do this step for you and save new users hours of confusion is that there are many models of computer hardware and software which all use the same kind of diskette, but which may format them differently. Therefore the manufacturers leave this step to you, knowing that your computer will format the disks correctly for its particular format.

YOUR COMPUTER'S ACHILLES' HEEL. One fact about disk drives that tends not to be emphasized by those who manufacture or sell them is that they are not immortal. In fact, they probably will not last as long as the rest of your computer. This is particularly true of your hard disk. The reason for this is simple. The disk drives on your computer are among the few parts of the computer that contain moving mechanical parts. While the rest of your computer just warms up and enjoys the quiet flow of electrons through its circuitry, your disks are whirling and clanking away, their arms moving tiny distances very quickly and very precisely, reading and writing data and wearing out.

The life of a disk is measured in "Mean Time Between Failures" (MTBF). This MTBF is usually reassuringly high, 60,000 hours for a hard disk, for example, which works out to something like seven years of

---

[12]More than one new user has been horrified to discover that just inserting a diskette into the diskette drive does not save their data onto that disk. You have to tell the computer to write your data to a diskette explicitly via a program.

continuous use. However, since the word "mean" means "average" you have to assume that some drives will fail before others and that it will probably be yours. This is one major reason that you must read and understand the discussion of file backup in Chapter 15. When your disk does go it may very well go with a bang or to be more exact, a "crash."

In a hard disk the read/write heads are supposed to float a couple of molecule-widths above the disk platters. If a head crash occurs, these heads touch the surface of the platter, scratching it and rendering it unreadable. If this happens, you might just lose a file or two. But if the head was positioned over a critical portion of the disk, as often happens, the whole disk may be rendered unreadable and you may need a new one.

What those who sell you disks also neglect to tell you, is that there is a simple step you can take to protect your disks from this kind of damage, particularly when you buy one of the less expensive models. The time your hard disk is most prone to damage is when you turn it off and the disk slows down from spinning at a high speed. It is then that the read/write heads have a higher likelihood of crashing or, if not crashing, of damaging the track that they are positioned over when the power is turned off.

If you read the material that came with your hardware you may find buried somewhere a paragraph that discusses what you should do when moving your computer. On cheaper systems this includes running a special program which is called a **park** program because it moves the read/write heads over a stretch of the disk that is not used for data and "parks" them there. If you have a cheaper system don't wait until you are moving your computer to use this park program. You should never turn the unit off at all without parking the heads, if for no other reason than that if the heads are left over a data track they may weaken its ability to hold a magnetic charge over time. All you have to do to "unpark" the heads, by the way, is turn the computer back on or just give it another command after you issue the park command.

More expensive disk units are built so that the read/write heads automatically spring away from the disk platters when power is turned off to the unit, making it unnecessary to park the heads manually, but parking these won't hurt. You can determine if you need to park the disk heads manually or not by reading the section in the operator's manual that came with your system, looking at what it instructs you to do before moving the system unit or by scanning through the material that comes with an aftermarket hard disk and controller.

What Is a File?

Disks can hold a lot of bytes. We mentioned that main memory, the memory associated with the processor may be able to hold anywhere from 512K bytes to several million bytes. But each removable diskette can hold anywhere from 360K bytes to more than a million bytes, and a hard disk holds anywhere from 20 million bytes to 200 million bytes or more on a single unit. Since you are going to be storing all sorts of related groups of bytes on these disks, whether it be the phone numbers of your contacts, a word-processing program, or the margin settings you like to use for your manuscripts, you need some way to keep related information together and to be able to locate it quickly when you need to find it. The way that we do this is by dividing the information stored on a disk into separate computer **files.**

A file is the basic unit in which we store information on disks. It is important to understand that we are only concerned with files when we are storing or retrieving information to and from disks, not when we are processing it in memory. Once a file is read into memory, the memory version of the data is no longer called a file.

A computer file is nothing more than a series of bytes one after the other that have some reason for being kept together. Every program you have on your computer is stored in a separate file; each manuscript you work on with your word processor is stored in a file; every database on the computer is stored in at least one file and perhaps a cluster of related files. So is control information that programs might need to look up, like your preferred margin settings or what dictionary your spell checker should use.

Each file has a **filename** and the usual way that a program finds a file is by asking for it by this name. Each file must have a unique name because operating systems may not be very bright in this area. If you name a second file with the name of an existing file as likely as not your operating system will simply replace your pre-existing file with the new one when you tell it to write the file on disk.[13]

Microcomputer file names usually have two parts, a name part and a so-called "file extension" which is usually used to indicate what kind of file the file is. For example your word processor may name manuscripts with a "DOC" extension so that your story named "Elephant" would actually be stored in a file called ELEPHANT.DOC. Lotus 1-2-3 spreadsheets are kept in files with the extension of "WK1" and many programs, when they see a file with one of these extensions, expect that the data in it is stored in a particular format. Programs on IBM and compatible systems are stored in files with the extension "EXE" or "COM."

A major job of the computer's operating system is managing these files. Each operating system on the market manages them a little differently, but all of them maintain some kind of index where each entry, like the index of a book, points to the actual place on the disk where that file can be found.

---

[13]Your word processor is, hopefully, brighter and will inform you when you are about to wipe out an older file with a new one of the same name.

This index is called the **directory** and is extremely important. You can look at it to see what files a disk contains. The computer uses it to find the files it needs to read or write to the disk. If the directory gets messed up for any reason, your file is for all intents and purposes gone, although there are some clever programs you can buy that may be able to recover your file in some cases.

Just to make your life more confusing, computers that have large hard disks subdivide their directories. Instead of having one giant directory listing thousands of files they let you set up many **subdirectories,** each containing a set of related files. This is great for keeping logically related items together. For example, your word processing stuff can be kept together in a word processor subdirectory and your outliner stuff in an outliner directory. But unfortunately your operating system may only work with the files in one directory at a time, which means that the programs you are using cannot find files that are not in the one directory that the current program is currently pointing at.

Directories are usually organized in a hierarchical pattern, as illustrated in Figure 5.3. This kind of organization, which, for whatever reason, mirrors the preferred method of organizing workers in American industry, works like this. For every disk there is a top or **root** directory that contains some files of its own, and in addition contains entries that point to several subdirectories. Each of these subdirectories contains its own files and also may include further entries that in turn may point to another level of directories. In the example illustrated in Figure 5.3, DATABASE, ORGANIZE, and WORDPROC are all subdirectories of the root directory ROOT. Each one of these directories has been set up to hold

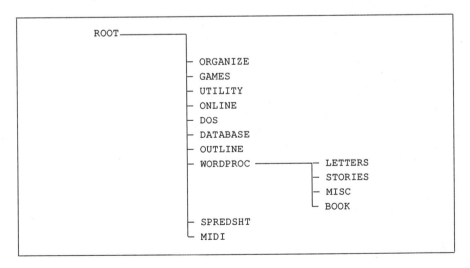

Figure 5.3: A Typical Directory and Subdirectory "Tree"

files that pertain to a particular program, like the word processor, desktop organizer, and database program. LETTERS is a subdirectory of the directory WORDPROC which is the word processor directory. It is set up to hold only letters created by the word processor. However there is no actual difference between one subdirectory and the others in terms of what they can hold.

If you want the computer to find a file in a subdirectory you have to tell it which intermediate directories are on the **path** to that directory. If you don't, the computer's operating system may come back and tell you the file you want doesn't exist, even though it does. In the example the path to LETTERS and all the files stored in that subdirectory would be C:\WORDPROC\LETTERS.

What are Ports?

We have now looked at the most important components of the computer and the software that runs in it, but there are a few more items to consider before leaving this brief introduction to computer concepts.

One of the most useful abilities of the computer is its ability to "communicate" with other machines. What this refers to is its ability to send a stream of bits and bytes down a wire or set of wires to another machine that interprets those bits and bytes in a useful way. Examples of machines that communicate with a computer are printers, remote computers (those reached over the phone), bar-code readers, mice, scanners, and MIDI compatible synthesizers, but these are just a few. Any machine that is capable of dealing with streams of electronic data can theoretically be attached to a computer.

In order to communicate with these or other devices, however, the computer may need another piece of hardware called a **port.** Ports are a gateway in and out of the computer. They come in several varieties. Serial ports send information out in a single stream of bits. On some computers, such as the Macintosh SE, it is possible to chain several serial devices together and hook them into a single port. On PCs, however, it is necessary to have a separate port for each serial device. Parallel ports send out a set of bit streams which travel simultaneously down separate wires. Yet another kind of port, the SCSI port, is used to connect a particular kind of external high density hard disk to computers. Your computer usually comes with a limited number of ports built in although not all do.

Slots, Boards, Cards, and Buses

What do you do if you want to add more memory, more ports, or some other hardware feature to your computer? Because the computer is assembled from components, adding more pieces to the hardware configuration is not a big deal. Most computers include slots on their motherboards. Found in the back of the unit, these are nothing more than places to plug in more hardware. This is one of the nicest features of current computer design, and you should absolutely refuse to buy a computer that doesn't include a good number of empty slots that you can fill up with hardware goodies once you have figured out what your computer is all about.[14]

The piece of hardware that fits into these slots is called a **board** or a **card** and it connects to the slot via a set of pins that slides right into the holes in the slot. In many cases, all you have to do to install such a board is take the cover off the unit, unscrew the metal plate that covers the empty slot in the back of the computer's case, and gently push in the board you want to use. I've done it myself, and I think twice before changing a light bulb.

There may be other things you need to do to get your board functional. You may have to plug in cables from a board to connect it to some other piece of hardware it communicates with, like a disk drive. You may have to set some switches or little staple-like objects called jumpers on the motherboard in order to inform the computer that it has a new configuration or more memory. But there is nothing very complex going on here.

Once the card is plugged into the slot it is able to communicate with the rest of the system. The only thing to be aware of is that you must buy boards that are designed to work with your particular model of processor—and not all will.

One determinant of whether or not a board will work with your system is the **bus** or kind of data path that the computer uses. This refers to how bytes are transferred around inside the computer from one component to the other. For example, some computers transmit 8 bits at a time over eight separate wires while others might have 16-bit buses or 32-bit buses. Some of IBM's computers use something called a **microchannel bus**, which requires boards designed specifically to work with that bus. The Macintosh II, a high-end Mac version, has its own design of bus called the NuBus, and yet other standards are on the drawing board. There are additional factors that have to be considered when looking at whether a board will work with a given system. You don't need to understand this in detail, but you do need to know enough to know that you need to find out.

Having slots available means that should some nifty piece of equipment be invented a year after you buy your system you will still be able to take advantage of it. It is even possible to replace your processor itself with a new one by buying a special processor board, and thus upgrade your computer at a price significantly cheaper than buying a whole new machine.

---

[14]The major exception to this rule may be the less expensive Macintosh models which provide few or no slots but are still very popular.

THE OTHER MACHINES THAT WORK
WITH YOUR COMPUTER

Printers

Before we leave this discussion of computer basics we should also look briefly at some machines you hook up to your computer: your printer and your modem.

The printer is not technically part of the computer and it will almost never be included in the price when you buy a computer, unlike the diskette drives, hard drives, memory, and keyboard which are pretty much standard now.[15] The different kinds of printers are discussed in Chapter 8. For now, the important thing to understand is how the printer and the computer work together.

Printers do what they do in response to certain "control codes" which computer software sends out through a port to the printer along with the encoded letters, numbers, and graphics that the printer is supposed to print out. These control codes are, not surprisingly, combinations of bytes that have special meaning to the printer. One printer control character might mean "eject the page" another might mean "change the font to elite."

Different manufacturers use different codes to perform different functions in their printers, although over the years Epson, IBM, and Hewlett-Packard Laserjet printer control characters have become a kind of "standard" for PC printers, meaning that these have become a generally accepted set of codes and meanings which other manufacturers' machines can also understand.

This ability of a machine to accept another machine's way of doing something is called **emulation**. If your printer, no matter what manufacturer it comes from, is able to emulate one of these popular printers, you will be able to use a wide range of software, since most software can send the codes appropriate for one of these popular printers, and your printer can receive them by emulating them. This is most useful when using unsophisticated programs. Most full-feature PC word processors include software to print using the precise codes understood by each of literally hundreds of printers. These programs do this by using something called a printer driver. The **printer driver** provides tables of code values and other information that the program uses to translate its own internally used codes into the format that the specific printer needs.

Modems

Modems are machines that take the strings of bits and bytes your computer works with and translates them to and from the sound-wave-based form

---

[15]The monitor is included with some systems but not with others.

that telephone wires transmit. The modem can either plug into a serial port on your computer, which makes it an **external modem,** or fill up a slot inside the computer which makes it an **internal modem.** Modems, too, respond to control codes. The current standard for modems is "Hayes compatibility," which means that they use the same codes as the modems originally designed by Hayes Microcomputer Products, Inc. Most do. Software that you are likely to use will work with the modems you are likely to buy without your having to know what you are doing.

The main difference between different modems is the speed at which they transmit data over the phone lines. This transmission speed is measured in bits per second, bps.[16]

It would seem obvious that where talking over the phone is concerned, and especially over the long distance line, the faster the modem the better, since this means that more information can be transmitted in less time, saving you phone bills. However the limitation on this is the fact that only certain speeds are supported by the machinery at the other end of the line you are calling on. So if your machine sends at 9600 bps but the system that you are calling can only receive at 2400, your modem will slow down and all that extra, expensive speed will be wasted.

The other limitation on the speed of your modem is the noise level on your phone line. Since you are sending very exact strings of bits translated into sound-wave form, a poor quality phone line means that your data may arrive unreadable. Your communications software tries to use error-checking logic to determine that it got what the sending system tells it that it sent, and some modems also have hardware error checking features, but the faster your transmission speed, the harder it is to correct these errors. In addition there can be echo problems on the phone line itself, especially if the phone company's line includes older equipment. This can cause further trouble with higher speed transmission.

However, at the modest price levels you are likely to be looking at when you get ready to buy a modem it is unlikely you will have to worry for now about the problems of high-speed transmission!

Software: The Soul of All Machines

In this chapter you may have noticed how every time we start out discussing a hardware topic we somehow end up talking about software, the programs that make the hardware do what it does. Although most texts try to separate these two items, to you, the computer user, they are

---

[16]There is another measure of transmission speed you may run into, the **baud** which is a measure that refers to the changes per second that the signal on the phone line goes through. With today's modems, baud is usually lower than bps however everyone confuses the two so don't worry about it.

inextricably interconnected. Where hardware leaves off and software begins is fuzzy enough that even experienced users may not always know where the boundary lies.

Yet being able to tell the two apart is extremely important. If you buy a computer because you see a demo that impresses you, flashing up screen after screen—only to discover that the demo is a program that simply displays pretty pictures on the screen with no ability to create or process these pictures (a common sales tactic) you will have fallen into the kind of trap that waits for the unwary. By the same token, if you buy a computer because you love the feel of its operating system—one, for example, that features easy-to-read menus—and then discover that it can't run the other programs you had intended to buy, you have fallen into another trap.

But for a deeper appreciation of what you are looking at when you sit down at a computer and begin to work with a piece of software you need to understand a little bit more about what software itself is.

We've talked about it at the level of bytes and at the level of logic, but there is another, higher, more compelling level. A decent piece of software is, believe it or not, a work of art—in the same way that a handmade piece of furniture or an architect's building is a work of art. The designers of a masterful computer tool do nothing less than make visible in very concrete form the very processes of thinking itself. Their program is an image of a thinking task and by creating a tool that amplifies your ability to perform those thinking tasks, they present you with a thing of compelling beauty.

As you get experience using computers, you will experience and respond to software with the same kind of subjective response that you do now when faced with a more familiar work of art—with the difference being that, more than is the case with most handiwork, you must spend some time learning the ins and outs of a piece of software before you really "see" it and are in a position to evaluate it fully.

That is why no reviewer can tell you conclusively whether or not you will like working with a certain operating system or piece of software. Because it will come down to whether you respond to its style and its creator's original conception as well as the quality of execution that was brought to it. Each of us responds differently to a particular piece of software.

There are, of course, programs that everyone agrees are awful: those that just plain don't work right or those that are designed in such a way that they are unpleasant for almost all people to use. But when you come to choose among the "good" stuff you will find that there are heated battles going on between the partisans of one operating system or software product and those who argue for its competition.

Each piece of software represents a designer's (or several designers') unique perception both of a task to be done and of the way to go about doing it. And so each computer solution will be unique in the same way that each person's way of solving complex problems is unique.

Certain products may come to "dominate" the market, perhaps because their style is closest to that of the people who dominate American industry. But you may find other less popular products that seem more in keeping with your style, just as you might not want to decorate your home with the "tasteful" graphics that are so popular in office building hallways.

Most of all, when you are using a program, you will be happiest if you can remind yourself that what you are using is nothing more than another human being's best effort at imagining how you, unpredictable creative individual that you are, work, and that it was crafted by programmers working within painfully strict limitations imposed by hardware and the nature of computer logic itself. The author of your program did the best he could to try to fit it to your mind. But because each of us is different, you will discover that the process of learning to use a program is really the process of discovering how the individuals that designed the software themselves think. Rather than working with machinery, when you enter the world of computer software you are really entering a new kind of relationship with a new group of creators.

The conscious utterance of thought, by speech or action, to any end is Art...From its first to its last works, Art is the spirit's voluntary use and combination of things to serve its ends.

Ralph Waldo Emerson 1803-1882
Society and Solitude: Art

6

THINKING ABOUT HARDWARE

Our inventions are wont to be pretty toys, which distract our attention from serious things...We are in great haste to construct a magnetic telegraph from Maine to Texas; but Maine and Texas, it may be, have nothing important to communicate.

Henry David Thoreau, 1817-1862
Walden

We have put it off long enough. We've looked at the software tools that might be of interest to you, and you've learned a little of what you will need to understand if you are going to use these tools. But that was all armchair traveling.

Now it's time to move on. You won't be able to take full advantage of any computer tools without putting together a computer system. And this means you must delve more deeply into the realm of hardware.

Hardware is a necessary evil. You can't get to the stage where, alone in your study, you can experience the power and beauty of a well-designed program until you have gone through the more earthbound process of acquiring a system.

Not everyone sees this as unpleasant. There are people—a lot of them as you will undoubtedly discover—who enjoy thinking about hardware, just as there are people who know the model numbers of their amplifiers and how many BTUs their air conditioners put out. In fact, if you spend much time around people who use computers you will discover that there is a whole population of computer users whose computers exist not primarily to solve problems or to serve as a platform for computer tools, but rather to fill the same kind of niche in their owner's lives now that a '57 Chevy with a broken engine did in their youths—something to tinker with.

Right now, though, you may feel that you have little in common with such people and that you find their chatter, filled as it is with acronyms and model numbers, irritating, and, what is worse, prone to make you feel like an ignoramus. This will change. If you can get your first computer up and working, you may well get hooked on your computer tools. Then you will begin to see the hardware enthusiast as a resource. You will realize that there is an important place in your life for a person who derives deep personal satisfaction out of resolving hardware problems for free!

So onward we go, into the realm of Hardware. As we said earlier, until now it was all armchair travel, but now we are entering the domain where we will be talking about spending real money. This makes it serious. Before we put on our shopping shoes, though, we need to get some things straight. First of all, it is not the intention of this book to tell you what to buy. It would be very tempting for me to tell you to go out and buy all the products that I use or that I wish I could afford. Many writers in the computer press do just that, recommending this and that high-ticket product as "indispensable." When you read stuff like that you should bear in mind that these writers get the products they recommend as review copies—for free.

Telling you what to buy would contradict my basic belief that selection of computer tools, like the selection of any craftsman's tool, is an individual kind of thing. On the other hand, I don't promise to edit out my own prejudices entirely. What is the point of writing a book if you can't lay down the law about the things that matter to you? Certainly, considering the pathetic royalties most books earn, being able to proselytize for the things you consider important is one of the few consolations left to the writer. But I will try to make it clear when I am speaking as an objective observer—if there is such a thing—and when I am sharing a personal preference with you.

The next chapters look at how to approach buying hardware, starting with the "principles" of buying hardware that experienced computer users know. Then you will learn the specific hardware decisions you must make. The intent of this section will be to determine which of these decisions are truly important and which are not, to ensure that when you choose a system you don't forget something essential. Finally you will find out where you should go to buy this computer hardware and where you can turn for more up-to-date information than any book can give you.

A BRIEF HISTORY OF HARDWARE

Computer hardware only became something that Joe Sixpack could go out and buy in the mid-1970s. Before then there was plenty of computer hardware available but it was priced in the same range as battleships, parking garages, and senatorial campaigns. These big-ticket computers, which continue to dominate the world of big-business computing, came in two major varieties: the larger ones were called mainframes and the smaller ones were called minicomputers. The mainframes tended to be priced in the multimillion-dollar range while the minis were cheaper, ranging from the tens of thousands into the hundred- thousand-dollar range.

Starting Off Centralized

These large computers were designed for business' workhorse applications: processing all the checking and savings transactions of all the customers of a bank, generating bank statements, or tracking every piece of product at every stage of its progress down a factory assembly line. Such computers lived in a climate-controlled computer room, tended by round-the-clock technicians, and were connected to hundreds of computer terminals—screens—that could be located anywhere in the world. These large computers ran all night updating millions of accounts and generating reams of reports about the updates they had applied.

The hallmark of these systems, whatever hardware they involved, was centralized control. Because hundreds of people with many different requirements were all sharing the same expensive, limited, computer resources it was very important that these computers be managed in a centralized way, both to ensure that the computer was used for the most remunerative possible uses and to protect the information on the computer from getting messed up by its many users.

Hunger for more computer power was a constant throughout this period. Computer manufacturers rolled out new models with the same kind of regularity that car manufacturers do. The only difference was that, unlike each year's new car, each year's new computer offered far more function and power than the previous year's model.

As a result of this, people whose job was to buy computers came to expect that this year's terrific breakthrough would be next year's unsalable trash. But because industry needed the new computing power so badly, and because there were always hundreds of people within the company clamoring for computer support that the company's mainframes still couldn't provide, corporate computer buyers had no trouble accepting the constant need to buy better and better hardware. And no matter how much they bought, there were still enormous backlogs of would-be computer users whom the mainframe still couldn't serve.

The Microcomputer Is Born

The microcomputer—the computer that Joe Sixpack can afford—came onto the scene in the later half of the 1970s. The first microcomputers were kit-built wonders, of interest only to the kinds of people who build their own stereos or pursue ham radio as a hobby. Building them took solid electronics know-how. Using them required some in-depth knowledge of the fundamentals of computing. These first micros were extremely limited in function. They had tiny memories, no disks, and in some cases no keyboards: their users entered data into these computers by toggling switches on the box's front panel. But these pioneering machines matured quickly, mostly because advances in the design and manufacture of mainframe computer chips were making it possible to put a previously-unheard-of amount of memory on a single chip as well as allowing more complex chip-based microprocessors to be produced.[1]

In only a few years Apple Computer, started, as everyone knows, by Steven Jobs and Steve Wozniak in Wozniak's garage, was selling to the public off-the-shelf microcomputers that featured monitors, keyboards, and—best of all—diskette drives. These were, for the first time, computers that looked like real computers, acted like real computers, ran lots of real programs, and best of all didn't cost hundreds of thousands of dollars.

By 1981 the media noticed this microcomputer revolution. It was not possible to pick up a magazine without reading about how everybody—or at least anyone who was anybody—would soon have a computer, and how these computers would change everything.

Enter the IBM PC

IBM wandered into this microcomputer market in 1981 somewhat as an afterthought, in response to the enormous success that Apple was having with its home computer. Originally IBM had figured the micros for nothing more than toys, but it was embarrassing to have a computer revolution taking place without IBM in the middle of it. IBM was supposed to *be* computers, wasn't it? IBM's first microcomputer was the original IBM PC. Its initials stood for "personal computer" a new term thought up by some IBM marketing genius which soon became the generic term for small computers.

---

[1]To get a feel for how fast this happened consider this: In the late 1970s a 4K bit memory chip designed for multimillion dollar mainframes was considered a big deal. By 1980 64K chips—still for mainframes—were big news. But only a few years later cheap PC clones manufactured in Third World sweatshops and selling for under $1,000 routinely used 256K bit memory chips, while the better machines by the late 1980s used 1 meg chips. This could happen because the process of manufacturing a 4K chip is not much different from that of manufacturing a 1 meg chip, once the design details are worked out. And, of course, the explosion of the microcomputer market brought about demand levels that allowed economies of scale.

The IBM PC was not significantly better designed than several other small computers already available. What was most different about it was DOS—disk operating system—the operating system it used, something IBM licensed from a small software company called the Seattle Computer Company, a company that is now, largely as a result of that deal, the industry giant, Microsoft. Up until IBM introduced the PC, microcomputers had run a different disk-based operating system called CP/M. Nobody has ever pretended that DOS was a well-designed operating system. But it was a step up from CP/M. The first PCs came with only 64K of memory—one tenth of what today's cheapie clones have—and used single sided diskette drives that could hold only 180K bytes of data.

A year later IBM introduced the first XT computer. It had more memory and a revolutionary 10-megabyte hard disk, revolutionary because until the XT's appearance hard disks were almost exclusively found in minicomputers and mainframes, while microcomputers used only the small, slow floppies. It also introduced double density 360K diskettes.

IBM itself had no idea of the demand that would emerge for the PC, expecting it to fill a niche in the "home computer" market. But in a world where to businesspeople the letters "IBM" spelled "real computer," the PC made it respectable for businesspeople to buy these new, cheap computers, and when they bought them they found things to do with them.

The single most important thing catalyzing the explosive invasion of IBM PCs into the business world was that they were able to offer the business community something utterly new and something not dependent on PC hardware either, but a software innovation. Dan Bricklin, a graduate student studying business at MIT, who had worked as a programmer, came up with the idea of a program that automated the accounting spreadsheet. His product, VISICALC, developed originally to run on the Apple, did something utterly new and powerful that businesspeople needed and did it elegantly.

Businesspeople brought PCs into their offices at first to run VISICALC for accounting and forecasting. But once they had the machine sitting there in their offices, it turned out that for a couple more bucks they could also use it as a word processor, and at that time stand-alone word processors could easily cost $10,000 apiece or more. All the PC owner had to do was simply buy a program that, while not as powerful as the expensive stand- alone word processor, *was good enough.* Best of all, once the machine was in his office, justified on the basis of its ability to run spreadsheet software, the businessperson no longer had to negotiate with the overburdened mainframe computer department for computer service—the same folks who had been postponing his requests for computer service for years. Nor did he have to waste time waiting for authorizations to buy expensive special purpose workstations or departmental minicomputers. All he needed to do to make his PC act like a word processor, a database machine, or anything else for that matter, was just buy a few software packages. Goodbye centralized computing and corporate-wide data processing strategies. The businessperson with a PC was home free!

Send in the Clones

The home computer market fizzled out as the general public grew bored with Space Invaders and never quite caught on to what else you were supposed to do with computers. But the IBM PC revolutionized computing in both large and small businesses. And with the PC's success a horde of imitators began giving IBM stiff competition, selling machines very much like the PCs to IBM's customers.

When IBM originally designed the PC they didn't start from scratch. They needed something quick. So instead of investing in a multiyear in-house design project, IBM's engineers designed the PC the way Dr. Frankenstein designed his monster: using readily available parts. The IBM PC was a hodge-podge of existing hardware supplied by other manufacturers, all hooked together, as we have seen, as a modular, plug-in system; the only thing uniquely "IBM" about it was the logo on the box.

Once the PC became a standard though, sharp engineers in other companies, who also knew how to shop for components, looked at the IBM machine and decided that they could put together a better set of pieces to do the same job. And there was no legal reason that they couldn't buy the same chip from Intel that IBM bought, pay Microsoft to license the operating system, and maybe put in a better disk drive controller and a better engineered motherboard. There were technical challenges involved. But eventually several companies were able to bring to the marketplace computers that functioned exactly like the IBM PCs, except that they were faster and had extra nifty features.

These were the clones, called "clones" because they were supposedly identical to the IBM machines. Even if they were not in engineering terms identical to the PC, they were able to run the PC's operating system and the PC's software. And that was close enough. The main incentive that the clonemakers at first offered the businesspeople who would otherwise have bought IBM machines was a significantly lower price.

But while the clone makers began by imitating IBM's PCs, led by Compaq they soon began to improve on the engineering of the IBM standard and surpass it. And business computer buyers began buying the clonemakers' machines, to the dismay of the IBM sales force which had owned the corporate computing market since time immemorial. IBM countered by hastily reengineering its offerings, introducing the PS/2 line and its microchannel bus, but the only real innovation these new computers seemed to offer was that their design, unlike that the original PC, was covered by legally defensible patents.

For computer buyers all this competition was excellent. If you wanted to buy an "IBM PC compatible" computer—one that could run the same software as those IBM sold—you could choose from any of dozens of worthwhile computers at every price and with every possible combination of features, all offered by a host of price-slashing vendors engaged in a snarling dogfight of competition.

The PC Software Explosion

And then, of course there was the software explosion. IBM started out assuming that, as they did in the world of the big computers, they would present the user community with a small selection of IBM software for the new machines and the users would have to use it. But these were not mainframes where it cost millions of dollars to develop a single program. Smart programmers who had been lurking around the corporate world, and smart kids who might otherwise have been fooling around with ham radios, could buy PCs and write programs for them at home—which was not true of the larger computers. Soon home-based programmers were churning out innovative and useful programs for these computers—marketing them, and even in some cases getting rich. By the end of the 1980s not a single one of the perennial bestsellers in the PC world was an IBM product and there was a whole new class of software multimillionaires.

With the combination of easily plugged-in hardware enhancements, thousands of available software programs, and a growing excitement about the new cheap computers in the business community, the PC took over. By the mid-1980s having a PC on your desk, whether you used it or not, was as important a status symbol in many companies as whether you had a window office or a mahogany desk.

But the dominant application that businesspeople used, the spreadsheets and databases, are designed in such a way that the more sophisticated the work you use them for the more processing speed and memory you need. So the forces were still there driving the computer manufacturers to provide more speed and more capacity, even though by doing so those manufacturers rapidly consigned their existing systems to the junk heap.

Hardware manufacturers raced to come up with faster and faster computers supporting more and more internal memory. By 1988 you could buy a personal computer that would sit on your desk processing at the same speed and with the same amount of memory as did multimillion dollar mainframes only a few years before.[2]

---

[2]But doing a lot less work since those mainframes used to support a hundred or more simultaneous users and ran at close to 100% of their capacity, while the desktop computer spends a huge percentage of its time just sitting and waiting for its owner to come up with something to do, or while he is working, just waiting for him to hit enter in response to a prompt.

Corporate computer users began linking these more powerful PCs together into networks, replicating the functions of the terminals connected to the company's mainframes, and putting even more pressure on computer manufacturers to beef up their products. Meanwhile, software companies that had concentrated on mainframe products began bringing over many of their products to the PC world, usually in versions that required the user to buy the most powerful, biggest, and fastest PCs to run them.

The Macintosh and the Graphical Interface Grail

The only serious threat to the hegemony of the IBM PC and its clones came with the introduction of the Apple Macintosh in 1984. Although Apple Computer was the first hugely successful microcomputer company, IBM's onslaught in the early 1980s almost knocked it out. The Macintosh was Apple's last gasp in the struggle to stay alive as a serious computer competitor and, as the home computer market died, to break into the business market. It worked. The Macintosh took on IBM head-to-head by taking a radically different approach to the design of every feature of the personal computer and, in the process, developed into a viable—and popular—alternative to the IBM standard.

The Macintosh carved out its own niche by realizing that many people found it hard to learn how to use the software that ran on the IBM machines. Seeing that this was IBM's Achilles' Heel, the Mac was designed and advertised as a friendly, easy-to-use "computer for the rest of us." By burying the seamy details of the operating system down a level where the user never really had to deal with it directly and by providing a carefully thought-out and well-designed Mac Interface that communicated with the user in a simple and, for many people, intuitive—that is, easy to learn—manner, the Macintosh made it easy for knowledge workers who had never seen a computer before to quickly master their new machines and go right to work.

Most innovatively, what the original Macintosh offered was a visually-oriented operating system. Instead of requiring that you tell it what to do with memorized commands like the IBM PCs, the Macintosh offered screens full of little pictures, called icons, which you selected using a pointing device, the mouse. This picture-based design, which was termed the graphical interface, let executives use computers successfully without having to type or read a manual.

To do this the Macintosh was built around a totally graphics-based approach, rather than the character-based mode that dominated the DOS world. Once the Macintosh's designers and programmers had managed to work out this graphic interface it was a logical extension to add some programs that were capable of simultaneously manipulating both words and complex graphic images, the kind of thing you would encounter on a magazine page. The final touch was adding to this system the LaserWriter, a laser printer—hitherto used only on larger systems—which produced near-typeset-quality printouts. The result was the first microcomputer capable of doing what became known as desktop publishing.

It was a success. The Macintosh wormed its way into the IBM-dominated corporate world because its ability to work with pictures and to print nice-looking copy—desktop publishing—could not be duplicated on PCs. Corporate buyers who would not have considered buying the older Apples brought in Macs for desktop publishing to feed the corporate hunger for ever-glitzier publications and for use in other graphics applications where the Mac was the incontrovertible champ. But once in the corporate workplace the Macintosh developed a core of fanatic mouse-waving devotees who proclaimed the superiority of its consistent, intuitive, graphics-based interface. A friendly rivalry broke out between PC users and Mac users with the latter typically suggesting that the only use for the PCs were as boat anchors and lamp stands and the PC users retorting that the Mac users were simply too chicken to handle a *real* computer. But the growth of a solid phalanx of Mac users in industry and their eagerness to use the Mac for all their computing needs built up confidence among software developers that the Macintosh was in the game for keeps and led them gradually to provide all kinds of business software for the Macintosh.

The impact of the Macintosh's innovative graphical interface extended beyond Macintosh users to the whole personal computing marketplace. In the short term it led to the development of powerful graphics-based desktop publishing tools for the PC and forced IBM to upgrade the mediocre graphics capabilities of the PC. In the long term it gave impetus to the development of graphics-based interfaces for PCs too, first the DOS-based Microsoft Windows and then the Presentation Manager, the interface portion of Microsoft's OS/2 operating system which was enough like Apple's Macintosh interface that Apple sued Microsoft, claiming patent infringement.

This shift toward graphics processing on both the Mac and the PC is yet another force pushing computer manufacturers to develop faster and more memory-rich machines. Graphics processing involves manipulating many more bits than text-based processing. The tradition that this year's machine has to make last year's machine look bad continues.

THE GREAT LAWS OF HARDWARE

Everything Is Junk

This is all very exciting, but it brings with it the single most important lesson you will learn when dealing with hardware: everything you buy, no matter how new it is, how good it is, or what it can do, will start looking like obsolete trash in a matter of months.

You also must steel yourself to deal with the fact that no matter how good a price you manage to find, in a few months the same amount of money you spent to buy your hardware will buy a much nicer system.

In fact it is not unusual to mail in the little cards that register your purchase with the manufacturer only to have his first mailing to you consist of news that a brand new version of whatever you just bought is now available with 15 exciting new features your version doesn't have, at a price no more than $75 higher than what you just paid!

This has been true of computers since the middle 1960s, and there is no reason to expect it to change.

Because this is true it has some important corollaries.

You Always Benefit by Waiting

Number one is that if you don't feel like buying a computer or some associated piece of computer hardware right now, waiting will not hurt you. There is no reason to take advantage of hard-sell "special opportunities." The chances are very good that if you delay your purchase you will be able to buy something nicer than what you see today for less money. In fact, the better an offer looks the greater the chance that what it offers is for sale cheap because the company is preparing to sell the upgraded version and is clearing out old inventory to prepare for this!

The second corollary is that you should buy computer hardware when you just can't bear not owning it any longer. Since the chances are that the price will either come down for the item you are interested in or, alternatively, that the same price next year will buy more function, it only makes sense to buy something when it seems ridiculous not to! Your reasoning in making a computer purchase should be what my mother counseled me about getting married: only do it when you absolutely can't stand not to!

If your financial resources are limited and you have no burning desire to participate in leading-edge technology, the sanest approach when considering computerization, is to decide what price level makes sense to you for a particular computer-related item and to buy it when it approaches that price.

You will miss out being on the cutting edge, no question about it, but you are more likely to be happy with your purchase.

If It's New It Won't Work Right

Another historically proven adage about buying both computer hardware and software is this: If it's brand new then it doesn't work right yet.

Any new technology needs to be exercised by thousands of users before it is really "clean." There is no way around it. It is inherent in the nature of complex system design. No matter how hard an engineer or programmer may have tried to imagine how his product would be used, there is always some joker out there who comes up with a great idea of how to use the machine or program *that doesn't work on the product as currently designed.*

This is important because you must resist the temptation to rush to get in on the very newest stuff. Let the guys at General Motors and Aetna have the fun of being the first to use new technology, whether it be a new printing technology, a new design for a processor, or a brand new kind of program. It is not for nothing that the press has come to call this "the bleeding edge."

Big, rich, companies can afford to try out things that may turn out to be bad ideas, and if they turn out to be good ideas that need more work, these huge companies have no problem buying the second or third version of the product that finally works. But you as a lone individual will be buying for keeps. When you are spending your own money, you want to buy something only after it has been tested, perfected, and most important, proven in the marketplace.

Someone Else's IS Bigger

There is a related issue that we should look at too in considering the headlong rush of hardware, because you will constantly be exposed to it when you read articles in the press, when you visit the computer store, or even when you just hang around with your buddies at the users group. I'm talking about Hardware Envy.

Extremely powerful forces are at work that make you feel there is something wrong with you if you don't have the most powerful machine possible. This, of course, has little to do with hardware. A 1988 issue of *PC Magazine* featured not one, but three, ads in which mild-looking computer users were getting their ties ripped off by the sheer power emanating from their desktop computers. Superman imagery shows up in a lot of these ads too.

Clearly the conflict between the demands of raw testosterone and the limitations of the corporate lifestyle still rages, but a faster CPU is not the solution.

The amount of press devoted to the so-called "power user" and the tendency of reviewers to call a new machine a "Screamer" or talk about revving it up as if it were a sports car should also clue you in to what is really going on. Beware! Prove your masculinity elsewhere unless you are independently wealthy, it is an insidious force and dangerous to your pocketbook.

The simple fact is that you, personally, don't need the kind of computer speed necessary to compute satellite trajectories. As a writer you will most likely concentrate your computer usage on fiddling around with words more than anything else. So much of the hardware and software down at the computer store is so utterly beyond what you need, or even what would be nice to have, that you must be very careful not to get swept away in the rush.

The absolutely bottom-of-the-line stuff available now could probably make you very happy and allow you to use a nice selection of computer tools. There are some areas in which going for the upgrades makes sense, and we will look at them soon. But you must resist the tendency to feel that if you are buying a bottom-of-the-line system this is somehow a statement that there is something bottom of the line about you.

THE GOOD-ENOUGH COMPUTER

The beauty of it all is this: right now at the start of the 1990s, for you the writer even the worst stuff is great! In the sections that follow we will concentrate on looking at a lot of small details that it helps to know when purchasing your own system. But even if you ignored most of what follows, went into the first computer store you saw, and bought the first system you could afford,the chances are excellent that you would still end up with a wonderful system whose power would blow you away!

The market is mature. The days of "orphaned" computers with no software are long past. Today there are clear-cut hardware standards, thousands of excellent programs, and millions of people who already own computers just like what you are about to buy.

Relax. Take with a grain of salt what you read in the press. Computer writers get paid to keep things interesting, and their salaries come from hefty ad rates paid by manufacturers who want you to buy the latest products. Let such people deride the lower end of the technology spectrum and look the other way when they suggest that only weenies use the kind of system you are about to take the momentous—and for you, expensive—step of purchasing. They get paid to bay in hot pursuit of this week's utter best.

There might be at any given time a "best" computer—and the best you will note changes every month—but the chances are that even the "worst" is still a very reasonable machine. In short, while you do have some decisions to make, no matter what you do, if you stick with a mainstream kind of computer you are not likely to make any horrible mistakes!

PUTTING TOGETHER THE BASIC CONFIGURATION

Given all this there is no way that this book can tell you which machine to go out and buy. By the time this book was printed most of its suggestions would be out of date. But in a hardware world that is always in flux there are some things that remain constant, and this permits setting out some general guidelines to help you when you do go shopping.

The questions that must be considered next are these: What choices do you face when shopping for a computer? How irrevocable are the choices that you are making? What pieces of hardware do you have to have? What is a frill? What can you postpone? Where are you most vulnerable to abuse? With the answers to these questions you will be ready to start shopping for hardware.

You will recall that a computer is a collection of components that work together. In computer terms the particular collection of components you select is called the **system configuration**. The process of putting the pieces together is called configuring the system.

CHOOSING A COMPUTER FAMILY

Once you have decided to buy a computer, the very first decision you must make is what kind of computer you are going to buy. By this we don't mean a big one or a pink one. We mean that you will have to choose between the few families of computers that have become standards over the last decade.

Since this is probably the biggest decision that you have to make it seems patently unfair that it should also be the first, and that it must be made when you least know what you are doing! But that is the way that it is, and as a result you will probably have to use some exterior criteria to choose the computer family rather than, as you would in an ideal world, choosing the system that was really and truly the best for you based on your experience using them all.

What criteria *do* people use to make this choice? The answer is probably that they use the same criteria they use to pick a car—they rely on anecdotal information, they buy what their brother-in-law has since he seems to like his, they buy what they use at work or school, they buy the kind with the snappiest slogan, or they buy what's cheap.

One approach is to weigh what software is available for a particular hardware family and how much the whole system, software and all, will cost. Price may be a reasonable criterion, particularly if you are one of those writers earning the $5,000 a year that professionals writers are reported to average. The objectively "best" computer is only a smart buy if you can comfortably afford it. However, coming into the computer market at the end of the 1980s as that market has matured you are in an enviable position since you can buy usable machines for as low as $1,000.[3] If you can go up into the $3,000-$5,000 range without massive feelings of

---

[3]If the phrase "only $1,000" makes you wince, and if minor items like buying a first car or a living room couch are first in line for your paltry savings, relax. Read the book, find out what's available, take a cheap course where you get some hands-on experience, and wait another year or two to buy. You'll either be better off financially by then or the prices will have come down.

guilt and fear, you can afford just about any type of hardware and can afford the luxury of making the decision entirely on the issue of how well you like the tools that are available for a given machine.

But no matter how rich you are, as a beginner with little idea of what you need or want, it might still be a good idea to start out with only a modest setup. In a few years, no matter what you buy now, you will be aching to buy a newer, more powerful system. By then you will have had enough experience using a computer to know exactly what it is you want when you next go out shopping. Or, alternatively, you may just keep happily using your first beginner's system for many more years until it dies. There are still people around using the very first PCs albeit with some significant upgrades.

This is probably the most realistic way to begin. No matter what you buy you will learn a lot about computers in the process of using it, and you will probably be able to find tools that are a great improvement over what you are using now. Even though you can afford the $5,000 system you might be better advised to wait and start with something simpler because it will take you a long time to get to the point where you are likely to be doing much that requires all the power of that expensive machine, and by then you will have a much better idea of what hardware you really need.

Currently the hardware families that are the more popular among people using computers for the kinds of things that you are going to do—word processing and personal productivity-oriented applications rather than engineering or academic computing—are the PC and the Apple Macintosh. There are several other computers that are popular as well, such as the Atari ST, the Amiga and the non-PC compatible Commodores, and the Apple IIe, but you will find, if you look at the magazines directed at owners of these machines and check out the software available for them, that they are more oriented toward recreational computer use, particularly games and music, or in the case of the Apple, school-oriented children's programs.

If you look at the software on the shelves in computer software stores you will notice that the "serious" software, the business-oriented stuff, seems to be almost exclusively available for the PCs and the Macintosh. This includes the full-featured word processors and many of the random information processing "thought extenders" we have been talking about. This is not to say that you can't get business functions out of these other machines. You can. But generally the word-processing and database programs you find for these machines are more of an afterthought than the finely honed tools available for the PC and the Mac. And you will not find the wide variety of choice in "thoughtware" on those computers that the business-oriented machines have spawned. What you may get with these systems, though, which will immediately strike you at the store, may be nicer looking pictures on the screens.

IBM and the Clones

The most popular family of business computers for almost a decade has been the IBM PC and compatibles family, which includes the computers manufactured by IBM itself and those made by a host of competitors. These are the computers that run the operating system called DOS.[4]

You might think that the best way to buy an "IBM"-style PC, would be to go into a store that sells IBM products and buy one of the machines you find there. But as simple as this sounds, it would not necessarily be the best way to buy an "IBM"-style computer. In fact, you might be able to buy a much better computer elsewhere.

If you go to an equally nicely appointed showroom that does not sell IBM products you will discover computers with the identical features you saw in the IBM showroom sporting lower price tags. Or—and this might be even a better solution for you—you may see computers with less flash at the back of the store, priced at half the price of the IBM system you saw before. This last system although it isn't "state of the art" might still have enough power to get the job done and still leave you enough money to buy some extra software.

Welcome to the incredibly confusing world of the IBM PC and its clones.

If you have decided to go with the IBM PC standard you may wonder why you would want to buy a cheap copy when you could have the real thing, a computer made by IBM? Well one reason is that some of the clone makers' machines are better designed than IBM's own offerings. There are clones and clones, but there is a solid core of respectable clone makers including, among others, Compaq, Zenith, AST, and Epson who have sold enough systems to be quite respectable. And these clone computer systems should not be equated with the cheaper but lower quality appliance "knockoffs" that you might be familiar with from shopping in discount stores. Clones are not knockoffs; rather they could be described as technologically similar alternatives.

But a most persuasive argument for most people when considering whose machine to buy is usually price. IBM stuff is expensive. IBM has a long-term relationship with corporate computer buyers. This makes it sensible for many of those buyers to buy from IBM, in spite of price, for reasons that are meaningful in the corporate environment but utterly meaningless to you. Because those buyers have incentive to buy from IBM, IBM can charge them premium "business" prices. But for the noncorporate customer IBM's only real selling point is its computer's superior reliability. But, lest this argument sell you, you should be aware

---

[4]DOS comes in two versions: PC-DOS which comes only with machines sold by the IBM corporation and MS-DOS, produced by Microsoft, the same company that produced PC-DOS, which is functionally identical to PC-DOS but runs on machines from all other manufacturers.

that the engineering differences in IBM products that form the basis for this claim are found only in the high—that is, expensive—end of IBM's product line, and recent experience has shown that the products that IBM offers at the lower end are often very poorly designed in terms of expandability and engineering compared with clone makers' products.

Clones vary to the extent to which they are utterly and completely IBM compatible. Clones made by manufacturers that have a reasonably large market share are all compatible enough that they run 99 percent of the software and a large amount of the hardware available for the PC line. But some clones have their quirks. These are sometimes caused by engineering improvements that may otherwise offer real incentive to buy the system. In most cases these show up only when you use a program that itself is quirky and does something it shouldn't at the lowest hardware level. But quirks in the popular clones—if you encounter them at all—usually just require that you make some small adjustment to get things working properly again, since software and hardware developers are aware of them.

Another thing to understand is the very large number of differing models available that fall under the PC rubric. IBM originally offered the plain PC in 1981. Soon after, it brought out the PC XT which was a PC with a 10 meg hard disk included that used double-sided, rather than single-sided disk drives. This was followed by the introduction of a more fundamentally different computer, the IBM AT. The AT had a different, faster, processor a wider bus, and featured high-density diskette drives. Its processor was rumored to have exciting new capabilities—to be able to do multitasking and support multiple users—but the vast majority of users just used it as a faster PC. IBM followed up the AT with the PS2 line which was supposed to be a "clone killer." But although several IBM computer models had "PS2" in their name, they had little in common with each other from an engineering standpoint.

The PS2 line was a dog's dinner. It included machines that had a supposedly revolutionary new engineering design, the Micro Channel Architecture, and a new high-resolution video standard, VGA, but at the same time the PS2 line also included other cheaper machines—lacking the microchannel architecture—that were basically just hard-to-expand PC clones, with yet another graphics standard. The company's advertising did not make this distinction clear.

Meanwhile the clone makers offered PC clones, XT clones, and AT clones, but they also introduced the so called "Turbo XT" clone which was an XT-type computer with a processor that was about twice as fast as the original. For AT clones, the speed of the processor chip got jacked up, leading to the appearance of 10, 12, 16, and even 20 Mhz AT clones.

Compaq computer took advantage of the introduction of a new Intel processor chip, called the 80386, or 386 for short, and instead of copying an IBM model, became the first manufacturer including IBM to offer a

386-based machine. This successful computer then immediately spawned a new phenomenon: the Compaq clone, as cloners cloned it.

It goes on endlessly, but the point is that to even figure out what "model" you are looking at you need to look beyond the label and interpret a lot of detailed product specifications. This is true whether you are looking at an IBM model or a clone, since you may well encounter 15 different flavors of PC/XT or AT, and 8 different flavors of PS2, all of them significantly different as far as what's going on inside them. We'll look at how you do this later.

The Mac Attack

When you step out of the radius of the IBM PC and family you enter the world of the Macintosh, or Mac for short. Be warned! The Macintosh adherent is an enthusiast. Sensitive in the extreme to the overwhelming numbers of PC users, the Mac user tends to become emotional about the virtues of what he claims is his superior machine. While most PC users just ignore the Mac, Mac users heap scorn on what they consider to be other makers' inferior machines and actively evangelize for their own.

You should expect then to encounter strong views if you have the temerity to ask a Mac user his or her opinion on what you should buy. Certainly they will probably claim that the Macintosh has more innovative programs. Without question they will gloat that the Macintosh programs are more consistent: that all the programs written to run under the Mac's graphical interface have to use certain conventions so that the same kind of user response causes the same effect in all Mac programs. And they will also point out that the Macintosh, unlike the PC, is easy to learn, so that getting productive on the Mac requires less effort than does the PC.

All this is true. In the PC world each program does whatever it feels like with the keys and the screen. There are some conventions that a lot of programs subscribe to, like using the F1 key to summon up a help screen and the Escape key to get out of the current screen. But using them is strictly optional and a lot of popular best-selling programs ignore these "standards" entirely. The Macintosh doesn't have these problems, and it is easier to learn. But then it costs a whole lot more for equivalent power too. There are arguments on both sides, but what you need to know as an innocent bystander, is that what it comes down to, more than anything, is an issue of personal style. Some people love the Macintosh interface. Others find it limiting. And the same goes for DOS.

The Mac world is one of elegance and style, while the PC world is a rougher, more diverse kind of place. The conformity of the software developed for the Mac makes it a lot easier to learn, and its visual elegance makes it superior for visually oriented work, but for the person who takes the time to master the quirks and nuances of the sloppier PC universe, the payoff is almost unlimited choice. Whatever way you like to do things, someone somewhere has probably programmed it in the PC world.

Would that it were only a matter of choosing which approach you liked better! Unfortunately, the problem with the Mac—at least for the impecunious writer—is that unlike the IBM PC design which was freely copied by the clone makers, the Mac is covered by fiercely defended patents. This is terrific for stockholders of Apple Computer, but it means that there are no clones and no competition within the Mac world to bring prices down. As a result, the Mac that you may very well want to buy is going to be much, much more expensive than the PC clones in the same class. And the price differential extends to a lot of other things you need to buy. The printers are more expensive. The hard disks are more expensive. Probably even the printer ribbons are more expensive. This is what happens when you don't have competition to keep prices down.

The other limitation on the Mac is that there are fewer programmers who know how to develop programs for it. This means that although what is available might be terrific, there isn't as much of it available. Even more limiting for the impecunious writer, is the dearth of industrial-strength public domain and shareware programs—the programs that you can get for free or very cheap. There are free programs available for the Mac, but only a few of them are in the same class as far as providing sophisticated function and feature as the big-time PC shareware and public domain programs are, nor are there the thousands of such programs available for the Mac that abound in the PC world.

The Mac users I know justify the greater expense of their Macintosh systems with the consolation that Ferraris aren't cheap either and that the Mac is a premium machine. They love their computers and their enthusiasm would suggest that a Macintosh may be worth every penny and more. So before you buy any system you probably owe it to yourself to at least check one out. But if cost is a prime motivator and you got interested in getting a computer in the first place because of the ads you saw for under- $1,000 PC clones, then, in spite of its benefits, getting a Mac may demand more of a sacrifice from you than you want—or need—to make.

Everything Else: Compatible How?

If you should happen to venture into a showroom of a computer store that sells a type of computer other than an IBM compatible or a Macintosh the salesperson may try to overwhelm your objection that such a computer can't run the DOS or Mac software you are interested in by claiming that in fact it can. Because of the huge variety of programs available for PCs and Macs, manufacturers of other microcomputers have begun to add to their boxes some kind of DOS or Mac compatibility. This may not be a satisfactory solution if your main reason for buying a computer is to run DOS or Mac software.

You should be particularly wary of any demos you see of these compatibility features, since they may be misleading. This software compatibility feature is called **emulation.** But having an emulation mode does not mean that the computer becomes a PC or a Mac. The emulating computer has its own processor and its own operating system. However it has a program that translates the PC program or the Mac program into something its own processor can run. This is a major effort requiring a lot of work by the computer so that often the DOS compatibility mode runs so slowly as to make it virtually worthless.

Emulation is emphatically not the same thing as the **compatibility** that the clones advertise. That kind of compatibility is hardware-level compatibility and means that the machine is using the same components as the machine it is copying and is functionally identical. Thus if you are tempted to buy a computer because of some feature like its superior ability to process graphics or music, and it is not a clone or a Mac, take along a borrowed copy of an IBM or Mac program you are planning to run on it, for example a word processor, and a computer- knowledgeable friend who can install it for you, and see if the salesperson will let you try it out to see how it runs, rather than trusting the store's demo disk which probably was set up to make the DOS emulation look good but is very lightweight in terms of the processing involved.

What's NeXT?

The NeXT computer was introduced with a lot of press fanfare in 1989. The product of a new company started by Steven Jobs, one of the original founders of Apple, it was originally announced as a ground-breaking computer intended for academic users. However, several months after these early announcements, Businessland, a chain of retail computer stores, announced that it would begin retailing the NeXT computer, giving it instant credibility in the business marketplace.

Sporting impressive graphics and world-class demos, the NeXT computer may well look like something that you would want to consider before making a choice. The NeXT computer uses its own version of the UNIX operating system—one developed by Bell Labs and preferred by the Federal government and many universities. It features a built-in large-capacity read/write optical disk, high resolution black and white graphics and symphonic quality sound generation hardware. For the writer NeXT offers a powerful built-in text search engine.

So what does this mean for you?

Not much right now, unfortunately. The NeXT has the potential to be a very exciting computer, but it is too new and unproven for you to even consider it. Right now the hardware is just being invented that hooks up to this computer and the bugs are still being worked out of the system software—to say nothing about the actual software packages you might want to run on it. Ignore the advertising and wait a few years. If the NeXT survives in the marketplace and attains a critical mass of users and of software products that work well on it, then it may provide another mainstream alternative.

7

CONFIGURING YOUR SYSTEM

As she frequently remarked when she made any such mistake, it would be all the same a hundred years hence.

Charles Dickens 1812-1870
Nicholas Nickleby

There are more decisions you must make before you can take your computer home and set it up in the den. How many of these decisions you make and how many you leave up to chance or to the manager of the computer store is up to you. This chapter takes a look at some important things that are open to choice when you buy a system and explains what the ramifications of making these choices might be. Once again, the goal of this is not to terrify you into immobility. Nor are you supposed to memorize what you see here. If you avoid the one or two very obvious pitfalls, for example, buying a cheap system that has no memory or the one with no disk drives at all, you will end up with a system quite capable of serving you well, at least for the year or two it is going to take you to get comfortable with using any system.

Much of the discussion that follows here refers to the PC. That is simply because buying a PC exposes you to making far more choices than buying any other kind of computer because of the diversity of the PC marketplace. Other kinds of computers offer four or five models to choose from, with each one clearly separated from the next by price, while in the PC world within a single price range you may find dozens of overlapping configurations and models for sale. But the underlying issues discussed below, like speed, hard disk size, and memory are relevant to any computer you may buy. Appendix B gives a Hardware-Buying Checklist which lists the most important questions you should ask about the hardware that makes up any computer you are considering.

Let's look now at the major hardware components and the choices they present to you.

CHOOSING THE PROCESSOR

Once you have decided what family of computer you want to buy into, your first decision will have to be what kind of processor you want your computer to have. Different computers in a vendor's line usually use different processor chips and the price of a computer rises with the increase in speed and the addition of capabilities to its processor.

While processors vary in important ways, speed is usually a major factor distinguishing one processor from another. What does this speed mean to you as a user and how much of it do you need?

Speed

When you see a computer advertised, its processor speed is usually given in megahertz (MHz). This is a measurement of the frequency of the waveform used to pace the computer's processing unit. This processor speed is one measure that reflects the total speed of a computer but it can be deceptive.

The original IBM PC ran at 4.77 MHz. This is as slow as it gets. The Macintosh SE model and the Macintosh II run at 16 MHz, while the AT class of IBM computers runs at speeds of 8, 10, 16, and 20 MHz. By 1989 the top-of-the-line processors were running at speeds of 33 MHz and above. However the true speed of the computer as a whole is not just a function of the computer's processor speed—sometimes called its **clock** speed. The speed of the memory chips and how they coordinate with the processor matter too. If your processor is faster than the rate at which the system's memory can move bytes in and out of it, engineers may have to slow down the processor by adding a "wait state" during which the processor idles, waiting for the memory to catch up. So, unless a processor is advertised as having a "zero wait state," it may not be able to take full advantage of its own speed.

Another determinant of the computer's real speed is the number of bits that the processor takes in at a time. The Intel 8088 chip, which was the first PC processor, works on groups of 16 bits; however, it brings them in from memory in groups of 8 bits at a time, using what is called an 8-bit bus. Thus it takes the 8088 two slurps to pick up the data it is going to process at one time. The next generation of PC chips, the 286 chips, have a 16- bit data bus. This means that the processor takes in at one time all 16 bits it is going to process. Thus a 286 processor running at the same clock speed as the 8088 is going to be a lot faster than the 8088 because it needs a lot fewer cycles to pick up the same number of bytes to process, so more cycles can be used to process these bytes. The Intel 386 chip has a 32-bit data path and thus requires even fewer cycles to bring data into the processor.[1]

How fast your computer will actually be is also largely a function of how well engineered it is as a whole. The processor, memory, and data path are only a part of the whole story. There are other elements, like hardware memory caches, which may make significant differences in the speed the computer delivers.[2] The Macintosh Plus and the Macintosh SE both use an 8 MHz Motorola 68000 chip but the SE is from 15 percent to 20 percent faster, again as a result of the total engineering of the system.

But no matter how fast the processor is, the slowest thing on your computer is always the disk because of its mechanical nature. And many programs do a surprising amount of disk access—reading and writing files on the disk. So a computer running programs that are constantly reading and writing files is going to seem slower than one running programs which work almost entirely with data in memory—which is how computer speed tests are sometimes run. This problem can be made worse if you don't have disk drives and disk drive controllers capable of taking advantage of a fast processor.

Consider this: While an AT running at 10 MHz is 11.7 times faster than the original 4.77 MHz XT, the disk drive originally sold with that AT was only twice as fast as the one that came with the XT. So when you are doing a lot of disk access—for example when running your spell checker—much of your processor speed is lost waiting for the sluggish disk to deliver! But judging speed can get even more confusing, because there are software techniques, not just hardware solutions, that can also speed up the computer's disk access, such as disk caching programs.

---

[1] Just to complicate things a little more there are several hybrids available in today's PCs too. The 8086 processor chip, is a version of the 8088 chip which has a 16-bit data path. The 386 SX chip, which sounds like it should be a foreign car, is a processor that can run all the instructions that the 386 chip does, but only has a 16-bit, instead of a 32-bit data path.

[2] A **cache** in computer terms refers to a portion of fast memory where the hardware—or perhaps software—stores data that the system figures might be needed again soon to avoid having to waste time inputting and outputting it. There are a variety of ways that systems try to determine what should be stored and each one works better under some sets of conditions and worse under others. It is by doing things like designing a caching scheme that engineers can show off.

As a result of things like this, manufacturers and reviewers have come up with many different ways of testing overall computer performance. You will often see these tests referred to as "benchmarks." Because each benchmark test measures speed in a different way it is not at all unusual to see two computers with the "same" processor get widely different scores on these tests. And because of the competitive nature of the computer business vendors will always, of course, mention only the results of the tests where their machines did well.

How Much Speed Do You Need?

In deciding how much speed you really need—and need to pay for—you must always keep in mind that the important thing is what exactly it is that you are going to be doing with your computer. If most of your time is going to be spent typing text in your word processor, processor speed is not all that important. Most of the time the system is not going to go much faster than you can type. The only times you are likely to wish for a faster system is when your word processor has to do a lot of formatting when you print a complex document, when your spell checker has to look up each and every word in a manuscript and suggest correct spellings for the misspelled words, or perhaps when using a sophisticated grammar checker.

But these operations, in all likelihood, will be performed only a very small fraction of the time you are using your system. Generally, when using a word processor you will find yourself doing these slower, time-consuming operations when you are all done working on a piece and are ready to print it. And when we talk about slow, we mean that you might have to wait 2, 3, or even, for a very long document, 10 minutes, very occasionally, while one of these operations takes place.[3]

This is not, in geological terms, slow. But computers evoke a funny response from people. You will find that when you are sitting in front of a computer—once you get over your initial beginner's terror—anything that is not practically instantaneous will cause the same kind of irritated reaction that you feel when the guy in the car in front of you sits at the intersection for five seconds after the light turns green. So when you consider the issue of speed in relation to a system that is going to be used primarily for word processing, you will have to ask yourself if it is worth an extra $700 to avoid a few moments of irrational irritation a week.

The standard thinking is that word processing doesn't require fast machines and that is why businesses regularly give their older, slower systems to the employees who use them for word processing. You should also remember that these slow word processor functions are very disk-intensive, which means that they involve a lot of reading and writing to the

---

[3]My "slow" XT clone is able to format a 100,000 word manuscript—including floating page references—in about 10 minutes.

disk so that a more expensive system whose disks are not the best still may leave you waiting for the spell checker or the formatter to finish. If it is the disk access rather than the processor that is slowing things down, you may be able to improve the speed at which a "slow" system works by using a software disk caching program or, if you have extra memory on that system, using it as a RAM disk. We'll discuss this further on page 135.

The real speed hogs that require faster machines are the spreadsheets and huge database applications that businesspeople use. A spreadsheet that computes three years of month-by-month manufacturing costs may do an enormous amount of calculation every time that you enter a single new number into the spreadsheet. As a result, the user of one of these, on a slow machine, can end up staring at the machine for a couple of minutes every time he presses the enter key. This would make using such a program difficult and frustrating and would certainly justify investing in a faster machine. A database program that has to sort twenty thousand records every time you enter some information about a new customer also requires a faster system. But unless you do a lot of work with scanned images and text, page layout, and documents that embody computer-generated illustrations, you are unlikely, as a writer, to be doing the kind of work that requires this extra speed.

However there are a few more issues involved with picking a processor than just speed.

Multitasking

One hot issue is the ability to multitask. Although multitasking is the farthest thing from your mind right now, this may well be something that a salesperson tries to snow you with. What is multitasking and why should you worry about having it?

A processor that can multitask is able to run several programs simultaneously, swapping them in and out of the processor and playing tricks with memory. This is a feature that mainframe computers have had since the 1960s. The 286 and 386 chip, used in PCs, and the Motorola 60020 and 60030 chip, used in the high end Macintosh IIs, are capable of multitasking.[4] But in spite of all the hoopla about this ability, few people take advantage of it, simply because multitasking is not a number-one priority for a system that only one person is using. Multitasking becomes useful when several people, each with their own terminal, share both a central processor and a set of files on a shared disk, or when a computer

---

[4]Note that though these chips are capable of true multitasking, the operating systems that came with the Macintosh, like the DOS operating system used in most PCs, are not. Apple announced it would provide such an operating system but by mid-1989 it was still not available.

is attached to a network and wants to run several programs at once to service requests coming through the network. The only use for one-user multitasking is to have some programs running unattended off the screen—called the **background**—while you work on another on the screen. As an example of this, you could be letting a database sort itself in background while you, on the screen, in what is called **foreground**, type up a memo. This is not exactly the greatest thing since sliced bread.

To make it more confusing, although the 8088 chip—the low-end chip used in the original PC and the XTs and XT clones—can't multitask in the strict definition of the term, it *is* able to run a type of program that *acts* somewhat as if it were multitasking, the so-called "pop-up" or TSR (terminate and stay resident) programs. If a program is one of these and is "resident," then you can use it even when you are in the middle of another program without losing your place in either program by just typing a few predefined key strokes. The Macintosh's MultiFinder, a part of the Mac Interface, also allows this kind of cooperation between programs.

Because only the more expensive processors can multitask and because there is a large population of low-end machines in the marketplace, developers have tended to stay away from writing programs that can run only on these higher end systems capable of multitasking. Their reasoning has been, why narrow their customer base? As it is now, only a very small amount of software now requires that you have a processor capable of multitasking. And most of these programs are directed toward specialized needs of business users in a corporate environment that includes mainframe computers. The best known of these programs demanding multitasking processors (and a lot of other things besides) is the OS/2 operating system, a much ballyhooed production of IBM and Microsoft which as of 1989 had given even the most enthusiastic of corporate users no clear-cut reason for using it. OS/2 requires buying very expensive hardware upgrades in return for few clear benefits.

There are several other programs that run only on the multitasking chips, including the PC versions of the mainframe and minicomputer database program Oracle and one version of Microsoft's graphics interface for the PC, Windows 386 (which will also run on a 286). The chances are, though, that more software will take this path as the 286 and 386 chips are coming increasingly to dominate the business computer population. But although this might be a future consideration it is not an overwhelming reason for a writer to buy a more expensive processor.

For the time being, 8088 chips are what you will find in the cheapest systems, so if a rock-bottom price under $1,000 is the reason you have been considering buying a computer in the first place, then it may not make sense to put out a lot more money than you had intended in exchange for these vague, future benefits. You may well reason that you are unlikely to want to communicate with mainframes and that word process-ing will constitute 98 percent of what you do on your computer. Unless you have serious intentions of getting into desktop publishing you don't really need anything beyond the 8088. Why speculate that some program sometime might come along that your cheapo can't handle when there are thousands that it can?

Which is not to say that having a fast, multitasking processor isn't great—I'm going to get one myself one day when my utterly adequate bottom-of-the-line machine breaks down! But for now it's doing every-thing I need.

Remember, the real determinant is how much you want to pay now for the features and programs that are available now. If you can afford a fancier, faster processor now, without its demanding sacrifices that will make it hard for you to relax and enjoy your new system, by all means get one, but if you can't, just remember that in two years you probably will be able to pick up today's top-of-the-line for what your cheap system costs today—or less. Probably the best course of action, if you are torn, would be to ask the salesperson in a store to let you test out a program that you are thinking of using, on the two competing models, the cheaper, slower one and the more powerful, more expensive one. This way you can see if there is a real difference that you can feel between the two computers' performance—a difference that is worth the extra bucks.

Desktop Publishing and Speed

The only real reason you, the writer, might consider buying a system with a faster multitasking processor is if you have plans eventually to do serious amounts of desktop publishing or to work intensively with other graphics-based programs. Graphics programs—which include the desktop publishing layout programs—must manipulate the individual dots on your screen or printer, rather than just use simple codes for letters and numbers, and as a result they do a lot more work to display a screen or print a page. If you intend to work with programs that build printer fonts dot by dot or manipulate graphics images brought in with scanners, you will need a speedier system.

Some of these programs will specify, right on the box, that the minimum configuration you should have to use the program is an AT class computer with a 286 processor chip. But other programs where this is equally true will say nothing, perhaps in the hope of getting you to try the program and then upgrade your hardware once you fall in love with it.

If you intend to do desktop publishing down the line it makes a lot of sense to buy a machine that has a faster processor now and that has the capacity to be expanded (which is discussed later), so that when you are ready to do desktop publishing you only have to buy the expensive printer and software, not a whole new machine.

Making the decision of what processor to choose—and by extension what kind of money to invest in your system—is not exactly like buying eggs, where there are rules of thumb about at what price it's smart to buy the extra large instead of the jumbo. You may, however, find that the amount you have to spend would allow you to choose between a top-of-the-line cheapie system and a more sparely configured faster-processor-based system. In such a case it is probably a better idea to get the faster system as long as it is expandable and includes the hardware options, like a hard disk and enough memory, that you need to get working now.

If, on the other hand, such a system is out of the question and the bottom of the line is all you can afford, don't worry. As we've stressed before, today's bottom of the line was an utter wonder only four or so years ago and is quite capable of blowing you away with its power to revolutionize the way you do your work.

MEMORY

Once you have decided which processor you want, the next question you should be asking is how much memory, or RAM, you will get with your system. This is an important consideration. Sometimes the only reason one system may look cheaper than another is that it has less memory on board.

Each system has a maximum amount of memory it can address, which is a function of the way it is engineered. For a DOS system the original limit was 1 meg, of which only 640K was usually usable, but schemes of using memory coprocessors allow many PCs to use much more. AT powerhouses, using DOS, not the memory-hungry OS/2 operating system, can make good use of 2 or 3 megs of memory. The Macintoshes can be configured to function with a whopping 8 megs of memory, which is the amount of memory that only a few years ago you would have found on a mainframe computer that supported 200 terminals on-line simultaneously.

It is probably safe to say that you can't have enough memory. Memory is where your programs sit when you are using them, it is also where many programs keep the data they are working on. For example, many word processors try to keep the whole manuscript file that you are working on in memory. Spreadsheet programs try to keep the entire spreadsheet in memory too. Even if your programs don't fill up what you have, it is by no means wasted. You can set up the extra memory to be a **RAM disk.** A RAM disk is a piece of memory that the processor is led to believe is a disk, although, of course, it isn't. The benefit of this is that once you have read in files from your real disks into the piece of memory that serves as the RAM disk, the system doesn't have to read or write files off the slow real disks but can read them from this pretend disk at memory access speeds which are many times faster than disk speeds.

Finally, the more memory you have, the more memory-resident, pop-up programs or Mac desk accessories you can have going simultaneously. This may not sound like much now, but you will appreciate it once you become dependent on a couple of these memory-resident tools. There are even programs that allow you to, in effect, turn all your programs into pop-up programs, so that you can pop up a database, word processor, outliner, and a spreadsheet—and anything else—all in one session. But these programs run effectively only if you have a lot of this extra memory. On the Macintosh the amount of memory you have can limit the number of items you can work on at the same time and more than 1 meg of memory is required to run the MultiFinder.

However, additional memory is one of the things you should think about fiddling around with only after you are a seasoned computer user. For the time being you have enough to deal with without having to configure memory, set up memory drivers, and define RAM disks. So in the store you, the beginner, really need concentrate on only two memory-related questions: Are you getting enough memory to use the computer for what you intended it for and can the system's memory be upgraded easily later on? Beyond this, the only time you should pay much attention to memory is when comparing two otherwise identical systems, one of which comes with more memory than the other.

The Macintosh Plus and SE models come with a minimum of 1 Meg of memory, which is the least amount needed to run the MultiFinder interface. They can accept more. If you buy an XT clone, the greatest amount of memory that most programs that run under DOS can work with without enhanced hardware and software is 640K. If you are getting an AT-type computer, the system can use 1 meg, so it is wise to get this much. If more comes with the system, great! Many XT clones come with only 512K installed, but the additional 128K is worth buying. It requires no additional software or effort on your part to use—as larger memory upgrades often do. You should insist on getting 640K. Any lesser amount may limit the size of documents you can work on or make it hard to use resident software—including the better organizers—with your word processor. If the system you buy comes with more than these base amounts installed the extra can be used as a RAM disk—at some future time when your understanding of the computer is more mature. Unfortunately, the beginner who uses memory to trick the word processor into thinking it is safely storing a document in a disk file for the sake of a little speed is likely to end up turning off the system without writing the file to a real disk, which results in an erased RAM disk, and the destruction of important work.

As a beginner, particularly if you are using your system mainly for word processing, consider additional memory as important as a future potential—an avenue for expansion on your system—rather than a present requirement. One additional note: A DOS system using more than 1 meg of memory requires that you have some software—and hardware—to manage it for you. And this extra memory can be used only by those programs that have been specifically designed to recognize it. Many programs simply can't take advantage of it. The Macintosh, on the other hand, has no problem using greater amounts of memory, but may have trouble running the standard Macintosh repertoire if only 1 meg or less is available on the system.

The limit on how much memory you get is the availabilty and the going rate for memory chips. Once cheap, in 1988 due to protectionist government intervention, their prices rose steeply and fluctuated widely enough that merchants sold them the way that restaurants sell lobster— you had to call for the daily price. Sleazy operators appeared out of nowhere at computer shows offering chips—possibly stolen—no questions asked, asking for checks now, and claiming the chips would be mailed later.

There are various ways to increase or upgrade the memory that comes with a computer. Some motherboards have empty sockets into which memory chips can be inserted. This is nice because it means that you won't have to fill up a slot with a memory card. Other systems have enough slots so that adding a memory board is not a problem. Systems also differ in what kind of memory chips they can accept. Some can only use smaller density ones while others can use memory chips that hold up to a meg on a single chip.

WHAT IS A BIOS?

If you buy a clone, one important feature to be aware of is what is called the **BIOS.** This acronym has overtones of some kind of basic life force, and for your computer this is what the BIOS is. The BIOS is a chip that contains, burned into it, a set of programs that control the most basic functions of the computer, such as communicating with the disk drives and the monitor. The BIOS, although it is a chip and therefore looks like hardware, functions as software. It contains part of the operating system. It is also the thing that makes a computer "compatible," since both the operating system and other programs call on the routines stored in the BIOS to perform these basic functions for them.

Computers sold by IBM use IBM's own BIOS, and there have been several versions of this IBM BIOS as the PC has matured. Clones use BIOS chips produced by chip companies, like Phoenix, Award, and Chips and Technologies, who produce chips that while different enough not to violate IBM's patents, function identically to the IBM BIOS chips. If you buy a clone you should determine whose BIOS chip the clone uses and stick with a name-brand BIOS to ensure that you are getting a compatible system.

DISKS AND DISKETTES

Once you have your processor and memory you are ready to decide what disk configuration you want. This is not the place to become stingy. You will need at least one floppy diskette drive since you get software into your computer by reading it in off the floppy that comes in the software box. A floppy is also where you will be storing backup copies of anything on your computer that is of the slightest value. If you have a hard disk on your system, all you will use the floppy drives for is transferring files and doing backup. Everything else is done on your hard disk. There are a whole lot of different kinds of floppy drives on the market, though, so systems at the same price level and that use similar processors may vary in what diskette drives they use.

Most existing PC and PC XT models have 5 1/4" diskette drives, which use double-sided diskettes that can hold about 360,000 bytes of data—the 360K diskette. Most programs are distributed on this size diskette. They are also cheap to buy blank, costing anywhere from 27 cents to $1 apiece. Even if you have a hard disk, you will still be buying a lot of blank diskettes as you will be using them to back up and protect your data as well as to exchange files with other computer users, including publishers. Five-and-a-quarter-inch diskettes, then, are convenient.

The older IBM AT computers also have drives that use 5 1/4" floppy diskettes but they are able to write more bytes of data on them. These are the so-called high density drives. Diskettes written by these drives can hold 1.2 megabytes of data. To confuse the issue further, the PS/2 family of IBM computers and many clones, as well as all Macintoshes, use a 3 1/2" plastic-jacketed floppy diskette which can hold even more data: 1.44 megabytes of data per disk, though some 3 1/2" diskettes only hold 720K. These plastic boxed diskettes protect data better than the older kind of paper-jacketed diskettes, but they are more expensive. In addition, when you buy software you may either have to pay a little extra or have to mail in a card to get the 3 1/2" version since a lot of software boxes come with only the 5 1/4" version in the box, though this is changing. As computers featuring the 3 1/2" drives become more prevalent this is becoming less of a problem and some of the very high-end programs are only distributed on these ultra high-density disks. But if the rest of your computer is a "low-end" machine it probably doesn't make sense to have a blue-ribbon diskette drive, since it means only that you will have to pay more for diskettes and programs, especially if you intend to have your second disk drive be a hard disk.

On a Macintosh Plus or SE model you won't have to worry about making the decision of what size diskette drive to buy. They all have high-capacity 3 1/2" diskette drives built into the unit.

Disk-sharing Considerations

But before you decide what kind of diskette drive you will get with your computer you should remember that a computer that has only a 3 1/2" drive cannot read 5 1/4" diskettes. This might seem like an obvious statement but if you work on projects that involve swapping diskettes around from one writer to another on different machines it suddenly becomes highly significant. If you intend to make electronic submissions—and publishers are beginning to ask for these more and more since it eliminates their typing step—make sure that there will be no problem with the diskette format you will be getting. If you collaborate with other writers this too is a consideration.

If you intend to use both a computer at the office and your computer at home to work on the same documents, make sure that the two machines are capable of reading and writing each other's diskettes. Some people get a computer with a 3 1/2" diskette drive built in and then add an external 5 1/4" drive to the system to solve this problem, but this is expensive. Disk- sharing problems are not insoluble by any means—in the worst case you might decide to transfer the files via an electronic bulletin board, for example—but it's one more thing to consider.

Your Second Disk Drive

You do not absolutely need two disk drives on a computer and plenty of vendors sell cheap systems where, when you read the fine print, you will see you only get one. But a computer with one diskette drive is a pretty sorry machine. Even a computer with two diskette drives and no hard drive is not much fun to work with. Diskette drives are slower than hard drives and limit you to programs that can be stored on a single floppy. But the real reason for getting a hard drive is that it allows you to work with all your stuff all the time, whereas a floppy system only lets you work with what is on the floppies you have in your drives at a given time.

Although millions of PCs with two floppy drives have been sold, the quality and price of hard disks today is good enough that it is senseless to buy anything less than a hard disk system right from the start.

In spite of what you might hear, a hard disk system is not hard to use. Once you understand some fairly simple concepts you can streamline your work easily and let several programs work together for you—but only when you have a hard disk. With a hard disk you are spared having to switch diskettes in and out of your drives every time you want to use your word processor's thesaurus or spell checker. The hard disk means that you can take advantage of utility programs with a few keystrokes instead of having to root through a pile of a hundred or more diskettes looking for the one that has the program on it you wanted.

You can also deal with your data better on a hard disk since having all your documents and research materials on a hard disk means that you can use programs that search all or part of them and that you can work on several documents at the same time, without having to switch diskettes in and out of the machine.

Finally, a lot of newer programs are getting to the point where you just about have to have a hard disk to run them. They are too big to fit on a single or even a few diskettes.

So, while the cost of the hard disk itself is not entirely trivial, you should consider the disk itself as one of the most useful parts of your system and worth investing in.

The big question when buying a hard disk is: how big? Here again, within reason, big is better. Hard disk size is measured in megabytes (megs). You might be wondering how you could ever fill up 20 megabytes. Twenty megabytes do, after all, hold some 21,204,992 characters—the equivalent of 10,500 double-spaced manuscript pages. But you will be amazed at how quickly that space fills up. The culprit is not your manuscripts—at roughly 2,000 characters per page an 800 page manuscript takes up only 1.5 megs. Your software is to blame. Today's garden-variety word processor, which includes a dictionary and complete thesaurus, can easily fill up a meg on your disk. A behemoth program like Lotus' Manuscript, a word processor with extensive facilities for producing graphics and tables in a quasi-desktop processing mode, fills up over three-and-a-half million bytes of disk space. If you are working with desktop publishing and graphics files then your disk requirements will skyrocket since a graphics file that prints out a single page will be many times the size of the 2,000-character text file that does the same thing.

Even without desktop publishing, by the time you have collected together all the programs that make your computer useful you may find half your hard disk filled up, and that's before you type a word. A desktop utility, backup utilities, disk utilities, an outliner, a random information database, a regular database for names and addresses, a full-featured communications program—or two—are just the beginning of what may fill up your disk. And you may easily end up with two word processors, or two databases, as you search for the one you like best, or even two versions of the same program if you install an upgraded version of the product next year but don't want to get rid of your old, working copy, until you make sure the new one is correctly installed.

Currently 30-meg disks are so close in price to 20-meg disks that it doesn't make sense not to have one if you are going to buy a disk. For desktop publishing you may need something bigger. But once you go above 40-meg disks you should expect to pay a lot more. This is because the larger the disk, the faster your access speed must be so that you don't get bogged down reading it. The very large disks that you see advertised, those above 100 megs in capacity,are not intended for individual users. These disks are for systems that manage huge databases on a network of PCs, and are intended for middle-size and large businesses.

While the size of the disk that comes with a system is usually clear, there are several other important measures of disk performance that you should note. One characteristic of a disk drive is its access time, the average time it takes the disk to find a specific track (or data location). A lower access time is characteristic of a faster drive. However you can't just go out and buy a disk with a faster access rate. The disk has to match the data path—the bus—that the computer uses. So if you buy an XT computer you need an XT-type disk drive.

When you buy a disk you should also be getting a disk controller, which is a piece of hardware that manages the task of getting the data to and from the disk. Some controllers are faster than others, and this is a significant factor in the apparent speed of your disk. What determines this apparent speed is the interaction between how the disk is formatted and how the controller card reads and writes the data.

There are other considerations too: This is where the engineering savvy of the people who designed your system comes into play—and where the ethics of the person who sells you the system come into play too. Since worrying about controller boards is not the sort of thing you should have to do when you are just getting your feet wet with computers, this is one reason it is important to buy hardware from the kind of outfit—whether mail order or a store—that has a reputation for quality and that will put the right controller together with the best disk for your purposes. This kind of attention costs money and is a reason to be suspicious of very cheap mail-order systems with hard disks.

The final thing you should do when buying your system is to make sure that you will get the hard disk both installed and formatted by the people you buy it from. A hard disk goes through two formatting steps. The first, low-level formatting, defines where the data tracks will be physically on the disk. The second, high-level formatting, writes information on the disk that is needed by the operating system before it can read and write files.

Some outfits, particularly low-ball mail-order companies, will ship you the components unassembled, leaving you to install and prepare the disk yourself. While this may be relatively simple for people who know what they are doing, it is not something you should have to deal with at your current state of computer expertise. The people who sell you your system should install and format your disk as well as install your operating system on that disk so that when you get the system home all you have to do is plug in the keyboard, monitor, and printer to be ready to go to work.

Most hard disks you can buy for a PC are built into the system, however you can buy external hard disks for the Macintosh which simply plug into a SCSI port. These are more expensive than internal hard disks, however they are easier to replace if they break and have the advantage of being portable from one system to another.

MONITORS

When you go into the computer store to shop you will see some beautiful-looking screen displays, images so crisp they almost look like printing, and waterfalls of changing pattern and color that look like videos. Unfortunately these demos are probably running on systems where the monitor alone costs what you intended to spend on the whole system. If you are planning to concentrate on word processing, collecting, and managing data, checking out a bulletin board or two, and experimenting with some "thoughtware," a fancy display like this is really a frill.

A standard merchandising dodge is to price the computer without the monitor, so make sure to determine whether any system price that you are quoted includes a monitor.

When deciding which kind of monitor you want, you have a lot of choices. First you will have to decide whether you want one that displays in color or a **monochrome** display—one that is either black and white, or black and amber yellow, or green. While almost all the ads you see in the magazines show the classy-looking high resolution color monitors, you can get along just fine with a monochrome monitor, and millions of PC users do.

Cheap monochrome monitors cost under $100 while the cheapest color monitors usually begin in the $300 range. But that is for the ugly-looking ones. The snazzy color monitors you see displayed at the store may well cost $700 or even $1,000, particularly the ones capable of the very high resolution color displays. **Resolution** means the number of dots per inch, and the higher it is, the better your picture will look.

Deciding whether you want color or monochrome is a decision you should make only after seeing examples of programs you intend to work with displayed on the monitors you are considering. Color is usually used in word processors to highlight format features in the text, for example red letters might be used to display some text that will print out in an italic font, and blue might indicate text that will print in smaller type. But some people find the color used in word processors distracting, particularly on the cheaper color monitors.

Color is also useful when creating graphic images, but remember that most printers do not print in color. If you are going to be producing black and white desktop publishing output you may well need an expensive high resolution display, but not necessarily a color one: your laser printer will be producing strictly black, white, and gray halftones. If you are going to do simpler graphics to be printed on a dot matrix printer again, a monochrome display may be fine.

What you see on a screen is dependent not only on your monitor but on a piece of hardware called a **graphics (or video) card.** Sometimes one is built into your system's motherboard. Other times it is a card that is plugged into one of the system's open slots. Wherever it is found the graphics card contains, among other things, a coprocessor which manages the image that appears on the screen. The kind of graphics card your system has, in conjunction with the kind of monitor you have attached to the system, determines the density of the graphics images you can display. Be very sure that the price you are quoted for a system includes this essential piece of hardware. Many low-ball prices do not and such boards can cost anywhere from $150 up.

In the IBM world there is a whole range of different graphics standards available. You will need to decide which one you want—independent of the decision to get color. Most monochrome PCs use the "Hercules compatible" monographics card, which is able to display graphics on a monochrome display. This kind of card can produce very respectable-looking graphics. But be aware that the only graphics programs that these cards can run are those specifically designed for the Hercules graphic display. If a piece of software specifies that some other video board is required, such as CGA, EGA, or VGA and doesn't list Hercules graphics (sometimes abbreviated HCGA) then you won't be able to use that graphics program on a system equipped with Hercules compatible graphics. Some word processors will let you use their WYSIWYG displays only with EGA or VGA graphics, or may require a special video board to display fancy typefaces on screen. If this is the case with software you are considering, it should be mentioned in the hardware requirement list usually found on the software's box.

If you want a color monitor, the PCs offer CGA, which is an old, low-resolution graphics standard, long abandoned by IBM, which looks clunky; EGA, which is a bit better; MCGA which is only offered with certain low-end PS2 computers; and, at the high end, the very impressive, and expensive VGA graphics. VGA graphics require that you use a kind of monitor called an analog monitor, rather than the cheaper TTL monitors that the other standards call for. VGA can also be used with black-and-white monitors, but they must again be analog monitors—expensive and not to be confused with the usual monochrome monitor—that allow the display of hundreds of different shades of gray, a feature useful for black-and-white desktop publishing. There are other even higher resolution special-purpose graphics cards available that require special software to do their tricks, but it is unlikely that you will be needing one of these.

The Macintosh world, as usual, is much simpler. In the low and mid-range models, the Macintosh Plus and the Macintosh SE, the screen is built into the system unit. There is therefore only one kind of display, one graphics standard, and for that matter, one set of colors: black and white, until you get to the very high end of the product line, with the Macintosh II, where color—and a range of hardware choices that resembles those you must make with the PC—becomes available.

The fact to keep in mind when selecting a monitor is that unless you are doing desktop publishing where, to be useful, your screen must exactly match your printer output, there is little compelling reason to buy a very expensive graphics display. Because of the huge number of machines in the business community that have the monographics displays, most programs work nicely on them, and even many game programs now come in a monographics form. If you have your heart set on something that only runs on CGA—which would most likely be a video game—there are programs available both as shareware and from commercial distributors that let you run CGA-only programs on a monographics card. These programs don't work on all CGA programs but they do work on a lot of them.

An upgraded display might be worthwhile to you if you intend to use a word processor like Microsoft Word or WordPerfect which offer a "preview" mode where you can look at pages of your manuscript formatted the way that they will print on the printer. Some of these preview modes display correctly only with EGA or VGA. And some programs can display special characters and on-screen fonts with an EGA or VGA display. Yet others require a different graphics board—the Hercules In-Color card. But unless you are going to be doing desktop publishing or academic writing involving a lot of complicated footnotes and charts so that it is important to see exactly where on the page a particular item might end up, this is just a frill.

There is no reason why you can't start out with the cheaper monochrome display and then later, if necessary, upgrade. Usually all that upgrading involves is buying a new monitor and perhaps a video card. However if you are thinking seriously about high-end graphics you should not plan to put them on a low-end machine.

We mentioned the vision problems that are reported by people who spend a lot of time starting at monitors. Whether the more expensive high resolution displays can prevent these sorts of problems is moot. Some people claim they can. However since much of the problem stems from your having to stare at points of light at a fixed distance and from glare, just upgrading the resolution and the color palette may not be enough to eliminate eyestrain and focusing problems entirely. Look for a monitor that has an adjustible stand that can swivel or tilt and remember when you set up your system to do all that you can to prevent light glaring off the screen.

KEYBOARDS

You are a writer. The chances are you have had a long and emotional relationship with at least one typewriter and have gotten used to the way that it feels. Your first encounter with a computer keyboard may, as a result, be upsetting. Computer keyboards don't feel like typewriter keyboards. In addition they contain a number of keys that are new. Finding a keyboard that you are comfortable with is important, but the fact of the matter is that you will probably have to get used to any keyboard you buy, and you probably won't start out liking any of them.

Still, when you test out a system you are thinking of buying, the feel of the keyboard is important. Reviewers routinely mention whether a keyboard feels "mushy" or "clicky." Keyboards are almost always included with a system, so you probably will have to settle for whatever comes with your system. But if you find that you absolutely hate it you can buy a different one for under a hundred dollars (or even maybe pick one up at a flea market.)

The Macintosh Plus comes with a standard keyboard. The SE model does not and you have choice of several models. If you don't like the ones Apple provides there is also a replacement keyboard, the Mac-101, made by a company called DataDesk which you can check out.

In the IBM world, again, as with everything else, nothing is standard.[5] The main differences between keyboards is where they put the nontypewriter keys. These keys include the function keys, which are the keys labeled F1 through F10 or F12, and the cursor keys, which have arrows on them and move the little underline character, that shows you where you are, around the screen. Some keyboards have the function keys on the side. Others have them on the top. This is not a big deal when you are buying your first system since you will get used to the key placement used by whatever keyboard you get. But it does get to be an irritant when you are used to using a different model. If you use a computer at work you may be happier if you have a keyboard that is the same as the one you are used to.

Some keyboards have separate numeric key pads and cursor keys which is great if you are an accountant and do a lot of numeric entry—and are used to an adding machine—but pretty meaningless to the writer.

---

[5]This diversity is what drives a lot of people nuts about PCs but, again, to others just reflects a world of choice.

Finally for reasons known only to IBM, each different model PC and clone keyboard has the "escape" key, the "Ctrl" key, the "Alt" key and the backslash (\) located in different places on the keyboard. Again, this is a problem only when changing computers after you have already learned a certain way of using one.

As a programmer I have had to cope with using a great variety of keyboards and have found that adapting to a new keyboard is much like getting used to a new pair of shoes. You notice the different feel a lot at first and then forget it.

DO-IT-YOURSELF HARDWARE CONFIGURATIONS

One subject that deserves a bit of discussion is the question of whether you should try to buy a complete package put together by a vendor, or whether you should get a "stripped down" base system and then buy the best components yourself and assemble them into a great system. You will hear a lot of experienced computer users arguing that the latter course is the way to go, and it is—for them! It may even, in another year or two, be the way for you. But unless you are already an electronics hobbyist you should resist the temptation to get too fancy when putting together a first system. You will have enough decisions to make even when buying supposedly cut-and-dried products.

Hardware can be fairly easy to master at the very elementary level where you choose options for a system that a reputable vendor offers. Putting together a more customized system takes a lot more expertise. Even though building a truly custom configuration can save you money, you need to know what you are doing to do it right. For now save your mental energy for mastering the details of the software you must learn. That alone will keep you busy for a while.

AFTERMARKET BOARDS

The one area in which you should not be too timid about hardware is the area of some—not all—aftermarket boards. This is because of the modular, plug-in design of most personal computers.

For example, if you want to add a MIDI interface to a PC you might be intimidated by learning that to do so you will have to install a board. But it would be foolish to cart your system to a service shop where it could sit for weeks until the technician installed such a board for you for $50. Installing such a board in a PC clone is simple. The whole operation involves unplugging your system, then unplugging the keyboard and monitor, taking the cover off your system unit, and plugging the board into a slot. It isn't much different from plugging in a lamp and if you have remembered to unplug the computer it's probably less dangerous. If you have an XT clone which has a clock on the motherboard, you might have to get a pair of tweezers and carefully pick up a small staple-shaped metal piece called a jumper whose "legs" rest in two little holes and move it to the next row of little holes. That's it. Put everything back and your system now has a MIDI board.

I mention this example since performing precisely this operation was my initiation into "doing" hardware. However to be utterly truthful I should add that when I put the cover back on the system, plugged the keyboard and the screen back in, and turned the computer back on, it no longer worked. This, it turns out, is typical. In plugging in the card I had bumped against another card which held the disk controller, and loosened the cable that connects the controller card to the hard disk. Since I had recently read in my computer users group newsletter of someone else's very similar experience when installing a card, I controlled my panic, reopened the system unit box and immediately noticed the loose cable. Once everything was plugged back in correctly the computer again worked.

An important factor that went into my decision to undertake this, to me terrifying, operation, was that I had a hardware "resource." At my PC user's group I had made the acquaintance of a man who puts together hardware for a living. He had assured me that installing this particular board was a reasonable thing for me to do, and I knew I could call him in a pinch. Until you develop this kind of "resource" you probably won't try this kind of thing on your own.

Instead, get the people who sell you your system to install everything including modems, extra memory, or other specialty boards that you want to add to your system to start with. But when you get to know your system and have developed your own resources, and are ready to add features to your system, you should feel comfortable doing much of the work yourself.

ENSURING THAT YOUR SYSTEM CAN GROW

Before you sign the check for the system that you have chosen there is one last thing you should determine: How many open slots come with the system. You may remember that these slots are the receptacles into which you plug cards. Having open, unused slots means that you can upgrade your system in the future. However even though a system supposedly has a certain number of slots doesn't mean that you can use them all. In some computers one slot will be filled with a hard disk controller card when you bring it home from the store. In others another slot may be filled with a video card. If you have bought extra memory it may have been added to your system on a card too. Some systems have their time of day clock—

used to give files the correct date and you the correct time—on a board, along with other things like all memory greater than 256K. An internal modem may take up still another slot, as may a mouse or joystick.

Where expansion slots are concerned, the more, the merrier. If you have to choose between two PC systems that are almost identical, where one has more slots than the other, your decision can be easily made on this feature alone.

If you are buying a middle- or high-end system, you may have to consider another characteristic of slots: the data bus they use. Because people who bought computers years ago usually already own boards, manufacturers of middle-range PCs usually give you a couple of slots that can be used for the older PC XT-type cards whose data path is 8 bits wide. To these they add AT-type slots with a 16-bit data path. In the top-of-the-line systems there are also slots that accept a 32-bit data path. The mix of data paths that the slots support is a concern, but mainly when you are upgrading.

Some machines are built so that some slots can accept only short, half-size boards. If this is the case for your machine, you might run into trouble even when you have an open slot because the board you want won't fit. Some PCs, most notably the Tandy 1000 from Radio Shack, require that you buy special boards rather than the off-the-shelf versions most PCs require.

A Macintosh can use only Mac boards, however you may not be using boards for the same kinds of functions you would be using them for on the PC. For example, with the Macintosh a hard drive plugs into a SCSI (pronounced scuzzi) port, rather than into a slot, and the mouse port is already built in. You probably will plug your modem into the machine's serial port. Memory doesn't go into a slot either. As a result, the Macintosh Plus at the low-end of the product line offers no slots, although it does make provision for you to expand memory. The next model up, the Macintosh SE, offers a single slot. Only when you reach the very expensive Macintosh II models—which in many ways are very different machines from the machines that built the Mac's reputation—do you begin to see a lot of slots.

Even if you don't intend to extend your system immediately, get the salesperson to tell you what it would cost to add a couple of features that might be interesting to you in the future, such as a scanner, more memory, or a mouse. This will help you get an idea of relative cost of such enhancements and ensure that you can make this kind of upgrade on the system you are buying.

8

PRINTERS, MODEMS, AND EXTRAS

Print it as it stands—beautifully.

Henry James 1843-1916
The Lion

YOU'RE ONLY AS GOOD AS YOUR PRINTER

You got into all this hardware in the first place because you are a writer. At the end of the whole process of putting these computer tools to work you are going to be producing a manuscript. The manuscript's intent may be to impress a professor, cajole an assignment from an editor, or nourish your sense of creativity. But the thing that will determine the manuscript's appearance is not the computer you buy but the printer you attach to that computer.

A crummy-looking printer attached to the best system will print out sloppy-looking junk. A good printer attached to a cheap system will print out professional looking manuscripts, though it may do so very slowly. But your reader doesn't see what went into producing your manuscript, just what he holds in his hands. The look of the print and the slickness—or lack of slickness—of your printed material all communicate subtle messages to your reader. Choosing a printer, then, is the part of buying a system where you express your personal sense of style.

Clearly, this should not be the place where you buy the special of the week to save a buck. But, on the other hand, this doesn't mean that you have to go out on a financial limb to get a decent printer either. There are a great number of printers available in a wide range of prices, and the differences in printer prices often result from things that matter only in the business environment and are of little importance to you.

What Should Your Printed Output Look Like?

You've probably been doing pretty well up until now with a typewriter and its predictable typewriter typefaces. Perhaps you have a more recent model which allows you to change the typeface by changing the printing element, or you may have just been using an old manual typewriter that gave your manuscripts a somewhat uneven look. You may even have been paying a typist to prepare your final, presentation draft, or you may just have have figured that as long as the manuscript was neat and readable its typeface was not going to significantly improve its chances of acceptance.

Now, by acquiring a computer, you can get a printer that makes it possible for you to produce printed material that looks exactly like the text you would see printed in a magazine. The world of fonts and differing type sizes is suddenly open to you. The temptation is great to buy this top-of-the-line technology. After all, getting words set in type has been the writer's goal, since Gutenberg invented the stuff.

But some thought is required here. Do you really want the stuff you produce to look like the slick junk mail you have been throwing away since you got your first apartment? Or do you, instead, want to keep it looking like a manuscript, albeit a clean, nicely formatted, error-free one? There is a subtle danger in having your printed material look too typeset when dealing with editors, professors, and other people whose response to your work is important.

If you are going to self-publish, you do need your printed output to look as much like set type as possible, but if you are trying to get someone else to publish your work, or if your main motivation for buying a computer is to take advantage of tools to organize your thoughts, simplify the creation of your manuscripts, and manage the information that goes into those manuscripts, then you might be better off avoiding the temptation to buy the printer that delivers the most impressive output. There is little reason to pay a premium price for a "corporate" image if that image will tend to make your reader read you with the same suspicious distaste with which he reads most corporate outpourings!

That said, let's look at the printer choices you face.

TYPES OF PRINTERS

Printers fall into a few clearly defined families, based on the technology used to transfer the image to the page. The good news here is that like all the other pieces that make up computers, the prices of printers have come down drastically in the last few years. This means that you will not have to impoverish yourself to get good-looking output.

Daisy Wheel Printers

When personal computers first appeared, the only way you could get anything approaching nice-looking printed output from them—by which was meant something that looked like what an expensive office typewriter could produce—was by using a daisy wheel printer. This type of printer used a spinning print element. Each letter was embossed on a little spine on this element and it worked much like the type ball in an IBM Selectric typewriter. The output looked crisp and clean and resembled the standard typewritten output people were familiar with, but these printers were slow and not able to print graphics. As the output produced by other printer technologies improved dramatically, these daisy wheel printers, which had been quite expensive in their heyday, declined in popularity, to the point where it is unlikely that you will see one now in a computer store. However you may find used ones for sale or see them at computer flea markets. There probably is little reason now to buy one.

If you bought an electronic typewriter a few years ago when they routinely boasted a "computer interface" among their features you may assume that you can use this typewriter as the printer on your new system. You may be able to, if you can hunt up the obligatory, expensive piece of equipment called a printer interface which allows the typewriter to be used this way—a piece of equipment that probably was not mentioned when you bought the typewriter. Unfortunately, if you can locate the interface, which often can be found only by writing to the manufacturer, you may find that the speed at which the typewriter prints when hooked to your computer is that of a hunt and peck typist. Waiting several minutes per page is probably unacceptable for the amounts of print your computer will generate. Since the output of cheap dot matrix printers is good enough to be acceptable for business correspondence, you might just leave your electronic typewriter alone, but keep it handy to address envelopes, a task that is a pain in the neck on many computer printers.

Dot Matrix Printers

If you read the paragraphs in *Writer's Market* where publishers list their requirements for submissions you will see publisher after publisher remarking that "dot matrix" manuscripts are just barely acceptable. Does this mean you can't consider one? Of course not. What these squibs are talking about is not the kind of dot matrix printer you will see in the store today, but the ones common four or five years ago whose output was characterized by hard to read, follow-the-dots style letters.

Dot matrix printers print an image, whether it be a letter or a graphic, by passing a print head across the paper very rapidly. The print head consists of a little bar containing a row of tiny pins. As it moves across the paper, the print head presses the appropriate pins against the ribbon to build a letter or picture out of the dots the pins make.

The cheaper dot matrix printers have 9-pin print heads. Junky-looking 7-pin printers are also available at almost the same cost as the 9-pin ones. In the older dot matrix printers these 9-pin printers made only one trip across the paper per line. This produced the characteristic "dot matrix" look most of us remember thinking of as computer output.

However, today's 9-pin printers are more sophisticated and usually include what is known as Near Letter Quality or **NLQ mode.** In NLQ mode the print head makes two trips across each line so that twice as many dots are used to build a single letter or image. As a result the characters produced in this fashion are fuller and less spotty looking. In NLQ mode most printers can produce a variety of typefaces. Most include a serif and a sans serif font. Most NLQ printers are also capable of printing tiny letters, known as condensed print, as well as italic print, bold print and other font variations. Samples of 9-pin dot matrix output are given in Figure 8.1. Dot matrix printers are also capable of printing out graphics images, including charts and graphs. Given the right software they can even do desk top publishing—although it won't have the crispness of laser printer output.

These newer dot matrix printers produce print that is crisp and neat. Because businesses frequently use this kind of printer for business correspondence, the print quality in NLQ mode strikes the eye as professional and completely acceptable for business communication.

This is a draft font.
This is a compressed font.
This is a NLQ sans serif font.
This is a NLQ serif font.
This is an elite font.
This is a pica font.
This is a NLQ bold font.
This is a NLQ italic font.
This is a NLQ wide font.
This is a NLQ subscript font.

Figure 8.1: Typical 9-pin Dot Matrix Typefaces (Epson LX-800)

At the same time this kind of output is clearly computer generated, which sends a subtle message to the reader about your technical sophistication. If you are a freelancer this obviously computer-generated output may signal an editor that working with you and your manuscript will be easier, since you have the capability of submitting your accepted manuscript in an electronic form, which requires no typing on the publisher's part.

How much you pay for a dot matrix printer appears to be a function of its speed, how sturdily it is built, the fonts it can print, what paper-handling features it includes, and the current phase of the moon. You may have steeled yourself to spend $400 or $500 on a "good" printer, only to discover that the $200 model is more than adequate for your needs.

The faster a printer is, the more it will cost, but unless you tend to print out 100-page manuscripts on a daily basis you can usually get along with a slower printer, printing your longer stuff out while you do something else. Speed is not an issue when you are printing out a short cover letter, a page or two long. The slowest printers will handle this task easily.

Printer speed is measured in **cps,** characters per second, but tests run by computer magazines would suggest that in real use all printers print much more slowly than the cps ratings given by the manufacturers. The manufacturers are not lying. They are simply measuring the printer's speed as it prints out something that was selected to optimize the speed rating. Use the speed ratings as a relative indicator.

The fastest speed you see listed in the specification list describing a printer is usually what the printer can do in draft mode. **Draft mode** is the term for when the printer prints in one-pass mode and produces rawer, but still readable, output. You probably will use this mode when you want to print out a lot of stuff quickly for your own use. It is usually quite readable. In the near-letter-quality mode the printer will go much more slowly, as it will when printing graphics, because of the extra passes and extra work that the printer must do to break the lines of print into the patterns to be printed on each pass.

Some dot matrix printers are able to print using a feature called **proportional spacing.** While most typewriters and dot matrix printers print each letter using the same amount of space, printers with proportional spacing can print a wide letter, like the letter "m" so that it takes up more space than a thin letter like "i." This gives your printed output a more typeset look.

There are several ways of getting paper in and out of the printer. Which ones a given printer provides will affect its price. Some printers print on **cut sheets,** which is a fancy term for what you have been calling, up until now, "regular old typing paper." Being able to feed such sheets into the printer is handy if you want it to print on letterhead. However, to print more than one sheet at a time you will need a separate cut sheet feeder which may not be included in the base price of the printer. Otherwise you must manually insert the sheets into the printer and spend a lot of time positioning the paper.

If you intend to do a lot of printing—and believe me, once you get your system up and running you will print, and waste, more paper than you ever dreamed was possible—you probably will prefer the familiar continuous form computer paper which has the detachable strip with little holes on each side. The device which pulls the paper through the printer using these holes is called a **tractor feed.** On some models it comes included. Other printers require that you pay extra for it, and still other printers don't need a tractor feed to use continuous forms.

The more expensive printers let you easily switch from computer paper to cut sheets without requiring that you remove the tractor feed or otherwise modify the printer set up. On the cheaper ones it is not a major production to change paper types, but it is enough effort that you will probably try to avoid it.

Since you can get very good quality continuous form computer paper with perforations that are almost invisible when you tear the sheets apart, there is no reason to avoid printing on these continuous sheets, particularly if you don't use letterhead. Remember, you can create a computer generated letterhead using special software or a graphics-capable word processor. This may make it unnecessary to use cut sheets at all.

Some printers make it a lot easier to print on envelopes than others. This can be very important if you do bulk mailings. If your mailings are limited to the occasional letter to a friend and manuscript submissions in manila envelopes you don't need fancy envelope handling. Many computer users either use their old typewriters for envelope addressing or even buy a cheap fleamarket printer which they use only for envelopes.

A reason that one dot matrix printer might be more expensive than another printer which appears functionally similar is durability. If you are in an office word-processing environment, where a printer will be pounding paper eight hours a day, five days a week, you need sturdier components than if you use your printer in short bursts, perhaps only for a half hour a day. The latter pattern is most likely how you will use your printer. Businesses are willing to pay significantly more for "industrial strength" 9-pin printers. You probably don't need one, unless you intend to run a word-processing business using your system. The reliability of even the cheaper machines produced by well-known companies is very good.

At the high end in the dot matrix line you will find the 18- and 24-pin dot matrix printers. These printers are similar to the 9-pin models but they use two rows of pins to produce the image rather than one. A single pass of the print head with these printers produces an image similar to the two passes of the 9-pin printers. In their letter quality, **LQ mode,** these printers make two passes across the paper, so the image is even more refined. These printers usually have more fonts available than 9-pin printers do. Some of them use plug-in font cartridges—a piece of hardware—to give you more fonts to print with, although you will have to buy these separately and they may be pricey. Others use **downloadable fonts.** These are fonts which are created by software and then sent to the printer. These give you maximum flexibility but you have to buy software to produce the fonts. These printers too can print graphics although they sometimes encounter problems printing with software that was written for 9-pin printers. There is software available to compensate for this problem.

The pins in the 24-pin printers' print heads are thinner and more delicate than the ones used in the 9-pin printers. This means that you probably shouldn't use cheap off-brand ribbons with these printers, since ribbon ink contains lubricants for the printer pins and the 24-pin printers are more prone to clog with inferior ink. You can even get Mylar printer ribbons, similar to the ribbons that office typewriters use, for even crisper looking print, which further enhances the look of the printout from your printer.

Some printer models, both 9- and 24-pin types, also allow you to do color printing by using special ribbons. Check out the quality of the output to determine whether you think it is worth the cost. Remember, too, that your software must know how to tell the printer to use its color capabilities in order to be able to use them effectively.

Printers come in narrow-carriage and wide-carriage models. The narrow carriage printers are designed for paper that is 8 1/2" wide with an additional inch added for the strip with the holes on it. This is usually adequate for most of your needs. The main reason people buy wide-carriage printers is to print large multicolumn spreadsheets. However most spreadsheet software can divide a wide spreadsheet up into separate standard-size sheets and print it on a narrow-carriage printer. If you occasionally need to print something that has more than 80 characters per line you can use the compressed or subscript typefaces that usually come with such printers to cram more characters into the inch. So you probably don't need the more expensive wide-carriage model.

How complicated you will find it to use a given printer varies. Some printers have a few controls on their front panel and that is it. Others require complicated combinations of button pushing to turn on particular features. While better-designed buttons may make one printer more attractive to you than another, you will probably end up setting up your printer not with these hardware controls, but through your software. Your word processor, for example, will most likely let you control the font, type size, and other printer features.

If you are buying a Macintosh and decide to use a dot matrix printer you probably will have to choose between the 9-pin Imagewriter II and the 24-pin Imagewriter LQ that Apple sells to go with their systems.

Because of the complexity of the Macintosh printer drivers—which are far more complex than the simpler code-driven PC printer interface—it is difficult to use printers designed for the PC with Macs. Doing this is only possible using slow, awkward, software solutions that most Mac users find too limited.

But whatever criteria you apply when choosing a printer, the most important thing is to give a lot of weight to your subjective reaction to the look of the printer's output. A printer that got a great magazine review and is priced just right is not the printer for you if you hate the look of its print. Every printer has a unique way of creating the different typefaces it uses, and some of them are better looking than others. Your printed material affects the reader in a subtle way and if you use a flamboyant typeface when you would be happier with a more demure one, or a cramped one when you would like something more flowing, you are doing yourself a disservice. As long as you buy a reasonably popular printer sold by a reputable organization you can pretty much give yourself the freedom to select the printer whose output you like the best.

Inkjet Printers

Inkjet printers produce an image by squirting tiny drops of ink at the paper as it goes by. These printers cost more than dot matrix printers but less than laser printers. You should add to your calculations of the price for one of these the cost of acquiring fonts—typefaces in different sizes— which ranges from $75 to $125 per font, and the cost of replacement ink cartridges which run around $20 and must be changed very frequently— after printing only 500 to 800 pages. The advertising for the inkjet printers often makes them sound as if they are identical to laser printers in function but with a cheaper price tag. This is not entirely true.

For one thing, inkjet printers don't use the same printer drivers—the routines that software packages include to control specific printers—as laser printers do. This could make it hard to use your printer's fancier features with some software. They also may have some limitations in terms of what fonts are available for them. Not all inkjet printers can print graphics and text on the same page, though the more advanced ones can. And inkjet printers print relatively slowly.

There may be other problems with these printers too. The ink from some inkjet printers is prone to smudge. This may make it necessary to use expensive paper with a special coating or you may find that the output comes out better when you print on a particular side of regular paper. Some inkjet printers pause between pages to let the ink dry which causes their overall printing speed to be slower than their listed page printing speed would suggest.

Nevertheless, advances in this technology are making it increasingly appealing to the person who needs a printer that produces sharper output than a dot matrix printer but who cannot afford a laser printer. Inkjet printers are usually priced below $1,000 and the technology is improving quickly. If you can afford to spend more than $500 on a printer you should investigate what the current state-of-the-art version of the inkjet printer can do.

Laser Printers

Laser printers use a technology similar to that used in copier machines. These printers use a laser beam to bond toner to paper where the image is to appear. Computer-driven laser printers have been available for mainframe systems for more than a decade, but they only dropped into a price range where they made sense for most personal computer users in the late 1980s, after a flurry of competition followed Apple's introduction of the Laserwriter printer for the Macintosh. Even now laser printers are not cheap, although the laser printer technology is improving so rapidly that it is possible that someday it might drop into the "got-to-have-it" range.

Currently, most laser printers are limited to printing in black, white, and shades of gray, created using halftones. Laser printers that print in colors, like color copiers, are still priced above $10,000 and may easily cost $25,000. Thus they are strictly for commercial printshops and as a result there is not yet much software supporting them.

Laser printers vary as to whether they can print on envelopes or on paper in sizes other than 8 1/2 by 11".

THE REAL COST OF A LASER PRINTER. You may see laser printers advertised in the newspaper for $1,700 or less, but this price does not include a lot of the real cost of setting up and maintaining one of these marvels. If the mere thought of spending $1,700 on a *printer* hasn't caused you to grow faint and think about buying a nice fountain pen, you should be aware that the initial investment is just that: initial. While your dot matrix printer will require nothing more than the occasional new ribbon, which can be bought for anywhere from $3.50 to $18 apiece, a laser printer will need a new toner cartridge every 1,500 pages. This cartridge, which often includes some of the moving parts most prone to wear out in a laser printer, costs about $90. Fifteen- hundred pages might sound like a lot of pages but it isn't. You can expect to routinely use up 4,000 pages of computer paper a year if you produce book-length manuscripts and print them out periodically. Part of the increase in paper use comes from the tendency to print out revised copies of your work, and from the ease with which the computer makes it possible to revise it. The other reason that you will be printing out more with a fancy printer, sad to say, is that it will take you a lot of wasted paper to figure out how to get the printer working right.

But toner cartridges aren't all you will need to spend money on. Worse is to come. Your laser printer may require you to buy font software if you want to go beyond the ubiquitous and rather boring Times Roman and Helvetica fonts that most come with. A single piece of font software can cost almost $100. *PC Magazine* estimated that over a five-year period, operating a Hewlett-Packard LaserJet Series II would end up costing an additional $3,300—about twice its purchase price—excluding paper. In contrast they claimed that a 24- pin Epson LQ-2500 would only require the additional expenditure of about $300 for ribbons during the same period.[1]

Buying a printer that is going to end up costing more than a good used car is a major decision. If you are going to be making money with your printer, as you may if you are going to go heavily into serious self-publishing, then you can probably justify this. But if money is a major concern, this is one purchase that you can easily put off for a few more years.

Some Other Considerations

Beyond the obvious determinants of what printer to buy there are a few more things to consider briefly. These are issues you might overlook which can make a difference in your long-term satisfaction with a printer.

The humble printer ribbon is capable of taking much of the joy out of your life if you can't find a replacement when you need one. You may have already experienced this problem with a typewriter ribbon. What happens is this: Just when you are about to print a manuscript that must be in the mail the next day, you notice that your ribbon is no longer printing legibly. You go to the local office supply store, K Mart, and three computer stores, only to discover that since your machine has been replaced by newer models its ribbons are no longer stocked but must be ordered—at an exorbitant price—from a wholesaler who, with luck can get them to you within the week. This is a major pain in the neck.

You will cut down the chances of having this happen if you buy a printer that uses one of the more common printer ribbons, for example the Epson FX 80 ribbon which is used by many other models of printers, including some made by other manufacturers. If you are looking at an otherwise attractive printer, check out what you will have to go through to get a ribbon for that printer. If it looks like there might be problems, and you just can't live without the printer, invest in a two-year supply.

[1]Robert L. Hummel, "Laser Printers: The Hidden Costs," *PC Magazine* Oct. 31, 1988, p. 184.

Similarly make sure that a printer you are considering doesn't require special paper. This is rarely the case anymore, but some inkjet printers, for example, will produce smudgy print on the coating used on some papers. A few printers require heat-sensitive paper.

Noise is another issue. The dot matrix printers are impact printers and make a characteristic whine and clatter. You can get covers to cut down somewhat on this noise if it is something that really irks you, or you can buy one that has been engineered to be a bit quieter.

Another issue you should consider is the software support available for your printer. If your printer has very fancy capabilities that are new and not like those found on other printers, it may be harder to use them in concert with word-processing and other programs. Most printers include some kind of "emulation" which makes them able to use the printer drivers developed for the most popular printers in their class, but in the emulation mode not all the unique features of a fancy printer will be available. You also may run into weird quirks when you run a printer that is not one of the market leaders—and so not as thoroughly debugged as they are. For example, a font different from the one you selected may print. Even weirder things may occur, such as finding that you can produce a certain font in the size you want only by turning off hyphenation.

The fancier your printer's capabilities, the more likely you are to run into problems. If you are just beginning and are willing to settle for decent looking output with few frills, you may be best advised to choose an inexpensive popular printer from an industry leader like Epson or Panasonic as your first one, for no other reason than to simplify your life.

Printer Cable

You will probably need to buy a separate printer cable to hook your printer up to the computer. This is not included with either the computer or the printer. If the person who sells you your computer can't tell you what kind of cable you need, you are probably buying your system in the wrong place. The cable will undoubtedly cost much more than you ever expected to pay for what looks like an electric cord. But it is actually a little more complicated. Don't forget to buy one or you will get your system all plugged in and ready to use only to find yourself unable to print.

MODEMS

What is the biggest mistake most first-time computer buyers make? The answer is simple: not installing a modem on their systems. The humble modem, a piece of machinery that can be purchased for a mere eighty bucks, converts your computer from a glorified typewriter into a device capable of connecting you with millions of computer users worldwide. At the least, a modem lets you submit copy to editors instantaneously, in computer-readable form. At its best, a modem lets you converse with people all over the world who share common interests. And what's nicest about this communication for the writer is that this computer communication is via the written word. As you get drawn into communicating on-line you will most likely find yourself writing terse but content-filled messages daily in response to notes from on-line correspondents who may well include internationally known writers and authorities in almost any field you are interested in, as well as plenty of interesting—and interviewable—average folks. Composing these daily messages is probably the best warm-up exercise a writer could do, comparable to the now-lost practice of daily letter writing which honed the pens of the great nineteenth-century authors. And on top of all these benefits, a modem enables you get answers to any hardware and software show stoppers you encounter as you get to know your system, as well as giving you access to lots of free software.

Save money elsewhere. Make sure that you get a modem installed when you buy the system, when it is easiest, rather than putting it off until later. The cost of the modem seems trivial when you are paying $1,000 or more for the system and start-up software. If you wait to buy the modem later, separately, its cost will loom larger and if you want the cheaper, internal board-based version, it may seem dauntingly complex to install.

When you buy a PC modem you have to make two decisions. The first is whether you want an internal modem or an external modem. The other is what speed modem you want. The benefit of an internal modem is that it is cheaper than the external kind and very simple to use. You just plug it into the phone line and use your communications software. The benefit of the external kind of modem is that it is portable. You can use it with more than one computer, for example one at work and one at home. You can also use it with your next computer which may not be the case with a card-based internal modem. The external kind of modem has lights and switches and gives you more idea of what is going on with it, but this may not be a benefit to you if you are already on the borderline of being overwhelmed by all the other things you have to pay attention to.

If you buy a Macintosh you will use an external modem that plugs into one of the system's ports.

Modem speed is important because the faster the modem the shorter the time you will have to spend on-line on expensive communications services and the quicker you can download programs from bulletin boards that may be a long-distance phone call from where you live. The fastest modem you can comfortably afford is the best buy. But if you are tempted to buy a very fast modem, something faster than 2400 bps, make sure that the services or boards you plan to call can communicate at the higher speeds. If they can't, your expensive 9600 bps modem may be forced to communicate with them at 2400 bps.

MICE OR IS IT "MOUSES"?

A mouse is a "pointing device." Popularized by the Macintosh, these little gizmos are used to select functions from lists of available program functions that are called **menus**. In graphics-based programs a mouse is used for drawing and for moving pieces of drawings around. A mouse usually fits into your palm and has two or three buttons you push to communicate with a program. You use it by rolling or sliding it around a cleared space on your desk top, or else on a special mouse pad. This causes a little arrow to run around your screen. The reason that a mouse is called a mouse is that the wire connecting the mouse to the computer comes off the back of the device giving it somewhat the look of a rodent with a long tail.

There are several different kinds of mice. Some are mechanical and use the rolling of a ball on your desktop to determine how far to move on the screen. Others are optical and use light reflected off a grid to do the same thing. Some communicate with your system via a card and others plug into a serial port.

You will get one included with the Macintosh, where its use is a major part of the design of all the software you will use. For other systems, however, the mouse is more likely an option. A few PC programs, most notably desktop publishing ones, require that you use one, but most don't. If you are a fast touch typist, moving your hand from the mouse to the keyboard and back again can be irritating, particularly in word processing applications where you might be clattering along typing text only to have to reach for the mouse to get a function that a mouseless program would let you get by with typing in a keystroke combination.

The mouse comes into its own in drawing and graphics-based work where the freedom of movement around the screen that it confers is a significant improvement over using cursor control keyboard keys. Unless you plan to make heavy use of such programs you can skip the mouse to start with.

There is one problem reported by heavy mouse users which might be of concern to you, particularly if you already any related problems: muscle and joint pains. Many users report that this, the computer equivalent of tennis elbow, can result from several hours of mousing around. An alternative to the mouse, the **trackball,** is a stationary ball that you move around with your finger. Using one might be easier on your elbow.

OTHER BELLS AND WHISTLES

We've mentioned most of the hardware basics now. There are many more things you could buy, but you don't need them to get started. Fax (facsimile) cards which let you send a document stored in a computer file to another fax machine over the phone are beginning to become popular. But you may be able to achieve similar effects for a lot less money if you are not a heavy fax user simply by joining CompuServe or MCI Mail and using the fax option on their electronic mail service. All you need to fax computer files this way is a modem.

Scanners are another group of machines where the technology is beginning to approach price levels where average folks can buy into it. The main thing to consider when looking at any of these newer hardware add-ons is where in the product development cycle does this the hardware lie. If it is touted as brand new, or revolutionary, remember that great law of hardware—If It Is New It Probably Doesn't Work—and give its makers some time to get the bugs out, the quality improved, and the price down.

Optical disk technology is another area where interesting things are *almost* available. The optical disk uses a technology similar, if not identical, to that in the CD player on your stereo. An optical disk can hold an enormous amount of data and is less prone to breakdown than a hard drive. But current optical disk drives only allow you to read data but not to write it, just like CD players do. An entirely different optical disk techology is currently under development. This technology allows the optical disk to be read and written but it is not compatible with the earlier CD technology. This kind of optical disk should be available for computers in the near future though it may be too expensive for the kind of system you will be considering.

Right now there is little available on optical disks worth the cost of the optical disk drive you need to use them. Some companies sell disks filled with reference works—but little of interest to serious scholars—and you can also get large collections of shareware programs on optical disk too, or sets of manuals for certain software products. But considering how often you would be likely work with the information available on these and the price of the drives it is unlikely that these represent a good investment. Once read/write optical technology is available—and after it has been in the marketplace long enough to work properly *and also* drop in price—optical disk readers might be a better idea.

PORTABLE COMPUTERS

If someone asked you which would you rather have, a computer that sits, chained to your desk, or one that you can take anywhere with you, your answer would be pretty clear, the portable one. Unfortunately deciding to buy a portable computer is not that simple.

Portable computers began as suitcase-sized items that were about as portable as construction site porto-potties. Over time they have gotten a lot smaller and some now weigh only a few pounds. There are now two different kinds of portable computers, **laptops** which are intended to be slipped into a briefcase, run on batteries, have small, flat screens, and have, in general, been optimized for small size, and larger **portable computers** sometimes nicknamed "luggables" which are larger than the laptops and may have better screens, and a conventional keyboard. Some of these run on batteries and others plug into the wall.

The trade off for the streamlining you find in the laptops is often a keyboard that is laid out quirkily, a display that is hard to see, and worst of all, batteries that are only good for a few hours of use before they require recharging. The major drawback of the better luggables, which might otherwise be very interesting to the writer, is price. They cost many thousands of dollars more than corresponding desk top units.

If you are planning to buy only one computer, buying a portable— particularly a laptop—as your sole computer may not be a good idea unless your need for portability is overwhelming. In all likelihood, you will be spending hundreds of hours working at the keyboard of the unit you buy, and peering at its screen, so you need a computer that has been designed for comfortable extended use. Most portable units are sold to salespeople and executives on the road who use them to run a quick program to give a price quotation or to download information from databases and analyze financial data. While they might use them to create a memo or two, they don't do the kind of extended word processing you are going to do.

Probably the only real justification for buying a laptop portable as your main machine would be if you are a roving journalist or if you do the bulk of your work in specialized research libraries where you must work with hundreds of pages of stuff that doesn't circulate. If you can get by with transcribing your notes and if you do the bulk of your writing and the planning for your writing in one place, you probably don't need to make the trade-offs the portable entails.

On the other hand, if you are one of those writers whose book cover biography notes that you make your home in London, Paris, and New York, then you probably can afford to buy both a desktop computer and a portable to take to the Hamptons on the weekend. Lucky you! If you should fall into this last, privileged, group your primary concern should be that the portable computer you buy can easily share diskettes with your desktop unit, since you will need to be able to move both programs and work from one system to the other. If you intend to use your portable in library settings, check out the noise level it generates. Some portables are reportedly so noisy that users report becoming the target of hostile looks or being asked to turn them off.

ACCESSORIES

Surge Protection

Before you leave the computer store don't forget to pick up a surge protector. What surge protectors do is act like a fuse to protect your electronic equipment from power spikes. Is this a hype? No. Power fluctuations can burn out computer chips. The only problem is that there is a lot of argument as to how effective surge protectors are in preventing this damage. Some experts claim that low voltages rather than spikes are what ruins your equipment. Still, a surge protector may help. If nothing else, you will feel better knowing that by spending twelve bucks on the surge protector you have made a good faith effort to avoid this kind of damage, a symbolic act if nothing else. Unfortunately, the kind of equipment that would really protect your system from all types of power fluctuations is called an **uninterruptible power supply,** and is priced around $1,000 or more, which doesn't make it a very realistic option for you now. These, like so much else, are intended for business users with much more sophisticated setups.

Printer Accessories

Another item you may see in a computer store is a plastic cover that quiets down your printer. You proably won't need one. You are unlikely to be running your printer enough to make it worthwhile, and it will probably just get in your way. You will see a lot of printer stands too. You probably don't need one of these, either. An old wooden chair with a slot in the back will work just fine until you figure out what computer furniture you need. Many computer desks have both a place to put the printer and a shelf for paper.

Computer Furniture

Which brings us to the subject of computer furniture. There is a lot of attractive furniture available for home computers that is utterly impractical. You probably don't need it. The problem is that all too often these units are beautifully crafted but don't have room for all the junk that is going to accumulate around your computer. What you need is a table the same height as a typing table, low enough for you to type at it comfortably. The computer table should have enough room for your monitor, keyboard, and system unit, so that you can easily insert diskettes into the system. There is no need to have a separate shelf for your monitor. A much better idea is to get a swivel stand for it that sits on top of the system unit and lets you adjust the height and angle of the screen. Sometimes such stands are included with the computer so don't buy one until you see what yours comes with.

Ideally, your computer desk should have a place for your printer. A PC printer must be within 25 feet of the computer if you want to use the usual kind of hookup, which is to plug the computer into the system's parallel port. It is possible to use the serial port to hook up a more distant printer but you need additional hardware to pull this off. The Macintosh uses a serial printer so distance is not an issue.

Don't plan to keep the computer on the desk you now work at, since it takes up too much room. Also remember that you need a place to put the reference materials you work with, manuals, odd bits of paper, notes, and your phone. If you plan to use a modem for telecommunications remember that you need a telephone outlet by the computer. The modem plugs into the phone line just the way a telephone would. You can get adapters anywhere phone accessories are sold that let you plug two phones into one outlet. This might be handy if you already have an office phone. You can also plug your modem cord into your answering machine.

You will also need shelves for your computer flotsam and jetsam: books, software, and floppies. You should also buy a decent box to protect the floppy disks that you will accumulate as you work, both those that contain the software you buy and the disks that contain backup copies of your work. Keep this floppy collection in sight, not hidden away. Having your backups in view helps you remember to keep up with the vital task of making backups.

My first "computer desk" was made from a filing cabinet and my old typing table. Not classy, but it worked. However, you can get a pressboard computer desk at a discount store for under a hundred dollars that will serve you adequately, if not aesthetically. As soon as you subscribe to a computer magazine you will be inundated with computer supply catalogs full of office furniture, some of it verging on the conceptually bizarre.

Paper

Finally, don't forget to buy paper! Bite the bullet and buy at least a thousand sheets. You will be using a lot of it, particularly in the first few weeks as you figure out how to use your word processor and printer. If your printer has a tractor feed you will need the standard computer paper with the holes along the side. The kind you want is called **microperf** and has a line of tiny holes punched along the tearing line. This kind of paper tears most neatly and doesn't leave a ragged-looking edge. Examine the paper, if possible, before buying it to make sure that it looks nice. Most of what you will find in computer stores is 20-lb bond which is fine for most uses. If you want continuous form rag paper or specialty paper you can find all sorts of paper variations in office supply stores or mail-order office supply catalogs. You will begin receiving these as soon as you subscribe to a computer magazine—particularly if you describe yourself as the principal of your own company. You can often find very good deals on the 20-lb paper in cartons of 2,500 sheets or more at discount office supply outlets.

9

WHERE AND HOW
TO BUY HARDWARE

It has long been an axiom of mine, that the little things are infinitely the most important.

Sir Arthur Conan Doyle 1859-1930
A Case of Identity

After you have decided what hardware you want to buy, you are still left with one more decision: where to buy it. The variety of places where you can get decent hardware is bewildering. On any given day you might see almost identical PC clones advertised in store ads in the newspaper business section, in the *New York Times* Tuesday science section, in mail order ads at the back of computer magazines, and even in a catalog house circular, right next to the clown statuettes, blenders, and children's toys. Because the items advertised seem so similar and the prices advertised seem so different, making the decision of where to buy your equipment is not simple.

DO YOU WANT USED EQUIPMENT?

When you see ads for used equipment in your local paper you might be tempted to save money by buying a used system. You may think that you can get a super-cheap system this way and then be able to buy a better, newer one later when you have a clearer idea of what you are doing.

Unfortunately, while this strategy works well with some other kinds of items, it is a bad one when it comes to buying computers.

The reason for this is the fast pace of technological progress and the constantly decreasing price of new technology. The person who bought a computer three years ago for $3,000 may well have bought the very same system that you can now get new for $1,200. As a result you will often see used stuff for sale priced higher than what you would pay for the equivalent new equipment. This is particularly true if the owner of the equipment has given up his system in disgust because he couldn't get it working and is not very current with what is going on in the PC marketplace.

Such systems, bought by people who had no clear idea of what they were doing, may be poorly configured and filled with poorly chosen software. You might not hesitate to buy a wedding gown that is advertised as "never worn" in spite of the tragedy the ad implies, but in such a case you at least know that the wedding was not called off because of flaws in the gown. A computer setup advertised as "used twice" is a different matter. A system that hasn't been used by its owner—unless he was hit by a train right after buying it—should be somewhat suspect.

But even if you buy a good used system at a good price, you still might have problems. When you buy something new you should get a warranty and a place to call if something isn't working right. This is very important if you are a new user and unable to factor out those things that aren't working right because they are broken from those that aren't working right because you did something dumb. When you buy used equipment you don't get this support. In addition, software you get used is likely to be an older version that does not include all the features that the current product offers.

The time to consider used equipment, if at all, is later on, when you know more about hardware and software. Then you will be able to spot a true bargain.

DEALING WITH COMPUTER STORES

Ensuring that you get the support you are going to need to get your system up and running is the best reason to go to a local computer store rather than a mail-order source or a store in a distant city—but only if your local store really will give you that support. In theory, if you buy from a local merchant you should be able to call them or their customer support department if the machine won't work right and get your problems fixed right away. Unfortunately, here as in so much else, there is often a gap between theory and practice.

The problem is that all too often computer stores are manned by people with only one goal in life, to sell you a computer and collect the commission. When you discover a problem with the unit you may be unpleasantly surprised to discover that you must go elsewhere for service—for example, a repair shop in a distant town. You are no better off then, than if you had bought the product through mail order. In fact you may be worse off, since some mail-order sources include a year-long contract for on-site service in the price of their systems, which means that if anything goes wrong with your hardware you get the repair done by a national service company that sends someone to your house. The only time that you do significantly better with a local store is when they have their own local service facility that has an impeccable reputation among area computer owners and when they provide free training in and help with using your new system. It is very much like picking a car dealership.

But buying a computer is more complex than buying a car, and here you encounter the biggest problem with buying from many computer stores: Poorly trained staff. This is a problem both after the sale when you call with problems and when you go into the store looking to make your initial purchase.

The problem occurs because there is a shortage of people with real computer expertise. Those who know enough to put hardware configurations together and recommend software usually can make a lot more money working as consultants, rather than walking the floor in the local computer showroom. As a result many of the people who greet you at the computer store know only a little bit more about the equipment in their store than you do, usually as the result of taking a quickie training program. This does not inhibit them from making definite recommendations about what you should buy. But it should make you very wary.

Because a salesperson is likely to be new and not know much about computers, he or she is likely to try to sell you one of the more popular products and models stocked in the store. This is not always bad, but you may run into problems when you try to determine exactly what comes with the package they want to sell you so that you can make fair comparisons with what other stores are selling, or simply so that you can decide what else you need to buy. The salesperson who sold me my system, for example, informed me that a printer I was interested in was not capable of printing graphics—which it was—and when asked about communications software for the modem I was buying, told me I would have to buy a software package, not realizing that the modem she was selling me *came* with a software package included. All this was not part of an effort to mislead me—the salesperson suggested I get the modem software at the local PC users group, not from her store—but she was new to the job and knew very little about the product she was selling.

Often you will find salespeople who can't get a floor model to work when you want to see a demo or who make totally inappropriate hardware or software recommendations after you have explained what you need your system for.

If you find yourself in a store with a good local reputation and get stuck with such a salesperson, don't give up! Usually there is someone in a back room of the store who does know the answers to the questions you have. You should ask to talk to the manager, in a polite way, if you feel that the salesperson can't answer your questions clearly and correctly.

But don't depend on salespeople for your buying decisions. Don't ask them what the best system is or what software you should buy. There are better ways to determine this. The people in the store should be your source merely for finding out what is in stock, how much an item will cost, what is included with a unit, and what the warranty covers. There are computer salespeople who are exceptions to this rule, but you don't yet have the expertise needed to ferret them out.

The other phenomenon that you may encounter in a busy well-known dealership is that since you are only a small-scale buyer you don't get the attention or service that their lucrative business accounts get. If you find yourself waiting half an hour at a big local computer dealership just trying to get waited on, while representatives of local businesses come in and get immediate attention from the busy sales force, this second-class treatment should make you wonder how you would be treated by their service department if you had to leave your machine there for any period of time for repairs.

Demos

When you go into a store you also need to be aware that many machines you see set up in these stores are running programs that are called **demos.** Demos are programs that are used to show you what a machine or piece of software can do. Demos are full of color and sound and rapidly changing dramatic screen displays. But such demos are often misleading. In many cases software demos are not running the program they demonstrate. They are just "slide shows" which display a series of screens one after the other as if the computer were running the real program. The graphics that the demo flashes will appear on your screen only if you spend hundreds of dollars on the software packages that generate them. Not only that, but when you run the actual software that generates these screens you may find that your system runs that software at intolerably slow speeds as the demo does almost no real processing, and runs much faster than the program it simulates.

Then too, the demos often run on systems equipped with expensive hardware and software options that are not standard with the unit you saw advertised in the paper. If all you see is demos and no one in the store is willing to show you real programs running on the machine that you plan to buy, you should probably go elsewhere.

Finally, if you do decide to purchase a system, make sure that you have in writing on the sales contract the details of everything you expect to receive with the system. If you are buying add-in boards or a modem or a hard disk, which may be items that the store adds to a basic manufacturer's model, have the merchant specify the manufacturer of each, and get in writing the warranty period for each add-in component as well as where warranty work must be done. Often when selling a fully configured system, stores add aftermarket products to the manufacturer's cheap base system. This is not necessarily a bad thing if the people running the store understand hardware. But you should be aware that this is what is happening and not think you are getting a system configured by the hardware vendor.

Warranties

The warranty that comes with your new system is worth some serious investigation. When personal computers first appeared they came with warranties that lasted for a brief 90-day period. Merchants justified this ludicrously short warranty period with the argument that most systems that are going to fail do so in their first few weeks. Nevertheless, the Leading Edge company sold a lot of PCs to buyers who saw this company's 18-month warranty as evidence that their machine wouldn't fall apart before the charge appeared on their credit-card statement. This put pressure on other vendors to follow suit and increase their warranty periods too. You will find longer warranties more often now.[1]

When investigating a system warranty find out exactly what components the warranty on the system covers. Also find out who will fix the system if it does experience problems and how long the service may take. In some cases you get only a manufacturer's warranty. That means the warranty period begins when the item leaves the plant, not when you buy it. If the item has been sitting on a warehouse shelf long enough, your warranty may be almost expired when you open the box for the first time. Ask the salesperson selling you the machine what happens if the company goes out of business. Will they still provide service for the unit through the period of the warranty?

The other problem you may encounter is that while the main part of your system is covered by a long warranty, the hard disk may have been added by the store and is covered by a separate, shorter, warranty. Since the disk drive is probably the most vulnerable part of your system particularly as it ages, it's a good idea to determine the length of its warranty period.

---

[1]Unfortunately, some Leading Edge warrenties lasted longer than did the company, which faced bankruptcy in 1989 as a result of bad management practices.

Getting a Delivery Date

Make sure when you order a computer that you get a firm commitment that the unit will be in your hands within, at most, a month. If you are having additional features installed you might have to wait a little longer, but what you want to avoid is paying for products that are not available. Unfortunately this happens. Companies announce "vaporware"—products that exist only in the planning stages—in order to depress the sales of a competitor whose currently available product doesn't have the bells and whistles the vaporware claims it will have, someday. This is more of a problem with software than hardware. But merchants have been known to take orders and deposits for systems that are backlogged at the manufacturing plant, leaving the buyers to wait for months for the system. If you give a deposit, specify that if the unit isn't delivered by a certain time you get your deposit back.

THE TROUBLE WITH DEPARTMENT STORES

You may be tempted to buy a computer through a department or catalog store where you have had good experiences buying other merchandise. Many appliance and TV stores are starting to stock PCs and are advertising them lavishly. What you will get from one of these is a cheaper PC clone, possibly at an attractive price which reflects the volume discount the store gets from the manufacturer. However, you will not be able to go back to this store for any of the hardware or software products you might want to buy, and you probably will be out on a limb for support and service too.

How good the systems are that these places sell is up for grabs. Some sell decent systems and others sell awful ones. It may be difficult to get anyone in the store to explain what the system includes. A clerk who is responsible for selling cameras, stereos, and computers all for a wage of four dollars an hour, is unlikely to be of any help to you before or after the sale. This, more than anything else, should make you think twice about buying from such a place.

MAIL ORDER

Computer magazines are full of ads for mail-order companies that sell both hardware and software. Some of these are great places to go for *software* and buying software from mail-order sources is covered later, in Chapter 12. Some mail-order sources are also good places to shop for hardware add-ons too, such as modems and special-purpose boards—the kinds of standard items that you buy by brand name and model number. But buying a system from a mail-order source is not for the neophyte, which is what you are right now. You don't have the expertise to differentiate between the great deals and the scams, nor do you want to have to go through what you might have to go through if you can't get what you order to work.

Many of the ads you see for mail-order computers are companies selling "no name clones," computers with brand names that appear today and are gone tomorrow, assembled from who knows what components of unknown quality. These are very different from the better-known clones sold by dealers. Most suspicious are those systems advertised at extremely low prices. Reading the descriptions of these systems often reveals that their low, low price is made possible because they come with almost no memory, no disk drives or a single diskette drive, no graphics board, and no ports. In short, you are buying a nice box with a processor in it—not a usable computer!

There are companies that have built very strong reputations selling mail-order systems whose offerings are routinely reviewed in glowing terms by the trade press. Dell Computer of Austin would appear to be an example of this kind of company. One thing that sets Dell apart from many other mail-order companies is that when you do buy a system from them you get on-site (that is, in your home) service if you do have problems with your hardware. But usually the mail-order firms with the best reputations, such as Dell, sell expensive, full-featured machines designed for business users, which may be more computer than you need and are priced out of your price range.

If you live in a remote rural area where there is a limited choice of computer stores and none of these stores has a particularly good reputation, you might ask local businesspeople where they got their systems and if they were happy with the service they got.

WHERE TO GET UP-TO-DATE INFORMATION

In our discussion of where to buy computer hardware we mentioned that computer stores are probably not the best place to go for the answer to the question: "What should I buy?" Well, then, where can you get this information?

The Jaded Trade Press: Computer Magazines

Computer magazines can tell you much of what you want to know, if you approach them carefully. *PC Magazine, MacUser, PCWorld, MacWorld, PC Computing, and Personal Computing* are all magazines you can probably find at any newstand. The larger public libraries often subscribe to them and keep back issues where you can look up reviews on specific products you might be considering.

These magazines are a good place to go when you already have narrowed down your search to a few contenders and are interested in getting some help in making the final decision. Unfortunately, starting out by looking through these magazines may overwhelm you.

The biggest problem with these magazines is that they are addressed to readers who are assumed to be sophisticated business professionals familiar with the intricacies of buying hardware and software. Occasionally these magazines will throw in articles of interest to the beginner, and these are worth looking at, but when they review hardware they are talking to people who are used to buying hardware and the discussion may quickly become too technical for you.

The other problem here too is that the people who write for magazines are, to put it plainly, jaded. They've been thinking about this stuff week in and week out for six or seven years now and it takes a lot to get them excited. The system that they dismiss as humdrum might be fine for your needs. These magazines compete against each other for readers and attempt to appear indispensable by developing stringent measuring systems with which to evaluate new hardware. There is a place for this, and the results of their testing can tell you much about the relative quality of a system you are considering. But all too often, battles of the boxes that pit 15 very similar computers against each other, pointing out the trivial differences between them, do little more than make the job of picking the best one seem even harder. In a subtle fashion, the frenzied need to find the "Best" of everything, which pervades these magazines, can end up confusing you. You end up not with a clear idea of what to buy, but with the suspicion that one false move and the system you do choose will turn out to be "the Worst."

Contributing to this is that the magazines tend to evaluate products in terms of the needs of the corporate business buyer—the so-called "volume" buyer—who they would like their advertisers to believe makes up the bulk of their subscription base. This is because any company about to plunk down $20,000 for a full-color ad in one of these magazines is spending that money in the hope of reaching people with the authority to buy several hundred of whatever they are selling. So, because these corporate volume buyers are of such importance to advertisers, the systems and software products that the magazines focus on are often chosen with an eye to things like hooking into mainframes, building PC networks, and producing ever-more-gorgeous pie charts and bar graphs— not the stuff you are going to do.

Finally, it is a good idea to remember that the magazines usually only review and compare the most recently introduced hardware. So an article entitled "Inexpensive Systems" or "9-Pin Printers" will not, in all likelihood, review all the available cheap systems, just those which have come into the marketplace in the last few months. Because of this, unless you look through back issues you may miss excellent products simply because they have been available for a year or more.

Once you understand how the magazines work, they can become an excellent source of information.

If you have seen a system advertised locally that interests you, you can check it out by going to the nearest public library that carries back issues of computer magazines and has a periodical index called the Magazine Index. The Magazine Index indexes many of the PC- and Macintosh-oriented computer magazines. You will find it either on microfilm or installed on a small computer. Look up the system you are interested in by its manufacturer's name. You can also look for articles on introductory topics by searching for the topic in the Index. The computerized version of the Magazine Index will even retrieve and print abstracts of product reviews for computer products, meaning that if you can't locate the back issue that has the review in it you can still get the gist of the article. This is worth a trip to a library in a nearby town if your own library doesn't provide it.

What you should come away with, when checking out a product, is a clear idea of how it compares to other systems in its price range and whether it has any fatal flaw you wouldn't have been aware of.

When you read computer magazines you will immediately notice the glossy ads. They are among the most impressive productions of the advertiser's art. But unlike most advertisements these often contain as much useful, educational information about the product as magazine reviews. Computer vendors are selling to smart, logical, people who simply won't buy something unless they understand what it is. As a result, the ads in computer magazines are surprisingly informative and even, unlike most ads, often tell you what the products cost![2] Remember, however, that a full-color, full-page ad in one of these magazines costs many thousands of dollars and that this means that cheaper, equally interesting products may not be represented in these pages at all.

Neither a Borrower nor Lender Be, and Don't Recommend
Hardware Either: Buying what Friends Have

If you have a friend who already has a computer system you might be tempted to find out what they have and then go buy it yourself. This is not necessarily a bad approach. But you should be aware that anyone who has spent $5,000 on anything, no matter how misguided, will tend to wax enthusiastic about it, if only to convince himself that he wasn't a fool.

---

[2]Although, of course the price in the ad is always higher than the price you should be able to get it at.

And, if you are trying to buy a cheap system, people with more expensive systems will tend to suggest that you need a system at least as good as theirs.

Most computer owners quickly develop wish lists of items they would like to add to their systems—often suggested by the very magazines we've just discussed. So the recommendations you receive may include all the bells and whistles and "nice to haves" that your friends are lusting for but getting along fine without.

Then, no matter what you end up buying, someone you know will undoubtedly manage to suggest, if only with their expression, that you could have done a lot better buying something else!

Part of the problem here is the tendency of PC fanatics to hold strong opinions and to debate them shrilly, as well as the human tendency to want to proclaim that one's own is the only possible choice.

If you intend to rely on a friend's advice you do need to be able to determine your friend's level of expertise. This is not as easy as it sounds. A great number of people who make their livings working with computers know almost nothing about PCs, and this includes about 90 percent of all professional computer programmers. Programmers who work on mainframe or mid-sized systems often are utterly ignorant about PCs. But their professional pride might make it difficult for them to admit this. People who use computers at work often, too, know only as much as they need to know to get their jobs done. They rely on professionals in the company to buy, set up, and install software on the computers they use, and may have little real understanding of what they use.

It's not worth destroying a friendship over a computer. Don't take a friend's suggestions if you will end up hating that friend if you hate the system. Nor should you expect your friend whose recommendations you take to sit by your side throughout the learning period as you get your system up and running, or to answer your agonized phone calls late at night!

Consultants

For a small businessperson a very wise decision may be to pay a consultant to choose and set up a system, *if* the consultant knows what he is doing. Such a consultant would interview the businessperson, then select the hardware and software he needs to get his work done. The consultant might also do a small amount of custom programming to make the system easier to use, and should be available to answer questions. Unfortunately, such consultants bill their services out at anywhere from $20 to $100 an hour. This means that unless you are a very successful writer hiring such a consultant is out of your range, although, as we will see later, if you use tact and common sense you can still draw on their experience. If you are able to afford a consultant, make sure that you work with one who can provide references to people who use their systems for the same kind of things you intend to do. Just as important as finding a consultant who understands computers is finding one who understands your needs—maybe even more important.

Going with Market Leaders

Many people just ignore all this decision making and buy whatever seems to be in the "top ten"—the best-selling stuff. When taking this approach remember that the products with the largest market shares are those most suited for the needs of big business. IBM dominates the business computer market not because of any intrinsic superiority of their products but because larger companies acquiring PCs often have long-term plans that involve tying their mainframes in with PC networks. IBM hints, subtly and not so subtly, that other vendors' hardware may not be able to function—in the distant, undefined future—as well with these mainframe systems as machines from IBM itself. Corporate buyers buy IBM products too because it is often easier. Because their company has been buying from IBM for a generation, they don't have to go through the elaborate justifications to buy an IBM product that they might have to resort to if they went with a less corporately successful vendor.

However, for the small buyer, IBM's systems are often a poor choice. They are almost always priced way above other similarly configured systems. They may not be well designed, either in terms of what components are included in the base model and of how they are engineered. Some IBM stuff is great. But you can't just go into a showroom of a company that sells IBM products and assume that what you will be sold will be great because it's IBM. You must apply the same tests and ask the same questions as you would with a "no-name" clone.

The Best Place to Get Advice: Users Groups Again

We spoke about users groups earlier, in Chapter 4. Users groups are the best place to get information about the merchants in your own community, a kind of information you probably can't get anywhere else. When you go to a users group make sure to go to the "New Users SIG" and feel free to ask anyone you meet where they would recommend that you purchase equipment. You will hear about the places that practice bait-and-switch and those that can't deliver what you order when they said they would. You also will learn who has good service departments and, perhaps, which store includes worthwhile introductory courses with their systems. You should also be able to find out if anyone local rents systems for a reasonable charge with a buy-later option. This can be a good way to get started if you aren't sure how much you will like using a computer.

Don't worry about being a complete innocent when going to a PC or Mac users group. The experienced computer users who go to these meetings get a kick out of answering beginner's questions. You may even be able to pick up tidbits from the very same consultants whose rates make them otherwise inaccessible to you.

When you go to a computer users group meeting you will probably find yourself surprised at the altruism with which people deeply involved with computers treat other users. Some of the people who show up at these are small businesspeople with computer-related products or services to sell, and you should not expect these people to give you their services for free. But a larger number are simply enthusiasts who go to these meetings to be with people similar to themselves.

In spite of the popular image of the computer enthusiast as a cold, logical and antisocial person, when you go anywhere such people cluster you will find that "real" computer enthusiasts show less competitiveness with each other and more of a tendency to share what they know, than any other group in our society. If there is competition, it is more likely to be competition between experts to explain something to you, the neophyte, in the clearest possible way. "Real" computer people love to explain and share their knowledge.

In our society, where those who have specialized knowledge tend to separate themselves from others and prevent their knowledge from being shared with outsiders, the amount of free help you can get from computer experts is mind-boggling—as surprising as the amounts of free or almost free software available to you, created by these same kinds of people.

Imagine what it would be like if you could go to the local physicians meeting and have three or four doctors listen while you explain in detail what exactly was wrong with your left arm and then vie with each other to suggest solutions. Not very likely. But at almost any users group you will be able to get two or three experts to diagnose any problems you have with your system.

Users groups generally meet once a month, with some holding extra special-interest group meetings at other times. These meetings may be announced in your paper. If they are not, call a few computer stores and ask if they know of any such groups. Finally if that doesn't help try calling the local representative of a company like IBM or Lotus since these companies often have sent speakers to local users groups and may be able to put you in touch with the people who run them.

The Power of On-line Help

Functioning somewhat like a national users group are the special-interest sections of on-line information services like CompuServe, and bulletin board networks like FIDONET. CompuServe has areas called forums dedicated to the discussion of hardware and software. Unfortunately, it is almost impossible to take advantage of such resources if you don't already have access to a computer that is equipped with a modem. But once you have bought your basic configuration you might want to turn here before buying anything else. The way that these on-line services work is simple. You post a message which asks a question. Over the next few days hundreds of people may see the title you put on the message. If they are interested in the title, which is known as a header, they will read the message and may reply.

When a friend of mine was considering buying a MIDI board for his system, he saw an advertisement for a hardware and software combination that seemed like exactly what he wanted. But the salesman in the local computer music store told him that the product in question was "buggy" and frequently crashed on his computer. This sounded pretty depressing, particularly since the system the store wanted to sell him cost several hundred dollars more. He posted a message on CompuServe's MIDI forum asking whether people had experienced problems with the software in question. A few days later when he checked back there were several messages from people who used the product. All claimed to be very satisfied with it. One person did mention a hardware problem that would not have applied to my friend's setup. Other messages talked about other systems in the same price range that were also worth considering. He bought the original package with a lot more confidence.

While you will have to develop some sophistication to be able to take advantage of this kind of resource, in the long term you can learn a tremendous amount, both by placing queries on-line and by reading other people's queries on topics you have an interest in. Because of the national nature of a service like CompuServe it is not at all unusual to get a response to a query from a person involved in developing a product you are interested in or from the author of a book about the product.

Beyond Advice

Once you have gotten a certain amount of advice and screened out the bad deals and the questionable merchants, the final decisions you make should be made by no one else but you. Ideally, the decision should also be made after you have a chance to try out the system you are thinking about buying, whether in a store, in a class, or by renting a computer for a month on a trial basis.

Given the current highly developed state of PC technology you have little to fear in buying almost any system. You can let your own, untutored, subjective responses play some part in the final decision without worrying unduly that you will end up stuck with some piece of junk.

The way the system feels, sounds, and looks should weigh in your decision since you may end up spending hours every day in front of it. If a system has a noisy fan that distracts you or makes it hard to hear conversations over the phone, the explanation that from an engineering standpoint the fan is performing a useful function by keeping components cool may not be enough to outweigh the anguish you feel trying to work on something that sounds like a motorboat.

Take the time to type a page or two on a system you are considering. See how you like the feel and sound of the keyboard. Is it too soft and mushy, does it clatter too much, or not enough? How about the screen? Can you imagine looking at it for hours on end? Can you adjust the screen angle to eliminate glare, or get a cheap monitor holder that will do this? You should expect to make a certain amount of adaptation to any new computer, just as you've done when you bought a new typewriter, but you should feel comfortable bringing these more subjective judgments into the decision-making process because, in the end, this is going to be your computer!

Renting a system or taking community college computer courses is often a way of getting the initial familiarity with a system and getting a feeling of what you personally would consider valuable in a system. If you have a close friend who has a system, ask if they would like to show you what it can do. Many people who own systems will not object to letting you try theirs out. And many people enjoy giving demonstrations of their favorite programs. Take advantage of these opportunities too.

WHY SERVICE AND SUPPORT SHOULD BE THE TIE BREAKER

Once you have made up your mind what system you want you will probably notice that there is no such thing as a set price. You will see a single manufacturer's computer advertised at a broad range of prices. Some of these price differences, of course, represent the cost of features that aren't included in the package price, as we mentioned before, but if you see the same identical system at different prices should you just buy the cheaper one?

No, no, a thousand times no. Not when you are buying your first system.

If all things are pretty much equal, there is a single factor you should throw on the scale when making your decision: Which seller has the best reputation locally for after-the-sale support.

You are not buying a washing machine but a complex piece of electronic equipment. Most computers don't have hardware problems. But a certain number do, and unfortunately the time that a computer is most prone to have problems is when it is fresh out of the box! Because of the stresses of shipment a certain number of computers arrive DOA (dead on arrival) at the very time you are least able to deal with such problems.

Being DOA can mean that the computer flat out doesn't work, or like my first computer, it may work only some of the time. In my case, since all my experience with computers had been with large mainframes where the first thing a programmer learns is never to blame the hardware for anything that seems wrong, I didn't suspect that the numbers that flashed on my screen periodically were a sign of a serious failure in the system. It took me several days of reading my manuals and fooling with the system to determine that something in fact was very wrong. Had I been a less technical person it might have taken me weeks or even a month to realize that I had some flukey hardware in my system.

I was fortunate enough to have bought my computer from a store with an excellent service department. After hearing my description of the problem the service manager told me to bring the system back to be replaced with another new one. The unit I bought was fixed and added to their rental inventory. A less responsive store could have made me take the unit I had just bought to a distant service center for warranty work, and it might have been weeks before I had a functioning computer. While this kind of thing probably won't happen to you, that it *could* happen means that after-the-sale support is vital.

It is not likely that you will have DOA hardware problems. However, it is extremely likely, based on the experience of millions of new computer owners, that in the first few weeks of computer ownership you will have a certain number of problems that *look* like serious hardware problems which, in fact, are software problems caused by your own inadvertence. These kinds of errors are discussed in detail in Chapter 14.

Because you are likely to encounter situations where your system digs in its heels and refuses to do what you want, being able to call on the people who sold you your system for support is essential. Some stores offer a period of free advice, a month, for example, with the purchase of the system. Others offer free classes during which you can learn the nuts and bolts of using your system. This is particularly useful if you bought a PC or clone and haven't taken some kind of introductory PC course first.

The first time your word processor tells you it can't find any of your manuscripts or your printer goes dormant when you are trying to make a deadline, you will see why good after-the-sale support alone can be worth as much as all kinds of engineering bells and whistles!

If you have any question about how the store handles after-the-sale questions, you might ask for the service number and try calling the help staff with a question and seeing how they respond. You will, if nothing else, get a good feel for how long you have to wait on the phone and what the attitude of the person who answers is.

Make sure to find out what happens if your machine does break during the warranty period. Will the company give you a new machine during the early period? If your computer needs extensive, time-consuming, in-shop repairs will the company provide you with a loaner machine?

This last question is very important, since after you use your system for a few months, being without it will be crippling. You should judge the service department just the way you would judge a new car dealer. Your dependence on your system, once you have gotten past the learning period will be just as intense as your dependence on a new car and being without your system will be just as devastating.

10

CHOOSING YOUR WORD PROCESSOR

*You may scold a carpenter who has made you a bad table, though
you cannot make a table. It is not your trade to make tables.*

Samuel Johnson 1709-1784

THE SANE APPROACH TO ACQUIRING SOFTWARE

Whew! We're done thinking about hardware, thank goodness. Hardware
is a necessary evil, you've got to have it before you can run software.
Hardware is final too—a sloppy hardware choice can profoundly limit both
what software you can run on your computer and what enhancements you
can add to it later. Finally, hardware costs enough that you have to do a
lot of ponderous thinking about it. But software is much more forgiving,
and software is what your computer is all about.

Software is why you buy a computer. Software to you, the user, *is*
the computer. Or at least, it's the computer's personality. When you feel
like kicking in your computer screen, the box itself is not the offender. It's
the program you are running, and ultimately the person who designed
that program who has occasioned your rage. When you love your computer and refuse to go to the beach because you can't take it along, it's the
programs on your computer and the way they interact with your thought
processes that you love.

Designing software is a creative endeavor that at its best becomes
an art. So, as with choosing any work of art, selecting your software tools
involves more than listing the features you need and then buying what-

ever program you find whose list of features matches your list of needs. Ultimately your favorite software tools will be those that reflect your own creative style and embody a useful paradigm of the way you think.

But notice the very important word that began that last statement: ultimately. You aren't there yet, and you aren't going to be there for months to come. Most introductions to computers assume that you will immediately assimilate everything that they throw at you and treat you as if you really were in a position to make informed choices when you acquire your first system.

This is nonsense. You are in no more shape at this point to choose software intelligently than you would be to translate Shakespeare into French after completing a Berlitz French class. If you do what many people do and rush out and buy a set of expensive computer tools now, without first getting the experience you need to make a wise choice, you may end up feeling stuck with what you have bought. This can take the fun out of buying software for good.

This book is going to take a rather different approach to showing you how to tool up than what you may encounter elsewhere. When we looked at buying hardware we argued that you didn't need a fancy system to start out with, just one powerful enough to run most of the tools we described, not one that runs at a blinding speed, and one without the latest bells and whistles. We asked you to assume that in two years or three at the most, you would have reached the level of experience and competence where you would be able to put together your own, perhaps more expensive, dream system. Our emphasis was on buying a system that would not cost so much that it would cause you to suffer an anxiety attack every time you walked into the room where you kept it, but one on which to learn.

BUILDING A CHEAP BUT USEFUL SOFTWARE
COLLECTION WITH DISPOSABLE SOFTWARE

Well, with software, our approach is going to be similar, but our task will be a lot easier, because of the unparalleled openness and decency of the community of computer programmers. The key to our strategy will be taking advantage of the enormous selection of public domain and shareware programs that you can try out for a nominal cost, as well as the offerings of the few commercial software vendors who offer programs priced for ordinary folks not fat-cat corporations.

Our emphasis will be on acquiring simple, cheap, software tools which you can use to get your "sea legs" in the world of computing. You will use these virtually disposable tools until you have enough experience using software to enable you to decide which, if any, of the more expensive software packages you really need. Little of what we suggest you buy is going to make you spend the kind of money where you won't feel free to throw the software away if you don't like it!

If you approach software this way, you will be much more relaxed about your system. Not only that, but if you take the cheap software route you will be able to try more than one product in each family of tools, and get a better feel for the variety of approaches that programmers take when designing that kind of tool.

Eventually you will know enough about what software feels like to be able to read a software review intelligently. You will know what features you like, which ones you need, and which design approaches drive you up the wall—independent of how successful a product has been in the marketplace.

But won't you be missing out if you don't buy the top-of-the-line programs that everyone else has? Well, you may be pleasantly surprised to discover that many of the cheapest programs available today have more features than you will begin to be able to master. In fact, if there is any real problem you will face it is that it is almost impossible to find good simple programs which would be the ideal tools for beginners.

The other thing to realize though is that because your personal needs are quite different from those of the business volume buyers whose purchases make programs "best sellers" you may be more than satisfied with programs other than the ones they use.

Unfortunately, this strategy is easier to follow with an IBM PC or clone than with a Macintosh. While there is great software available for the Mac, very little of it is cheap shareware. Most shareware available for the Mac falls into the utility catagory, or comes in the form of Hypertalk "stackware," computer applications built using the Mac's hypertext language, rather than the full-fledged programs serving every function under the sun available for PCs. If you want to explore the different families of software that might be of use to you as a writer, you will usually have to buy products after reading reviews in magazines, rather than using the free shareware sampling method.

It is beyond the scope of this book to tell you how to select every type of tool in every family. That would be ample subject matter for not one, but several, separate books. Instead, the focus here will be on how to get yourself the software starter set you need in order to have something to begin working with. You will learn about the tools you need to get started and the features those tools should ideally include. Much of what is said about these tools is true of other tools and tool families not covered here and should help you when evaluating them.

Finally you will learn where to find these tools, particularly the cheap and useful shareware tools that are produced by smaller software developers who don't have the resources to pay for glossy advertising.

WHAT SHOULD BE IN YOUR STARTER SET

The starter set is a well-balanced group of software tools that lets you get to work and begin enjoying your computer. It will also give you enough experience with software that you will be able to move on comfortably to other tools. Of course, what you need to have in your starter set will vary depending on what kind of work you want to do with your system. Since you are a writer, you will start with a word processor. The word processor is the tool you will use more than any other. You will need some basic utilities too, things that take care of the files you create with your other software and prevent disasters from occurring. Beyond these basics there are several other items you ought to try out, because they are the ones that writers universally recommend, such as an outliner and desktop organizer. We will also look a little at databases and personal information managers. Once you have picked out a word processor, deciding what to get next becomes a more individual decision. Because of this there really is no cut-and-dried list of indispensable software—except, of course, for the backup software that protects your work, without which you should never operate your computer.

Once you have identified a type of tool that you think you might be interested in, you can try out a shareware version or two, at a cost of anywhere from $3 to $10 apiece, to see if the tool really is useful to you. In cases where such a program fits the niche under discussion the book will point it out, particularly if it is one that is not featured much in the magazines you might otherwise turn to for software recommendations. However, mention of such a program is not to be taken, necessarily, as a recommendation that you rush out and try it. The programs I enjoy using are not necessarily going to appeal to you, any more than do the paintings I hang on my wall.

CHOOSING A WORD PROCESSOR

However, having stated that our policy will center on cheap shareware products, it's time to violate that policy. Although I'm going to suggest that you start with shareware for all the other tools in the tool box, the word processor is a special case, and a different approach is called for when choosing it.

The word processor is, without question, the king of the jungle, at least as far as the jungle on your hard disk is concerned. Many writers have no other program on their computer except a word processor. It is the single most powerful program you will use, and beyond that, the single most convincing reason for the writer to buy a computer. However the sheer number of word processors available is mind boggling and picking one soley on sane carefully reasoned grounds is impossible.

You must give up the idea that you will somehow get the "best" word processor. So many word processors are so very good that this is not possible. What you need for your first word processor, more than anything, is not the best word processor, but one that is reasonably easy for you to learn.

Without a smoothly functioning word processor on board, your computer is going to be dead in the water and utterly worthless to you. So your goal with your first word processor should be to get it working fast. That means it's worth spending the extra money it takes to get a commercially distributed word processor that comes with bound manuals, a tutorial, and most importantly, a phone number to call for customer support.[1] With the more popular word processors you can probably find an adult education class somewhere local too.

This still doesn't mean that you must either spend hundreds and hundreds of dollars to get a word processor or else settle for the "starter" products designed to let executives create one-page memos. Sprint, introduced by Borland in 1988, is available for a street price of less than $150 for IBM PCs and clones. Sprint is a word processor that includes almost every feature writers need including some not found in much more expensive programs. On the Macintosh side you can buy word processors WriteNow, Microsoft Write, or the outline-oriented MindWrite, for around $100. Though not as full-featured as Sprint these word processors may well have all the horsepower you need for professional writing. If you insist on buying one of the industry leaders you can get Microsoft Word, WordPerfect, or Xywrite III +, word processors used by many professional writers, for only another hundred dollars or so, if you do some judicious comparison shopping and don't mind buying through mail order. While this is not cheap, it is not that much to pay for the tool that will be your constant companion. Any of these heavy-duty word processors is quite capable of doing far more than you are ever likely to need it to do, and all are popular enough in the marketplace that you can find courses, books, and people to help with using them.

You should expect to spend a few weeks getting comfortable with your word processor. Only then should you start experimenting gingerly with the tools in the other tool families. Then you can start looking into shareware, since working with your word processor should have taught you some of the basic software-using lore you will need to know to use these other programs.

These secondary tools should be tackled only after you have mastered the rudiments of using the word processor. But using them should turn out to be a much less anxiety-provoking operation, simply because failure

---

[1]There are decent shareware word processors, especially Quicksoft's PC-Write. But few beginners have the skills needed to get one of these up and working properly.

to get one of them working is not going to ruin your relationship with the computer, the way having problems with your word processor might.

Going with the Horrors of the Known

The rest of this chapter reviews some features to consider when selecting a word processor, but by the time you get ready to buy your own system, the chances are good that you may already have learned how to use a word processor, whether at school or at work, and would prefer to use the same program rather than start out with something less familiar, no matter how good it is. That's fine!

The guidelines given in the next section are intended to show you how to find the most useful writer-oriented word processor, but if you already know how to use one, then that one and not some distant ideal is, by definition, the most useful word processor for you. Having experience with one program may very well outweigh any other program's richness of feature, since it means that you can take your computer home, install the word processor, and get to work. After you've gotten completely comfortable with your word processor there may come a time when you pine for a more powerful product and have the maturity as a computer user to undergo the learning period involved in mastering a new word processor. There is no need to add the additional stress of learning a new word processor to the natural anxieties with which your first few weeks with your computer are likely to be filled.

When preparing the 400-page manuscript of my first book for publication I used the word processor that I had learned at work. It was designed exclusively for corporate memos, is regularly beaten black and blue whenever it is reviewed, and should rightly rank at the bottom of the writer's scale. It forced me to insert hard coded page numbers in each chapter, it couldn't index, it created footnotes that were virtually unusable (and which disappeared unaccountably from time to time), and required, besides, that I manually repaginate a chapter every time I entered a few words, a task that was so slow that I usually did it during lunch.

But doing my book on this word processor *still* filled me with wonder and impressed me with the ease with which I was able to work, compared to doing the same task on a typewriter!

Now I have a new, even more wonderful, word processor. But, as is the nature of software owners everywhere, I tend to be more picky and less easy to please with my new streamlined wonder than I was with my first, awful one.

How Hard Is It to Switch?

Many people take the attitude that once you have learned a word processor it becomes somehow engraved on your brain, and so claim it is important that you start out by learning one of the two or three powerful, best-selling programs. Countering this argument is that any new word processor you decide to change to after using another one should be so well designed that learning it will be a pleasure. Its functions should be cleverly integrated, its keystrokes should be close to intuitive, and therefore moving away from your investment in your earlier system won't be such a big deal after all. If a new word processor doesn't meet these criteria there is no reason on earth for you to switch to it!

There are, of course, some very popular programs that are miserably hard to learn if you are used to anything else. People who began using these programs years ago are used to them and tend to shrilly defend their quirks. But there is so much function available in other programs that there is no reason you should feel that you have to force yourself to deal with one of these.

In fact, when starting out, a good attitude to take is this: If you can't sit down in front of the computer, and after reading the first couple of chapters of the books that come with the software, type in the command that gets you to the word processor and figure out what to do with the help of whatever screens appear in front of you, you probably don't want to buy it!

THE MOST VITAL FEATURES OF YOUR WORD PROCESSOR

Now let's look in depth at what makes a word processor suitable for use by you, the writer. Read what follows and think about it, but don't use what follows to depress yourself with the thought that the word processor you may already have chosen doesn't live up to some ideal. Eight years ago writers wealthy enough to afford word processors were spending $20,000 for systems that provided only the functions you would find in today's worst word processors.

Focus on getting comfortable with your software and let those who have so little to write about that they have to babble in print about how rotten your favorite software is waste their creative energies on finding the perfect tool.

You just need to get to the point where you understand the tools available to you well enough that you can use them effectively. Then, thankfully, you can stop thinking about software features and put your energy back into working on your writing, where it rightly belongs.

Help Screens

We will start by looking at the single most important feature of your word processor. But this feature is probably not one you will see prominently featured on the box. The most important feature you should be looking for in a word processor at this point is *not* microspaced kerning or the ability to rotate graphics images. What you should be looking for is the ability to figure out from the program itself what on earth it is that you need to do to use it.

All well-designed programs have what are called **help facilities.** These let you, right in the middle of using the program, stop and ask how to do something you need to do. There are many approaches to designing help facilities. Some programs let you go into a **tutorial mode**, a special part of the program where you are walked through instruction in how to use the different features of the software. Such tutorials may take you through screen after screen of helpful information arranged by topic, pausing at times to let you answer questions that test whether you have taken in what the tutorial is trying to teach.

Other programs have what is called **context-sensitive help.** Context-sensitive help means that at any given point in the program, pressing a help key, for example the F1 key, will display a help screen that contains information relevant to what you are in the middle of doing. For example, if you are looking at a print menu, pressing the help key with context-sensitive help will immediately display a list of help topics that describe the different ways you can print your document.

Programs vary widely in the quality of their help services. But some programs are much easier to use than others, and it is one of these that you should be looking for.

There are still going to be things you need to look up in the manuals that come with your system. And if you are a new computer user who has never used any computer programs at all, there is still, sad to say, a certain learning curve you will need to go through that has more to do with learning how to use a computer and any software rather than the merits of any particular word processor. But the quality of the built-in help that a program supplies can do a lot to simplify the learning task.

Menus and Other Interfaces

The second important feature that you should consider before all the bells and whistles that the software companies tend to brag about, is how the program communicates with you. This is what is described as its interface. There are several different commonly used ways of designing this interface.

Older programs that emulate mainframe systems, such as older versions of MultiMate, use a flat menu interface. With this kind of interface the program shows you a screen listing the things that you can choose to do when you first enter the program. Once you have selected what you want to do, the program gives you more screens which require you to fill in information, until the program has enough information to do what you want it to do. This approach is not bad, but over the years several better types of PC menu interfaces have developed that take advantage of the unique PC programming environment.[2]

One of these kinds of PC interfaces is called the **pull-down menu.** What happens here is that in response to some keystroke that means "show me a menu" you will be given a little box that pops up over whatever you were working on. You can select an item on this menu either by putting the cursor on it, or by typing the first letter of one of the choices on the menu, or perhaps, by clicking a button on a mouse. Selecting one of these options either causes something to happen right there or causes yet another little menu box to pop up over the first. This kind of system is very easy to work with, particularly since, if you select a couple of menu entries, you see all the little menus, stacked on top of each other like solitaire cards, giving you a clear idea of how you got to the menu you are looking at. This ability to see how you got somewhere is a major advantage, particularly when you are just learning how to work with software. When you are done with a menu, some key, perhaps the Escape key, gets rid of each menu you have "pulled down."

A slightly different interface is the **moving-bar** menu. Here what happens is that the program gives you a list across the top or bottom of your screen of words showing what operations you could do now in the program. You choose a particular one by moving your cursor (or a mouse) to the word you are interested in. A brief explanation will be displayed on a line near the menu to remind you what the menu item does. Selecting a menu item may cause a new list of things to display across the top or bottom of the screen.

Not all programs do things one of these ways. A much more complex interface to learn is the **function key-driven** interface. In this kind of program each of the function keys (F1–F10) has a function that it invokes and you must memorize each one. All you can hope for here is that the software company will at least give you a little cardboard overlay that you tape to your computer near the keys, which briefly recaps the function of each key. You may have to spend a lot more time reading the manual to learn this kind of system. However, in all fairness, once you have learned this kind of program, it can be a lot faster to use than those which force you to use multilayer menus.

Finally there is one last interface that is rare in the PC world, the **command-driven** interface. Here you type in a word or a few letters to get specific functions performed. Few programs in the PC world are command driven but the glaring exception to this rule are the two word processors that many people consider to be the ultimate writer's word

---

[2]Recent versions of MultiMate allow you to use one of these newer interfaces instead of its original one.

processors, Xywrite III + and Nota Bene, so you can't ignore this approach. Here you need to memorize the commands before you can get to work. However, since the commands usually are English words or derive from English words, like "del" for "delete," this kind of interface is not as hard to learn as you might expect.[3]

Many programs offer a single interface. However it is becoming fashionable to offer alternative interfaces. You may have a choice of using a pull-down menu or of skipping the menu entirely. You may be able to get to a function using a keyboard shortcut combination, such as pressing the Ctrl key and then pressing P for print, rather than going to a menu. Some word processors even let you fool around with the interface to make it work more the way you want it to. Many let you reassign the functions that go with the different function keys. Others let you create new functions for the function keys yourself, so that, for example, you could set up a particular key to cause a document to print double-spaced with a particular typeface. This ability to customize the program's interface is a very nice feature to have, but may require a little more savvy about using software than you start out with.

The only way you will be able to get a feeling for the user interface of a new word processor is by sitting down in front of a computer that has the program installed on it and trying it out. Unfortunately, it is not always possible to do this with many of the software programs you might want to buy. But when you are considering a word processor, the center-piece of your entire software tool collection, you owe it to yourself to try out the program before you buy.

FEATURES THAT ALL "REAL" WORD PROCESSORS HAVE

There are a certain core of features that are common to just about every word processor designed for adults. These features include the ability to type in text, and then copy, move, and delete (that is, remove) letters, words, sentences, paragraphs, or larger sections within a document.[4] Word processors also should allow you to search through a single document looking for a particular word or words. Once you find the word it should allow you to change each incidence of the word you find to a different word, a feature called search and replace.

---

[3]Recent versions of these programs offer you the option of using menu interfaces instead of the comman- driven one.

[4]**Document** is the word processing term for a word-processing file. The word refers to any manuscript-type item created by a word processor and does not carry the more common meaning of an important legal text.

TABLE 10.1 Common Word Processor Features

Basic Features	Utilities
Text Entry	100,000-Word Spelling Dictionary
Copy Text	Continuous Spell Checking
Delete Text	* User-Defined Spelling Dictionary
Move Text	Sophisticated Thesaurus
Search and Replace Text	Convert to/from WP Formats
	* Convert to/from ASCII
Help Facility	Automatic File Saving
Built-in Tutorial	Keystroke Recording
* Context-Sensitive Help	Built-In Outliner
	100,000 Word Spell Checker
User Interface	**Book Length Manuscript Features**
Pull-Down Menus	* Unlimited Document Size
Moving-Bar Menus	* Treat Set of Files as Single Work
Full-Screen Menus	* Unlimited Footnote Size
Function Key Driven	* Endnote Capability
Command Driven	* Automatic Footnote Numbering
User-Modifiable Interface	* Automatic Figure Numbering
* Rich Cursor Control	* Floating Reference Capability
	* Style Sheets
Formatting Features	Bibliography Management
Set Margins	Index Generation
* Number Pages Automatically	Automatic Table of Contents
Change Fonts	**Desktop Publishing**
* Automatic Headers and Footers	Font Control
* Store Formats	Line Drawing
	Embed Graphics
File Management Features	Display Graphics on Screen
Copy Documents	Multiple Snaking Columns
Delete Documents	Spreadsheet/Database Compatibility
Search Documents for Text	**Miscellaneous**
* Redlining	Allow Nonprinting Comments

Features Preceded by an Asterisk are of Particular Interest to Writers

Word processors almost universally allow you to prespecify the format you want for your document, including margins, tabs, line spacing, and often, the size and style of type to be used for the whole document. These formatting specifications should be easily modifiable, and many word processors let you store particular format combinations for future use. Most word processors will number your pages for you. The word processor should also make it easy to print your document. Many word processors include some kind of file-management features to help keep track of the document files you create with the word processor.

Beyond this, almost all the word processors you encounter nowadays include a spell checker. At a minimum this should flag misspelled words, and preferably it should suggest the correct spelling for an unrecognized word with a high degree of accuracy.

Most word processors allow you to automatically generate a header or footer, which is the term for a line that appears on every page or on alternate pages at the top or bottom. These often contain the page number and perhaps a chapter title. Such page numbers are usually numbered automatically by the word processor.

Finally, and this is more important than you might think, a word processor should have the ability to translate a document it has created into a universally understandable form, such as an ASCII file, that other word processors (and typesetting systems) can use—albeit somewhat clumsily.

These are the rock-bottom things you should expect to find in a word processor.

VITAL FEATURES FOR WRITERS

Once you move up from this basic set of functions you get into the area in which word processors begin to differ significantly from each other. Most word processors have many more features than the basic ones we just mentioned. But exactly which features you will find in each word processor varies. Unfortunately, there are so many features buried in a given piece of software that it is often very hard to find out before buying which ones come with the program. Most programs list features on the outside sleeve of the software box, but they often list only the highlights, and may ignore a feature that is of vital interest to you, the writer, since it is likely not to be much of a selling point to the memo scribblers in the corporate world who buy the bulk of word-processing software. You encounter the same problem in reviews too, since a reviewer only has room to comment on what is new and exciting in a program and either may not have noticed some particularly useful writer-oriented feature or may not consider it of much interest to a business audience.

Therefore, when you consider a word processor, the only way you can usually figure out what it is really capable of doing is by looking through the manual that accompanies the software or a book about it. And even here you may discover that features included with the software are not described!

There are too many features to describe all of them here, but there are some features of particular use to writers and some that are virtually worthless. Looking these some of these should give you some kind of feeling for what you should be looking for when choosing a word processor for the different types of writing tasks.

Book-Length Manuscript Handling Features

There is one set of features that you may need as a writer that may very well *not* be included in many of the popular word processors you encounter. These are the features useful in preparing book-length manuscripts, particularly academic and nonfiction manuscripts. As you have probably noticed, very few people create book-length manuscripts. Consequently, many popular word processors have ignored this set of features in favor of providing features more useful to generating business correspondence or snappy flyers.

This is particularly true of several of the "beginner" word processors touted for their ease of use.

If you routinely write things that are longer than 20 or 30 double-spaced pages, or if you need to use scholarly footnotes, endnotes, indexes, and other such textual paraphernalia, then the features that fall into this category are significant and, if possible, you should buy a word processor that provides them.

It is possible to write a book with almost any word processor, but if a word processor was designed mainly to produce simple business memos you will have to do by hand many of the tasks that better software would do for you, such as numbering your pages sequentially, calculating the manuscript's word count, or generating an index.

You want a word processor that doesn't impose any arbitrary limit on the size of document you can create. You should be able to create single chapter files 100 pages long if you want to. If you must buy an inexpensive word processor, be extremely careful in this regard, since some of the "starter" word processors promoted heavily in the software stores will limit you to creating document files containing at a maximum only 30,000 characters, or about 15 double-spaced pages. Other word processors may allow longer documents but slow down painfully when attempting to work on them.

Even if you have a word processor that provides long-document handling capabilities, you probably will still want to create a book-length manuscript in the form of a set of chapter-length files, rather than as a single huge file. No part of a book can be larger than what you can store on a single floppy disk for backup. Smaller files are easier to manage for other reasons too. This means that ideally you ought to have a word processor capable of treating a set of files as a single work and letting you work on more than one chapter file at a time, so that you can move easily from one chapter to another without delay. Many word processors do not have these abilities.

The word processor you are looking for should be able to correctly number pages sequentially in a work made up of a set of independent chapter files and should make it easy to use the same layout for all your chapters, including specialized layouts you create yourself.

Spell Checker and Thesaurus

Most word processors include spell checkers. The first spell checker you see will probably blow your socks off no matter how poorly designed it is, so impressive is it to see a program find and correct misspelled words. However, as the old story goes, once you have gotten over your astonishment at seeing a dog play chess, you will rapidly find that you don't think much of a dog that loses most of its games. So it is with spell checkers. A spell checker that is not very bright about finding misspellings will not be very useful to you.

By the same token, although you can usually add your own list of words to the dictionary the spell checker uses to look things up, a well-designed spell checker dictionary will contain some 100,000 commonly used words, including names, and will not flag everything in your document as a misspelled word simply because of its own limited vocabulary.

How important this will be for you has a lot to do with how well you spell and how accurately you type. Some writers—those who can spell—disdain using such aids. For others they are lifesavers. I considered myself a very good speller until I got a good spell checker and discovered a whole phalanx of words I had been consistently misspelling all my adult life with no suspicion at all that there was anything wrong with them. These were words I would never have considered looking up because they looked right to me. But I had been mailing them out to editors for years! Most spell checkers have to be run against a piece of text or a whole document after you have finished it. However some including those in Sprint and PC-Write offer the option of having the spell checker check each word as you type and beeping immediately when you make a mistake, which eliminates the need for lengthy spell checking sessions.

Spell checkers have one fatal weakness: they can't find a mispelling which results in a word which happens to be in the dictionary, for example, when you misspell "and," "an." To find these typos you will need to use a powerful grammar checker, such as Grammatik III, and put up with having it flag a lot of correct constructions as errors.

The on-line thesaurus is a more recent addition to the word processor list of standard features, so although many programs now have them, they are by no means available in all word processors. Here the quality varies more than with spell checkers. Some thesauri are designed for business users with limited vocabularies. These are of almost no use to a writer since they offer a very limited choice of words. If you can't come up on your own with the same synonyms that these programs turn up, you probably ought to give up all thoughts of being a writer. Other thesauri are more useful. The best offer synonyms grouped together within meaning groups, like a real thesaurus, and are rich enough to be useful to you when you are momentarily stuck for a word. If your word processor does not include a spell checker or thesaurus, both of these can be bought as separate programs that can be used with almost any word processor. Shareware spell checkers are available too.

Footnotes, Figures, and Floating References

If you write nothing but fiction you probably don't need any further features at all. However if you write nonfiction or do scholarly work there are some additional features that can make your job easier. At the head of the list of such nonfiction-oriented features is the ability to create footnotes. This feature is available on several word processors but the actual implementation can range from the virtually worthless to the very impressive indeed.

Virtually worthless, in this respect at least, are those word processors, that limit the size of the text of your footnote to a certain number of characters. This makes such a feature useless for any scholarly work. The better word processors are able to format footnotes so that they spill over to the next page, the way they would in a book. However even better than this are word processors that allow you to create different kinds of footnotes, including numbered, asterisked, and most importantly, endnotes—notes that appear at the end of the chapter.

A feature related to this is bibliography management, which is useful if you write highly researched manuscripts. This is not commonly found but is available with Nota Bene, which is a top- of-the-line word processor designed for academic scholars. Nota Bene can automatically generate a bibliography that conforms to the requirements of particular academic journals or publishers, and just as easily modify it to another format should the first publisher reject it.

Nota Bene also lets you have floating cross-references, as does Sprint. This means you can refer to a figure by number before you know what number it will end up having in the final version. This lets you generate text that says "As you can see by looking at Figure 4 on page 83 in Chapter 3..." in such a way that if you insert a few more figures or add another chapter the numbers in the text automatically adjust when you reprint and it reads "As you can see by looking at Figure 6 on page 96 in Chapter 4." This can save you hours of grunt work.

Another feature that may be important to you is the ease with which you can generate and modify tables. If this is a very important part of the writing you do, read through the manual that accompanies the word processor or a book about it, to see what, if any, features the word processor provides for this task and how hard they appear to be to use.

Finally, some word processors let you caption figures in a consistent fashion and generate figure lists as part of their table of contents generation routines.

Saving Yourself from Yourself

One important feature is built-in document security. This is not the kind of security that protects you against other people—which is what busines people usually mean when they talk about computer security—but the kind that protects you against yourself.

What is the point of entering 50 pages' worth of text into the best word processor if it will vanish without a trace when you trip over your computer's power cord, pulling it out of the wall. Similarly, should you have a brief power outage, which in my neighborhood occurs any time there is a brisk wind, a heavy rain, or an overwrought squirrel, you can also lose everything you have worked on for hours. You will also lose work when you run into the kind of software bug that causes your system to freeze up, and most programs have a few of these buried in them. Finally, it is not unknown for the writer, in the throes of a creative fit, to hit a combination of keys that accidentally deletes whole pages of a document.

Any feature that can protect you against this kind of disaster is worth real money!

The main reason that you might lose your document is that many word processors work on your text in the computer's main memory, which, as you remember, loses its contents whenever the system is turned off or rebooted. Word processors may write your work to the safe disk file only when you are about to exit the program, at which point you may be asked whether you want to save your work or not.

In a perfect universe you would, of course, remember to save your work to disk every ten minutes or so, manually. But this is Planet Earth. So the chances are very good that unless a program does this kind of save for you automatically—**an autosave**—it is not going to get done. Some kind of Save facility should be high on the list of features you insist on. A few word processors, most notably MultiMate, save each page as you move through your document, but a word processor that keeps the whole document in memory needs to have a built-in feature that kicks in every few minutes and writes your latest stuff to disk. Failing this, make sure that the program at least forces you to remember to save the file before you end an editing session, rather than leaving it up to you to remember to do the save. You don't have to have this feature. But if you don't have it, it is virtually guaranteed that you will write the greatest chapter of your life and then get into some fumble-fingered fugue state and obliterate your entire file!

Besides the autosave feature, another lifesaver is the "undo" which allows you to back out of a series of steps you regret or to "unerase" something you just deleted. This is one of those features that you will find yourself grateful for again and again, since you will find that deleting huge blocks of text is something that all word processors make all too easy.

Rich Cursor Control

Another important feature that may not be among those touted on the back of the word processor box is cursor control. This doesn't sound sexy, but it is one of the things that if your word processor is designed right, will do a lot to get you hooked on it.

Some cursor control commands let you dart all over your document with just a couple of keystrokes. You can go back a word or forward a word, or to the top of the paragraph or the end of a line with just a flick of your finger. This makes it very easy to work with text, particularly if you are a touch typist. Other cursor control commands let you delete a word or a sentence as a unit, again, with just a few keystrokes. Mouse-based word processors, in contrast, may use the mouse movements in the place of cursor control.

Where cursor control will become a joy or a sorrow is in the degree to which the program you are using uses fairly standard cursor control commands. Many PC programs use the cursor control commands popu-larized by the Wordstar word processor, one of the earliest available on the PC. For cursor control these programs use combinations of keys pressed simultaneously that are somewhat like piano chords. For exam-ple, you might have to press the Ctrl key and an arrow key to move directly to the next word, or the Ctrl key and the letter "t" to delete a single word. These combinations seem a bit strange and hard to remember until your fingers learn them. Then they seem very obvious and second nature, since for keyboard control they use motions that, for a touch typist at least, are natural and easy to use.

Being able to dart all over the keyboard and quickly delete an erroneous word or a bad line here and there is great. The problem that you will encounter, however, emerges when you begin to use several programs and one of them refuses to respect these cursor control conventions! PC-Outline, an otherwise brilliant program, for some reason uses the Ctrl-arrow sequence to *delete* the word at the cursor rather than to skip to the next word, as a great number of other programs do. This can lead to a lot of accidentally deleted words if you use PC-Outline after using a word processor that uses this sequence for cursor movement. Fortunately, PC-Outline does have an option that allows you to change the definition of the keys which it uses, so you can set it up to match your word processor; however, how you must go about doing this may not be entirely obvious to a beginner. Switching between programs that have painfully conflicting cursor functions is a real inconvenience and the kind of thing that gives Macintosh owners the right to make snide remarks about PC software!

Compatibility

The last thing that is important to you as a writer, if you intend to make electronic submissions to a publisher, is that your word processor be one that the publisher can work with. If you can submit your manuscript in the same form that it comes out of the word processor, without having to run any translation routines against the word processing files, you will have that much less to worry about. Most typesetting systems can now take input from the more popular word processors, but you should inquire about the one you are thinking of buying if yours is not one of the best-selling few.

If your word processor is not one that can go directly into the publisher's typesetter, you will have to submit your manuscript in ASCII form. This usually involves running a translation utility against your word processor document. However, the result of this transform may be messier than you would like. Complicated formatting will be lost, as will all typefaces that you have embedded in the text (like italics) and even, possibly, footnotes and section headings.

However, if you do mostly magazine work, with magazines that use the ATEX system (as many do), you may have to submit all your work in ASCII form anyway.

Which brings up an important point. Many of the word processors you see advertised emphasize rich typesetting features, most of which are designed to work with laser printers, and the ability to include graphics images in the document. If you are writing primarily for a magazine audience, however, you won't be allowed to use these features in the electronic manuscripts you submit. The same may be true too when you submit a book to a publisher who will be using the electronic form of the file as an input to a typesetting system. Therefore, you may find yourself spending valuable time stripping out all the fancy formatting you paid so much for. The only time you will use those features will be when creating your own promotional materials. Unless you decide to provide

camera-ready copy and own the requisite laser printer and font software—
and don't plan to use one of the more powerful desktop publishing packages—
you won't ever use most of the fancier formatting capabilities of today's
word processors. And if you do use a desktop publishing software
package, *it* will forbid you to use the fancier features of your word
processor!

WORD PROCESSOR FEATURES THAT ARE NICE
BUT NOT VITAL FOR WRITERS

Redlining

Those were the basics. But there are some other features that are also
nice to have that deserve mention. First among these is redlining.
Redlining is the ability to compare two versions of a document and
highlight the changes. Sometimes a redlining feature will put vertical
change bars next to the portion of your text that is new when it prints.
This is useful to you if you keep various versions of a work lying around
and then can't remember which is which.

Comments

Another useful feature is the ability to stick nonprinting notes into a
document. With this feature you can put in a few lines specifying what
additional research you need to do on a topic, or suggesting an appropriate
illustration, or just reminding yourself of something related to a particular patch of text, without having any of these comments print out. (Of
course if you submit electronic copy they will be included.) This is
particularly useful if you work with another writer or editor who uses the
same word processor as yourself, since it makes it possible to stick
nonprinting electronic post-its all over your work.

Index Generation

Yet another nice feature although, sad to say, one that is not as nice as it
looks, is the ability to generate an index. Generally, to use one of these
what you must do is enter some kind of tag at the point in the manuscript
where the item to be indexed appears. When the document is printed, a
properly laid-out index, generated from these tags, is printed at the end,
including the page numbers where the indexed items can be found. Some
word processors have very sophisticated index generators that allow you
to specify indented sublevels in the index and let you include with the tags
special text that appears only in the index, not in the body of the
document. Less sophisticated indexers will just pick up the words found
in your text and slap them into the index.

This sounds terrific, especially if your publisher's standard contract charges you for the costs of creating an index. It is terrific too, if you are going to be doing self-publishing, using the output of the word processor as your camera-ready copy. However, if you are writing a book for publication, this feature is of little use since the page numbers on your final typeset proof pages will not in any way correspond to the page numbers on your manuscript. You could index the manuscript this way anyway and then go through your page proofs to find the real page numbers for each item in the index, which would be no worse than doing the index from scratch, but you still have a lot of miserable dog labor in front of you.[5]

Table of Contents Generation

The feature that creates a table of contents is another feature that is better sounding than it is. Usually these merely strip out your chapter and section headings and list them with page numbers. Unless you are very careful about how you write your subheading, you will end up with a table of contents more appropriate to a painfully dull business report than anything you are trying to sell. Some such facilities only create numbered table of contents, the kind with stuff like "1.3.2.1" before each entry. Again, this is a format only suitable for a captive audience. The page numbers in this table of contents will have no relationship to typeset proofs either.

Line Drawing

If you use an IBM PC or a PC clone and a printer that can print IBM graphics characters, one feature you might find useful from time to time is the ability to generate simple lines and boxes. This is not worth spending money for, but if it is included in a word processor you already like, it can be very handy for designing simple diagrams and charts. I designed all the illustrations in my first book with one of these. These line/box drawing features are not creating real graphics (that is, pictures made out of dots) but instead are using combinations of a couple of special characters called the IBM graphics characters, a set of characters which includes items like — , ⌐ , ⌐ , ⊥ , — , and ▓ . To print these you need to have a printer capable of printing the IBM graphics character set. These can be used to draw simple boxes with single or double lines but such illustrations will probably have to be redone in order to be considered camera ready.

[5]Rather than doing this you might find it easier to go through your page proofs filling in database records using a simple database program, like PC-File, where each record would contain the index entry text, subentry text and page number(s) from your proofs. You could then have the database sort these and print out the resulting list.

EQUATIONS AND NON-ROMAN ALPHABETS

If you do the kind of writing where you must be able to use equations and symbols, or foreign alphabets, only certain word processors will do. You will have to decide whether the amount of such work is enough to justify buying a special-purpose word processor that has these abilities or whether you will buy a more general one and muddle through without these specialized features.

If you do a lot of work in Russian, Greek, or Hebrew you are in luck. If you can afford Nota Bene and some Nota Bene accessories, which will cost around $600, you can have a top-of- the-line word processor and use the non-Roman alphabets.

If you absolutely must work in Urdu or Thai you will have to make do with one of the few word processors available that support their alphabets, like the versatile word processor Duang Jan from Mega-Chomp. This is a word processor that supports not only Urdu and Thai, but also English, Armenian, Bengali, Greek, Khmer, Lao, Punjabi, Sinhales, Tamil, and Viet. Other word processors are also available such as one from Gamma Productions, Inc., that claims to handle a wide variety of languages without requiring that your computer have a special graphics board.

If your writing involves displaying significant amounts of equations, then you may need to select one of the special scientific word processors. There are several, and each features a different way of approaching the task of formatting the equation, making it necessary to choose the one you are most comfortable working with. If you need one of these you most likely already move in the kind of circles where you know people who use scientific word processors. Their recommendations may be useful in finding what you need.

Built-in Outliners

Several word processors have begun including an outliner within the word processor itself. This can be a mixed blessing. Outliners can be a great help to you in organizing your work. It's great to have the ability to make portions of your work "disappear" so that you can look at your section headings or topic sentences without having to look at the rest of the text. This makes it easy to check your logic flow. The only problem here is that the outliner that you find included with the word processor may not be particularly easy to use, which may sour you on using this useful type of tool.

On the other hand, if you always work from an outline, you may end up using a powerful outliner as your word processor of choice, particularly a piece of software like the Access Technology's MindWrite Express for the Mac.

Font Control and Fancy Layout Features

The ability to use all the typefaces available on your printer directly from your word processor can be a nice plus, *if* you remember what we said before when discussing preparing text for a publisher's typesetting system: You may not be allowed to use them for electronic submissions since your publisher's printer or typesetting equipment most likely uses different control codes than your printer.

But you can use printer font features to produce professional-looking cover letters, folders, brochures, or even newspaper ad copy, so the more mileage your word processor can get out of your printer the better. Many word processors will allow you to lay out your text in columns that snake up and down the page like those in the newspaper. Some let you set aside areas for illustrations, or even, as we mentioned, let you include an illustration from a graphics file in the document itself. While you may not be sending this to a publisher, it can be of great value to you when promoting the stuff the publisher puts out.

The limitation here, of course, is not the capabilities of your word processor so much as those of your printer, since most of the truly impressive things that today's word processors can produce require the use of a laser printer or even, beyond that, the use of a laser printer equipped with a postscript formatting language interpreter.

The other thing to be aware of is that the fancier you get in using formatting services, complex font arrangements, and interesting layouts, the more time you will find yourself wasting trying to get it all to work, and the higher the piles of waste paper that you will generate! In spite of the rosy picture painted by software vendors, getting desktop publishing output to look right, whether you are using real desktop publishing software or a fancy word processor, requires a significant amount of trial and error.

Keystroke Recording

A nice touch that many word processors include is the ability to record a series of keystrokes and then assign them to a key. This means that if you find yourself doing a certain thing over and over again, like setting up a document to print in a particular manner or doing a complicated set of search-and- replace functions, you can record them and then have the software automatically run through the whole set of keystrokes whenever you type in whatever keystroke combination you assigned to the function. For example you might set up Ctrl-P to set a document to double spacing, set the typeface to a sans serif font, and print the document immediately, thus freeing yourself from having to go through a format menu, a set of font menus, and a couple of print menus. Some programs call such a set of recorded keystrokes **a macro.**

Style Sheets

Similarly useful is the ability to store style sheets and use them for new documents. Stored in the style sheet would be the margins, tabs, font, spacing, what type of headings to use, the kind of page numbering and footers to use, and similar formatting information that you want to use over and over again for a certain class of documents. For example, you could have a style sheet for letters and another for manuscripts. The power of these style-sheet facilities varies, with some of them being powerful enough to allow you to produce professional-looking business documents even if you know little about how to lay out business correspondence.

FEATURES THAT ARE FRILLS FOR THE WRITER

Here, finally, is a brief list of the features you probably don't need at all. However, just because you don't need them doesn't mean you won't get them anyway, since many of these are at the top of the business memo scribbler's wish list.

At the top of this list is the mail merge. Mail merge is the feature that lets you create junk mail. A mail-merge utility merges a text file containing the stuff that goes on every letter with another file containing the information that is unique for each. These utilities may be complex and hard to master. But you are unlikely to ever want to bother with one.

It is not that you won't use your computer to generate a lot of repetitive mailings. You will probably end up creating a lot of junk mail of your own—letters begging book reviewers to accept a free copy of your book or proposals to editors, for example. But you will not be very likely to do this using a mail merge. For the kind of mailings you will probably be doing, you will probably just need to copy an existing letter and change the relevant names and text by hand before printing the letter out. Mail merge makes sense when you must generate a hundred almost- identical letters. Nevertheless, almost every word processor you buy will have this feature whether you want it or not.

Another potentially useless feature is the ability to work directly with files created by Lotus and dBase, respectively the most popular spreadsheet and database programs used on the IBM PC. This is very useful to businesspeople whose writing is often just an excuse to display something lifted from a spreadsheet or database report. But you are not likely to be doing this. A business math feature that allows you to add up columns of figures right there on the page is probably another such worthless feature, as is the ability to maintain files full of canned text, which you can import with a keystroke, things like "If I can be of further assistance please do not hesitate to call."

Another questionable feature is one that lets you define abbreviations that the word processor then expands into a full word as you type. You could, for example, instruct the system to translate MC into Martin Chuzzlewit, thus saving yourself some keystrokes, but such features are probably thrown into products to allow salespeople to give demos that impress vacuous executives who have trouble typing. You can achieve the same effect with the search-and-replace function if you really feel like you have to do this kind of thing.

Finally there comes the thorny question of the graphics-based, rather than character-based, interface, which increasingly is being promoted as something you "gotta have." While there is no question that many writers love to work with the graphic interface that prevails both on the Mac and some PC programs like Microsoft Word, not all do. Unfortunately, in our video culture there is a frightening tendency for pundits and decision makers to proclaim that if something is visual—as opposed to verbal—it must be the wave of the future, and this attitude is having a profound effect on the direction developers are taking in designing PC software. Personally, I find it hard to understand why a writer would be attracted to writing with software that replaces words with little simple-minded pictures scattered over the screen, like a toddler's abandoned toys. Literacy is fading out so fast, we as writers should oppose anything that erodes it further![6] Still, there is little question that graphics is the direction in which the top-of-the-line PC word processors are moving—and of course the Macintosh word processors have been there all along—driven mainly by the effort to provide more and more fancy typesetting and illustration features, and, I suspect, reflecting the deep-seated belief of our society that people shouldn't have to read text that isn't full of pictures.[7]

Still, the need to see your words in Technicolor and fancy fonts, which is what the graphics interface provides, is not likely to be a primary need of the impecunious writer, who would settle happily for seeing them in print, at least as long as the graphics interface requires a more expensive, speedier CPU and expensive monitors to be effective. But if these features appeal to you, they are certainly available.

---

[6]But then, I'm one of those utterly nonspacially- oriented souls who can't tell left from right, and I find it hard to remember what those little pictures are supposed to mean.

[7]I find it interesting however, that the word processor that is used by the graphics-hailing writers at PC Magazine itself is Xywrite III + which, as we mentioned before, is one of a tiny number of command driven—i.e., word driven—programs.

11

ACQUIRING MORE SOFTWARE TOOLS

One half of the world cannot understand the pleasures of the other.

Jane Austen 1775-1817
Emma

TOOLS TO ORGANIZE YOUR THOUGHTS

Although there are variations in the features that you will find in word processors, by and large there is agreement about what it is that a word processor should do. But when you begin to look at other tool families you find less agreement about function and less catholicity of design within the tool family.

The software tools intended to organize your thoughts vary the most. Each program that bills itself as a random information processor takes an idiosyncratic approach to processing random information and offers a different set of functions than does its competitors. This makes it hard to make broad statements about what features you should look for when choosing such a tool, but it also means that you can choose from a selection of tools, each crafted to serve a slightly different purpose.

Demand Intuitive Design

Though there is no one list of features to look for, there are some characteristics you should demand from such tools. First and foremost is that the program embody **intuitive design.** Intuitive design means simply that a person of normal intelligence who has been fooling around on a computer for a few weeks and has mastered how to insert diskettes and how to invoke a program, should be able to get productive with the new tool, be it "information manager" or "random information processor" within no more than half an hour.

Getting productive doesn't mean that you have mastered all the features that come with the program, but it does mean that you can do something useful that you couldn't do before you loaded the program.

Unfortunately, a program that is ambitious in concept and design may be hard to learn. And such a program, no matter how great its power, will languish unused—a piece of expensive "shelfware"—unless you can get enough of a feel for its benefits, the first couple of times you try it, that you are motivated to keep on using it.

Yet often the most powerful thought tools are surprisingly simple. Their brilliance is in their underlying conceptual imagery, the way that they embody a thought process, not in how much function they stuff onto a single screen. These intuitive programs fit so well into the way you already think that learning them is like buying a piece of ready-made clothing, already fitted to your body, where using more poorly designed programs require that you make an effort more akin to sewing your own clothing from a pattern.

There is a place for the more complex program, because it is quite possible that once you have mastered it, it can offer you far more function. But at the stage you are now, as a beginner still most likely trying to get reasonable results out of your word processor, you probably don't have the energy to invest in mastering one of the more complex products.

So when looking at reviews of these products, look closely for statements like "if you have an aversion to manuals you'll get along fine just by following the help screens"[1] and save for later those where the reviewer harps on the program's long "learning curve."

Also, too, look for programs that offer flexibility in their interface. You will be using this kind of program when you are trying to structure your thoughts and pull together complex but jumbled bits and pieces. This makes it imperative that the program not consume more than a tiny amount of your mental energy. Ideally, you should be able to invoke a function in one of these programs in any one of a number of ways so that you can choose the one that is most natural to you. PC-Outline and Grandview, one of whose designers created PC-Outline, offer you the choice of using menus, which can be invoked using a variety of keystrokes, or of using fast keystroke combinations to get the identical functions. And

---

[1]*PC Magazine* review of Grandview (Symantec) December 13, 1988. Page 113. Bruce Brown "Personal Information Managers."

you can use a built-in function to assign your own keystrokes to a function if you don't like the ones that came with the product. When you use the menu interface on these products the menus also show you the keystrokes that accomplish the same tasks, which serves as a subtle tutorial. This is good design.

Determine a Program's Real Function

The next thing to keep in mind when evaluating such a program is the "real" function that the program was designed to serve. Unfortunately, when personal information management emerged as a hot new software category, a lot of software companies jumped on the bandwagon by taking old products that they were already marketing as something else and redefining them as personal information managers.

It is depressing to discover that what you thought was supposed to be a thought organizer really is a calender manager meant for tracking business appointments or that what you thought would be a great tool for keeping track of the junk that floats through your head really was designed for managing uniformly formatted abstracts downloaded from an on-line service.

A useful question to ask when evaluating these products is what is the basic unit that they operate on. Some programs work with only small chunks of text, and their displays may be limited to a few lines, though they may let you link this manipulatable unit to a longer piece of text somewhere else. Such a tool can be useful, but only if you had intended to use it for the kind of information that can be reduced to a few lines.

Other tools, like the better outliners, let you work with text items of any size. And some are not limited to handling just text but, like Owl International's program, Guide, a hypertext program, or the Mac outliner, More, allow you to integrate pictures with text.

Some of these programs are designed to work with the actual contents of your existing files, which includes the stuff you create using your word processor and databases, while others work only with files that they themselves create. For example a text search utility like GOfer or ZyINDEX, goes out and searches through all your existing documents and files for some word or combination of words you specify, and then displays for you what it has found. This means that you can find strings of words buried anywhere in any of your files. ZyINDEX, in addition, lets you define fairly complex relationships between the words you search for. A very different approach to managing random information is embodied in IZE, which is also sold as a personal information manager. IZE looks at your documents long enough to strip out information about them and then builds indexes pointing to the things you tell the program you are interested in. If a piece of information doesn't contain a keyword you have told the program to search for, then the program will not be able to retrieve that text later. The shareware random information database Instant Recall works only with what you enter into its screens, but it indexes every word you enter. Programs that take this kind of approach only manipulate and display information about what they have stored in their own files, rather than manipulating and searching the actual documents themselves. This approach is most useful for manipulating certain types of stuff—primarily huge amounts of text— when you already have a clear idea of what you will want to retrieve later.

Some information managers only manage the information you give them in their own very particular format and are not intended to work with other existing documents, although such programs may allow you to **import** pieces of existing documents, which simply means copy them in. Outliners and products like Lotus Agenda fall into this category.

Some programs, including Agenda and Grandview, boast the ability to give you "multiple views" of your data. This may be of tremendous use and allow a kind of reshuffling of your thoughts. But you do need to determine who defines the views that you get of your data, you or a built-in routine in the program, and if you find that you must define the view yourself you need to determine just how much work is involved in setting up such views.

Memory Residence—Pros and Cons

One question to ask is whether or not a program can be **memory resident.** Memory-resident programs are the kinds of programs that can "pop up" when you hit a special keystroke sequence in the middle of using some other program. This can make a program much more useful than one that only runs in stand-alone mode. For example, when using a memory-resident outliner you can effortlessly switch back and forth between looking at the outline and working on your manuscript. But there is a price for this versatility, and that price is filled-up memory. A memory-resident program sits in a piece of your computer's memory for the rest of your session after you start it up, even when you are not using it. If the memory-resident program is large, you may not be able to run the other programs you want to run it with, particularly your word processor. So although you will see many programs advertising them-selves as being able to run in memory-resident mode, not all of them are very useful when run this way.

Try Shareware to Determine What You Need

Unfortunately, many of the most interesting thought-organizing tools, like Agenda, IZE, and Grandview, cost as much or more than a word processor, making it impossible to explore them in a lighthearted way unless you are rich.[2] Since you won't know if one of these potentially useful tools is going to be useful to you until you try one out, and since no one can be objective when trying out something they have just spent $350 on, you would do best to avoid looking at big-ticket commercial programs at this stage. Instead, consider these kinds of tools as the ideal tools with which to begin your shareware collection.

In the PC world you have many excellent shareware programs available that provide at least some of the functions that the commercial programs do. What you want to do is try to find a shareware program that shares key design components with some of the expensive, well-advertised thought-management tools that you read about. Try these out, rather than the expensive advertised versions. You can't find a direct match for every one of the more interesting kinds of programs available commercially, but you might be surprised at how many programs embodying significant amounts of an expensive program's function you can find.

Shareware programs may not have all the bells and whistles of the more expensive commercial programs but they generally supply the same kinds of functions. If you find that the primary function of such a program is not particularly useful to you, for example the ability to search all your files for specific pieces of text or the ability to manipulate an outline, it is unlikely that a more expensive, more feature-filled program that does essentially the same thing will be worth much to you.

On the other hand, if you find yourself using a shareware program all the time you can then register it—often for a tenth of what the commercial program would cost—or you can evaluate a more feature-filled commercial program that shares the same niche with the shareware. In addition, shareware programs are likely to be useful to you because of the way that shareware is distributed: without benefit of ads or printed manuals. In order to be successful in the marketplace a shareware program *must* be easy to learn and to use.

If you have an IBM PC or clone you might begin your shareware collection by picking up a copy of PC-Outline which will give you a good idea of the power of a well-designed outliner, or you can look at PC-Hypertext to get a feeling for what the hypertext approach is all about. If you are interested in text search software you can try PSearch or the highly rated FGREP utility, either of which can quickly locate a word or set of words anywhere in any of your files, giving you a feel for how useful this kind of function might be for you. As an example of random information management you might try out Instant Recall, a memory-resident free-form database or, for a different approach, get 3BY5, a free-form

---

[2]An exception to this rule is the Mac PIM/outliner Acta which can be bought for under $40.

database based on an index card format with index and search capabilities. These are just some of the shareware software tools in this category that are available. There are more.

TOOLS TO ORGANIZE OTHER KINDS OF INFORMATION

It is not necessary to buy a database program as part of your starter set either, particularly not the $500 kind you are likely to see in the software store. The best solution for you for handling your information management needs right now is probably either to use the notepads provided by a good desktop utility or an inexpensive random information database like Tornado Notes. These are not the structured kind of database that you find embodied in products such as dBase or Rbase but, as you saw earlier, using structured databases takes a kind of expertise that you are unlikely to have right now. The notepad storage concept conforms more to the way that you are used to storing data.

For the phone number and address database you probably need right away, you can use the address/phone number database that comes built into a desktop utility. If that isn't enough, you can try out some of the contact tracking systems that are available as shareware, such as Contact Plus.

Using a formal database such as dBase, Paradox, or RBase requires mastering some concepts that are not difficult to understand, but which are far from intuitive. Worse,when you use such a formal database, you must design and set up your database correctly at the very beginning before you put any information in it. Setting up such a database is a rigorously precise operation. Once you have defined your database, making major changes to the way you have structured it requires a lot of work.

If you would like to try out a structured database, this is where you might want to try an excellent shareware database like PC-File Plus or File Express. If you find that these popular and relatively simple databases are useful for the kind of information you use, you can register them—for under $100 as opposed to the $500 plus prices of the commercial programs. Then you can begin looking into the intricate commercial database programs to see what else they might give you. When looking at the powerful "industrial strength" databases, make sure that you ask yourself whether you will be able get more out of one of them than you get out of the shareware database—without having to pay a consultant to set the database up for you the way most businesspeople do. There are many books available about these database programs. Reading or, more likely, attempting to read one of these should give you the flavor of what is involved.

PC-File Plus, by the way, comes complete with an address database that is already set up to produce mailing labels.

If you have a Mac you might look into what is available as shareware hypercard stackware or else, if you want to use a more formal database, try the Reflex database product, which can be bought for around $100.

TOOLS TO ORGANIZE YOURSELF

The tools that fall into the desktop utility class of programs are extremely popular in the marketplace and deservedly so. Whether you need such a tool at all, or which one you would be happiest with, is again a matter of personal style. Commercially available programs include SideKick and SideKick Plus available in PC and Mac versions, and Lotus Metro, among others, but there are also perfectly adequate shareware programs for the IBM PC and clones, including the powerful Homebase and PC-Deskteam. There is even a shareware product available for the Mac—MockPackage+. Tools from other families are beginning to look more and more like desktop organizers too. For example, the reasonably priced set of disk utilities PC Tools Deluxe includes an editor, cut and paste, calculators, and calendar, which are all desktop utility features, besides including such utilities as a DOS shell, file defragmenter, and backup and unerase programs which fall into the utility family discussed later in this chapter.

When looking at one of these, you should make sure you understand what features the desktop organizer includes, since each package usually has a slightly different mix of function.

A good desktop organizer should have the ability to create and manage **notepads.** This means that while working in one program, for example your word processor, you can hit a quick combination of key-strokes ("hot" keys) and get a notepad screen where you can jot down random thoughts. The better notepad programs allow you to keep lots of different notepads on different topics, and may let you search the text or titles of these notepads. This kind of search feature makes them, in effect, behave like free-form databases.

Most desktop organizers include calendaring functions, which may or may not excite you. Many include a file manager which is very useful. But beware: Such facilities can allow you to damage your files if you don't fully understand what you are looking at. This is because such utilities, besides letting you edit text, allow you to delete files— often in one fell swoop—and switch directories, which can confuse your software.

Many such programs include phone dialers—databases of phone numbers which, if you have a modem and a phone near the computer, will find and automatically dial a number for you.

Editors are another kind of program that you may find included with a desktop utility. An editor is a program that lets you look at a file and change it, no matter what program originally created it. This kind of program is particularly useful if your word processor can't deal with ASCII files. You will need such an editor for changing things in control files later when you have a little more understanding of the computer environment.

A useful feature is **cut and paste.** This is a feature that lets you pick up text displayed on the screen by one piece of software and write it, as a unit, into another program's screen. Among other things, this lets you take an address stored in a database and transfer it into a letter in your word processor. Unfortunately not all programs will accept pasted-in text, and sometimes using one of these can lock up your system. Whether you can use such a feature with a new program must be determined by trial and error, when you are *not* working on something important, of course.

Memory Hogs

Because these desktop organizers are by definition memory-resident programs, the issue of how much memory they require in resident mode is not trivial. If you plan to use a memory-resident random database and a memory-resident outliner, for example, the addition of a desktop organizer might push the amount of remaining memory below the amount you must have free to run your word processor. If you have additional memory installed on your machine this may make life easier, but only if your organizer, like Sidekick, is able to use this extra memory to run in.[3]

To avoid memory problems don't use the usual procedure, which is to start the desktop organizer every time you bring up your system. Instead, just invoke it when you know that you will be doing the kind of work where it will be useful.

Incompatibilities

The other thing to be aware of is that there are some programs—not a lot, but some—that run into trouble coexisting with one of these organizers, particularly if the problem program is trying to use the same keystrokes as the organizer. In addition, some disk utilities specifically note that you shouldn't have any memory-resident software running when you run the utility. Don't forget that your desktop software falls into this category. If

---

[3]As you won't be surprised to learn, IBM PCs have not one, but two, different kinds of extra memory—extended memory and expanded memory—and programs that need one kind may not be able to use the other. In addition, many other programs just ignore both types.

you encounter strange results when using a new program, bringing your system up without the desktop utility and running the problem program again may be all you need to do to fix the problem.

Style Analyzers

It is hard to make generalizations about grammar and style analyzers. The bad ones are worse than useless since they waste your time and offer little in return. But the good ones, such as Grammatik III, are getting pretty close to being useful tools for the writer. Ignore what you read about such programs and do your best to get your hands on one you can try out. The best test is to run 20 pages of your best stuff through one of these programs and see if the program comes up with anything useful.

When I did this recently with one such product, the software at first got me laughing with antics such as flagging "pregnant women" as sexist word use and telling me "new" was a verb used incorrectly. But I was sobered a few minutes later when the program identified four real errors in the same piece, which I had not noticed when I mailed it to an editor. Most of these were typos that slipped past the spell checker, but one was an incorrectly used word and another was a verb that didn't agree with its subject, a collective noun. And after I got over being irritated at the software for flagging so many sentences as overly long, I reluctantly agreed that perhaps some of them would benefit from restructuring.

Because of the complexity of what such programs are trying to do—which is nothing less than speak English—the signal- to-noise ratio in these programs is quite high. This might make a potentially helpful program too irritating for you to use frequently. You may also find it more irritating than you had imagined to have a program make suggestions about your prose, even when its suggestions are right. After all, being able to construe syntax has long been what sets us apart from the lower animals. Given such subjective factors there is no alternative to testing these programs yourself and judging their usefulness by your own subjective response. Just be sure to give such a program a comprehensive enough trial to let it show what it is capable of doing.

Such programs are also available on the IBM PC as shareware, including PC-Stylist. Mac users can buy MacProof or Sensible Grammar.

TOOLS TO GET INFORMATION

If you have decided to get a modem and plunge into the world of computer communications you will need to make several important choices.

First, you will need to decide whether you want to sign up for any of the commercially available communications services, and then you will

TABLE 11.1:   Some On-Line Services of Interest to Writers

CompuServe	(800) 848-8990 (United States)
	(614) 457-8650 (Ohio)
Delphi	(800) 544-4005
GEnie	(800) 638-9636
BIX	(800) 227-2983

need to look at the communications software available that works with your modem to handle the communications session.

Picking A Communications Provider

There are two questions to ask when deciding which service to sign up with: What kinds of services are available on-line and the how do you pay for the service. You must weigh both these factors if you are going to enjoy your on-line experience.

ON-LINE OFFERINGS. The question of what is available on-line is vital. A service like PRODIGY, which offers the on-line equivalent of USA Today—news bites, sports scores, and a preponderance of shopping-oriented services—will be worth little to you no matter how cheap it might be, since it is not oriented toward getting real information or communicating with intelligent people. Such a service is nothing more than an attempt to sell you, as a consumer, to merchants who then pay hefty fees to the service.

The better services are built around the concepts of allowing communication with interesting people in tandem with giving you access to rich information sources. Such on-line services also offer access to specialty databases. If you intend to use one of these you should make sure that the service you are considering can get to the database you need to work with. If you are looking more for friends, contacts, and the opportunity to interact with people all over the country, CompuServe might be a good choice. CompuServe is also the service where you will get the best product support. Many software companies maintain forums on CompuServe devoted to answering your question and maintain libraries of programs and free add-ons for their software. You can get shareware and public domain software on CompuServe as well as on other services like Delphi and GEnie. But you can also get these programs from local bulletin boards, which makes getting them much cheaper, or from user's groups and shareware services. Both of these might be better sources.

Delphi has a writer's group on-line that features live writer's conferences held each Thursday night, and claims a membership heavy in, among other genres, serious science-fiction writers. Bix and CompuServe also feature popular on-line writer's hangouts.

ELECTRONIC MAIL. If an on-line service offers electronic mail it can be very useful to you, but only if the people you intend to communicate with use that service or can be reached electronically from it. MCI mail is one such electronic mail service that you may find useful. You can sign up for it directly or you can send messages from CompuServe's Easyplex to MCI mail customers for an additional charge. If you are interested in electronic mail, you should also find out whether you can use the service to send files to subscribers. File transfer can be a fast way of submitting copy to an editor in electronic form. You may also be able to use one of these electronic mail services to fax pages stored on your computer to an editor or other businessperson who has access to a fax machine but not to a computer. This can be a great time saver, contribute to your image as a professional, and best of all, only cost a few dollars per transmission—far less than buying your own fax equipment would cost.

HOW ON-LINE SERVICES BILL. The way that you are billed for using these services varies. Some services charge a flat monthly fee, which you pay whether you use the service or not. Some charge this flat fee and then bill you in addition for your **connect time**, the time you spend on-line using the service.

Other services, like CompuServe and GEnie only charge you for the time that you actually use the service. The total amount you pay varies, depending on whether the number you use to get into the on-line service is run by the service itself or whether you are using a network service like TYMNET or Telenet which takes you to the on-line service. If you are using a network service you will be billed a by-the-minute rate for both the network and for the on-line service. Unfortunately, the quality of the service you get from these networks can vary. In the worst case the network response can be so slow that you end up running up high on-line charges because of the time you spend sitting waiting for the network to respond. You will do best, usually, if you can access an on-line service directly.

Besides these charges, some of the databases that you access on-line have their own charges, which are added in on top of these other charges. These can be quite stiff, ranging from a couple of dollars for every database search to $60 an hour for some specialty databases.

Finally, don't forget that you will be using your telephone to access these services, which means that you must pay all the necessary phone charges besides. Using on-line services extensively can cause some nasty surprises at billing time if you have the kind of phone service where you pay for local calls, since you can easily add a hundred calls per month to your bill using such a service, even though each call might last only a minute.

If you don't live in a major population center, there may be no local phone numbers for these services either, so you may have to add long-distance rates into the calculation. In this case, it is often cheaper to call an access number that is in a neighboring state and thus get the advantage of lower nighttime interstate long-distance rates, rather than calling a nearer in-state long-distance number.

JOINING ON-LINE SERVICES. There are several ways to join an on-line service. You can buy starter kits for several of the on-line services in a software store for a price of $25 or more. These usually include a credit toward some on-line time, so they aren't as expensive as they look, and usually a book is included to help you get going. However, before you rush out to buy one of these be certain that none of the programs you have bought includes a free on-line sign up. Many of them do. Borland includes a free on-line sign-up package for Compu-Serve, which includes $15 of connect time, with its Sprint word processor. Borland provides this in order to give users access to their excellent customer service people. Some modems and some communications software also include such free sign-up packages. The only thing these packages lack is the book that comes in the regular Compu-Serve sign-up pack, and you can order this on-line or get something close to it at the public library.

In addition, if a new service is trying to recruit users they may offer free sign-up periods to people identified as likely prospects. If you are a member of a computer users group you are likely to hear about these opportunities before anyone else. Some companies are also able to offer their employees trial subscriptions. Free sign-up offers are also advertised in computer magazines.

In short, don't shell out real money for a starter kit until you've made sure that you can't get one for free.

Here, as in so many other areas, you probably can get much more information about available on-line services and what they offer from members of a local computer users group.

FREE BULLETIN BOARDS. Of course, you don't have to use commercial communications services to get on-line. There are plenty of free bulletin boards all over the country. If you can get to a local one and avoid having to pay long-distance charges, using one of these may be a good way to learn the basics of on-line communications and pick up the shareware and computer buddies you're looking for. Here, too, getting recommendations from people at a local users group is a good idea. Bulletin boards vary widely in terms of their focus and the kinds of people and programs that you will find on them. A FIDONET bulletin board may be a great place to start if there is one in your area. These boards form a national network, allowing you to send messages around the country, and have fairly high standards for what is available on-line.

Communications Software

In order to use one of these services you will need a modem and communications software. There are two kinds of communications software. General-purpose software is designed to let you call any other on-line computer, be it a mainframe in Omaha or a bulletin board down the street. In contrast, special-communications software is designed to streamline the use of a single on-line service. Let's look at both types.

GENERAL-PURPOSE COMMUNICATIONS SOFTWARE. If your modem came with software it is undoubtedly one of these general-purpose packages, such as Bitcom, Procomm, or Crosstalk. These packages usually allow you to store the phone number and settings you need for each on-line service or bulletin board you might call. Often they include a **script language** which allows you to speed up and automate procedures you always use with a given service. For example, after you write your user ID and password into one of these scripts—items most on-line services require you to enter before you can get into the service—the software can automatically sign on to the service for you. You might also have your script automatically enter the commands necessary to take you to a particular message area or file library. This can be very useful, but unfortunately most of these script languages are more complicated than what you, as a brand new computer user, are prepared to deal with.

These general-purpose software packages also can create a file containing all the stuff that scrolls across your screen while you are on-line, so that you can look at it later when you are not on-line and not paying charges.

Such packages usually contain routines that let you upload (send) and download (receive) files from bulletin boards and communications services. These routines use something called **file transfer protocols** to transfer data to and from other computers. The protocol you use must also be used by the computer at the other end of the transfer. Popular protocols used on bulletin boards and other communications services are **XMODEM,** and **Kermit** (named, I believe, after Kermit the Frog) but there are others. As you can only upload and download using a protocol that is supported by the software in use on the computer you are calling, having a selection available is a good idea.

Some of the fancier programs include something called **terminal emulation**. This is not a feature you are likely to need unless you are going to be accessing certain kinds of non-IBM mini- and mainframe computers. With terminal emulation you can set up your computer so that it behaves like certain popular mainframe and minicomputer terminals. If you have been thinking about accessing the computer at work or school and that computer is a large IBM mainframe, however, you will need more than one of these communications programs to be able to access the mainframe in the mode where your computer behaves like a mainframe terminal. Here you will need an expensive hardware card with its own software to access the mainframe—something you should get your employer to pay for or go without.

One feature that may be worth looking for in general-purpose communications software is the ability to manage on-line conferencing. Procomm, a PC shareware program, makes it easy to participate in an on-line conference. Less sophisticated packages may end up mixing up outgoing and incoming messages.

But when picking a general purpose program you can feel secure that almost any package available will be adequate for your needs. You needn't agonize nor need you spend big bucks for top-of-the-line products, since you are unlikely to need the business-oriented features they provide. In fact, in this one area, communications software, the programs that reviewers rate most highly are, as often as not, shareware! The highly rated package, Procomm, is available as shareware, as is Boyan D3. On the Mac side there is the popular Red Ryder package. Don't spend money buying a commercial package until you have tried out one of these.

SPECIAL-PURPOSE COMMUNICATIONS SOFTWARE. Such is the popularity of CompuServe that several programs have been developed to run on a wide range of hardware to access it most effectively. If you have any intention of using CompuServe Forums as a tool to meet people and exchange information you should get one of these, since the software simplifies what is otherwise a far-from-painless experience, and makes it cheaper too.[4]

What programs like TAPCIS and Autosig for PCs and Navigator for the Mac do, is allow you to do as much as possible of your CompuServe work off-line where it costs you nothing, rather than in an interactive mode. These programs let you read and write messages at your leisure on your computer on your own, free, time, with plenty of time for revisions and thinking out your message, rather than during the on-line minutes for which you pay an arm and leg. The messages, when complete, go into files that you upload and download to CompuServe. These programs also

---

[4]However, before you rush out and get one of these to cut down your CompuServe costs, be warned that because of how easy this software makes it to exchange information you may very likely end up using the service more.

feature automatic scripts, which let you go on-line and automatically scan the message headers on various forums and pick up messages others have sent you as well as sending the messages you have composed off-line.

TAPCIS, a powerful shareware program, allows you to use Compu-Serve's electronic mail service easily, makes it a bit easier to download files, and tracks the time you have spent on-line so that you can estimate your monthly expenses. Autosig does less. It automates reading and sending messages on CompuServe forums, but doesn't handle electronic mail. But Autosig is public domain software, which means that you don't have to pay to use it. These programs can both be downloaded from CompuServe, but they are so large that downloading them may be chancy and prohibitively expensive. It may make better sense to order them from a shareware distribution company or to copy them from another user.

None of these packages is intended to work with the specialty databases available through CompuServe. There are also packages available for other services such as Lotus Express for MCI Mail and Aladdin for GEnie. On the Mac you can buy Desktop Express, a package that semi-automates access to Dow News/Retrieval and MCI Mail.

TOOLS TO PRODUCE PUBLICATIONS

It would be beyond the scope of this book to give you the kind of information about desktop publishing that you need in order to do a professional job. The key to the whole subject is professionalism. While you can get great results from inexpensive software coupled with inexpensive hardware in almost any other area of computer use, there isn't any way you can get camera-ready output from a computer without investing in very expensive professional hardware: fast processors, top-quality scanners, and powerful laser printers. There are no cheap stand-alone desktop publishing systems that can produce output of the quality that you will need if you intend to replace the typesetter in a self-publishing operation, though you can, it is true, do as well with some of the newer word processors, like WordPerfect 5.0, Microsoft Word, and Sprint that include font management, scaling, and the ability to layout blank areas on the page, as you might with a separate cheapie desktop publishing package.

If you are able to afford the thousands of dollars needed for the hardware required for a professional desktop publishing setup, you should spend some more money on courses in how to use one of the professional packages, such as Aldus Pagemaker and Ventura Publisher, which are the standards for desktop publishing. While there are some shareware font-management packages, you won't find professional quality desktop publishing shareware, at least not now.

This is one area where a strategy of starting simple and cheap and working up is not the way to go. And this is probably a clear sign that desktop publishing is not something to get involved with in your first year or so of computer use! Unless you already have experience with this kind of thing and are comfortable using a PC, you should concentrate on mastering the essentials first, and save desktop publishing for when you are a more experienced user.

While you get comfortable with your starter set and your reasonably priced hardware, you might consider treating yourself to a hands-on course or seminar on desktop publishing. You should also read all you can about it in the computer press. This is a definite case in which the more you know the better off you will be. Pay the typesetter this year, or use the services of the local copy shop that invested in PC technology and can do desktop publishing for you. Then relax in the secure knowledge that if you wait another year you will be able to afford a much nicer setup than you can get now and that your familiarity with computers will have advanced to the point where you can evaluate the necessary hardware intelligently.

TOOLS TO MANAGE THE COMPUTER

There are many other computer tools, but we don't have room to discuss them all. You do have enough now to get started using your computer creatively. But there is one more family of tools that must be discussed: tools whose only purpose is to manage the computer itself. You will need at least a couple of these to use your computer productively and safely. Fortunately, this is the area where you will find the most shareware and public domain software.

The Utilities You Should Own

SHELLS. The first program that many new computer users encounter is what is known as an operating system shell. In the Macintosh this is designed into the system, and it is the presence of such a shell that makes the Mac appear more humane. But most PCs equipped with DOS will not have such a feature. What a shell does is give you a menu interface into the operating system. Without a shell when you turn your system on, DOS itself greets you by displaying on the screen nothing more than what you see in Figure 11.1.

Figure 11.1: The Infamous DOS Prompt

Needless to say, this doesn't give you much idea of what to do next. With a shell installed you usually get a menu screen that lists the programs you can run and lists operating system features like copying, deleting, and viewing files. Several low-end PC clone computers such as the Tandy 1000 and the Headstart include such a shell with the system. The only problem here is that the free shell may point to the programs that come bundled with these systems, rather than the ones you may want to use. Not only that, but with the Tandy at least, the shell is pretty much welded to the system and eats up memory, so that you can't get rid of it even if you want to.

You can buy shell software as part of general-purpose utility packages, such as the Norton Commander, or PC Tools Deluxe or as separate stand-alone products. Usually they have an installation procedure that prompts you to tell them which programs you want to see on the menus they construct. Shell programs are available as shareware too, such as the very popular Automenu.

You don't have to use one of these to use a computer, and if you take some courses and become familiar with your PC, you may not even need or want one of these. There are other ways of arranging your programs for easy use that you might prefer. But if you are new to computers, having one of these will infinitely simplify your initial experience.

FILE RECOVERY. The next utilities don't sound like much until you need them. These are the file-recovery programs. There are several varieties of these. The simplest form, the "unerase" or "undelete" program, attempts to recover a file you erase accidentally. This may or may not work, depending on whether you have written out other files since doing the accidental erase and how much you wrote. If you catch yourself right after doing the erase, such utilities usually are effective. The chances are very good that you will find yourself carelessly erasing at least one important file in the course of your computer usage.

But unfortunately you often don't realize that you have erased something important until it is too late to recover the file with the first kind of utility. Disk Optimizer, which you can get for under $40, is an example of a second kind of recovery software. It tries to protect you from this kind of thing by doing a "pretend" erase when you ask the operating system to erase a file. Disk Optimizer saves copies of files you erase, which it keeps for some specified period of time before it really erases them for good. This slows things down somewhat, and is a little intrusive, but if it prevents you from losing work, this or something like it, can be a good investment.

Finally, there are utilities that allow you to recover from the biggest mistake of all, accidentally reformatting your disk. When you reformat a disk you effectively erase everything on it. This is sad when you do it to a diskette, but tragic when you do it to your hard disk.

It would seem like a good idea never to format any disks at all, but unfortunately you have to format almost all the diskettes you buy in order to use them! So there is always the potential of getting confused and formatting—and clobbering—your hard disk. I haven't done it myself (yet) but I have seen other people do it. The Norton Utilities, and The Mace Utilities are among the better disk utilities that can restore a disk that was accidentally formatted. If you don't buy such a program now, at least be aware that they exist, in case you do find yourself with an urgent need for one. If you do accidentally format your disk, you will need one of the recovery programs that doesn't require that you run it before the damage occurs, as several do.

These utilities are also useful if you experience hardware problems with your disk because they can often recover files damaged by head crashes. On the Macintosh you will find tools that can recover damaged files included in the MacTools portion of Copy II Mac and the Symantec Utilities.

BROWSE UTILITIES AND EDITORS. One of the most useful of utilities is what is called a browse utility. This is a piece of software that lets you look at a file without being able to change it. One important thing you do with a browse is look at files that contain the instructions on how to use shareware programs. They are also useful for looking through word processing files and other files quickly, since browses are much faster than word processors or editors. Since they don't give you the ability to modify what they read, brouse utilities don't have to do a lot of processing that word processors do. Besides showing you what's in a file a browse utility lets you search a file for some particular word or piece of text. Browses are good for looking at control files too, since, thank goodness, you don't run the risk of accidentally changing something you look at with a browse—which is all too easy to do with an editor or word processor.

There is an excellent public domain browse program available for PC's called LIST, written by Vern Buerg, who asks for a small contribution if you like the program. It's certainly worth it. LIST has a slew of features and lets you selectively print off pieces of a file as well as browse it. It is quite fast.

Editors, as mentioned in our discussion of desktop utilities, are primarily useful to you if you have to fix control files. There is a miserable editor included with DOS, called EDLIN, but you would be best advised to ignore it. Word processors that can edit ASCII files containing no special word processing codes, not just their own word-processing files, can take the place of such an editor, but if you are using a program, like MultiMate, that cannot, you will eventually need to pick one up. There are many decent shareware editors available.

BACKUP SOFTWARE. The utilities we mentioned before are nice to have but having backup software is a necessity. So important is backing up your system that the subject is covered in its own chapter, Chapter 15. Ninety-nine percent of the truly awful tales you will hear about lost data occur because people neglect to set up a file backup system.[5]

Not backing up your system almost guarantees that somewhere along the line you will destroy an important document and not be able to get it back. So, while learning how to use many other computer functions can be deferred to a later time when you are more comfortable with your system, file backup should begin, in rudimentary form at least, the day that you create the first word processor file not named "TEST.DOC."

You can find out more about the software you need for backups in Chapter 15. For now, just remember that *some* backup software must be on your shopping list.

Other Utilities That are Nice to Have

After a while you are going to start accumulating a lot of stuff on your computer. At that point you may find a use for some utilities that can help you find things that are lost. This is particularly true because unlike with manuscripts stored on paper you can't riffle through stuff stored on your computer when you are searching for something whose whereabouts you only dimly remember. Among the programs that come in useful to help you keep track of what you have on your computer are file finders, file comparers, and the text-search utilities discussed on Page 211. A text-search utility is most useful when you know what you wrote but not which file you put it in. The file finder, on the other hand, is useful when you know what a file is named—or part of its name—but not where on your hard disk it can be found. This is useful in troubleshooting, as will be seen in Chapter 14, where you need to make sure you haven't "clobbered" an important file by accident. Some shareware file finders available for the PC are Whereis and Findit. Findswell is a highly recommended file finder for the Macintosh.

A file-compare utility allows you to compare two files to see how their contents differ. These vary in how good they are, but may be able to help you sort out which revision of a work you have stored on a backup diskette.

LAST BUT NOT LEAST. You don't need to buy the following utilities, but you ought to know that they are available. If you have a PC or clone with Hercules-compatible graphics, you will discover that a lot of public domain

---

[5]Only rarely does disaster occur because an adequate backup system exists. The single, but shining, example of this occurring is the case of Oliver North and John Poindexter. Their schemes to subvert the U.S. government were revealed only because they planned their escapades in documents that they erased, not realizing that the system had already been backed up.

computer games require CGA color graphics and won't run on your system. There are programs, including the excellent shareware program HGCIBM, which allow you to run many of these color graphics games on a Hercules type graphics board. However, there will still be several games that won't work, including some of the more interesting commercial games. These will continue to hang up your machine and cause it, perhaps, to emit a piteous squeal. Such utilities also won't let you run games that require the more expensive EGA or VGA color graphics.

Another popular group of utilities is the family of keyboard utilities. These let you redefine the keyboard. With one of these you can use your PC keyboard as a Dvorak keyboard, or you can cause one key to act as if you had typed in a whole bunch of keystrokes. This last facility is called a keyboard **macro**. But much more important, if you have physical limitations that make it hard to type some of the keystroke combinations used in many programs, there are special programs available that let you modify the keyboard to make the most of your physical abilities. For example there are programs that enable you to type one key after another rather than your having to play keyboard chords.

If you have low vision there are also special programs you can get, possibly from agencies that help the visually impaired, which will display extra large characters on your screen or print them on your printer.

Hard-disk utility software is available that optimizes the performance of your hard disk. It does this by rearranging the files on the disk so that they can be read more quickly. This is a fine idea, but I don't recommend it to you at this point in your computer career, simply because these utilities are too powerful and may allow you to mess things up. In the same category are programs that speed up your disk via caching schemes. These can be very useful, but they sometimes run into problems. When they do, the result will be to make your hard disk make such awful noises that you won't want to go near the computer for a week.

If you don't understand what you are doing at a technical level, the benefit of powerful but dangerous utilities is dubious. This is also true of utilities like the Norton Utilities Advanced Edition, which make it possible for you to clobber vital control files you don't even know exist. These utilities are tremendously valuable but only in the hands of a person who knows enough about computers to know how to use them properly.

Another group of utilities, often called context switchers, are programs that allow you to run several programs simultaneously, turning each such program, like your word processor, into a pop-up program, or even providing true multitasking. Desqview is a program that will let you multitask your programs if you have extended memory. Software Carousel turns all your programs into pop-ups. If you have extra memory installed in your system one of these may be useful.

However, if you buy one of these programs for a standard PC with 640K of memory because you hear that the program can use a piece of your hard disk in place of extended memory, you are in for a big disappointment. These utilities can swap programs from memory to a hard disk, but the speed at which a PC XT clone will do this is sluglike, and your computer when running these programs will seem drugged.

12

HOW AND WHERE
TO BUY SOFTWARE

Well now it is public, and you will stand for your privileges we know:
to read, and censure. Do so, but buy it first. That doth best
commend a book the stationer says.

John Heming d. 1630 and Henry Condell d. 1632
Preface to the First Folio of Shakespeare

Buying software is very different from buying hardware. The places where you find good hardware are by no means the best places to buy software nor are the things you have to watch out for the same.

THE ROLE OF SUPPORT

In buying hardware we stressed that the support you received from the seller was of paramount importance. With software the situation is different. You still need support, but you won't necessarily find it in the same places. There are thousands of software products for sale, each with its quirks and eccentricities—such as hardware incompatibilities. It would be unrealistic to expect the service department of any retailer to be able to keep up with the details of all the programs in stock.

Because of this you will end up using the same sources for software help no matter where you buy your program: the manuals and on-line help included with the program, books written about the program, help lines maintained by the company that developed the software, and special-interest groups devoted to the software, both on-line and at a users group.

Nor do you have to worry about the quality of individual units when you buy software the way you do with hardware. Programs are standard. The program you get from the discounter is identical to the one you get from the store in the mall. Also, unlike machines, programs almost never arrive DOA, and if they should arrive on a defective diskette, getting replacement diskettes should not be the big deal that getting a hardware replacement is. After all, replacing the diskettes only costs the manufacturer pennies.

COMMERCIAL SOURCES

What this means is that there is no reason at all why you shouldn't buy software through mail order, as long as you stay away from fly-by-night firms. It also means that if you are trying to decide between two stores you can let yourself be guided by price. But let's spend a little time here considering the dynamics of software pricing.

How Mass-Market Software Is Priced

The list price of popular mass-market software is usually the absolutely most ridiculously high amount that the vendor imagines anyone would ever pay for the product. It is printed on the box so that you will feel that you got a great deal whatever you really pay. The discounts that software vendors give to retailers (including mail-order firms) are traditionally very deep, much deeper in fact than the 40 percent off cover price that publishers give bookstore chains. This is probably so that you can walk away feeling you got a great deal in spite of having paid hundreds and hundreds of dollars for something that you know, and they know, can be copied for free!

You should expect then to get a hefty discount off the product's so-called list price. But when you see ads with extremely low software prices listed you must remember that the retail merchant is not selling software because of an altruistic desire to flood the world with these wonderful products. The software merchant needs to make a profit, some amount of money above the amount the software costs him. With this in mind you can see that there is a reasonable price range for every mass-marketed software product. This is the price around which all the advertised prices should fall and this is what you should expect to pay. A price that is considerably lower may be a loss leader, but it is just as likely, experience has shown, particularly in the mail-order arena, that it is a sign that you are dealing with a scam artist.

Once you determine the "real" price, which you can find by looking through the mail-order ads in the magazines, you can usually feel right about buying the program any place whose price is in the same range.

Why Are Programs So Expensive?

If you can get a book or record for a couple of bucks why is software priced like mink? There are several reasons. One is the very high cost of supporting software. Supporting a software product is a complex undertaking involving fixing the bugs that turn up after it is in the marketplace, answering users' questions, and adding new features that take advantage of the flood of hardware and software advances that occur after the product is originally designed.

While most successful programs start out as the work of a single smart programmer, by the time the product has sold a couple hundred thousand copies, hundreds of people may be required to keep the program up to date in the dizzying world of hardware advances, and hundreds more must provide support to the product's users in the form of answering questions and solving bugs.

Another reason for the high prices characteristic of software is that the market for software is not a mass market and is limited compared to, say, the market for rock and roll CDs. But the real reason that software is so expensive is probably that the main customer for software is the corporate manager to whom the random hundred dollars here or there is no big deal. Because a significant proportion of the larger population can barely read or write and has no information of any kind that needs to be processed by a computer, it is not likely that the "home" market for serious software will ever really mature. And truly low prices emerge only when a product appeals to that wider general market. In software, that market has proved as chimerical as the legendary China market.

Only a few vendors have attempted to take the low road in pricing, with mixed results. At one time, what cheap products were available provided only a limited number of features compared to the high-priced stuff. Then Borland introduced cheap, well-designed, full-featured, computer language compilers several years ago that were every bit as good as more expensive ones and that were wildly successful among impoverished computer students and hackers. Borland followed these up with the introduction of its Sprint word processor which entered the marketplace priced in the same tradition, at a street price close to $100, putting it among the best deals in commercial software.

A few other companies, particularly those producing utilities and simple accounting packages that have a potentially huge market followed suit, introducing software priced under $100.

Unfortunately though, the business volume buyers tend to stick with the high-priced products, and you often get the feeling when reading the computer magazines that reviewers think only a jerk would use any but the more expensive products.

Buying Safely with Mail Order

If you do decide to buy software from a mail-order firm there are a few guidelines that will keep you from grief. People in the mail-order industry, such as Peter Haas, a manager at PC Connection, a Marlow, New Hampshire, mail-order firm, suggest that you charge your purchase on a credit card rather than sending a check, because if you do this you will not end up paying for something that never gets delivered. If the charge for something you never received appears on your card statement, you don't have to pay for it. You just write the card company explaining that you didn't get delivery, and that should be that. Haas claims that the banks tend to side with the customer in these cases and notes that piling up too many such problems will cause a mail-order merchant to be dropped by the banks who administer the cards or cause the fees that the merchant pays to the card companies to go up. All merchants do pay a percentage of the sum charged on a credit card back to the credit-card company for the priviledge of having been the agents of getting you into debt.

Another suggestion from the same source is to order only from companies that have real addresses, not post office boxes or phones. It is all too easy to set up a company that consists of only a mailbox and a WATS line. People have been known to place an ad and hope they could acquire the inventory needed to fill orders after the checks poured in, and have skipped town when it didn't work out. If you are thinking of using a mail-order source now advertising in a magazine, you might see whether they were around a few years ago by checking out the magazine's back issues. But magazines usually let anyone advertise that can meet their rates. Some computer mail-order scams have been advertised widely in the better magazines before going under.

Finally, it is best to ignore advertisements that offer everything at prices significantly lower than what they cost elsewhere. Remember, mail-order merchants are not in business for their health.

Once you subscribe to a computer magazine, you will be flooded with direct-mail offers to purchase software by mail from the vendors. Just be careful that you don't end up taking advantage of one of these offers and paying the list price when you can buy the same product down the street at a hefty discount.

Software Vendors Who Don't Discount

There are some excellent programs, among them the word processor Nota Bene, which are sold by small companies who have succeeded by targeting a particular niche in the market and charging a price that keeps the company going. Where there is a small but clearly defined market for a product you should not expect to get the kind of discount that a more widely marketed product would get. To offer that kind of discount would be a poor business move on the part of the software company. It is the programs that sell in the hundreds of thousands of copies that can be discounted deeply.

If a program you are interested in is not marketed by the mail-order discounters it doesn't necessarily mean that there is anything wrong with it; rather, it just means that there is not enough demand for it to justify the room it would take to list it in the ad, or that the profit the merchant makes selling it isn't enough to cause him to bother with it. In this case you should try ordering the product from the vendor directly, using the address supplied in reviews of the product that appear in the computer magazines.

Turning to Crime

Given the high cost of software and the fact that all it takes to turn one copy of a $450 software product into two copies of a $450 software product is a couple of 59-cent floppies and a PC with a single floppy-disk drive, it is not surprising to discover that there are a lot of unofficial copies of commercial software packages floating around.

Copying software in this manner is illegal. But few people end up doing time in the pen for it.

Software vendors have tried numerous schemes to copy protect their products. Unfortunately, these schemes are usually more trouble for the honest software owner, who occasionally gets locked out of using a program for which he has shelled out his hard-won cash, than for anyone else. Devious hackers see undoing copy protection as a challenge, and foiling copy protection is considered a worthy arena for the display of dubious programming talents. As a result, few products are protected by such schemes anymore.

If you should come into possession of an illegal copy of a commercial program you should be aware that you are committing a crime right up there with duplicating videos. If nothing else, this should cause you to think twice before calling the company's technical support number to complain that some feature of the software doesn't work. The person who legally buys such a program registers his name and address with the vendor along with a serial number from the program's master disk. Few support personnel will have anything to do with anyone who can't provide this registration number when calling for help.

If anyone tries to sell you extremely cheap versions of commercial software that are packaged suspiciously, you should probably pass them up. There are whole factories in the Orient devoted to producing pirated versions of popular software. As we are about to see, there are so many software products available that you can legally copy for free and that are at least as good, or even better, than many commercial packages, that there is no need to stoop to crime in order to fill your software toolbox.

But beyond that, by stealing a program you are denying the people who created it the fruits of their labor. You wouldn't like to see your work plagiarized or published by people who paid you nothing for it, so you shouldn't use someone else's software without paying for it either.

THE SHAREWARE ALTERNATIVE

But you don't need to turn to crime to get your hands on lots and lots of software. The single biggest difference between buying hardware and software, particularly for IBM PCs and clones, is that there is a very viable alternative to using standard marketing channels. When it comes to buying software you are able to take advantage of one of the very few heartening innovations in the wasteland that is twentieth-century marketing: shareware.

Shareware is generally described as "try before you buy" software. The programmers who write shareware are the buskers—the street musicians—of the computer world. Where buskers play their instruments on the street, their guitar cases open in front of them, in the hope that you will toss in a buck as you pass, shareware authors put their programs on bulletin boards in the hope that if you find the programs useful you will send them a check to make your ownership of the program official, a process called **registering** the program.

As a programmer I find it depressing that the authors of what are in many cases brilliant programs have to give them away for free, because of the difficulty of getting into the mainstream distribution channels dominated by a limited number of rich corporations. But as a writer whose lifestyle leaves me very little disposable cash to invest in commercially distributed programs with their inflated price tags, I am deeply and devoutly grateful that shareware exists and that it lets me acquire and try out the programs I need without resorting to crime.

Shareware changes the rules of the buying game, not only because its existence means there is a large pool of almost free software that you can use to get your bearings in the world of computers, but also because it lets you develop your sense of discrimination. You can try out 20 shareware programs, where you might be able to try only one commercial one; this lets you get a feel for the design of the kinds of programs you like to work with as well as what kinds of features are really useful to you.

The Rules of Shareware Use

Shareware authors let you try their offerings for free. But there are a few rules that you must observe when using shareware. Observing these rules means that the shareware route can continue to be a viable way for programmers outside of the corporate rat race to develop and distribute programs that serve as an alternative to the expensive software that the big guys sell. Shareware authors don't have the legal resources that rich corporations do to go after you if you break these rules. But to take advantage of the shareware alternative and ignore these rules puts you somewhere to the south of slime on the great chain of being.

The first rule is that anyone can copy a shareware program freely and *give* an unregistered version to a friend to try (within the United States and Canada). However shareware—unlike public domain software—is copyrighted, and this means that you must respect the stated desires of the owner of the copyright. Notice of copyright and any description of limitations on the distribution of the software should be distributed along with the software, and you must respect these limitations. Usually shareware authors allow third-party distributors to *sell* a shareware diskette but only for a price that doesn't exceed a modest fee, usually $10. This is to allow shareware distributors to make some money with which to cover advertising, packaging, postage, supplies, and the wear and tear on their hardware. But the point of shareware is not to make money for middlemen. All shareware that is sold should clearly indicate the author's name and address and what cash amount should be sent to the author to register the software. Distributing shareware for high profit *is* stealing, as is distributing shareware without providing the author information.

The second rule is that the author of a program doesn't get paid unless you pay him by mailing a check to the address specified somewhere in the files that come with the product. So if you end up using the software as a regular thing you should pay the registration fee. The money you pay a disk distributor does not, emphatically not, get passed on to the author. Therefore, if you find yourself becoming dependent on a product, you should register it. Some products specify a time period during which you can use the product freely. If users support a product by registering it, the programmer who wrote it is more likely to improve it and add more features to it. The most popular shareware products have respectable numbers of registered users and manage to provide both upgrades and support as good or even better than what you get with commercially supported software.

Unfortunately, only a handful of authors get the kind of financial support from their users that lets them extend their programs. One shareware author, whose excellent utilities are found on every bulletin board, reports that it took more than three months for him to receive two registration fees for one of his products. Now he makes about $200 a week in registrations from a whole set of widely used programs, but when you consider that a programmer of his caliber can easily make $1,000 a week or more as an employee of a software development corporation, and that executives in big software companies make millions, shareware authors are hardly cleaning up.

Where Do You Get Shareware?

That's how it works. Now where do you find this wonderful stuff? You can find shareware in a variety of places. Users groups often sell shareware as a fund-raiser at their monthly meetings and by mail. This is an excellent way to get such programs. CompuServe and other commercial on-line services are a good source for shareware too. Private bulletin boards have shareware; however, you are not guaranteed that you are getting the latest version when you get a program from a bulletin board. Unfortunately, too, with smaller bulletin boards there is the chance of picking up programs that have viruses embedded in them, left by unscrupulous troublemakers. This is not a problem with the commerical communications services, which check uploads carefully, or with the better shareware distribution services.

Many of the most interesting shareware programs are big, which makes downloading them from bulletin boards an expensive proposition. An alternative to getting large shareware programs on-line is to order them from one of the larger, ethical, shareware distributors. The Public (Software) Library (PSL) run by shareware author Nelson Ford is one such outfit.[1] These distributors publish newsletters and provide catalogs describing the software. There is a cost to join these groups, which covers the cost of the monthly newsletters, but it is worth paying because of the access they give you to hundreds of the best shareware programs. Ford's PSL newsletter contains notes on bug reports as well as other items of interest to shareware users, and is slowly developing into a magazine. You can find other distributors through advertisements in computer

[1]PSL can be reached at P.O. Box 35705, Houston, TX 77235-5705, and will mail you a free newsletter listing their inventory.

magazines, though to be safe, it is a good idea to check up on them either at a users group, on-line, or by reading about them in articles about shareware that periodically appear in the computer magazines.

Recently shareware has been cropping up in software stores, in fancy boxes with generic-sounding labels. Often these packages are not clearly labeled as shareware and may make it sound as if by paying what is really the shareware diskette fee you are buying the software, which you aren't. If you do buy such a product, you will undoubtedly pay more buying it in the fancy packaging than if you got it elsewhere. And remember, the author still doesn't get paid unless you pay him. The distributors have no responsibility to pay him, and indeed may be distributing the product without the author's permission.

Occasionally a shareware product becomes so successful that it moves into the commercial category when a new version comes on the market. PC-Outline has taken this path. In this case you can still distribute and register the shareware versions of the program but the commercial versions may not be copied and sold.

Shareware Does Get Reviewed

You may not realize it when you read a computer magazine, but shareware products get reviewed side by side with commercial products in places like *PC Magazine* or *MacWorld*. However, it is sometimes hard to tell from the review that the product under discussion is a shareware product. The review will give the registration price. After all, programmers like to make money too, and as a rule don't want their products to remain shareware a minute more than necessary. However, if you see an interesting product with a relatively low price reviewed in a magazine you ought to check a shareware catalog to make sure that the product isn't distributed as shareware.

Getting Shareware Working

Shareware is distributed on diskettes or copied from bulletin boards, so unlike commercial programs, it doesn't come with a printed manual. But this doesn't mean that you don't get instructions on how to use these programs. You do, but it is usually contained in a file that comes on the diskettes that contain the software. Consequently, you may need to understand a little bit more about how to use a computer in order to get shareware up and running. However, after you have used one or two shareware programs and gotten used to the way that they are distributed, you will probably find commercial manuals a pain in the neck, and wish that the commercial programs were simple enough that you could use them without needing to read through what looks like an encyclopedia to get started. You will also find that the quality of shareware manuals is often as good or better than those found with commercial programs, particularly the cheaper commercial ones.

Always copy the files making up a shareware program into their own subdirectory on a hard disk to make it easy to get rid of the whole mess if you don't like the program or if you don't find yourself using it. Putting a piece of shareware software into its own subdirectory also protects you against accidentally wiping out a preexisting file you might have that has the same name as a file that comes with the shareware.

Many shareware programs are distributed in a special compressed format in order to fit more stuff on a single diskette. Files in this compressed format are called archived or **ARCed** files. You can tell if a PC file is ARCed by looking at its file name. An ARCed file has ARC as part of its name. In order to use such a program you need to unARC it, which you do by running an unARC program. If you got the program from a users group or distribution service, the unARC program is often on the distribution disk, along with instructions on how to use it. Otherwise, for PC programs, you can download Wayne Chin and Vern Buerg's shareware ARCE program from a bulletin board, or get a copy from your local users group. Running the unARC program will create a set of files out of the single compressed file that you started out with, so be sure to unARC shareware into its own directory.

Look at the list of files making up your shareware product. There should be a file named READ.ME or README.DOC or something of that nature. Look at it with a browse utility like LIST which is often included on shareware diskettes. This file will tell you what you need to do to get the program working. There will also be a manual which you can either print out, or look at on- line with a browse utility. This manual file usually has a name that has "DOC" (for documentation) or "PRN" (for print file) somewhere in it.

Getting Help When Using Shareware

Most successful shareware programs are easy to use, because a confusing program wouldn't get very far with this kind of distribution system. Explore help screens, read the supplied manual, and relax. You've only spent about $6 or perhaps some phone charges, so it's not the end of the world if you decide you hate it. If you do run into a brick wall with such a program and can't get it working at all, it is possible that you have a hardware incompatibility. For example you might need to have a particular kind of color graphics card installed on your computer. But shareware that you get from a reliable source usually indicates what its hardware requirements are and usually works very well. For most problems you can use the same troubleshooting strategy that we will cover in detail in Chapter 14.

If you run into a problem you can't solve yourself, there are several approaches to getting help. If you have been using the product for a while and love it, then it's probably time to register it and get support from either the author or from the company that currently supports the product.

If you are not ready to register it, there are still some avenues of help. Should you get stuck, feel free to ask questions of SIG leaders at your local user group. If they don't know the program in question they might well know someone else in the group who does.

The CompuServe forums are another excellent place to get advice, although if you are a PC user you will probably need to get one piece of shareware—TAPCIS or the public domain program, Autosig—working correctly to use them efficiently. If you don't want to wear out your welcome with your computer-expert friends, the best thing you could do would be to get one of them to install a program that accesses CompuServe for you and have them hold your hand until you understand how to send and receive messages on-line. You can then stop pestering your computer-expert friend and start posting messages about software problems in forums where experienced users who are familiar with the program can give you answers. The best places to turn for help for using PC software, especially shareware, on CompuServe is the IBMNET set of forums, especially IBMNEW—the new users forum—and the TAPCIS forum. Macintosh users can find Mac shareware and help on CompuServe in the several MAUG forums; however, experienced Macintosh users suggest that there may be more Mac activity on GEnie, a competing communications service.

There are even books available about some of the most popular shareware products, such as the word processor PC-Write and PC- File. Unfortunately though many other potentially useful shareware programs have not attained the kind of market share that makes it worthwhile for publishers to put out books about them.

Shareware and Viruses

Recently a lot of attention has been paid to computer "viruses," and because software from bulletin boards has been associated with the spread of "viruses" many people have become loath to use such programs, thereby making harder the already difficult situation of shareware developers.[2]

---

[2]The situation for these programmers is reminiscent of the situation for violin playing street musicians in the old days when violin cases (at least in the public imagination) were thought to be where gangsters hid their guns: not good for business.

A computer virus is nothing more than a computer program that has been hidden inside some other program by a prankster. Its purpose is to mess up your system. These programs were originally named viruses because some of them wait until a certain date, for example Friday the 13th, before doing their damage, meanwhile copying themselves every time the harmless program is run on a new machine. The term "virus" was applied to these prank programs because the replication they attempt is similar to what a virus does while hanging around in a cell. These so-called viruses are just pieces of computer logic that take advantage of the way your operating system works. There is nothing mysterious about them.

Most viruses are more of a prank than a malicious attempt to damage unknown people's computers. A lot of viruses simply freeze up the machine and display "Gotcha" on the screen, but a few maliciously conceived ones will mess up the directory on your hard disk. Unless you have been religious about taking backups (which you should be) this can mean destroyed data. Recovering from a virus involves identifying the program containing the virus, removing it from the computer, and reloading the operating system from its distribution disk. At worst, you might have to reformat your hard disk and copy your files back from your backup copies.

Unfortunately, in the age of AIDS, the idea of machines getting viruses has been very appealing to the legions of technophobes who never liked computers much anyway and are thrilled by the thought of them getting sick. Enormous amounts of nonsense have appeared in otherwise reasonable newspapers about these viruses, most of it characterized by a complete lack of understanding of what viruses really are and how they affect computers.

In the PC world many of the best-known viruses have been spread by means of illegally copied software passed from corporate user to corporate user. The wide distribution of these viruses shows the extent to which such illegal copying takes place. Many other virus tales fall into the category of urban legends, tales like the one about the lady who dried her poodle in the microwave. They are part of the vast body of stories that everyone thinks happened to the friend of a friend and assumes are true but that no one really can verify. In short, they are neo- folklore.[3]

Because of the amount of publicity about viruses, anyone running a commercial communications service or shareware distribution company is very aware that viruses exist. A competent programmer has

---

[3]The viruses that began "infecting" huge academic and military networks in late 1988 are another story. These virus programs merely exploited the fact that the UNIX operating system that the military and universities favor has some well-known security holes, places where you can bypass all the password checking routines that are supposed to keep strangers out. That the U.S. government insists that this UNIX operating system be used on all its computer projects rather than others which have been proven impervious to invasion has to make you wonder.

several tools at his disposal to inspect a new program and look for such buried subroutines. As a result you are quite safe if you get your shareware from a service like CompuServe or a reputable distribution company. And if weird things do start happening on your computer, don't assume you have a virus—unless you see the "Gotcha" on the screen. It is far more likely that whatever weird thing you are seeing was caused by you yourself, using your software in some way you had not intended.

In short, if you get your software from reputable sources you have little reason to worry about viruses. Besides, the best protection against viruses, as against every other form of computer mishap, is to back up your system, which you should be doing anyway. In the unlikely event that the worst happened and a virus destroyed your hard disk directory and took with it access to all of your files, you should be able to rebuild your entire system by reformatting your hard disk and reloading your backups right back onto that disk. But it is far more likely that you will cause damage to your system yourself by making some sloppy mistake than that a virus will get you.

And finally, in spite of what salesmen at software stores may tell you, don't think that you are more likely to find viruses in shareware than you are in commercial packages. Viruses have turned up in some of the most expensive commercial software packages, introduced somewhere in the manufacturing cycle by disgruntled employees or competitors, though it's not known exactly who. Avoiding shareware and paying full price for everything is not going to improve your chances of avoiding viruses. If you really worry about viruses a lot just pick up a copy of the shareware antivirus program FLUSHOT. It protects your system against programs that attempt to modify a key piece of your operating system, which is how most PC viruses seem to work.

HOW TO GET HELP CHOOSING SOFTWARE

Magazines

The best place to find out about new programs or to read about established ones is in magazines like *PC Magazine, MacUser, Personal Computing,* or *MacWorld.* These magazines routinely review all major new programs and new releases (that is, versions) of programs. They also feature "bake-offs" where all the programs in a single category are described and compared against each other.

Chapter 9 discussed at some length the nitpicking spirit of petty jadedness that tends to overwhelm software reviewers too long in the field and causes them to utter wearied "ho hums" when confronted with yet another terrific and powerful program. As long as you keep in mind that a review shows you as much about the reviewer as it does about the product, you can get a lot from these reviews. They are, in fact, very similar to book reviews. If you read a couple of reviews of the same software package, you will begin to get a feel for its style and function. Just keep in mind that there is not room for any reviewer to describe all the interesting features of a complex program so reviews are slanted toward the needs of the ubiquitous corporate volume buyer.

Your best entry into the magazines is the Magazine Index, an index which is available at many public and academic libraries on microfilm, and, most recently on InfoTrac, a CD-ROM-equipped computer. As of 1988 the on-line Magazine Index began storing abstracts of product reviews from the major computer magazines which makes it even easier to find what you are looking for and may even make it unnecessary to hunt up the volume of the magazine that carries the review.

Users Groups, Yet Again

You are probably tired of hearing about users groups by now, but they are a good place to hear about new programs, not only because you can chat with other users, but because the representatives of software companies routinely come by to give product demonstrations of their latest offerings. Since there is no substitute for seeing a program in action these demo sessions are worth attending.

If your users group publishes a newsletter it probably reviews the "Shareware of the Month" too. Be sure to ask if there is a catalog of all such reviews that you can browse through since this is where you will find the best descriptions of the shareware that is in your users group library.

Trade Shows

If you can stand going into crowded civic centers and battling for a parking space downtown you might try attending a computer show. Vendors set up booths and demos here and have lots of brochures for you to look at. This is probably not the best environment for finding out about new products, but it might be fun to go to one just for the experience.

Shareware Distribution Companies

Shareware distribution companies usually sell disks containing descriptions of their offerings the same way they sell the disks containing the programs. If you join one of these services, it is worth getting the descriptions of the existing library (a **library** is the computer term for a collection of programs). Usually the monthly publications of these groups only have room to briefly mention new offerings, and there may be a hundred or more programs already in the library. The only way you can get the details about these may be to look in the catalog. Remember, too, that shareware does get reviewed and look up shareware programs by name in the Magazine Index to see if you can locate a recent review.

On-line Forums

If you want information beyond what is available in the magazines, you can post a message on a bulletin board or an on-line-forum asking for suggestions for what kind of software to use for a particular task and addressing your query to people with your own interests. For example, if you are deeply involved in raising tropical fish and are looking for a way to store information about your collection, a query on FISHNET, which is the name of a real forum on CompuServe, might bring you news of a program that some other fish fanatic had written and was willing to share, as well as suggestions of how you could use standard products for this specialized task.

My queries about writing tools on CompuServe's LITFORUM, a forum devoted to writing, evoked a heated debate about the worth of spell checkers and the names of several outliners that various writers on the forum claimed were the best.

If you are looking into buying a product from one of the big software companies that maintain their own customer support forums, then browsing through some of the problems that users have sent to customer support might be instructive too, first of all to see how they are handled and second to see if any particular kind of problem seems to dominate the message areas.

THE MOST IMPORTANT QUESTION TO ASK
ABOUT A PIECE OF SOFTWARE

It is important to know what a piece of software does and whether its features appeal to you. You should attempt to answer these questions before you plunk down your money for any software package. But there is one very, very basic thing you need to know about every piece of software you buy, which is even more basic than what functions it provides. That is, *what hardware and software does it require to run!* The best graphics package in the world is useless to you if it requires EGA graphics and you only have monographics. The best word processor in the world is useless if it requires that you have 640K of memory installed and you only have 512K. Most programs list their requirements right on the box and you should make sure that you note them before you buy. If you are buying from a knowledgeable source, such as some of the better mail-order houses, quiz them about the hardware and software requirements of the package you are thinking about buying.

And just because a package can run on your configuration doesn't mean that you will be happy with it. A program that requires CPU speed and memory, such as Microsoft Windows or a program that runs under Microsoft Windows, will run on your old 4.77 Mhz IBM PC, but you may be able to balance your checkbook between the time you hit Enter and the time the next screen displays. A reputable dealer should be able to warn you about programs that are not suited to your setup.

A bare-bones PC XT clone equipped with a hard disk, monochrome graphics, and 640K of memory can run almost all the PC programs around. The Macintosh Plus can run most of what you might need too, particularly if you have installed more than 1 meg of memory. But whatever machine you have, make sure to verify that you haven't picked up one of the few pieces of software that have extreme requirements. Usually the ones most likely to cause you trouble on the PC are programs that require EGA or VGA graphics, programs that required extended or expanded memory, which is memory above the 1 meg DOS limit, graphics mode programs, programs that require a printer able to receive commands in the Postscript document description language, programs that require a mouse, and programs that use megs and megs of hard disk storage.

The other place you might run into trouble is the release of the operating system that you need to have installed on your system to run the program. Most DOS systems that you buy come with DOS release 3.1 or higher, and most programs for DOS machines require only DOS release 2.0 or higher, so in most cases you are fine. But some programs require that you have installed a DOS version with a release number greater than the version you have installed. In this case you will not be able to run the new program until you upgrade your system with a new release of DOS. Nor will you be able to run PC OS/2 programs on a system that doesn't have the OS/2 operating system running on it. Likewise, check what release of the system software a Macintosh program requires and how much memory it requires to run well.

13
USING YOUR SOFTWARE TOOLS

Glendower: I can call spirits from the vasty deep.
Hotspur: Why so can I, or so can any man; But will they come when
*   you do call for them?*

Shakespeare, 1564-1616
Henry IV, Part I

You've brought your new computer home. You've taken it out of the box. The booklet that came with it was obviously written by people who were not native English speakers. You may wonder if they spoke any language at all. Still, using a combination of interpreting the manual and looking at its pictures, you've managed to hook the monitor into the system unit, plug in the keyboard, and locate the on-off switch. You turn the computer on and wait nervously as it goes through its warm-up exercises. The diskette drive hums. The light flashes on your hard drive. The screen comes to life. Your computer is up!

What do you do now?

What you do now is sigh a great sigh of relief, turn off the computer—after you look up how to park your hard disk if it isn't the self-parking kind—and then do something that as a writer you should enjoy tremendously: read.

The task that lies before you is to learn how to work with your new computer software. The first thing you need to do is familiarize yourself with the books and other material provided with your software. Then, fortified with some knowledge, it will be time to explore.

GETTING YOUR BEARINGS WITH THE MANUAL

What the Manual Can Show You

As you begin to read computer magazines and talk to computer users you will begin to notice that everyone seems to assume that *nobody* can make sense out of manuals. The hottest selling computer books today are books that essentially duplicate, at $25 or more, what you get for free in these manuals. Some manuals are awful, but these are the exception, not the rule. Software vendors know that if people can't understand their programs they won't use them, and as a result they spend a lot of money paying professional technical writers to produce usable books.

The reason that most people take such a negative view of manuals is not, then, because the manuals are poorly written—it is because so many people in our video culture find it difficult to read anything! Since as a writer you fall into the tiny segment of the population that actually enjoys using the printed word for the transmission of knowledge you may find the manuals that come with your programs more palatable.

The place to start, of course, will be with your word processor, which, incidentally, is also the most confusing and complicated piece of software you will encounter in your career as a computer user. There is no reason you can't take a look at some of the books devoted to your word processor at the public library. There may be great tips in them and they may show you how to do things that the manual does not make clear. But before you shell out your hard-earned bucks to buy one of these, at least make a good-faith effort to see what useful information you can get from the books that came free with your software.

You are not going to be reading the manuals in order to memorize what is written there about the software. This is what people who hate manuals tend to try to do, and it is utterly unnecessary. Manuals are primarily reference works.

What you will do as you skim these books is learn what is in them, locate the sections in these manuals that describe the different functions, get a broad overview of what your software can do, and look for a tutorial that will walk you, step by step, though the process of using your software for the first time.

If you have already used your word processor at work or in a class it is still worth taking the time to look through the books that come with your software. The chances are very good that whoever taught you how to use the software never mentioned the manual, again owing to the presumption that most people hate to read and are not very good at it. But since you are by definition a word-oriented person, reading the manual is a very good idea. And even if you have experience with the software, the chances are very good that in browsing through the manual you will discover at least one or two useful things that your software can do that you didn't know about—perhaps a lot more.

The manuals that come with your software are usually divided into two sections. One section is intended to introduce you to the software. It should walk you through what the program can do, step by step, with ample illustrations, giving you a sample document to work on as you read through this section.

The second part of the manual, which may be in a separate volume, is usually the reference section. This part of the book is for you to use later, when you are more familiar with the program. It is arranged so you can look up a particular thing you might want to do and find out how to accomplish it.

The Missing Section in Most Manuals

Some manuals include a very brief section listing the error messages that the software might give you, along with an inadequate description of what each message means. But what is almost always missing from these manuals, unfortunately, is a section detailing the common problems that new users run into with the software, and showing how to recover from the common errors that new users make. Even when a troubleshooting section is provided, it usually covers only a fraction of the errors that all new users make.

The lack of such a section is not due to its being impossible to write one. Perhaps the software companies just want to keep the feeling in their manuals (and product) upbeat. As a result, software manuals are like those medical books that never mention death. And even the software books you find in the bookstores aren't much better. Sometimes potential errors are discussed in the course of the text, under the topic they relate to, but this is of little use to you when trying to solve one of these problems. If you remembered the section where you saw the error description you probably wouldn't have made the error.

However, in reading through the manual you may at least subliminally note some of these warnings, and this may be of use to you when you run into a problem later.

GETTING STARTED

Installing the Program

Once you have read through your manual, looking to see what information it provides, you are ready to get started. The first thing you need to do is install your program.

Installing a program is really no big deal. Installing a program just means copying the program itself and the control files it needs from your distribution disk—the one that comes in the package—onto the disk you are going to run it from. If you have a hard disk on your computer, installing the program usually means creating a subdirectory and copying the program and its control files into that subdirectory. If you use a system with only floppy disk drives, installing the program means copying the program onto what is called a **bootable** diskette. A bootable diskette is one that has a piece of the operating system on it so that you can bring up your computer and get to work using only the program diskette, dispensing with a separate operating-system diskette.

You should *never* run your program from the distribution diskette. After you install your program, save it in a safe place in case you clobber the copy you do use, which may be easy to do. Make a copy of each of the distribution diskettes. These are the copies you will use later if you need to restore corrupted control files, a process we will discuss in Chapter 14.[1] The only time you should ever use the distribution diskette is when you install the program and when you create the backup copy. Resist the temptation to use the distribution diskette itself for restoring files, because it is all too easy to get confused and mess it up, which will leave you without a word processor.

Most commercial programs now come with an installation procedure— a program that automatically copies the files the program needs from the distribution disk onto the disk you will be storing it on. This procedure prompts you for the information it needs to install the program properly.

Since the installation procedure is usually automated, it takes on a certain air of mystery, but there is nothing mysterious going on. All that is happening is that the files containing the program(s) and control files are being copied from the distribution disk to the disk you will run them from. Perhaps a few control files are being written on that disk to give the program information about the peculiarities of your own system, for example which kind of printer you have attached or which kind of monitor.

Sometimes, after the program is installed, you will have to go through an additional step of setting up what are called the **defaults,** the settings that you want the program to use all the time unless you explicitly change them. Out of the box, your word processor might automatically assume that you want all documents to have 65 characters per line and print in pica characters, while you want your margins to always be 70 characters wide and your document to print in elite rather than pica type. Many word

---

[1]If you don't know how to make a copy of a file you are not ready to start working with your word processor. Go out immediately and read an introductory book about your operating system and find out what you have to do to make such a copy. And make sure that you sign up for an introductory course too. Otherwise you are unlikely to enjoy using your computer. See Appendix C for a list of some of the other things you should be able to do *before* you buy your own computer system.

processors will have some way that you can enter in these settings once and then not have to change them each time you start a new document.

Most word processors come with a large number of distribution disks and the installation procedure will tell you which one to put in when it is time to copy specific files. If you get confused during the installation procedure and answer a question or two wrong, don't panic. Just end the installation and start it over from the beginning. This is usually all you have to do. If the installation procedure won't let you do this and you are using a hard disk system you will have to get into the subdirectory that the program installed itself into, which you can determine from the manual, and erase all the files in that subdirectory, and *then* begin the installation procedure again.[2]

If at any time your word processor, or any other program for that matter, starts behaving very weirdly there is a good chance that you can fix whatever is wrong merely by reinstalling it, after having backed up your documents, style sheets, and your personal spelling dictionary.

Looking at What You've Installed

Once you have installed your program it is a very good idea to find out which files the installation program has put on your disk and where it has put them.[3] Many manuals list what files you should see in this display and what they contain. Print this list of files and keep it in a safe place, because when you run into trouble, knowing what files are *supposed* to be on your disk is one of the things you will need to know to straighten things out. Notice that each file has a date on it. After you have used your word processor for a little while, you should list its files again and note which files have acquired new dates, showing that they have been modified, and which ones still have the date they came with. This tells you which of the files that make up your word processor get updated when you use the program and which ones are only read. This, too, can be useful information to know when trouble strikes. Often your problems result from corruption of one of these modifiable files.

Looking for Update Information

When you display your list of program files you may see a file with a name like READ.ME. If you do, browse through it. Often what you will find there is information about last-minute changes that have been

---

[2]Being able to go from one directory to another and knowing how to delete files are two more of the basic competence skills that are listed in the list of basic things you should be able to do on a computer before you attempt to own one. This list can be found in Appendix C.

[3]Looking at the lists of what files are on a disk is yet another skill you should have mastered.

included in the software. These usually result from bug fixes that didn't make it into the manual. You will also find corrections to the manual itself. Many of these will be trivial, but some may be very important and being aware of them may save you hours of hair-tearing confusion. So look through this file and copy any important changes into your manual in the appropriate places.

Walking Through the Tutorial

You are finally ready to start using the program. If the manual contains a section that walks you through the process of using the word processor step by step, now is the time to use it. It is likely that the tutorial will assume that you are a secretary. This just reflects the reality of who uses word processors in the business world. It also means that the tutorial is likely to cover in depth things you don't need to know how to do—like lining up decimal points in a table or creating form letters—and that it won't mention things you do need to know, like how to generate a multichapter work with correct page numbers.

But don't despair. Since corporate report writers love to generate painfully long and needlessly complex documents—documents that use all the features you will need to use and then some—the manual probably *will* cover all the topics you need, somewhere, perhaps in a section labeled "for the advanced user." Just ignore the sections on the stuff you know you will never use and keep working through the examples, at least until you can't stand it any longer.

Mastering Cursor Control

One area worth considerable attention in this initial learning phase is the ways of controlling the cursor. The cursor is the little line or block that points to where you are on the screen. Most word processors (and many other programs) have many different ways of moving this cursor. One command will move to the beginning of the next word, one to the previous word, one to the beginning of the current sentence, one to the top of the screen, and yet more to the beginning and end of the current line. Take the time to learn, at a minimum, how to get to the next and previous words and to the beginning and end of the current line. These commands make revising as you write much easier.

Most word processors have a fast way of erasing the current word, line, sentence, and paragraph. Make sure you learn these, as they, too, speed up your writing considerably. Another reason to know these is that because hitting one of them by mistake can cause you to erase something you didn't mean to erase—one of the standard new-user traumas. These cursor control commands may be initially difficult to remember, but after using them for a few days they will become second nature and will infinitely simplify the mechanical task of entering and revising your text.

Customizing Your Word Processor

The last thing you should do before you are ready to begin serious work is to look over the word processor manual to see whether there are features of your word processor that you may need or want to change to suit your own tastes.

Programs vary in the degree to which they allow you to set things up your way, as opposed to their way. The majority of programs allow you to customize the way you want your documents to appear. For example you may be able to set up a default format that points to the typeface you prefer using on your printer, the line spacing you usually use, the margins and tabs you use, and other such information. Some programs allow you to set up several such formats so you might have one for business letters and one for manuscripts.

It is a good idea to set up these format defaults when you start using your word processor and try printing out a few samples to make sure that you like the way the format you set up works.

Other programs allow you to customize more than the documents you are working on. Some may even allow you to customize the way that the program itself works. This kind of program will let you change the way that the various keystroke combinations and function keys cause the program to respond. Before you attempt to change these, you should make a serious effort to use the program the way it came out of the box and to make sure that you are familiar with what the keystrokes were designed to do before you reassign them. This is particularly true if you are not familiar with word processing in general, since you will find that after using the program for awhile you will have a much better idea of which keystrokes are just fine the way they are and which ones in the current setup you don't use. When you do get around to customizing your word processor what you will want to do is assign to the function keys the functions you use a lot, replacing ones you don't use with ones more useful to you in your work.

With any word processor that allows you to do a lot of customizing, you should make sure to back up the word processor control files after you get the system working the way that you like it in case later you mess it up.[4] These files, which are among the modifiable control files we mentioned earlier, are where the word processor stores the changes you made to the way that the word processor works.

With any word processor, remember that if things get out of control and you customize more than you had intended, you can just reinstall the program from the distribution disk to get back to the original system.

---

[4]Chapter 14 discusses how to determine what control files you need.

Most word processors that have spell checkers allow you to add your own words to a special personal dictionary. To build this personal dictionary you just need to spell check your documents as you create them. Any word not in the spell checker's base dictionary will be flagged as misspelled. You then use the spell checker's built-in "add" function to add these words to a personal dictionary. This personal dictionary is a separate file from the standard dictionary that came with your system. Just remember to back up this personal dictionary file from time to time in case it gets messed up, to ensure that you don't have to reenter all your personal words.

Perhaps the most irritating thing that can happen when you use a spell checker with a personal dictionary is that you inadvertently add a word that you commonly misspell to your private dictionary, thus ensuring that it will never again be flagged as wrong. If you know that you have added such a word there is usually a way to remove it. If your manual doesn't tell you how to do this, you might simply be able to edit the user dictionary with your word processor or other editor and delete the offending word. Just make sure that you made a copy of the dictionary file before beginning this procedure in case, as may happen, the editing causes the dictionary to stop working properly. Some word processors provide a special function that lets you look at, add, and delete words in the custom dictionary.

Getting Comfortable

Now it's time to get comfortable with your word processor. If you bought other software or have gotten some shareware to try out, leave it alone for now. You will have enough on your hands just mastering the word processor, and this should be your first order of business. The key to doing this sanely and comfortably is *not* to begin by working on anything truly important. Use the word processor to generate short business letters and to work on manuscript items that are not required by an editor the next day.

Attempting to do important work from day one is asking for trouble. In a week or two you will be able to do important work well with your word processor, but during your first few days and weeks of use you should be experimenting, and trying out different features. This means that you should not be putting most of your energy into thinking about what it is you are trying to say, but rather into using, and thus mastering, the wide range of functions your word processor provides. You should feel free to stop and look at the help screens provided with the system, and should take the time to look up in the manual the details of how to do anything that occurs to you to try as you experiment.

Make sure that you can move a paragraph or a sentence from one place to another. Try replacing one group of letters with another. Try taking a piece of one document and putting it into another one. Experiment with typefaces, such as bold and italic. Find out whether there is some way to count how many words there are in your document. Try changing the margins and seeing how the printout looks. If your word processor lets you create headings and chapter titles that automatically generate a table of contents, try them out and see if you like the way they look enough to use them in your real work. Test out the footnotes that the word processor creates. Do they fit the standards you need to meet?

If your word processor includes an outliner, try it out a few times and see if it is useful to you. In fact, once you have mastered the basics of your word processor you should go through the reference part of your manual and try out anything that looks like it might be of use to you. Even things that sound ridiculous might turn out to serve some purpose later.

Remembering What You Did Right

Always print out a sample of your efforts just to make sure that you did correctly what you were attempting to do. Often things look great on the screen but don't print out properly without further fiddling. If you generated a printout by using a particular setting of something that is not a default setting or by using a special command that you just unearthed from the manual, write down on the printed sample exactly what you used to get the effect you produced and then save it. It is very unlikely you will remember what you did later when you want to repeat the procedure.

Likewise, if you run into trouble trying to use a certain feature and finally figure out what you have to do to get it to work, write down what you did in a special word-processing document that you keep, entitled something like "FIXES." You will appreciate having this when you encounter the same problem late one night when you have a deadline to meet. You can then browse the FIXES file and use a search command to look for the problem and its previous solution.

Keeping It Fun

Stop when it stops being fun! If you start feeling overwhelmed, it's time to do something else. Resist the feeling that you have to master it all right away. You may be able to spend only an hour here or there comfortably with your new system when you first get it. But that's fine! You have alot to assimilate, and it is supposed to take time. Approaching the task with a fresh, relaxed mind and a sense of play rather than a grim determination to fight your way through, is the key to a long-term happy relationship with your system.

If you take the time to exercise the features of the word processor before you attempt to do real work, later you will be able to turn out nice-looking copy that incorporates them. What you will avoid, more importantly, is what most new users do: writing an important work under a deadline using the word processor's fancy features for the first time, only to discover, when printing out the manuscript, that nothing will print out because of some error, somewhere, caused by one of these features—who knows which one.

Using your word processor or, indeed, any new program, is usually hard for some initial period during which you do have to make a very conscious effort to remember what will, eventually, become utterly natural and automatic. If you can convince yourself that in time you will be at ease with it, it is a lot easier to get through the first few days.

Moving On Beyond the Word Processor

The time to begin looking into the rest of the tools in the writer's toolbox is when you are starting to enjoy using your word processor and have gotten past the stage where you have to keep stopping to look things up. You should have also gotten to the point where your fingers remember which keystrokes do what without a lot of intervention from your brain. If you are still trying to remember how to do a delete or how to move a block of text from one place to another you do not need to further complicate things by using another program that may do the same things differently.

Only begin working with a second piece of software when you feel that you have mastered your word processor. The rest of the programs you will use are probably not going to be as complicated to master, but they will require some attention and the same kind of poring over help screens and perhaps a manual. Of course, if they are shareware, you will benefit by having the manual contained in a file in your system, since when you run into a question you can use the "find" feature of the browse to locate quickly the portion of the manual that contains the instructions you are looking for. Once you get comfortable doing this you will wonder why the commercial software developers don't put *their* manuals in electronic, searchable form.

REGISTERING PROGRAMS

Whenever you buy a piece of software be sure to fill out the registration card that comes with the product. These are not the same as the warranty cards you are accustomed to getting with small appliances. Often you will need to have mailed in the registration card in order to get support from the software company's customer service department. You may also need to have sent it in to be eligible to get cheap upgrades to your software when the company comes out with a new and more powerful version of the product.

The registration card associates your name and address with the serial number stamped on the distribution diskette. Until your program is registered, the software vendor has no way of knowing whether you have a legitimate or pirated version of the software.

Upgrades

Periodically, software companies put out new releases of successful software products. These releases generally incorporate a lot of tiny fixes as well as new features that have been on users' wish lists for awhile. If you are a registered owner of an older version of the software you usually can get the upgraded release for less than what it would cost to buy it new. Nevertheless, these new releases will cost money, and if you are still reeling from having spent hundreds of dollars on the original product you may balk at spending even more, no matter what it gets you.

It is often a good idea to upgrade when you can. Usually the upgrade is available at the cheap rate only for a limited time, and it is quite possible that after you become more familiar with the software you will want the additional features (and the fixes). When you receive notification of such an offer find out when the latest date is that you can take advantage of it, and note it on your calendar.

HOW TO TELL WHEN YOU'RE NOT A BEGINNER ANYMORE

Your first weeks and months with the system are a breaking-in period. You will have moments when the whole thing looks like a dreadful mistake. You will have moments of excitement and pride. Somewhere along the way it will start making sense to you and you will begin to enjoy what you are doing. You can tell you have ended your apprenticeship when you start looking through computer magazines and lusting for products you see described in them because you understand what it is that they do and how they could make your system even more powerful. When this lust for more tools becomes stronger than your fear of what you will have to go through to get them working, you know you are a computer regular!

On the way to this point you will encounter crises. In fact, until you encounter—and solve—crises, you aren't done with the training period. Part of being an experienced user is getting the confidence that there is nothing that can come up on your system that you can't deal with or find help for.

Take your time, keep it fun, and remember that the breaking-in period does come to an end. Then your only problem will be talking yourself out of buying all the hardware and software that could make your system so much better!

14

WHEN THINGS GO WRONG

"And what is hell? Can you tell me that?"
"A pit full of fire."
"What must you do to avoid it?"
I deliberated a moment; my answer, when it did come, was objectionable: "I must keep in good health, and not die."

Charlotte Bronte, 1816-1854
Jane Eyre

It never fails. You are typing away at your latest work, you have gotten to the point where you have stopped thinking constantly about THE COMPUTER, you are even, almost, starting to enjoy working with your word processor, when out of the blue something awful appears on the screen. It may be just an error message. Your software may politely inform you—in English—that something is not quite right. Or it may not. The screen may just fill up with garbage or your computer may freeze and reply to anything you type with ear-splitting squeals.

Something has gone wrong.

This is the moment of truth. You may deal with it by turning the whole thing off and walking away. This is not cowardice, by the way, but a proven strategy that will solve the vast majority of such problems! When you get the courage to come back to the machine later everything may work just fine.

But the problem you encounter may not go away. More work may be required to fix what has gone wrong. If you are to be comfortable committing your work to the tender mercies of a computer, you are going to have to learn something about computer troubleshooting.

This is not going to be painless. People who have worked with computers for years can still get a sick feeling in the pit of the stomach when their computer manifests some new and terrifying symptom. The only difference is that the more practiced user has enough experience to know that no matter how dreadful the computer looks or sounds, what ails it is probably something that they can easily remedy—as can you.

But you have to be prepared for a certain amount of tooth clenching.

It helps a little if you understand why computer malfunctions feel so scary. A large part of the problem is that things rarely go wrong with most of the machines you are familiar with. But with these other familiar machines when something *does* break down dramatically you may find yourself in real physical danger. If your car stops dead and refuses to budge, the result can be a five-car pileup. If your toaster makes a horrible sound you may discover that the kitchen is on fire. Computers are different. Computers constantly break down—or rather, their software does—but unlike other machines, when computers break down it's rarely anything serious.

Computers are different from other machines because they are animated by software. Whereas even a machine as complex as an automobile follows a very simple plan, computers are much more complex. They respond to complex software, built out of human logic, which frequently runs into trouble. When the logic embodied in a piece of software fails, the result is usually dramatic behavior on the part of computer hardware. But what is broken is not the computer itself, but only the programming logic animating it.

If you can realize that it is human logic that is failing in 95 percent of all computer problems—not the machine—you will in time be able to thoroughly enjoy using your computer. If you cannot come to terms with this, you will not.

To understand just how frail is the human ability to think logically, you should try programming. Programming is an ideal pursuit for monks as it furnishes endless opportunities to humiliate the intellect. While programmers may be portrayed in the media as brilliant and all-powerful dominators of the machine, in real life most programmers develop a deep respect for the limits of their own intelligence and a deep appreciation for the fact that they cannot possibly think out in advance all the combinations of behavior that their software encounters in real life. Good programmers know that their best programs will have bugs, and they do what they can to try to find them before their programs' users do. But good software development companies know that some problems will still slip through, which is why they pour money into providing customer support.

No matter how good a program's designers are, the statistical probability is about 100 percent that some things are going to slip through the program's test phase and be revealed only when you and hundreds of other software users demonstrate your own ineffable individuality by using the software in some manner not envisioned by its designers.

In short, bugs, glitches, and even system crashes are part of the territory.

But by mastering a few essentially simple techniques you can learn to deal with most of these problems unaided. The goal of this chapter is to show you how to approach troubleshooting.

DEVELOPING A TROUBLESHOOTING MENTALITY

The very first thing you must do when confronted by a problem on your computer is assure yourself that you probably did not break the machine. This is easy to say but hard to do. You may have to print "I Did Not Break the Machine" on a piece of paper you keep taped to your monitor the first few weeks that you use your system because it is almost guaranteed that every time something does happen you will assume that you did break it.

The second thing you must do is remind yourself that most of the problems you encounter are not caused by bugs in the program you are using. Most problems are caused by your misunderstanding what the program does and how to use it. This is called "user error" and hilarious stories of such mistakes lighten the otherwise heavy load of those who make their careers in customer support.[1]

Finally, when you encounter situations where work seems to have disappeared—usually some vital piece you need immediately—you must remind yourself that the chances are that it really is still there and that the problem, again, is your own ignorance.

There are a few situations in which your hardware or software really may be broken, and this chapter will show you how to identify these situations and get help for them. But if you work, as good programmers do, from the assumption that the problem is probably something you did, and follow the steps presented in the next few sections, you will be able to handle most of the bone chillers that your system dishes out and eventually get to the point where you can calmly, routinely deal with and solve the vast majority of all computer problems that can occur.

Although the following discussion is about problems you may encounter using your word processor (since that is the first program you will use) the troubleshooting strategies illustrated here work the same for any other program you may use.

---

[1]Consider, for example, the user who, when told to get a "clean diskette" washed one in the sink.

THE TROUBLESHOOTING COOKBOOK

The following sections show you what to do when you have scary-looking problems. The solution almost always is to pursue a cut-and-dried strategy. The strategy works because there are a few prevailing causes for most problems that new computer users encounter, particularly those problems that result in new users' making terrified phone calls to customer support or computer-using friends. This troubleshooting strategy is summarized in figure 14.1. Detailed discussion of the

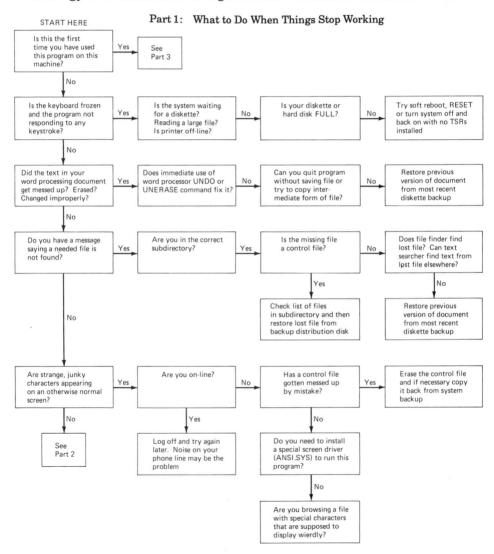

Figure 14.1: Troubleshooting Cookbook.

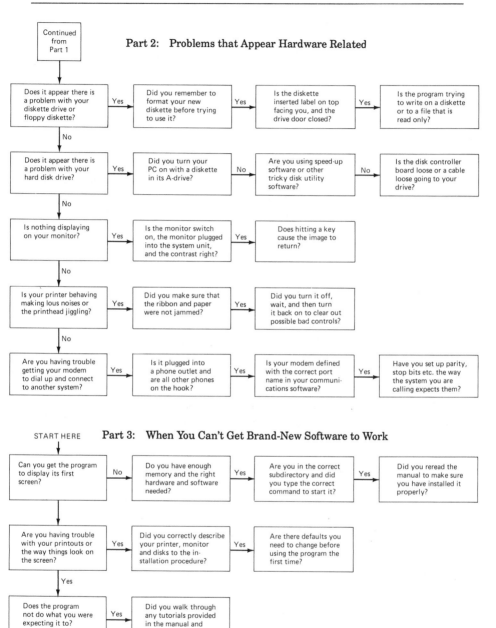

Continued from Part 1

Part 2: Problems that Appear Hardware Related

| Does it appear there is a problem with your diskette drive or floppy diskette? | → Yes → | Did you remember to format your new diskette before trying to use it? | → Yes → | Is the diskette inserted label on top facing you, and the drive door closed? | → Yes → | Is the program trying to write on a diskette or to a file that is read only? |

↓ No

| Does it appear there is a problem with your hard disk drive? | → Yes → | Did you turn your PC on with a diskette in its A-drive? | → No → | Are you using speed-up software or other tricky disk utility software? | → No → | Is the disk controller board loose or a cable loose going to your drive? |

↓ No

| Is nothing displaying on your monitor? | → Yes → | Is the monitor switch on, the monitor plugged into the system unit, and the contrast right? | → Yes → | Does hitting a key cause the image to return? |

↓ No

| Is your printer behaving making lous noises or the printhead jiggling? | → Yes → | Did you make sure that the ribbon and paper were not jammed? | → Yes → | Did you turn it off, wait, and then turn it back on to clear out possible bad controls? |

↓ No

| Are you having trouble getting your modem to dial up and connect to another system? | → Yes → | Is it plugged into a phone outlet and are all other phones on the hook? | → Yes → | Is your modem defined with the correct port name in your communications software? | → Yes → | Have you set up parity, stop bits etc. the way the system you are calling expects them? |

START HERE

Part 3: When You Can't Get Brand-New Software to Work

| Can you get the program to display its first screen? | → No → | Do you have enough memory and the right hardware and software needed? | → Yes → | Are you in the correct subdirectory and did you type the correct command to start it? | → Yes → | Did you reread the manual to make sure you have installed it properly? |

↓

| Are you having trouble with your printouts or the way things look on the screen? | → Yes → | Did you correctly describe your printer, monitor and disks to the installation procedure? | → Yes → | Are there defaults you need to change before using the program the first time? |

↓ Yes

| Does the program not do what you were expecting it to? | → Yes → | Did you walk through any tutorials provided in the manual and reread topics? |

Figure 14.1: Troubleshooting Cookbook (*cont'd.*)

topics illustrated follows below. Read this section now, when you are not facing a real emergency, and use it as a reference later when you might be.

WHEN A PROGRAM THAT USED TO WORK
STOPS WORKING

By far the most common problem you are likely to encounter is getting stuck somewhere with your computer refusing to do anything at all. If you are working with a piece of software that you have used successfully even once, the chances are that the problem is not a major one. If the problem occurs when you are using a program for the first time, look at the discussion about new programs that won't work, on page 267.

Sometimes the reason that your computer seems to have frozen up is that it is waiting for something to occur. If you are working on a long document and ask your word processor to look for a word that it turns out isn't in the document anywhere, the system will freeze up while the word processor examines everything in the file. In this case you just need to wait a bit longer until it is done. You may also have to wait for a very long time if you ask your word processor to load in a very, very long document, for example a formatted version of a 400-page book.

It is a very good idea to make sure your system is really hung before taking radical action, since such action can result in your losing the work you have done in your current work session, or even worse, can destroy important files. Make sure that the diskette and hard drive lights are not flashing, a sign that the program is reading or writing something, and give the program a few minutes to see if it will come back to you with an explanatory message before assuming that it is really hung up.

Sometimes the problem is that your program is waiting for a response from an attached piece of equipment you have inadvertently turned off. This might happen if you are trying to print a document but haven't turned the printer on or if your program is attempting to read a diskette in a diskette drive when no diskette is in that drive.

In these situations the computer will often sit doing nothing—hung—for a few minutes until it finally issues some kind of error message. The message, which is trying to say—"turn on the machine, dummy!"—is often confusing and obscure.

Waiting for a Diskette

A program will not be able to read a file that is on a diskette unless you have put a diskette in the drive and put the switch or lever on the drive in the closed position. And just because you personally don't want to read anything on a diskette doesn't mean that the program doesn't! If you see the read light on your diskette drive come on when the system is hanging (after the system has booted up) your system expects something to be in that drive and the best solution is often just to put any formatted diskette into the drive.

Waiting for the Printer

If you are trying to print and nothing is happening, make sure your printer is not only turned on, but has the on-line light lit. When you take the printer off-line so that you can eject a page, the computer is not able to send printed output to the printer until you switch it back on-line. If your computer is turned on and the printer refuses to come on-line, make sure that the cable that attaches the printer to the computer is firmly seated in the plug receptacles on the back of the computer and the printer itself. If the cable is all right, try turning the printer off for a minute and then turning it back on. This can reset the printer if its internal program has gotten bollixed up, as occasionally happens.

Bad Logic

If the system is really hung, and there doesn't appear to be a hardware wait going on, then you have probably run into some flukey logic, either in the software or in the way that the software interrelates with other software, including the operating system and resident programs. Most of the time all you need to do is what is called a **soft reboot.** A soft reboot is very much like what you do when you turn the computer on, in that a soft reboot sets everything in memory back to where it is when the machine is started up. However, a soft reboot doesn't perform the memory-testing routines that occur when you turn the machine on. With the soft reboot you don't turn the power on and off either. Turning the power on and off can be hard on your hardware since it can expose it to fluctuating power levels and should be avoided where possible. On an IBM PC running DOS you accomplish a soft reboot by pressing and holding down simultaneously, in a "chord," the Alt, Ctrl, and Del keys.

The soft reboot doesn't always fix logic-caused system crashes. If it doesn't, your next line of approach is to press the "reset" button on your computer if it has one. This will cause your computer to do exactly what it would do if you turned it off and then on but it avoids the dangers of turning the power on and off and thus slowing and speeding up the disk drive. If your system doesn't have a reset switch, turn the system off, wait two minutes for everything to slow down and come to a halt, and then turn the system back on.

Once the system comes back up you can try going back to the program that you were using when the system hung. Most of the time everything will work just fine. If your word processor does its work in memory and doesn't do automatic file saves for backup, you will probably have lost the work that you did between the time that you did the last "save" of the file you were working on and the time the system hung.

If your word processor does have an automatic save you will lose only a few minutes of work.

If, when you attempt to bring the system back up, you are greeted by an error message from the word processor, follow the procedure described in the section "When Your Program Tells You Something Is Wrong" later in this chapter.

Often when the system freezes up like this and you bring it back up, everything is fine—except perhaps that you have lost hours of work—and you never again have the system hang in the same way. However, if the system freezes up every time you do some particular sequence of things, you may have encountered a bona fide bug. Note the sequence that causes the problem and refer it to the software's customer support staff as described in the discussion on customer support on page 279. You might jot it down in your "FIXES" file where you describe problems and solutions. Some of these bugs result from trying to use more than one program at the same time, whether the culprit is a resident program or another program you invoked from inside your word processor.

When Your Document Gets Screwed Up

Sometimes, when you are working away, your system doesn't freeze but you suddenly find yourself in a disaster situation all the same, because the document you were working on has gotten messed up. Even though the computer is still working, the thing you are working on has been effectively destroyed. You may swear up and down that the word processor just went and zapped what you were working on, but the chances are slim that this is really what happened. What probably occurred was that you inadvertently hit some random keys, probably without noticing it, and activated some advanced feature of your software.

All is not lost. In many programs there is an "undo" feature that will return your document to the state it was in before it got messed up. Read up on this now, before you run into a problem, to see if your software does have such a feature (or features). If such a feature exists, immediately undo what you just did and see if the problem is fixed. Many programs allow you to "undelete" erased lines. If what you did was delete to the end of the file, when you were on page 2 of a 50-page file—which is often easily done with just a few keystrokes—the undelete may have to be done immediately, before you do anything that would cause the stuff you just deleted to be replaced with something else. In some software the undelete works only for the last thing you deleted.

If your software doesn't have an undo or undelete, all still may not be lost, depending on how your word processor is designed. If you didn't make any major changes in the document in this work session, just exit out of your word processor but **don't save the file** when you exit. If you don't save the file after you mess it up, most word processors will leave you with the version of the file you had *before* you started working on it this session.[2] Some word processors automatically save your file when you print or format it. So if you didn't discover that your file was messed up until after you did one of these operations you won't be able to get the old version back even if you don't save it when you exit.

If your software does automatic saves or lets you save your file while you are working on it, you may be able to recover this intermediate form of the file after a major screw up. Read your manual to see if it includes a section on using such "save" files.

Here is an example, using a document named CHAPTER1.DOC, of how you might be able to restore such a file from a saved version. Let's say that the program automatically saves the file to a file named CHAP-TER1.BAK. If you mess up the version of the file you have been working on don't exit and don't save the file. Instead, if your word processor allows it, go to a screen where you can manage files.

Look for the backup version of the document which should be in the subdirectory you are working in. If you find it, compare the time and date on the backup with the time and date of the file that bears the full name of the document. If the backup is more recent than the document file it *may* be the version of the file you want to restore. Browse it if you can, to make sure. Then, if it is the version you think you want, rename the backup version "CHAPTER1.XXX," to keep it from being automatically erased—which may occur when you exit the word processor—and then go back to your word processor and quit without saving the document.

Now all you have to do is rename the old, unedited version of the document file from "CHAPTER1.DOC" to "CHAPTER1.YYY." Don't erase it in case you run into trouble with the backup file you are trying to use. Now rename the backup version from "CHAPTER1.XXX" back to the name that the word processor uses for documents: "CHAPTER1.DOC." Start your word processor back up and see what you get now when you try to edit the document.

If what you have is what you want to work on, you can delete the CHAPTER1.YYY version of the document—after you have made a backup on diskette of the new version.

If your document really is a dead loss—when the bad version has been saved and has replaced the good version—what do you do? Well, if you have absorbed anything from this book you will have a backup version of the document on a diskette, which you will have created using the backup procedures we described in Chapter 15. You will copy this to your word-processing subdirectory and try again.

---

[2]Unfortunately this is not true of word processors like MultiMate, which save individual pages each time you move on to a new page.

WHEN YOUR PROGRAM TELLS YOU SOMETHING IS WRONG

Often trouble begins with a simple-looking communication from your word processor or some other program. In the middle of an otherwise ordinary editing session, or perhaps when you attempt to start the program, a message politely informs you that the program can't find something it needs and the program refuses to proceed. The something it can't find is usually a file. What you do next depends on what file it is that the program is telling you it can't find.

Clobbered Control Files

If the missing file is not anything that you have ever heard of, in other words is not one of the document files you yourself have created with the word processor, the chances are very good that what the program is looking for is one of its own control files. If your system has recently crashed and had to be rebooted, it is quite possible that the lost file got destroyed or rendered unreadable at the time the system crashed. If this is what happened, you need to reload a new copy of the control file from the disk that holds the backup version of your software.

Before doing this make sure that you are positioned in the word processor's subdirectory and list the files in that subdirectory. Recall that Chapter 13 advised you to print off a copy of this list of files. If you are in the correct subdirectory but can't find the missing file and if your old, saved list of control files shows that it used to be in that subdirectory, you can be pretty sure that a clobbered file is the problem.

You may discover, when you list the subdirectory looking for the file that the word processor couldn't find, that you are not pointing to the subdirectory that you should be pointing to when the word processor runs. If that is the case you must change directories to get to the usual subdirectory. It is very possible that the file you are looking for will show up when you are in the right subdirectory and that your problem was caused by trying to run the program while in the wrong one. In this case all you have to do to fix things is to run your program again from the correct subdirectory.

If a missing control file is the problem, you will need to pick up a new copy from a backup copy. You can find the file's full name either from the message, the control file list in your manual, or from looking at your saved directory listings. To find a replacement copy of the file, look through the directory lists of your backup diskettes until you locate a copy, or, if you didn't back up the control file, look through the directories of your copies of the software distribution disks until you locate the correct file. Then copy it into the subdirectory that holds the rest of the program's control files.

Even if you do find the control file listed in the correct subdirectory you might want to replace it with the backup version because it might have gotten damaged when your system crashed. Just erase it and copy over the backup version.

When you retry your program, you should find that it works again; however, you may find that your program has reverted back to using its original default values for whatever it was that the file controlled. This may or may not be evident depending on whether you ever changed the default values. If your margins in new documents change or if your printer setup isn't right, just go back and use the appropriate functions provided by the software to set up your own values for these.[3]

Lost Documents

If the system is telling you that it can't find one of the document files you yourself created, your approach should be different. First, make sure that you typed in the name of the file correctly. Enormous amounts of panic are caused by people assuming that their files have been destroyed when in fact they have simply mistyped the file name. Remember that the computer does a byte-by-byte compare. If you type a single letter of the name wrong, the computer will not be able to find your file.

If after typing the name correctly your file is still reported missing, you need to make sure that you were looking in the right place for it. Make sure that you are pointing to the correct drive and subdirectory. If you still can't find it, it is worth looking for it in all the other subdirectories on your system on the assumption that you might have been pointing to another subdirectory the last time you saved the file. You use a file finder utility to do this. On a PC the public domain progam WHEREIS works well, as does Norm Patriquin's shareware PSearch. Or you can use one of the file finders that come with commercial utility packages.

If you have a text search utility such as FGREP or GOfer you might try searching your files for the contents of your lost document, looking for a unique word or phrase that occurs in the file you are looking for. Perhaps

---

[3]If you are using a PC and want to get fancy and confirm that you did clobber the file there is one further step you can take. You can run a simple diagnostic program that is included in your operating system whose job is, among other things, to look for clobbered files. This is the DOS command, CHKDSK. You run it by typing CHKDSK at the DOS prompt. Running this program will show you if there are any "file fragments" lying around your disk. If there are, you can turn these fragments into a file by typing CHKDSK /F at the DOS prompt. When CHKDSK completes, there will be a file in the root directory named FILE0000.CHK containing whatever was in the file fragments that the routine found—probably your control file. You can delete this file. Don't worry if CHKDSK turns up more than one such file fragment. Sometimes you will get these when no data has been lost.

you renamed it something entirely different from what you remembered, or you combined it with another file, perhaps by accident.

If this doesn't find your file, you may have to face the fact that your document is gone. You have several choices at this point. If you (or your program) erased the file completely you may be able to recover the file if you have an unerase utility such as those we discussed on page 223 in Chapter 11. The most important thing to remember here is not to do any computer operation that will write to a file before you run the file recovery program. This is because the unerase can work only if the system hasn't already reused the space used by the erased file. Any new file writes are likely to reuse it. Therefore you should run your unerase program the minute you think that a file may have been erased accidentally.

Your software may have some recovery routines of its own. If it does, give them a try too. Otherwise, all you have left is whatever you saved on diskette as a backup. Is the word "Backup" starting to stand out to you? Good. It's supposed to. If you remember nothing else from reading this book, you should remember that files *do* get clobbered in the ordinary course of computer use, and that you must back up every new version of every document you ever work on.[4]

Nice Screens Full of Junk

Sometimes your document seems to be fine, but when you go to perform some function with your word processor it displays a screen that looks like the normal screen you usually see, except that where you expect to see information on that screen, you see what looks like alphabet soup. For example, if your word processor builds a print queue—a list of files waiting to print—you might be told that you can't print a document because the print queue is full, even though you haven't got any other documents printing. When you look at the screen that lists the documents in the queue, the screen is filled with junk.

What has happened here is that the screen displays what it finds in a control file—supposedly the list of files. Unfortunately, that file has been overwritten with garbage. So that is what the screen obediently displays. Often this occurs as a result of conflicts between two programs both of which use the same area of memory. This kind of thing is particularly likely happen when you use resident programs. You will still see the control file listed in the directory list—because it is still there—but if you

---

[4]If you are on a PC, you can try running CHKDSK to recover fragments of a document file if it was destroyed in a system crash, and the pieces are still lying around, as described in footnote 3. You can rename the recovered fragments and edit them but they probably won't contain all of what the file contained. Using good backup procedures is a much better idea!

look at it with a browse program you will see that it contains the same junk that you see on the messed-up screen display.

Here, to solve the problem, you must erase the messed-up control file and try the program again. If the program then tells you it can't find the file you just deleted, load a new copy of the control file from the backup copy of your distribution disk. The program may not need you to restore any control files however. There are many control files that your program builds and uses which do not need to be restored if you erase them. These are files, like a print queue list, that the program can build itself from scratch if it doesn't find one in the subdirectory. This kind of control file is different from the kind of control file that must be replaced, one that contains information that the program cannot rebuild on its own from defaults if it gets destroyed.

Disk Full

One thing you should always be aware of is how much room is left on the disk or diskette you are working on. Unfortunately some, although by no means all, word processors cannot deal with the situation that arises when the document you are working on in memory gets bigger than the amount of space left on your disk. Should you add the fatal sentence to a manuscript that pushes it over the size limit of what your current disk can hold, the word processor may hang and in the process destroy the latest version of your document. The possibility of this occurring is low if you are working on files stored on your hard disk, but if you are working on a diskette file it is all too easy for this to happen, and the chances are very good that it will occur just as you finish the final keystrokes of an assignment that is due the next morning.

You can avoid this problem on a hard disk system by making it a point never to make changes to the diskette version of a document but only to a version stored on your hard disk. Keep your hard disk from overflowing by occasionally printing out a list all the files in all the directories and erasing those that you determine are junk.

On a system that has only floppy drives, you will have to remember to monitor the amount of space left on your current diskette. Save your work frequently, and copy a large document file to an empty diskette before beginning work on it so that you don't run into space troubles.

IF YOU CAN'T GET A BRAND-NEW PROGRAM
TO WORK

Up until now we've been talking about problems that arise with programs that have been working fine and then stop working. But what about the brand-new program that you can't get to work at all?

There is nothing more profoundly depressing than spending a lot of money on a software package, breaking the shrink-wrap, reading the manuals, installing the program, typing the command that brings it up and then having your computer shriek, moan, or just sit there stone silent and dead. It is just as depressing to get the program up and apparently working only to have it refuse to print, come up missing some menu you expected to see, or otherwise behave in a manner very different from what the manual says it should do.

This doesn't happen a lot, but it happens. And again, there is usually some solution to your problem short of calling up the place that sold you the software and having a tantrum. What do you do?

The first thing you should do, of course, is reread the software manual's section on installing the program to make sure that you really did what you are supposed to do to install the program. You may have neglected some screen you need to fill out after the program is installed, or you might need to run some special setup routine the first time you run the program. The next thing you should do is list the files on your copy of the software's distribution disks, looking for READ.ME-type files containing some vital piece of information that didn't make it into the manual.

If you can't get to the first screen of the program at all, you may have a hardware or software incompatibility which you didn't realize when you bought the program. This is not very likely with the big popular mainstream word processors but might happen with other software. If your program requires CGA or VGA graphics and you have only a Hercules-compatible graphics board, then running the program will result in a hung system. However, if you look through the manual you may discover that there is a different command used to run the program on a system with a Hercules-compatible graphics board and that you can run the program just fine if you type in the correct invoking command.

If you have a PC clone you may very occasionally have trouble with programs that are supposed to work with PC compatibles. If the clone you have is one of the popular ones, such as Leading Edge, or Epson, the sheer number of other users of that machine in the marketplace means that there is probably a fix for the problem. Get in touch with the customer support department at the software company and find out what they can tell you. CompuServe is another excellent place to go looking for such a fix. If the software is from a company that supports a forum on CompuServe (which includes many shareware programs) you can go to that forum and leave a message asking about your problem. If it isn't, you can go to the forum for your hardware, such as IBMNET or MAUG, the IBM and Mac forums, and ask for help, specifying the brand and model number of your computer as well as any hardware you have had added.

Usually, the problems you have getting a program running the first time come not from hardware incompatibility but from your having neglected to read the manual and perform some necessary setup step in your haste to get the software up and working. Many programs install automatically but still require you to fill in some screens before you can get to work. This should be documented in the manual, so go back and read through your books again and make sure that you performed all the necessary installation steps.

A common reason for not being able to run a program the first time after installing it is that the program installed itself in a new subdirectory and you are attempting to start the program without having changed your current directory so that you point to the new directory. This should be covered in your manual, but all you need do is point to the new directory and then attempt to start the program again.[5]

Another reason a program won't run is that you have too many resident programs and there isn't enough memory left for your program to load into memory. Some programs can tell you when they encounter this problem, others just hang. Follow the procedure described in the section labeled "Removing TSRs" on page 275.

If your documents do not print out correctly when you start using a new piece of software, you probably haven't installed the necessary printer driver. The printer driver describes what control characters your particular printer needs to receive to do particular printer functions, so that the word processor can translate its codes into the correct printer control characters for your particular printer. Read the section in your manual that covers installation and double-check that you filled in any necessary screens that describe the printer you will be using.

PROBLEMS THAT LOOK LIKE YOUR HARDWARE IS BROKEN WHEN IT ISN'T

The most terrifying problems you are likely to encounter are those that make it look as if your hardware is broken. These are the situations where your hard disk clatters or whines shrilly, or where your printer acts like it has St. Vitus' dance, where your modem goes incommunicado, or your cursor streaks across the screen and won't stop.

These errors are frightening because you immediately picture huge repair bills and long waits for your machine to come back from the repair shop. Fortunately, again, real hardware problems are rare, and most of the things that cause your hardware to misbehave are actually software

---

[5]Your manual should show you how to avoid the need for this by adding the new directory to your path in your start- up procedure.

problems. Let's look at the various ways your hardware can frighten you and how you can fix, or avoid, these problems.

Fatal Diskette Error?

Nothing generates messages quite as horrible as a PC floppy disk that needs to have something trivial adjusted. If you get a message claiming "FATAL DISKETTE ERROR" or something equally terrifying, the chances are that one of a small number of easily remedied problems has arisen.

Remember that every floppy disk you use must be formatted before you use it. If you attempt to read or write to a diskette that has not first been formatted, your software will give you a message suggesting that your diskette drive is broken. It isn't. You just need to format the diskette using either an operating system command or, if it is provided, the equivalent function within your word processor.

Another very common reason that your machine will report something wrong with your diskette *drive* is that you have inserted the *diskette* sideways or backwards. A 5 1/4-inch floppy diskette can be read only when it is inserted with the label face up and with the labeled edge pointing toward the computer user. If you insert it any other way the drive light will come on and the diskette drive will whir, but eventually you will get a message that seems to be saying that the drive isn't working.

Don't forget, too, that your diskette drive can't read what is on the diskette unless you have closed the drive door. You do this either by pressing down the lever on the front of the diskette drive, or perhaps by pushing in a button. Doing this engages the diskette so the drive can read it.

Another thing that may cause your software to shudder in horror and refuse to go on is if you have either a whole diskette or a single file that has been marked "READ ONLY." If a file or diskette is marked this way, the system will permit software to read it but not to edit or otherwise alter it. If your word processor encounters such a file it may be at a loss as to what to do.

There are two ways to make something read-only. You can make a whole diskette read-only if you put a write-protect tab over the notch on a floppy diskette. The write-protect tab is nothing more than a little piece of paper. This mechanically prevents the disk drive from writing to the diskette. You can make a single file read-only by changing a bit in the directory entry for the file that marks it—in the directory—as a read-only file. Various utility programs let you do this, and if you have been experimenting with one of these you might have done it by accident.

In either case, attempting to read a file that is thus protected can confuse your software and cause it to tell you that your diskette drive is broken. This may occur even if when the write-protected file is on your hard disk! This happens because many older word processors contain, deep in their innards, routines from long ago that were written before you could write-protect a file on your hard disk. These routines assume a write-protected file is on a diskette and thus give you a diskette error message when they encounter one. In either case you must unprotect the file to prevent the error message. Take off the write-protect tab, if that is the problem, or use an operating-system command if the directory bit has been set. In DOS, the command is "ATTRIB."

Boot Failure

If you have a hard disk system, you may bring your computer up one morning only to be greeted with an error message that tells you that the system can't find the boot disk or that there is a disk error.

Don't panic! Your boot disk is your hard disk, but many hard disk-equipped systems are not very bright when they power up and always look for a boot disk in the diskette drive before looking for the information they need on the hard disk. All the message means is that you left a floppy diskette in your disk drive and the system is trying to boot off it, which won't work. Remove the diskette and try again.

Weird Disk Sounds

If your disk is making weird sounds it is not necessarily broken. Hardware mavens on CompuServe report that a simple vibration problem that can be fixed with a dab of silicon gel is often the reason for whining disks. If your disk is whining then, don't worry. Many disks also clank as a natural part of their functioning. However, running a particular program may cause your disk to clatter for relatively long periods of time whenever you read a file. The sound your disk makes in this situation is not a normal one and sounds alarming. Sometimes all that is happening is that the program—for reasons known only to its designers—is doing a terrific amount of reading and writing. Sometimes this is part of an extensive setup routine.

But what might be happening is that the software is using some recondite piece of information the programmer knew about the way that disks work to play tricks with the disk reads in an attempt to speed things up. Unfortunately the programmer may not have known something important about your disk controller. As a result, his program may cause the disk-read mechanism to encounter more errors as it tries to read. When such errors are encountered the system will often reread the problem sector over and over again, which causes the chattering sound your disk makes.

Usually the programs that cause this kind of problem are resident utilities whose aim is to speed up your system. Once installed, all your programs will be affected when they read. If you install some speed-up routine and then find that your word processor begins taking much longer to read in a file than usual and that the disk makes these protesting sounds, get rid of the speed-up software, reboot the system, and the problem should go away.

Display Problems

If your screen remains blank after you turn on the system, it is quite possible that you have forgotten to turn on the separate monitor switch. In some systems, turning off the main unit will cause the screen to go off too. But if you switch off the monitor using its own switch you will need to also turn it back on with its own switch.

Check, too, that the monitor is plugged in, because the plug may have come loose. If that doesn't work, make sure that you—or a curious toddler— haven't rotated the brightness controls on the monitor to where they suppress any image. If the screen goes blank after you have left your computer sitting turned on but unused for a period of time, don't panic. This is good. Some software automatically blanks the screen after a period of time to protect the monitor from getting patterns burned into the phosphor that coats the tube. Just hit any key and the screen image will return.

There are several reasons why odd characters may appear on your screen, making it look broken. On a PC system a very few programs require that you have a particular screen display driver installed before you run the program.[6] If this driver is not installed and you run a program that expects it, you will see a lot of odd letters and characters at the beginning of each line and here and there around the screen. Read the manual for the software you are trying to use. It should tell you what to do.

If you call up another computer for the first time (or the first time using new communications software) and just get connected when your display suddenly begins to display junk, the problem may be that the settings you have chosen for your modem, (that is, the parity and stop bits you have selected), don't match what the receiving computer is expecting. Do what your communications software requires to get off-line, and then change the modem settings to a different parity setting and try again.

Sometimes you will get a messed-up screen display while communicating with another computer because the computer you are communicating with assumes you are using a type of terminal different from what you are using. There is usually some way of telling another computer what kind of terminal you are using.

If you are calling a communications service that you routinely call without problems and suddenly get junk on your screen, the problem is probably not in your computer at all. You may be suffering from a noisy

---

[6]This driver program is called ANSI.SYS. You install it by typing "DEVICE=ANSI.SYS" on a line in a file called AUTOEXEC.BAT, which contains all the commands that are executed when you boot your system.

phone line, which has made it look as if you transmitted something to the other computer that you really didn't, or the other computer may be having some problems of its own. In that case just sign off and try again later.

Violent Printers

Usually printers are calm and well behaved. However, if you run into a problem while your printer in the middle of printing in the dot-oriented graphics mode and later try to print text, your printer may begin behaving hysterically, emitting shrill squeals as the print head jerks back and forth in one place at high speed. This, believe it or not, is a software problem. What you will need to do is this: Turn the printer off. Wait until your word processor gives you a message telling you something is wrong with the printer and ask it to quit printing. Save your word-processing file and get out of your word processor. Then turn off the computer. Wait two or three minutes, and then turn the printer and the computer back on again. Everything should now work fine.

Another simple reason for hysterical printer behavior is that your printer ribbon has gotten jammed or twisted. On some printers this can cause the printer to emit a dreadful noise. To check whether this is the problem, turn off the printer, remove the printer ribbon following the instructions that come with the printer, check that the ribbon is able to unwind freely, and then reinstall the ribbon.

Your printer may also refuse to print if your paper has gotten stuck or jammed. Unfortunately, more often it will continue to print quite happily when the paper is jammed. It's a good idea therefore when printing a long work to keep an eye on the printer. Otherwise the printer may print 20 or 30 pages of text out on a single line of jammed paper.

When Your Modem Won't Respond

If your computer has a modem installed and you try to call another computer but nothing happens, there are several things you should check. First, make sure that the phone cord from the modem is plugged into a phone outlet. The modem needs to be connected to your phone line just like a telephone would be or it can't use the phone line to dial out. Then make sure that there is a dial tone available. You can't use the modem if a phone on your line is off the hook.

If the modem is plugged into the phone line and there is a dial tone then you need to check which port your communications software thinks your modem is hooked to. On the PC, if your system came with a serial port built in an internal modem is probably installed as COM2, leaving the serial port, which you can use for a printer, mouse, or external modem as COM1. If you are using an external modem plugged into the serial port the modem should probably be COM1. Somewhere in your communications software there is a screen where you tell the software which port to use for the modem. Make sure it is pointing to the correct one. If COM1 and COM2 don't work, try COM3.

If none of these work and you have an internal modem you might want to open the system unit and make sure that the modem card is pushed down securely into the plug receptacle. If you have an external modem look at its lights and check them against the manual that came with the modem to make sure that it is turned on and hooked up to the computer correctly.

Runaway Keys

Occasionally you will press a key, particularly a cursor key, and the key will just keep on moving by itself. Usually you can fix this by tapping the key a few times, since it is merely stuck. If this doesn't work turn the system off, wait a few minutes and start it up again. If keys stick very frequently you probably need to get the keyboard serviced. However, if you are out of warranty get an estimate, since buying a replacement keyboard costs under $100 and might be cheaper and faster than getting an old one repaired. Make sure to buy a keyboard that is compatible with your machine.

You may also see weird things happen on a PC keyboard if you have installed a pop-up utility that lets you play tricks on your keyboard. Such utilities sometimes interact weirdly with other programs resulting in peculiar responses when you try to type things in. To check if this is the case, try starting your system with no resident software installed. Then type the alphabet in at the DOS prompt and see if the screen displays what you typed.

Address Conflicts and Switch Settings

If you install a new board and bring your system up only to discover that your time-of-day clock doesn't work right or that you can't use the new board, you may have inadvertently run into an address conflict. Hardware uses things called interrupts and addresses for various purposes that you don't need to understand. What you do need to understand is that if two different pieces of hardware are trying to use the same address or interrupt you may have major problems.

Your best approach in this situation is usually a call to the people who sold you the board, explaining what kind of machine you are using, what other boards you have installed and what is not working.[7]

[7]For example, most PC MIDI interface boards use an interrupt called IRQ-1. The Leading Edge PC uses this same interrupt for its time-of-day clock. If you want to install a MIDI board on the Leading Edge you will need to switch the time-of-day clock from IRQ-1 to IRQ-2. You do this by moving a small jumper on the Leading Edge motherboard from one set of holes to another.

You may occasionally have to set little switches, called DIP switches, on your motherboard when you install something new in order to inform the hardware about the addition. These switches and their settings should be described in the manual that came with your computer. Setting them incorrectly may also cause your hardware to act broken.

Removing TSRs

If you get to the point with an IBM PC or clone where you just can't get a program working, and call a service person the chances are that whoever you call for help is going to tell you to remove all TSRs and try the program again, leaving you, perhaps, wondering what they are talking about. **TSR** is short for Terminate and Stay Resident, which is the technical term for the pop-up programs discussed before. These are the programs that are able to perform their functions while you are in the middle of another program. Unfortunately some of these cause problems with other programs and may make it look like your system is broken.

There are two ways to remove TSRs, depending on how your system is set up. If you start one of these programs by typing a command at the DOS prompt, then all you have to do to remove it is reboot the computer.

However, if the program is always there whenever you turn on your system, the chances are that either an installation procedure or a clever friend typed in an extra command in the special control file which is called AUTOEXEC.BAT. This file contains commands that are executed every time you turn on your system.

If this is the case what you need to do is a little more complicated. Copy the AUTOEXEC.BAT file to a second file with the name AUTOEXEC.BAK. Then edit AUTOEXEC.BAT and remove the line that contains the command that starts the TSR program. Save the file and then reboot. Your TSR should be gone. When you are all done fixing your problems and want your TSR to automatically load again, simply rename the AUTOEXEC.BAT file something else and rename the AUTOEXEC.BAK file back to AUTOEXEC.BAT. Your TSR will install automatically the next time you boot the system.

TSRs are often to blame when a system locks up unexplainedly, particularly cut-and-paste functions and keyboard utilities.

SIGNS THAT YOU REALLY MIGHT HAVE A HARDWARE PROBLEM

Parity Check Error

If your computer suddenly displays a message on the screen saying "Parity Check Error" you may really have a hardware error. However, if you have installed some memory speed-up software, the speed-up software itself might be causing the message to occur, so first get rid of any such speed-up software.

If your system continues to get this kind of message you may have a bad memory chip. You can determine which chip it is by running the diagnostic programs that came with your system, following the instructions that should be in the computer's manual and running the memory test. This test should be able to pinpoint which chip is bad. It is not a major big deal to replace the problem chip, but it does take some dexterity and, most important, you must know enough not to fry chips accidentally with static electricity. If you have a friend who really, truly knows what he is doing and is willing to help, you can do this at home, but to be on the safe side it is probably best to take the system unit to a good repair shop.

If your system is still under warranty, this will be covered by the warranty and you should let the shop do it, although you might have to pay for the labor involved depending on the way your warranty was written.

Numbered Error Messages

If you have a PC or clone you may get a number flashing across your screen when you boot it up. These numbers refer to hardware errors which are, unfortunately, not documented in your hardware manual. PC mavens usually can get you the list of what these errors mean, and many PC users groups distribute this list. You can also call a hardware repair shop and ask to speak with someone in service who might also tell you what the problem is.

Unreadable Diskettes

Flipping the little lever or pushing the button on your diskette drive causes a mechanism inside the drive to engage or release the diskette drive. Unfortunately, as all too many computer users have discovered after exultantly ripping a diskette out of the drive after typing the last line of a long project, if you don't wait for the drive to stop spinning before pulling the diskette out, you can render the diskette unreadable. Always wait until the light on your diskette drive goes out before pulling out your diskette.

If you do ruin a file on a diskette this way, all may not be lost. Some word processors will let you read the file in and will just display garbage in the section where the drive scratched the recording surface. You can then fix the words that got destroyed and save the file onto another diskette.

Broken Diskette Drive

Since so many other errors can make a diskette drive look broken, how do you determine when it really is broken?

One symptom of a truly broken diskette drive in a hard disk system with a single floppy drive is that when you boot up the computer the diskette light doesn't come on the way it usually does, and the computer can't boot. If a secondary diskette drive, signs of real failure would be if it can't read files on any diskette you feed it, not just a single one—assuming, of course, that you are inserting all the diskettes properly. Strange noises coming from the drive are another sign, as is the lack of any noise at all or the failure of the drive light to come on.

If the drive doesn't function at all, it is worth checking whether the cable attaching the floppy drive to the floppy controller, which may be on the motherboard, has come loose. And remember that the diskette system contains several pieces: the drive itself, the cable, and the controller, so your problem could be in any one of these components.

Disappearing Hard Drive

If you turn on your hard disk PC system one day and see a number 1701 on the screen and a message telling you that the system can't find the boot disk, you should insert the diskette containing the **diagnostic** programs that came with your machine and go to the routine that lists the hardware you have installed. The chances are good that it will only show your system as having a floppy drive and not a hard disk.

Don't panic. Your hard disk is still there. It is also quite possible that you have nothing worse wrong with your computer than a loose cable connecting the disk controller card with the hard drive. This is particularly likely if you have opened your system unit recently and possibly bumped against a connector cable.

The way to check for this and fix it is this: Unplug your system from the power outlet, then unplug the monitor, and keyboard, and take the top part of the case off the system unit. The cable you are interested in is a flat ribbon-like affair that stretches from the sealed hard disk to either a card installed in a card slot or perhaps to your motherboard. The end of the disk cable should be firmly seated in a multiprong receptacle. If it is loose, give it a firm shove, like you would when plugging in an electric plug. Just in case, press the controller card straight down into its socket to make sure it hasn't come loose. Then put the top back on your unit, plug in the monitor and keyboard and try bringing up the system again. If it still doesn't respond then you might have a more serious hardware problem, perhaps with your controller card, and should take your unit in for service.

Hard Disk Failure

You can tell that you have a real problem with your hard disk if you get messages telling you that you have had a general drive failure or that the system is unable to read the drive, no matter which program you try to use or which files you try to work with.

If you receive this kind of message only when working on a particular file or files you may simply have a bad spot on your disk. In this case you may be able to continue using the disk after running a disk optimizing utility which analyzes the disk and marks the bad spot as unusable. However, if you run into several such rotten spots on your disk you better be sure that your backup procedures are impeccable, because the next region to go bad could be your disk directory.

However your hard disk may still be salvageable—although your data won't be—even if many attempts to read the disk result in messages that the disk is unreadable. The problem may be that as your disk has gotten older the read/write heads have drifted away from the data tracks on the disk platter. If this is the case, it is worth trying a maneuver called a **low-level format** before throwing away the hard disk. A low-level format is different from the usual formatting you do. That kind of formatting involves writing to the tracks on the disk the information that the operating system uses to store and retrieve files. Low-level formatting, in contrast, redefines the location of the tracks on the disk. If your disk heads have wandered away from your old data tracks, low-level formatting, by defining new data tracks under the current position of the read/write heads might fix the problem.

You redo the low-level format on your hard disk using a program that should come with your hard disk controller, following the instructions that should be in a manual that accompanies this equipment. You might want to get a hardware-smart friend to help with this. After you have finished the low-level format you will need to do a high-level format. Then you must reload all the files that used to be on the disk, including your operating system, onto the disk from your backups, since the formatting process destroys all your data. Obviously you should only do this as a last resort.

If this doesn't work you will need to replace the hard disk drive. If you want to do this yourself you might consider buying a card-based disk drive which you install just by plugging it into an open slot, though these are more expensive than the usual kinds. Or you might be brave and try taking a do-it-yourself approach to installing a regular hard disk. Some of the more humane vendors sell their disks with a video demonstrating the installation process. In all cases make sure that you buy a drive that can work with your current type of system and your current drive controller, unless you plan to replace the controller too.

Monitor Problems

A truly broken monitor will simply not come on. Make sure however that you have plugged the monitor in (many plug into the system unit) and that you have turned on the monitor's own switch, not just the system unit switch. Also check that a video card that controls the monitor hasn't come loose in its socket.

Dead Power Supply

If your power supply is dead, no lights will come on on your computer at all when you turn it on. Make absolutely certain that you do have the system plugged in and switched on before you assume that this is the problem. Professional computer consultants report that an unbelievable number of customer complaints turn out to be caused by systems that have come unplugged. Also, make sure you haven't inadvertently switched off your surge protector since this is the same as unplugging the system.

A failing power supply may cause weird problems. For example, your hard drive may start turning itself on and off as the power supplied by the power supply fluctuates. Power supplies are cheap and if yours breaks, just get a new one installed, or do it yourself if you are brave. You can find descriptions of what you need to do in books and magazines.

PEOPLE TO CALL FOR HELP AND HOW TO CALL THEM

Hardware Problems

If you are really facing a hardware problem—not a piece of hardware that is misbehaving because that is what your software told it to do—your first resort should be the place where you bought your hardware. This is why we made such a point about buying hardware from a place that provides high-quality service. Print out any screens that display when you encounter your hardware problem. On a PC you can do this with a print key or a shift-prtSc key combination. Dig out your sales slip and verify the date that you bought the hardware and the length of the product's warranty and then call the service department.

Software Problems: Customer Support

If you are having problems with a piece of software you have bought and paid for, you should be able to call on the customer service department of the software company for help. Whether this is an option should be a factor in your decision to buy a product or not, particularly if you are not an experienced user.

As an example of the kind of support you ought to insist on when you pay full price: WordPerfect is famous for having a toll-free help line open to buyers of their products. Other companies have help lines, but unfortunately, they are not toll free and may ring busy for hours at a time. Borland, which has such a non-toll-free line, gives another kind of free help. They send you a free CompuServe sign-on pack and $15 (about an hour's worth) of free connect time so that you can exchange messages on CompuServe with an excellent product support team that responds immediately in writing to your problems.

Some companies may require you to pay a hefty additional fee to receive phone support. Still others may put you on hold for 20 minutes on a long-distance, non-toll-free number when you need help. Obviously it's a good idea to try to determine what kind of help is available for the word processor you are planning to buy before you purchase it.

When you call a help line you should expect to wait for awhile. You need to have the registration number of your software, and you may need to have mailed in a registration form so that your name is associated with the registration number on the product. The registration number is printed somewhere on your distribution diskettes. If you can't supply this number many customer support people will not answer your questions because they will assume that you are trying to get help for pirated software.

Before calling you should try to print out the screens that display any relevant error messages. Have your computer in front of you, turned on, so that you can run any tests that the customer service representative would like you to try.

Before calling, make sure that you are prepared to give customer service answers to the following questions:

1. The brand and model of your computer
2. The operating system and release number of the operating system you are using
3. How much memory is installed on your system
4. The size of your hard disk and how much of it is filled with files
5. The kind of diskette drive your system has
6. On a PC you should be able to describe the contents of the following files which you can find out by printing the files on your printer using the PRINT command:
   a. CONFIG.SYS
   b. AUTOEXEC.BAT

Be prepared to describe your problem briefly and then let the customer service representative ask you questions. If you get good service, ask the representative for his or her name. The next time you have a problem ask for that person specifically by name. But remember that these people have brutal jobs and spend their entire day on the phone with hundreds of inarticulate and often disconsolate customers, so don't expect them to remember you or your previous problems.

And be aware, too, that customer service people have been known to give wrong answers or to be unaware of the solutions to what are known bugs. Customer support is not among the more highly paid jobs open to people with real computer expertise. So you have to accept that sometimes such representatives' responses are less than ideal. If you don't get a working solution try calling a different person in customer support. If all else fails, don't forget the help available on-line or at a near by user group, especially in a new user SIG.

Help with Shareware

If you register a shareware program you can usually get help by contacting the person with whom you registered the product. However, if you are trying to install a program in order to test it out, this is not always possible. Some of the larger shareware companies such as Quicksoft, the company that supports PC-Write, will answer whatever questions you need answered in order to get the package up and running, even if you aren't registered. You can also get help on CompuServe from shareware developers and other users of the product. For PC shareware problems you can also leave messages on IBMSW, the CompuServe IBM software forum. And again, don't forget you can call on people who distribute the shareware at your PC user's group.

15

BACKUPS: The Single Most Important Chapter in this Book

Okay. Up until now you've been meandering along thinking about computers, learning some basic concepts, and getting a feel for what it would be like to use the tools in the writer's toolbox. It's all been pretty relaxed. You've been exposed to a lot of concepts and a lot of information but all of it has been imparted with the underlying assumption that you don't have to master any of it now and that with a modicum of common sense you will get along just fine with a computer, no matter what you do.

Well that's been true up until now, but now the rules change! You could skim most of the previous chapters with the understanding that if you needed the information in them you could come back later. But that isn't the case here. In fact, if you don't read this chapter with rapt attention and take it seriously, it is almost certain that you will experience one of those disastrous episodes that give computers a bad name.

I'm talking about data loss. In simple English: ruined work. Clobbered files. Erased text.

You can put off mastering a lot of things about your computer, but if you put off learning how to back up your system effectively you will eventually lose an important manuscript just as thoroughly and effectively as if you had left the only copy of that manuscript in the back of a gypsy cab.

You wouldn't entrust your only copy of a manuscript to the U.S. mail without keeping a copy would you? No, of course not. Well, by the same token, if you are going to prepare your work on a computer you must observe religiously the simple but necessary practices of file backup. All the time. Not next week, not when you get comfortable with your computer, but from the very first time you create a single document whose name is not "TEST.DOC."

You must never forget backups, because, as any computer professional can tell you, the day that you don't back up your manuscript files is the day that some unpredictable event is going to clobber them, leaving you bereft of all the work you put into them. And experience shows that these events are most prone to happen when you are approaching the end of a major project and working under deadline pressure. The more tired you are, the more likely you are to inadvertently destroy your manuscript files. The more important your work is, the more likely it is that your hardware will fail as you near the finish line, or that a squirrel will commit suicide in your neighborhood power substation, blacking out the neighborhood and crashing your word processor, or that one of any number of other unpredictable data- destroying events will occur.

LIVING EACH DAY AS IF IT WERE YOUR SYSTEM'S LAST

You must use your computer with the explicit understanding that each session might be its last. Every time you turn on your computer you should feel confident that if the machine comes up dead you could keep right on going with a loaner machine with only a pause to load in your files. Every time you run a new program you should be assured that if that program contained a virus that destroyed your hard disk directory and with it your access to everything on your hard disk, you could simply reformat the disk and reload your system right back from backup diskettes. Every time you begin to edit a manuscript with your word processor you should be certain that if you happened to accidentally hit some keys that would delete all the text in your file and then save the empty file, that you could get back to where you were on that manuscript in minutes.

In short, you need to keep a carbon of your whole system!

WHY DATA GETS DESTROYED

Oceans of ink have been spent discussing the destruction of data that hacker-instigated viruses inflict on computer systems. But the amount of damage done by hackers pales to insignificance when compared with the damage done every day by ordinary folks to their own systems!

Data loss is not something that people like to talk about, but it happens constantly, for a variety of reasons.

Businesspeople who maintain computer systems know this, and in any well-managed computer center it is standard procedure to back up the system every night, copying vital files to tape backups and sometimes making backups of the backups. Companies that maintain data centers spend vast sums on planning for disaster recovery. At IBM, for example, the computer centers periodically run drills similar to a fire drill where they pretend that a data center has been destroyed and time how long it takes to get the whole thing up and running again on new machines reloaded with copies of their old data retrieved from a secret vault.

This reflects the fact that IBM is well aware that their data is valuable—if it wasn't, why would they be wasting all their time and resources processing it?—and that they well realize that disaster can strike at any moment.

You must know this too.

Anything that is entrusted to a computer is open to destruction from two powerful forces, entropy and human cussedness. Entropy expresses itself in the gradual breakdown of machinery.[1] Although your computer is a high quality machine with few moving parts it is not eternal. Eventually disks will crash, memory will fry, and data will be destroyed. But even as a paper-based writer, you faced this kind of threat. You always knew that your house might burn down, taking with it your manuscripts. You may have even taken this seriously enough to store copies of important writings in the safe deposit box or maybe with your mother.

But when you begin working with a computer system the possibility of damage goes way up, and not because of anything wrong with the hardware. No, the problem comes when you take a human brain and body developed in response to 3.4 million years of wandering through the forest looking for fruit, and sit it in front of a tool of the complexity of any modern piece of software. The plasticity that the computer confers on your productions, the very ease that makes working with a computer so attractive, enables you, with a single reflex finger movement, to destroy hours—if not days'—worth of work.

Everybody does it. It is not just the inexperienced user who erases vital files, though the inexperienced user tends to do it more often. No. It is just a side effect of the enormous power that computers give us, and testament to the fact that, as human beings, a lot of what we do is controlled by low-level instinct and whatever else it is that lets us drive when we are almost sound asleep.

It doesn't work on the computer. If you are editing along in that semicomatose state in which you might be able to drive home safely, trusting to low-level motor intelligence, you will probably wreak havoc on your computer system.

---

[1]Software, built as it is of logic, partakes more of the ideal than the material and does not break down as it ages. However, human systems generally do become more complex as they age, and since software interacts with human systems, eventually the complexity of the human system outpaces the usefulness of the existing logic, forcing the software to be rewritten or discarded.

When it comes to destroying data the enemy 99 percent of the time is yourself.

Data gets destroyed because you forget the name of a document and decide to tidy up your files one day and erase the wrong one. Data gets destroyed because you meant to select the menu item that lets you edit a file but the phone rang so you selected the one that deletes it. Data gets destroyed because you mark a group of files to be copied to a floppy disk but just before you copy the marked files you see one you don't need so you type in delete to get rid of it—and watch all your marked files disappear. Data gets destroyed because you hit the keys on your word processor that in your outliner move the cursor but here deletes the paragraphs. Data gets destroyed because you forget that you already have an 80-page chapter file named "NOSES" so you save a memo with the same name and thus erase it. Data gets destroyed because you forget that you have almost filled up your diskette and you add one more page to the final version of a magazine article due the next morning, only to get the DISK FULL message and have the machine freeze. Data gets destroyed, in short, because humans were not designed to be logical for more than a few moments at a time.

Which is not meant to drive you into a frenzy of paranoia, nor to take away the good feeling about computers that you may have begun developing as you read this book. It is just to get you motivated enough to slog through the rest of this chapter, which covers the very pedestrian steps that you can, and must, take to prevent the standard, predictable disasters that strike most new computer users, no matter how bright.

TYPES OF BACKUP FOR A HARD DISK SYSTEM

Image Copy

There are several different approaches to taking system backups on a hard disk system. One way is to periodically back up everything on your hard disk by making what is called an **image copy.** In this kind of backup you produce an image of the entire disk, including its directories and control blocks. The ideal way of doing this is to use a high speed tape backup unit which is able to dump your whole 20 or 30 (or more) megs worth of hard disk files onto a tape cassette in a few minutes. There are various products that come with software to do this kind of backup. They vary in the degree to which they let you pick out a particular file to be restored as opposed to restoring the whole disk. There are also machines that let you do image copy backups to VCR tape.

But these solutions require additional hardware that is expensive. They are practical for corporate users who are storing data worth thousands or millions of dollars on their systems and don't have any problem with spending $1,000 on backup hardware, as indeed they shouldn't. But this solution is probably out of the question for you.

It is also possible to do image copies onto floppy diskettes using commercial backup software. However a little basic calculation reveals that it will take about 30, 360K diskettes or 9, 1.2 M diskettes to back up each 10 meg of hard disk, making this kind of backup a painfully time consuming-operation and not one you are likely to do very often.

Taking an image copy of your disk using a reliable backup software package is the officially recommended way of preserving yourself from harm. Everything on the system is preserved this way including files you may not even know you have. These include the control files and work files that your software builds and the files that result from any customizing activity you perform on a software package. Backing up this way will also save other things you may not know are there, like footnote files that some word processors keep separate from document files.

This kind of backup works, but in practice few people have the patience to practice it regularly.

File Copy

The quick and dirty method of backup is to copy to floppy diskettes only those specific files that you have identified as important, and only when these files have changed. You can do this several ways. The easiest is to buy either a commercial or shareware hard disk backup utility that lets you specify which files or subdirectories should be subject to backup. Such backup packages include PC-Fullback and Corefast for the PC; HFS Backup, Flashback, and DiskFit for the Mac; and Fastback, which comes in versions for both the PC and the Macintosh.

These programs usually have sophisticated menus that lead you through the process of selecting the criteria to be used in choosing files for backup, doing the backups, and, of course, restoring files from the backed up versions when you need them. Many of these utilities store the backed-up files in some kind of compressed form so that they take up less room on your diskettes. If your software does this it means that you must always use the backup software, not a straightforward copy command, to retrieve a backed up file back onto your disk since the stored file is stored in a format only meaningful to the backup program.

You don't have to go out on a financial limb to acquire this kind of software. Several of these utilities can be bought for around $50 through mail order. If you don't want to spend that much for backup alone you can use your fifty bucks to buy PC Tools Deluxe, mentioned earlier, which provides a backup utility together with a slew of other useful utilities.

There are numerous PC shareware programs available to help you with selective file backups, too. Public (Software) Library, for example, carries two disks full of small utilities as well as ABF, a larger shareware backup package. So you can't claim poverty as an excuse for not getting backup software!

Selective backup schemes often makes use of a handy built in operating system feature: the **archive attribute.** The archive attribute is merely a bit switch which can be turned on and off. Each file on your disk has one as part of its directory entry. Anytime that you modify a file the archive attribute is turned on. Therefore, if your backup software turns it off when you backup the file, you have a very simple way of isolating those files which have changed since your last backup and thus need to be backed up again.

But you don't even need a special backup utility to do backups using this feature. If you are a bit more sophisticated you can build a very adequate backup system using a generic copy utility, such as Norm Patriquin's excellent shareware PCopy which is able to test and set the archive flag. PCopy also allows you to specify date ranges for the files you want to have backed up, so you can back up all the files you have modified in the last week with a single command.

Using this kind of backup strategy protects you very adequately against "user error," in other words, your own stupidity, finger fumblings, and accidental deletions. All you have to do is locate the diskette that contains the most recent backup copy of the file you've messed up and copy the diskette version of the file back into the correct subdirectory.

However, if you suffer a hardware problem with your hard disk or if your disk directory gets screwed up, restoring your system from a file-oriented backup will be more complex than if you had saved an image of the whole disk. If your disk fails you will have to reinstall all of your software off of the copies that you made when you installed them the first time, and, if you haven't backed up the control files that go with this software, you will have to enter in all the default information and customization information that those control files contain.[2]

If you do have to restore an entire hard disk, don't forget that you must install the operating system back on to it first.

Minimalist Backup

If even this kind of partial backup is beyond your current computer skills, but you just have to use a word processor, make absolutely sure that you make a diskette copy, preferably from within your word processor, of every

---

[2]Obviously it would be a better idea, though more time consuming, to include the control files in the list of files to be backed up, and as some people do, to back up whole directories together as a unit.

word processing document you create, every time you work on the system. The reason you should do this from within the word processor is that some word processors may store a single document in several files and saving them from within the software ensures that all the files making up the work will be copied. That way at least your work should be safe.

And, for anything else you'd ever like to see again, there is always the system copy command. All you have to do in a DOS PC to copy a file to a diskette, is put a diskette in the disk drive, close the drive door, make sure you are in the subdirectory that contains the file you want to save and type the following at the DOS prompt:

```
COPY filename.ext a:
```

leaving the spaces where you see them and replacing "filename" and "ext" with the actual name and extension of the file you want to copy. That's all there is to it.

BACKUPS FOR THE FLOPPY DISK SYSTEM

Just because your system doesn't have a hard disk doesn't mean that you don't need to take backups! Floppy disks are subject to failure just like hard disks. And of course, you are just as likely to erase or otherwise mess up a document you are working on when it is stored on a floppy as anywhere else. All you need do to back up floppy files is to make copies on another diskette of each diskette you work on using a diskette-oriented command like DOS's DISKCOPY which makes a diskette image copy.

MAKING BACKUPS WORK

Scheduling Backups

The single most important law of system backup is this: The BEST backup strategy is one you really use.

A wonderful image copy utility that preserves your entire system is not much use to you if you only run it once a month. The chances are that the one time you will really need to restore your system will be on the twenty-ninth day since you took your last backup. This means that you will have lost a month's worth of work.

A much better idea is to use a backup procedure which you can comfortably run before you turn off your system every time you use the system. This probably means a selective file-oriented backup procedure that backs up only those files you changed in the current session. Its up to you whether you want to exclude control files or not. At the bare minimum, you should plan to make a copy on diskette of the file you created with your word processor each time you finish using it.

Printing out what you write is not enough. It is better than nothing, but it makes little sense to put yourself in a situation where you may have to retype many pages of material when a simple copy command could make you a diskette copy you could reload in seconds.

Another caution: Many word processors will prompt you with a question like "Save current file?" when you exit your word processor. All this means is that if you say "yes" the word processor will copy the document that you have been working on from the computer's memory where changes have been made to it back into a file on the computer's hard disk. It does *not* mean that a backup copy is being taken, as new users often erroneously conclude. Nor will just placing a diskette in the diskette drive automatically cause the word processor to write the file back onto the diskette. In a hard disk system you usually do all your reading and writing to your hard disk and you must specifically instruct the word processor to write a file onto the diskette in the diskette drive since the word processor usually writes to the hard disk. Watch to see that the diskette drive light comes on to ensure that the diskette version is really being written.

Rotating Backups

While making a copy of your latest efforts every time you use the computer is a good idea, there is one further step in creating a really foolproof backup system. This is to keep backups of your backups. The goal of this kind of backup system is to preserve the last three versions of any file you back up. Some backup software lets you do this automatically, renaming the older versions of your backed-up files to indicate which version they hold. Another way that you do this is simply to keep three separate sets of backup floppies and rotate them, always copying the latest version of your documents on the set of floppies that has the oldest set of backups on it. This way, if you back up daily, you will have the version of your document you created today, the version you created yesterday, and finally the version you created the day before.

Why go through this?

Because this protects you from the situation where you have screwed up a file but don't realize it. If you have deleted 10 pages in a file by accident and don't notice it, you will probably copy *that* messed version of the file onto your daily backup diskette. If you keep only one backup then you will be replacing a good copy of the file with the messed-up version. However if you keep rotating backups you will have two earlier versions of the file left from which you can get back the pages you deleted by accident.

The other reason that this makes sense is that unlike writing on a typewriter, when you work electronically you don't get to keep the intermediate drafts. All too often in a fever of revision you make changes that later on you realize were not really what you wanted. If you keep the intermediate stages of your work you can easily revert to the earlier version. But if all you keep is the latest version you will only have whatever printouts you generated to guide you.

If you are working on a major effort, like a book, it is a good idea to save a complete version of the work in progress every month, a version separate from your usual set of rotating backups. And it doesn't hurt to store your diskettes in different places, including a safe deposit box or a friend's house in case the house does burn down.

Diskette Labeling

One very trivial step you can take to make your backups much more useful, is to get a hold of a program that creates a detailed list of what is on your file in a format that fits inside the sleeve of the floppy diskette, or on a label you can stick on the diskette. COVER is a public domain program that does a nice job of listing files on a piece of paper that fits inside a 5 1/4" sleeve. It runs on printers that accept Epson or IBM control codes. myDiskLabeler is a fancy label program for the Mac. You want one that includes the names of each file on the diskette and preferably its date of creation. Some such utilities will print the size of the file instead of its date which is also useful.

If you have these labels or listings it is much easier to look at the diskettes themselves and see what your collection of backup diskettes contains. Since, as time goes on, this collection will come to include 30 or 40 or more diskettes, anything that prevents you from having to load each one and look at its directory to see what is on it is a benefit. How likely you are to stick to a backup regimen religiously is pretty closely tied to how easy your backup system is to use. Making it easy to keep track of what you have on each diskette without requiring that you put in a lot of additional time is one way to make your backup system easy to use.

YOUR COMPUTER FIRE DRILL

Don't wait for disaster to strike to see if your backup strategy works! Try a fire drill of your own. Create a test document with your word processor and then do whatever you plan to do for backup before turning off the system. Back out of the word processor and erase the test file you just created. Then turn the system off. See how long it takes you to get to where you are looking at the restored test document with your word processor. If you have trouble with this test, you know that you have some serious work to do before you commit any important real work to your electronic tools!

The key to happy computer use is providing yourself with an easy-to-use backup system and using it until it becomes a reflex action to use that backup system every single time you use the computer. You can give yourself lots of time to master the intricacies of your word processor and you can wait to master most of the other tools in the writer's toolbox, but remember that the day that you write your first piece of real writing on your computer is the day you should begin making backups.

APPENDIX A

SOFTWARE MENTIONED IN THIS BOOK[1]

Type of Software	Product Name	System	Software Company	Comment
Backup	Fastback	Both	Fifth Generation Systems	Fast
	DiskFit	Mac	SuperMac Software	Backs up all or changed files only
	Flashback	Mac	Mainstay	Backs up HFS hard disks
	HFS Backup	Mac	PCPC	Cheap and flexible
	ABF	PC	Querty Development	Shareware
	COREfast	PC	Core International	Highly rated
	PC-FullBack	PC	Westlake Data	
Bulletin Board System	RBBS	PC	*	Public Domain
Database	dBase	Both	Ashton-Tate	Heavy duty industry standard programmable database
	Foxbase +	Both	Fox Software Inc.	dBase-like database
	Filemaker Plus	Mac	Nashoba Systems	
	File Express	PC	Expressware	Shareware
	Paradox	PC	Borland International	Powerful database with language
	PC-File +	PC	Buttonware	Shareware. Simple to learn standard database

[1]All software products mentioned in this list are mentioned for illustrative purposes only. While every attempt has been made to mention only useful products, mention in these pages is not to be taken as a recommendation to buy any product. Products not listed here may be as good or better than those listed.

Type of Software	Product Name	System	Software Company	Comment
Database (*cont'd*)	RBase	PC	Microrim	Popular with small businesses.
Desktop Publishing	Aldus Pagemaker	Both	Aldus	An industry standard
	Ventura Publisher	PC	Xerox	Industry standard, especially for long documents
Desktop Utility	SideKick Plus	Both	Borland International	Ed, Out, File manager, phone, notepad, sched, etc.
	MiniWriter	Mac		Public domain notepad
	MockPackage+	Mac		Shareware. Editor, text printer, comm, charts, men
	MockWrite	Mac	CE Software	Notepad
	Top Desk	Mac	Cortland Computer	Cut and paste etc.
	Homebase	PC	Brown Bag Software	Shareware. Notepad, File mgt, Cal, Phone, C+P etc.
	Lotus Metro	PC	Lotus Development Corp.	
	PC Deskteam	PC	Alternative Decision Software	Shareware. Calendar, notepad, DOS commands, phone.
Desktop/Notepad /Database	Tornado Notes	PC	Micro Logic Corp.	Super note pad with indexing and search
Environment	Desqview	PC	Quarterdeck Systems	Multitasker
	Microsoft Windows	PC	Microsoft Corp.	Provides graphic environment for special programs
	Software Carousel	PC	SoftLogic Solutions	Turns all programs into popup—needs extra memory
General Purpose Comm	Red Ryder	Mac	Freesoft	Shareware
	Bitcom	PC	Bit Software, Inc.	Included with many modems
	Boyan D3	PC	Telecom	Shareware
	Crosstalk	PC	Digital Communications Assoc.	
Grammar Checker	MacProof	Mac	Lexpertise, USA, Inc.	
	Sensible Grammar	Mac	Sensible Software, Inc.	
	Grammatik III	PC	Digital Marketing	Good and getting better.
	PC Stylist	PC	Buttonware	Shareware
	Rightwriter	PC	Writesoft, Inc.	
Graphics	Cricket Draw	Both	Cricket Software	
	Adobe Illustrator	Mac	Adobe Systems Inc.	

Type of Software	Product Name	System	Software Company	Comment
Graphics (*cont'd.*)	Aldus Freehand	Mac	Aldus	
	MacPaint	Mac	Claris	
	Pixel Paint	Mac	SuperMac Software	
	SuperPaint	Mac	Silicon Beach Software	
Graphics	Freelance Plus	PC	Lotus Development Corp.	
	Harvard Graphics	PC	Software Publishing Corporation	
	PC Paintbrush	PC	Z Soft Corp.	
Hypertext	Guide	Both	OWL International	
	PC-Hypertext	PC	MaxThink	PC-Hyperlink, PC-Hypertext & Houdini, together
Outliner	Acta	Mac	Symmetry Corp.	Desk accessory
	More	Mac	Symantec	Powerful
	PC-Outline	PC	Brown Bag Software	Shareware. Everything you need in an outliner.
Outliner/Random Database	MaxThink	PC	MaxThink	Extremely powerful, includes brainstorming aids
PIM	Agenda	PC	Lotus Development Corp.	Manages short bits of info you enter. Complex.
PIM/Outliner	Grandview	PC	Symantec	PC-Outline with new bells and whistles.
PIM/Text Search/Free-form	askSam	PC	askSam Systems	Powerful text management system
Random Database	3x5	PC	Softwhell Corporation	Shareware. Searchable index cards, reference mgt.
	Instant Recall	PC	Precept	Shareware. Indexes everything it its files.
Special Purpose Comm	CompuServe Navigator	Mac	CompuServe	Access CompuServe automatically
	Desktop Express	Mac	Dow Jones Software	Access MCI/Dow Jones News Service
	Autosig	PC *		Public Domain (free) Automate CompuServe forums
	TAPCIS	PC	OMNI Information Resources	Powerful CompuServe Access program

Type of Software	Product Name	System	Software Company	Comment
Specialty Database	EndNote	Mac	Niles and Associates	Bibliographic database
	Publish or Perish	Mac	Park Row, Inc.	Bibliographic database
	Writer's Workshop	Mac	Futuresoft System Designs	Track income, manuscripts, income, publishers.
	Bilio-file	PC	Dean Madar	Shareware bibliography manager
	Contact Plus	PC	Ed Trujillo	Shareware contact data base
	Muses	PC	Louie Crew	Shareware tracks articles and publishers
	Reflist	PC	E. J. Shillitoe	Shareware. Does ref. list for sci/tech ms.
Spreadsheet	Excel	Both	Microsoft Corp.	Graphics-oriented
	MacCalc	Mac	Bravo Technologies	Powerfull full-featured spreadsheet
	Multiplan	Mac	Microsoft	Basic spreadsheet
	Lotus 1-2-3	PC	Lotus Development Corp.	Industry standard spreadsheet
	PC-Calc +	PC	Buttonware	Shareware. Enough spreadsheet for home businesses.
	Quattro	PC	Borland International	Inexpensive and powerful
	Qubecalc	PC	Formal Soft	Shareware. 3-D spreadsheet.
	VP Planner	PC	Paperback Software	Cheap but effective spreadsheet
Text Search	GOfer	Both	Microlytics	Memory resident text search.
	Fgrep	PC	Christofer J. Dunford	Free Shareware text search
	IZE	PC	Persoft	You tell it what to index. Powerful.
	PSearch	PC	Norm Patriquin	Shareware. Simple, fast text seach utility
	ZyINDEX	PC	ZyLABS	Extremely powerful
Utility Packages	Copy II Mac	Mac	Central Point Software	Backup/Recovery
	Symantec Utilities	Mac	Symantec	Disk/File recovery programs
	Mace Utilities	PC	Paul Mace Software	From the man who first restored a crashed disk
	Norton Commander	PC	Peter Norton Computing	More powerful disk utilities
	Norton Utilities	PC	Peter Norton Computing	Very useful, maybe too powerful for beginners

Type of Software	Product Name	System	Software Company	Comment
Utility Packages (*cont'd.*)	PC Tools Deluxe	PC	Central Point Software	DOS Shell, Backup, Undelete, Unformat, Notepad etc.
Utilities etc.	myDiskLabeler	Mac	Williams and Macias	Snazzy disk labels
	WordCount	Mac		Public domain Desk Accessory
	ARCE	PC	Wayne Chin and Vern Buerg	Shareware. Uncom presses ARCed files
	Automenu	PC	Magee Enterprises	Shareware. Menu/ DOS Shell
	COVER	PC		Public domain diskette lable maker for Epson/IBM
	Disk Optimizer	PC	SoftLogic Solutions	Reorganizes hard disk, prevent erasures, unerase
	Flushot	PC	Ross M. Greenberg	Shareware anti-virus utility
	HGCIBM	PC	Athena DIgital	Shareware runs CGA graphics on mono grapics board
	Letrhead	PC	Technical Service Associates	You design your own computer-printed letterhead
	LIST	PC	Vern Buerg	Shareware. Powerful easy-to-use browse utility
	Pcopy	PC	Norm Patriquin	Shareware copy utility. Use it to do your backup.
	Whereis	PC	*	Public domain file finder.
Word Processor	Microsoft Word	Both	Microsoft Corp.	Graphics-oriented word processing bestseller
	WordPerfect	Both	WordPerfect Corp.	Bestselling PC word processor. Great support.
	Fullwrite Professional	Mac	Ashton-Tate	Graphics and out-lining. Needs memory.
	MacWrite	Mac	Claris	Simple word processing
	WriteNow	Mac	T/Maker	
	DisplayWrite 4	PC	IBM	
	MultiMate	PC	Ashton-Tate	Page-oriented word processor popular in offices
	Nota Bene	PC	Dragonfly Software	The ultimate academic word processor
	PC-Write	PC	Quicksoft	Shareware. Most powerful shareware word processor

Type of Software	Product Name	System	Software Company	Comment
Word Processor (*cont'd.*)	PFS: Professional Write	PC	Software Publishing Corp.	Basic word processing for executives
	Q&A Word	PC	Symantec	Easy-to-learn word processor
	Sprint	PC	Borland	Powerful, easy-to-learn, customizable and cheap.
	Wordstar	PC	MicroPro International	Historically, first PC Word Processor.
	XyWrite III +	PC	XyQuest, Inc.	Powerful word processor used by many writers.
Word Processor/ Outliner	MindWrite	Mac	Access Technology	Word processing and outlining combined

APPENDIX B

HARDWARE-BUYING CHECKLIST

When shopping for a computer you should get the information necessary to fill in each blank below. Use this as a way of comparing competitive products too.

Manufacturer:
Model Name or Number:
Store:
Salesperson's Name:
Delivery Date:
   (Guaranteed?)
Price: (total):

   1. **System Unit**

      a. **Processor** chip type:
         Speed in Mhz:
         Wait state?
         Memory in K (included with base unit):
            Room for more memory on motherboard?
            Maximum size of memory supported?
            Size of upgrade chips supported: Cost of upgrade chips

      b. **Diskette Drive**
         How many?
         Size (in inches):
         Bytes diskette holds (in K or megs):

   c. **Hard Disk**
        Size in megs:
        Included in base price?
        Installed?
        Formatted?
        Access speed?
        Controller included?
        Manufacturer:
        Separate Warranty?
   d. If PC clone, who manufactures BIOS?
        Is it guaranteed 100% PC compatible?
   e. Available **expansion slots?**
        What bit data paths do slots support (8, 16, 32)?
        Does system require special boards?
   f. What **ports** does system include:
        At least one serial port?
        At least one parallel port for printer if PC?
   g. Built-in time-of-day clock?
   h. **Keyboard** type:
        Separate cursor keys?
        Function keys where?
        Included in package price if Mac?
   i. **Upgrades** installed by vendor:
        Memory?
            Cost:
        Disk drives:
            Cost:
            Manufacturer:
        Type of controller:

2. **Monitor**
        Included with system?
        Cost, if not included:
        Graphics board included?
        Video standards supported (Hercules, CGA, EGA, VGA)?
        Color?:

3. **Printer**
        Typefaces included:
        Type sizes supported:
        Prints graphics?
        Prints IBM character graphics?
        If not IBM, Hewlett-Packard LaserJet, or Epson, what
        emulations supported?

What paper handling included?
Tractor feed needed or included?

4. **Modem**
   What speed in bps:
   Error checking?
   Internal
   Installed at sale?
   External
   Does system have serial port?
   Software included?

5. **Mouse**
   Included with system?:
   How attached to system?
   Software included?

6. Is **software** included with system purchase?
   Is software built in?
   Can it be removed?
   Is this software sold separately from this system?

7. **EXTRAS** to remember:
   a. Surge surpressor
   b. Printer cable
   c. Paper
   d. Diskettes (at least 20)

APPENDIX C

COMPUTER COMPETENCE CHECKLIST

ENSURING BASIC COMPETENCE

What you have read in this book should help you begin the process of understanding computer hardware and software. But it shouldn't take the place of getting some guided, hands-on experience. If you are serious about acquiring your own computer system you need to get some further education before you begin. Take a class. Read some good introductory computer books. Go to a users group meeting. Look at some computer magazines at the library. Take the time to do it right.

To help you know when you are ready to start spending your hard- earned money on your own system, here is a list of the basic operations you should be able to perform—with some fuzzy idea of what you are doing—before you attempt to buy or run your own computer. Nothing in this list is hard or requires that you have technical skills. Everything listed here should be covered in an introductory course.

If you make the effort to master the few operations that are listed here before you go out to buy your own computer, you will save yourself hours of pain and misery, and you won't end up placing one of those classified ads that say "PC For Sale, $2,000, Used Twice."

You can find a discussion of where to get the education you need to master these items in Chapter 4.

COMPETENCE CHECKLIST

On any computer you are thinking of buying you should be able to:

1. Turn on the unit.
2. Know how start up a program that is installed on either a floppy diskette or on the computer's hard disk.
3. Know what to do if the computer freezes and won't respond to keystrokes.
4. Be able to generate a list of the files stored on a diskette. Know how to generate a list of files on a hard disk, listed by directory.
5. Understand what a directory is and know how to move from one directory to another.
6. Know what a system commmand is.
7. Know how to copy, rename, delete, and print a file using operating system commands.
8. Know how to create or delete a directory.
9. Understand how to format a diskette and why it is necessary to do so.
10. Know whether there is a control file your system runs every time you boot it up, and if there is, know what it contains.
11. Know how to look at the contents of a file with a browse utility.
12. Know how to direct the computer to point to the diskette drive and how to get it to point to the hard drive.
13. Know how to tell when the computer is writing or reading to your disk drives.
14. Know what you must do when working with a file to make sure that your changes are kept.
15. Know how to turn off the computer safely and what you must do with the stuff you are working on before turning it off.
16. Know how to make backups of anything on your computer, particularly the files containing your work.

APPENDIX D

LIST OF COMPUTER USER GROUPS IN THE U. S. A. AND CANADA

The following is a list of the mailing addresses of some user groups catering to PC and Macintosh users. It is by no means exhaustive. Some users groups (like Houston's HAL PC and The Boston Computer Society) have hundreds or even thousands of members and meet regularly. Others have only a score of members and meet sporadically or not at all.

The best way to find an active users group in your area is to check with salespeople at local computer stores and with staff at college computer science departments, to read bulletin boards at computer stores and schools and to check local newspaper listings for notices of upcoming user group meetings.[1]

ALABAMA

B.I.P.U.G., INC.
Dave Chanslor
P.O.Box 19248
Birmingham, Alabama 35219

F.A.O.U.G
Ed Burquez
303 North Hwy-47
Columbiana, Alabama 35051

MONTGOMERY PC USER'S GROUP
Kerry Butler
3505 McGehee Road
Montgomery, Alabama 36116

ALASKA

ALASKA COMPUTER SOCIETY
George Harper
2042-East 3rd Avenue
Anchorage, Alaska 99501

[1]Many thanks to Dennis C. Lozen, author of FastBucks Home Finance Manager (Software Expressions, P. O. Box 301002, Houston, TX 77230-1002) for sharing his list of PC User groups.

ARIZONA

TUSCON APPLE CORE
P. O. Box 41706
Tuscon, Arizona 85733-3176

TUCSON COMPUTER SOCIETY
Rice Bullock
P.O. Box 1489
Tucson, Arizona 85702

CALIFORNIA

CALIFORNIA PC USERS GROUP
Dave Goode
150 S. Magnolia Avenue, Suite 248
Anaheim, California 92804

KERN INDEPENDENT PC USER
  GROUP
Jim Harper
P.O. Box 2780
Bakersfield, California 93303

BMUG, Inc.
1442A Walnut Street, Suite 62
Berkeley, California 94709

SACRAMENTO PC USERS GROUP,
  INC.
Rick Hellewell
P.O. Box 685
Citrus Heights, California 95611-0685

FOG INTERNATIONAL COMPUTER
  USERS GROUP
Ron Forsythe
P.O. Box 3474
Daly City, California 94015

VALLEY BLUE IBM-PC CLUB
Cherie Jo Paternaude
Lila Chase, LLNL, P.O. Box 808 L-321
Livermore, California 94550

LOS ANGELES MACINTOSH GROUP
12021 Wilshire Blvd, #349
Los Angeles, California 90025

UCLA PC USERS GROUP
Richard Katz
Attn: Schroth, UCLA, NPI 77-365, 760
  Westwood Plaza
Los Angeles, California 90024

MODESTO PC USER GROUP
Loyd Reedy
P.O.Box 5122
Modesto, California 95352

MBUG-PC
Bob Stephen
177 Webster Street A-354
Monterey, California 93940

OKOK
Lionel Soracco
P.O. Box 40429
Pasadena, California 91104

PASADENA IBM USER'S
  GROUP
Steve Bass
711 East Walnut Street #306
Pasadena, California 91101

REDDING AREA PC SOCIETY
Ken Daniels
2615 Park Marina Drive #6
Redding, California 96001

IBM AT/XT CLONE USER GROUP
  & PC CLONE NEWS
Edwin Rutsh
P.O. Box 15000/324
San Francisco, California 94115

SAN FRANCISCO PC USERS
  GROUP
Dave Eden
3145 Geary Blvd., Suite 155
San Francisco, California 94118-3316

SAN FRANCISCO COMPUTER
  SOCIETY
Ralph Callagher
P.O. Box 783
San Francisco, California 94101-0783

LABORATORY PC USERS GROUP
Glenn Ouchi
5989 Vista Loop
San Jose, California 95124

SAN JOSE IBM/PC CLUB
Jim Ward
D74/B21, 555 Bailey Ave.
San Jose, California 95141

MARIN/SONOMA PC USER
  GROUP
John Hawkins
P.O. Box 6476
San Rafael, California 94903

STANFORD PALO ALTO PC USERS
  GROUP
Corwin Nichols
P.O.Box 3738
Stanford, California 94305

SOFTWARE NATIONAL USERS
  GROUP
Ken Fowles
1111 West El Camino 109 - 402
Sunnyvale, California 94087

CONSOLIDATED COMPUTER
  CLUBS
David Nussbaum
14200 Polk Street #53
Sylmar, California 91342

SEQUOIA COMPUTER USERS
Mark Richmond
463 E. Cross Ave.
Tulare, California 93274

HIGH DESERT OSBORNE
  GROUP
Ron Davidson
7185-A 29 Palms Hwy
Twenty Nine Palms, California 92277

DIABLO VALLEY PC USERS
  GROUP
Doug Blackburn
P.O. Box 8040 #117
Walnut Creek, California 94596

COLORADO

DOG COMPUTER CLUB
Dale Cochran
2140 Braun Dr.
Golden, Colorado 80401

P.A.S.T.E.
George H. Heymann
1822 Settlers Drive
Pueblo, Colorado 81008-1814

CONNECTICUT

HART/PC
Bob Zurek
P. O. Box 1054
Glastonbury, CT 06033

PC-COMP
Jeff Levesque
P.O.Box 4408
Marion, Connecticut 06444

CONNECTICUT IBM PC USERS
  GROUP (CPC)
John McGinley
P.O.Box 291
New Canaan, Connecticut 06840

SOUTH EAST CONNECTICUT PC
  USERS GROUP
Catherine Winslow
P.O.Box 180
West Mystic, Connecticut 06388

DC

CAPITOL PC USERS GROUP
51 Monroe Street
Plaza East Two
Rockville, MD 20850

FLORIDA

MANATEE PC USER GROUP
William M. Harrier
4411 - 100th St. W
Bradenton, Florida 34210

MIAMI AMATEUR COMPUTER
  CLUB
David Bobo
4705 W. 16 Avenue
Hialeah, Florida 33012

MIAMI PC USER GROUP
Jeffrey Feinberg
4651 Sheridan Street, Suite 300
Hollywood, Florida 33021

SPACE COAST APPLE USERS'
  GROUP INC.
Elmer Whalley
P.O. Box 542112
Merritt Island, Florida 32954-2112

GREATER ORLANDO COMPUTER
USERS GROUP
Martyn W. Simpson
8142 Steeplechase Blvd.
Orlando, Florida 32818

TRI-COUNTY COMPUTER USERS
GROUP
Benjamin Soskel
2 Don Quixote Ct.
Port St. Lucie, Florida 34952

BREVARD USERS GROUP
Lee Jones
P.O.Box 2111
Satellite Beach, Florida 32937-2111

PINELLAS IBM PC USERS GROUP
Richard Kellerman
1331 Sea Gull Drive South
St. Petersburg, Florida 33707

FT. LAUDERDALE COMPUTER
USERS GROUP
Steve Matus
8461 N.W. 31 Place
Sunrise, Florida 33351

TAMPA BAY OSBORNE GROUP
David Hardiman
P. O. Box 14331
Tampa, Florida 33690

U.S.F. PERSONAL COMPUTER
USERS
Steven W. Phillipy
SVC 409, UCS Info Center, USF
Tampa, Florida 33620-7250

GEORGIA

ATLANTA IBM PC USERS GROUP
Jack Bolton
P.O. Box 28788
Atlanta, Georgia 30358

ILLINOIS

NORTHERN ILLNOIS COMPUTER
SOCIETY
Bill Budde
1271 Dundee Road 25A
Buffalo Grove, Illinois 60089

CFOG
Rand Gerald
P.O. Box 1678
Chicago, Illinois 60690

CHICAGO COMPUTER SOCIETY
Mary A. Dolce
P. O. Box 8681
Chicago, Illinois 60680

INDIANA

NORTHEAST INDIANA PC USERS
GROUP INC.
Dave Simone
9904 Goshen Road
Ft. Wayne, Indiana 46818

NORTHERN INDIANA APPLE
USERS GROUP
Edward Szymoniak
930 Highridge Drive
Schererville, Indiana

IOWA

HAWKEYE PC USERS GROUP
Shelley B. Plattner
P.O. Box 2966
Cedar Rapids, Iowa 52402

QUAD CITIES ALL COMPUTERS
USER'S GROUP
Robert H. Lay
P.O. Box 2456
Davenport, Iowa 52809

SIOUX LAND OSBORNE GROUP
Gary Shaner
Box 2193
Sioux City, Iowa 51104

DES MOINES AREA IBM PC USERS
GROUP, INC.
John Williams
1804 Hillside Street
West Des Moines, Iowa 50265

KANSAS

MIZOG
Russ May
7400 Hadley
Overland Park, Kansas 66204

WICHITA PC USERS GROUP,
INC.
Harry Hodson
P.O. Box 781200
Wichita, Kansas   67210

KENTUCKY

CENTRAL KENTUCKY COMPUTER
SOCIETY, INC.
Arthur A. Abshire
Suite 160, 2050 Idle Hour Center
Lexington, Kentucky   40502

KENTUCKY INDIANA PC USER
GROUP
Elliot Mcguire
P.O. Box 3564
Louisville, Kentucky   40201

POWELL COUNTY PC USER
GROUP
Neal Miller
Route 3 Box 144-F
Stanton, Kentucky   40380

LOUISIANA

NEW ORLEANS MACINTOSH
USERS GROUP
Box 5991
Metairie, Louisiana   70009-6991

NEW ORLEANS PERSONAL
COMPUTER CLUB
Gary Shurman
P.O. Box 8364
Metairie, Louisiana   70011

MAINE

ISLAND/REACH COMPUTER USERS
GROUP
Rowan A. Wakefield
P.O. Box 73
Deer Isle, Maine   04627

MARYLAND

BALTIMORE PC USER GROUP
Jeff Forman
1910 Trout Farm Road
Jarrettsville, Maryland   21084

CAPITAL PC USER GROUP, INC.
(CPCUG)
Jerry Schneider
51 Monroe Street, Plaza East II
Rockville, Maryland   20850

NATIONAL CAPITAL PC CLUB
Lowell Denning
13231 Hathaway Drive
Silver Spring, Maryland   20906

MASSACHUSETTS

BOSTON OSBORNE GROUP (CP/MS
DOS)
John J. Demeritt
John J. DeMeritt, 32 Willow Street
Belmont, Massachusetts   02178

THE BOSTON COMPUTER
SOCIETY
One Center Plaza
Boston, Massachusetts   02108

IBM SUB GROUP/BOSTON
COMPUTER SOCIETY
Mike Rohrbach
One Center Plaza
Boston, Massachusetts   02108

BOSTON COMPUTER SOCIETY
IBM USERS GROUP/SOFTWARE
EXCHANGE
Mike Rohrbach
385 Elliot Street
Newton, Massachusetts   02164

PIONEER VALLEY PC USERS
GROUP
Mort Sternheim
P. O. Box H
North Amherst, Massachusetts   01059

MICHIGAN

WUPCUS
Bruce Graham
P.O. Box 7508
Ann Arbor, Michigan   48107

HEATH USER'S GROUP
Jim Buszkiewicz
P.O. Box 217

SOUTHWEST MICHIGAN PC USERS
GROUP
R.K. Schmitt
2320 Crosswind Drive
Kalamazoo, Michigan   49008

MINNESOTA

TC/PC
Scott R. Young
P.O. Box 3163
Minneapolis, Minnesota   55403

MISSISSIPPI

MISSISSIPPI COMPUTER SOCIETY
Winnfred Smith
P.O. Box 16417
Jackson, Mississippi   39236-0417

MSU MICROCOMPUTER USERS
GROUP
Dr. Gene Boggess
P.O. Drawer CC
Mississippi State, Mississippi   39762

NORTH BAY PC USERS GROUP
Larry Corran
216 Barbara Circle
Ocean Spring, Mississippi   39564

IBM USERS GROUP
Doyle Brant
3004 Hwy 90
Ocean Springs, Mississippi   39564

MISSOURI

JOPLIN REGION PC CLUB
Deborah Cable
3323 Highland
Joplin, Missouri   64804

ST. LOUIS USERS GROUP
FOR THE IBM-PC
Andy Swartz
P.O. Box 69099
St. Louis, Missouri   63169

NEVADA

LAS VEGAS PC USER GROUP
Al Sexner
1415 S Arville Street Suite B
Las Vegas, Nevada   89102

NEW JERSEY

SOUTH JERSEY APPLE USER'S
GROUP
P. O. Box 4173
Cherry Hill, New Jersey   08003

AMATEUR COMPUTER GROUP
OF NJ, INC.
Bob Todd
P.O. Box 135
Scotch Plains, New Jersey   07076

NEW YORK

BIBMUG
Walt Sydoriak
P.O. Box 1487
Buffalo, New York   14221

NIAGARA FRONTIER OSBORNE
GROUP
Edwin Swan
238 Sterling Avenue
Buffalo, New York   14216

NORTHWESTERN NEW YORK PC
USER GROUP
Jim R. Cummins
181 Goode Street
Burnt Hills, New York   12027

U.G.U.G
Mike Borzumate
631 West 3rd Street
Fulton, New York   13069-3124

LONG ISLAND COMPUTER
ASSOCIATES, INC.
P.O. Box 71
Hicksville, New York   11802

MICROCOMPUTER BUSINESS
USERS GROUP
Laird Whitehill
c/o MBS 161 W. 75 Street
New York, New York   10023

NEW YORK PERSONAL
COMPUTER, INC. (NYPC)
Frank Bolton
40 Wall Street, Suite 2124
New York, New York   10005

SUFFOLK COUNTY COMPUTER
ASSOCIATION
James Edwardson
236 German Blvd.
Yaphank, New York 11980-9772

NORTH CAROLINA

IBM-PC USERS GROUP OF ASHEVILLE
Bruce Rogers
P.O. Box 2942
Asheville, North Carolina 28802

FAYETTEVILLE PC-USERS GROUP
Nick Lipe
5713 Water's Edge Drive
Fayetteville, North Carolina 28304

RALEIGH OTHER COMPUTER CLUB
Michael Rulison
3256 Lewis Farm Road
Raleigh, North Carolina 27607-6723

NORTH DAKOTA

FARGO IBM-PC USERS GROUP
Calvin Paulson
P.O. Box 9121
Fargo, North Dakota 58109

OHIO

ATHENS PC USERS GROUP
David Dabelko
P.O. Box 776
Athens, Ohio 45701-0776

ACORN GREATER CINCINNATI PC
USERS GROUP
Bill Bolduc
P.O. Box 3097
Cincinnati, Ohio 45201

CINCINNATI IBM PC USER GROUP
William Radock
P.O. Box 3097
Cincinnati, Ohio 45201

CLEVELAND COMPUTER OWNER'S
GROUP
Peter Tipett
2135 Renrock Road
Cleveland, Ohio 44118

OHIO STATE UNIVERSITY IBM PC
USERS GROUP
Art Krumsee
1050 Carmack Road
Columbus, Ohio 43210

NORTHERN OHIO BUSINESS
USERS GROUP
Michael Sura
571 East 185th Street
Euclid, Ohio 44119

PENNSYLVANIA

CLIFTON HEIGHTS USERS
GROUP
Alan Richter
P.O. Box 235
Clifton Heights, Pennsylvania 19018

EXTON PC COUNCIL, INC.
Gabe Preston
Exton Square Parkway
Exton, Pennsylvania 19341

THE HARRISBURG PC USER
GROUP
Tom Miceli
1195 Fairmont Drive
Harrisburg, Pennsylvania 17112

LANCASTER MICRO USERS
GROUP
Roger Kresge
3624 Horizon Drive
Lancaster, Pennsylvania 17601

MIDPOG
John W. Reinhardt
P.O. Box 287, 69 North 5th Street
Lemoyne, Pennsylvania 17043

GENCAP
George Garrettson
Microdoc, 815 Carpenter Lane
Philadelphia, Pennsylvania 19119

THREE RIVERS OSBORNE
GROUP
Alex Botkin
P.O. Box 23152, 4th Ave Station
Pittsburgh, Pennsylvania 15206

SOUTH CAROLINA

PALMETTO PERSONAL COMPUTER
  CLUB
Skip Williams
P.O. Box 2046
Columbia, South Carolina 29202-2046

SOUTH DAKOTA

APPLE CORE Of SIOUXLAND
William J. Reynolds
P. O. Box 90002
Sioux Falls, South Dakota 75105

TENNESSEE

CUMBERLAND MICROCOMPUTER
  USERS GROUP
Joel Seber
P.O. Box TTU 5071
Cookeville, Tennessee 38505

MEMPHIS OSBORNE GROUP
Isaac Kullman
2753 Woodland Hills Cove
Memphis, Tennessee 38127-8820

MEMPHIS PC USERS GROUP, INC.
Bob Sayre
P.O. Box 241756
Memphis, Tennessee 38124

TEXAS

AGGNOG
Eric Laine
1118 Georgia Street
College Station, Texas 77840

NORTH TEXAS PC USERS GROUP
Jim Hoisington
P.O. Box 78066
Dallas, Texas 75378

HAL PUBLIC SOFTWARE LIBRARY
Jim Nech
P.O. Box 35705
Houston, Texas 77235-5705

HOUSTON AREA LEAGUE OF PC
  USERS (HAL/PC)
Jim Nech
P.O. Box 61266
Houston, Texas 77208

PERMIAN BASIN PC USERS GROUP
Eldon Reedy
Odessa College 201 W. University
Odessa, Texas 79762

TEXAS USER GROUP
Ken Holcombe
178 Tipperary
San Antonio, Texas 78223

THE ALAMO PC ORGANIZATION
  INC.
Frank A. Synder
P.O. Box 791030
San Antonio, Texas 78279-1030

UTAH

UTAH BLUE CHIPS
Don Kaufer
P.O. Box 510811
Salt Lake City, Utah 84151

VIRGINIA

NORTHERN VIRGINIA APPLE
  USERS GROUP
Dave Harvey
P.O. Box 8211
Falls Church, Virginia 22041

BLUE RIDGE EXPRESS
Webb B. Blakman, Jr.
P.O. Box 34446
Richmond, Virginia 23234

RICHMOND KAYPRO USERS GROUP
John Alwood
P.O. Box 3892
Richmond, Virginia 23235

WASHINGTON

PACIFIC NW IBM PC USER GROUP
Rollie Cola
P.O.Box 3363
Bellevue, Washington 98009

PC-MAJIC COMPUTER SKILLS
  ASSOCIATION
Wayne I. Moore
186 East Satsop Road
Elma, Washington 98541

SOUTH KING COUNTY
OPERATIONS GROUP
David Pierce
316 S. 193rd
Seattle, Washington   98148

TACOMA OPEN GROUP
FOR MICROS
Jim Cooke
1808 Lenore Drive
Tacoma, Washington   98406

MEDICAL COMPUTER USERS
GROUP
Roger B. Lee M.D.
Dept OB/GYN, Madigan Army Medical
Center
Tacoma, Washington   98498

WEST VIRGINIA

PC-HUG
Levi Lauvray
P.O. Box 1958
Huntington, West Virginia   25720

MINDLESS ONES BBS
Frank Salerno
P.O. Box 2601
Weirton, West Virginia   26062

WISCONSIN

MILWAUKEE AREA IBM PC USERS
GROUP

Matt Brzeski
P.O. Box 2121
Milwaukee, Wisconsin   53201

WYOMING

BIG HORN BASIN COMPUTER
USERS GROUP
Paul Card
P.O. Box 2353
Cody, Wyoming   82414

CANADA

PERSONAL COMPUTER
ASSOCIATION
R. Mc Lelland
P.O.Box 235
Ajax, Ontario   LIS 3C3

PERSONAL COMPUTER CLUB
OF TORONTO
Thomas Koschate
P.O.Box 5429
Toronto, Ontario   MSW 1N6

VANCOUVER PC USERS SOCIETY
Paul E. Porter
P.O. Box 48297
Vancouver, BC   V7X 1A1

IBM PC USERS GROUP
OF WINNIPEG
Dennis Bayomi
P.O. Box 3149
Winnipeg, Manitoba   R3T2N2

GLOSSARY

ARCHIVE ATTRIBUTE A bit found in the directory entry for a file that is used to indicate if the file has been changed and thus needs to be backed up.

AT IBM PCs and clones that use the Intel 286 chip and high density disk drives.

AUTOSAVE A software feature that automatically makes a disk copy of the file that is currently being edited.

BACKGROUND Term used to describe where a program is running when it is running in a computer while another program has control of the screen.

BACKUP The practice of making diskette copies of computer files.

BATCH FILES Files used in DOS systems to invoke programs and to perform series of often-used system commands.

BAUD Measure of modem speed. Technically baud rate is not identical with bits per second, but in practice it is often used this way.

BIOS Computer programs that control basic computer operations, such as managing the screen or reading disks. The BIOS routines reside on a BIOS chip usually on the computer's motherboard.

BIT The fundamental form in which computers store information. A bit is a switch that can be set on or off.

BOARD Collection of electronic components often including processor chips. Expansion boards can be plugged into the main computer board (the motherboard) via expansion slots.

BOOT The process of loading the BIOS and operating system into a computer's memory. Booting occurs when the computer is first turned on and can also be performed to reset the computer after the computer has gotten hung up.

BOOTABLE DISKETTE Diskette that contains several operating system files, which are needed to boot the computer, as well as some program you might want to run after the computer boots.

BPS Bits per second. A measure of the speed at which a modem can transmit bytes over the phone line. Typical speeds are 1200 bps and 2400 bps.

BROWSE To look at the contents of a computer file without changing those contents.

BULLETIN BOARD Computer that is running special bulletin-board software and is hooked into a phone line. Usually bulletin boards contain libraries of software that callers may copy and allow messages to be stored for other users to retrieve.

BYTE The basic unit in which computers store and process information. A byte is simply a group of eight bits. A single byte can contain a single letter or special character, or it can be an instruction that tells the processor what operation to perform.

CENTRAL PROCESSING UNIT (CPU) The component of a computer that moves, compares, modifies, and stores, bytes of information.

CHARACTER Computer term for a letter, decimal number, or other item that can be printed. A character set is a group of characters. For example, the Greek letters and symbols used in equations constitute a special character set.

CLONE Computer that is engineered in such a way that it can execute all programs that run on a different manufacturer's computers at a similar or better level of performance. Usually used to refer to computers that function like IBM's PC.

COMPATIBILITY Ability of a machine to use the hardware components and programs designed for use on a different machine. Software compatibility means the ability to work with files created by a different program.

CONTEXT-SENSITIVE HELP Technique for displaying screens containing information about how to use a program. With context-sensitive help, invoking the help facility causes the program to display a help screen on the subject of the feature the program's user was currently positioned at.

CONTROL FILE File used by a program to hold information the program needs to use.

CONTROLLER Piece of hardware, usually on a board containing processing chips, which manages some piece of hardware.

CPS Characters per second. A measure of printer speed, which rarely corresponds to the actual number of characters the printer prints under normal printing conditions.

CRT Cathode ray tube. A computer screen or monitor.

CURSOR The little line or box that highlights the current position on the screen.

DATABASE Collection of information, usually text, arranged and indexed in a prespecified way, so that the information can be retrieved and analyzed. Also, the program that creates, updates, and reports on such a database.

DEFAULT A value supplied by a program for use when the user hasn't indicated what value should be used.

DESKTOP PUBLISHING Production of near-typeset- quality, camera-ready copy using a computer and a laser printer.

DIAGNOSTICS Programs usually supplied by the hardware vendor that can determine whether or not hardware is operating correctly.

DIRECTORY List of files contained on a disk which includes the date and size of the files and some switches used to indicate the status of each file.

DISK Device used for permanently storing computer files.

DISK DRIVE Hardware that reads and writes to a disk.

DISKETTE A removable disk.

DISTRIBUTION DISKETTE Diskette that comes in a software package, containing the files that make up the program.

DOS Disk operating system. The most popular operating system used by IBM PCs and compatibles. It comes in several versions differentiated by release numbers, such as DOS 2.0 and DOS 3.1.

DOT MATRIX PRINTER Printer that creates an image using a set of pins that pass back and forth over the paper.

DOWNLOAD To copy a computer file from another computer.

DOWNLOADABLE FONT Typeface whose description is defined by software and sent to a printer that has its own computer on board, which takes the software description, interprets it, and prints it.

DRIVER Routine that a program uses to work with a specific piece of hardware, such as a printer, monitor, or mouse.

EDIT To modify the contents of a file.

EDITOR   Piece of software that is capable of modifying the contents of a file.

EMULATION   The ability of a piece of hardware to act like a different piece of hardware in response to software.

FILE   Unit in which data is stored on a storage device such as a disk, and the unit by which the operating system indexes such data.

FLOPPY DISK   Mylar removable diskette.

FLOPPY DRIVE   Disk drive used to read floppy diskettes.

FONT   Strictly, a particular size and face of type, such as 12-point Times Roman.   Often used to refer to a typeface in a more general fashion.

FOREGROUND   Referring to a program that is sharing computer resources with other programs but has control of the screen.

FORMATTED DISK   Disk that has had a program run to write certain control information on it.

FORUM   On CompuServe, an area where a particular subject is discussed and where files related to that subject are stored.

FUNCTION KEY   Set of special keyboard keys whose functions are arbitrarily assigned by software.

GRAPHICAL INTERFACE   Method of designing programs that uses pictures (often called icons) rather than words to communicate with the user.

GRAPHICS   Used most frequently to describe charts used in business presentations; less frequently it refers to any dot-generated image.

GRAPHICS BOARD   Piece of hardware that allows the computer to send an image to a monitor.

GRAPHICS MODE   The video or printer mode in which an image is built dot by dot rather than by using stored character formats.

HYPERTEXT   Method of presenting text and graphics in which specified points in one piece of data are linked to other points in an other piece of data in a relatively free-form manner.

IBM GRAPHICS   Set of characters provided on monitors and certain printers to allow the drawing of boxes in character mode.

IMAGE COPY   Process of copying the entire contents of a disk onto another medium, such as tape or diskette.

IMPORT   To bring data in to one program from a file created by a different program.

K   1,024, the power of 2 closest to 1,000.   Often used to stand for 1,000.

LAPTOP COMPUTER   Portable computer designed to fit into a briefcase, weighing only a few pounds, and powered by batteries.

LASER PRINTER Printer that produces a page image by bonding toner to paper in a fashion similar to Xerography.

LQ MODE The ability to produce printed output that compares with the output of office electric typewriters.

MACRO Often, a recording of a series of keystrokes that can be played back by invoking a particular sequence of keystrokes within some piece of software. Used to perform frequently repeated tasks.

MAIL MERGE Word-processing feature that creates customized junk mail.

MAINFRAME A powerful multimillion-dollar computer usually used to store and process institutional or corporate databases.

MEG 1,048,576, the power of 2 closest to 1 million.

MEMORY Where data must be stored for the processor to work with it. Usually embodied in memory chips that may be installed on the motherboard or on expansion slots.

MEMORY RESIDENT PROGRAM Program that is able to install itself in such a way that it can run side by side with other programs.

MENU List of options displayed on a screen by a program.

MICROPERF Continuous form computer paper separated by lines of tiny dots which separate leaving a clean edge.

MIDI Musical instrument digital interface. A protocol used by electronic instruments and tape recorders to communicate with each other.

MODEM Piece of hardware that converts bytes stored in digital form to the analog form used to send electronic information over the phone line.

MONOCHROME Term describing monitors that display in two colors, usually amber/black or green/black.

MOTHERBOARD A computer's main integrated circuit board usually containing a system's CPU, BIOS chip, and main memory. Other components may be on the motherboard too.

MOUSE Pointing device that is moved around some surface to control a pointer on a computer screen. It contains buttons that can be assigned functions by software.

MULTITASKING Ability of computer hardware to run more than one program in same the time period.

NLQ MODE Near letter quality. Usually used to describe the dot matrix fonts.

ON-LINE Describing the connection of a terminal or PC to another computer in such a way that data can be transmitted.

OPERATING SYSTEM Master program that controls the use of a computer's resources and lets other programs run in the computer.

PC Personal computer. Trademark of the IBM Corporation for its 1981 microcomputer product, now rapidly becoming a generic term.

PIM Personal information manager. Catchall term for the class of "thoughtware."

PROGRAM At the lowest level, a series of computer-readable instructions that tell the computer's processor what operations to perform on what data. Also, the file containing such instructions. Also, a series of instructions written in a human-readable computer language such as Assembly language or BASIC, which can be translated into computer-readable form.

RECORD Unit in which a database program stores information within a computer file.

RESOLUTION Number of dots per inch that a printer or monitor uses to create an image.

SCANNER Piece of hardware that can convert an image on a printed page into a text or graphics file, which can be stored and processed by a computer.

SHAREWARE Coyprighted computer software that can be copied and used freely with the understanding that if the user continues to use the software after testing it out, he will send a registration fee to the owner of that software.

SHELL Computer program that provides screens and menus which simplify using the commands supplied with a computer's operating system.

SIG Special interest group. A group of people who meet at a computer users group or electronically via a communications service to discuss a topic of mutual interest.

SLOT Receptacle into which add-on boards can be plugged, allowing them to communicate with the motherboard.

SOFT REBOOT Using a software command to cause a computer to clear its memory and reload its BIOS and operating system. On a PC this is accomplished by pressing Alt-Ctrl-Del at the same time.

SOFTWARE Computer programs.

SOFTWARE LIBRARY A collection of computer programs.

SPELL CHECKER Program often included as part of a word processor package, which finds misspelled words and suggests correct spellings.

SPREADSHEET Grid of columns and rows, every element of which can contain a number, a descriptive phrase, or a formula relating other grid elements to each other. Also, the software that creates, prints, and stores such spreadsheets.

SYSTEM COMMANDS Set of commands, such as COPY or ERASE, which are really utilities supplied with the operating system.

SYSTEM CONFIGURATION The specific combination of hardware components that make up a computer system.

TEXT Data that is made up of letters, numbers, and special control characters stored in character format.

TEXT MODE Mode used by monitors and printers in which an image is made up of a stream of characters, with a predefined image used for each character. This is in contrast to graphics mode where an image is made up of a stream of dots, which are either on or off.

TRACKBALL Mouse substitute consisting of a ball in a stationary mounting which is swiveled with the fingers to control an on-screen pointer.

TRACTOR FEED Printer attachment that pulls paper through the printer using holes punched in the sides of the paper.

TSR Terminate and stay resident. Program that can run at the same time as other programs, being invoked by a special key which causes it to "pop up."

TUTORIAL Computer program that teaches you how to use some other computer program.

UPGRADE New version of a piece of software, usually with additional features. Hardware may be upgraded too, usually by replacing chips.

UPLOAD To copy a file from one computer to a library on another computer.

UTILITY Program that is useful for managing the computer's resources. Also, small program that performs a useful function.

VDT Video display terminal. A monitor or computer screen.

VIRUS Program routine that is hidden in another program and intended to cause malicious damage. Such viruses may be written in such a way that they install themselves in a host computer and then copy themselves into other files or communicating computers.

WORD PROCESSOR Complex software package used to create, edit, and print manuscripts.

WYSIWYG What you see is what you get. A term describing a program that displays a file exactly the way it will print out on a printer.

XT A kind of IBM PC or compatible characterized by having an 8088 or 8086 chip, a 5-1/4" 360K floppy drive, and usually a 20- or 30-meg, 65-millisecond hard drive.

INDEX

A

ABF, 287
Academic journals, 30
Accessing, disk, 97
Access time, 141
Accounting, and spreadsheets, 46
Acta, 36
Addiction to computer use, 62–63
Address conflicts, 274
Adobe Illustrator, 34
Adult education, 74
Advertisements, 175
Agenda, 40
Aladdin, 221
Aldus Freehand, 34
Aldus Pagemaker, 53, 221
Alphabets, non-Roman, 16, 203
American Optometric Association, 69
Amiga, 121
Analog monitors, 143
Apple Computer, 111, 115
Apple II, 76
Apple IIe, 26, 121
ARCE, 237
ARCed files, 237
Archive attribute, 287
Artform, software as, 105–7
Artificial intelligence, 93
Artist, self image and computers, 59
ASCII, 200
    code, 88
    files, 214
    format, 194
AskSam, 43
AT, memory, 136
Atari ST, 121

ATEX, 54, 200
Autoexec.bat, 275, 280
Automatic backup, 198–99
Automenu, 223
Autosave, 198
    restoring from files, 263
Autosig, 220–21, 238
Award BIOS, 137

B

Background, 133
Backup, 263, 266, 282–91
    and disk failure, 99
    automatic, 198–99
    before customizing software, 250–51
    defense against viruses, 240
    file copy, 286–87
    for floppy disk systems, 288
    image copy, 285–86
    of long documents, 196
    minimal, 287–88
    software for, 286–87
    when to schedule, 288
    why needed, 283–84
Backup software, 225
Bar code readers, 102
Bar graph, 33
BASIC programming, 75
Batch files, 95
Baud, 105
Benchmarks, 131
Better Business Bureau, 73
Biblio-File, 43
BIOS, 137–38

Bitcom, 219
Bits, 87
BIX, 52, 216, 217
Bleeding edge, 118
Boards, 103
  half size, 148
  installing, 146–47
  problems with, 274
  sales contract, 171
Book-length manuscript handling features,195–96
Book promotion, 19
Books:
  about computers, 73–74
  about shareware, 238
  word processor features for writing, 195–96
Boot, 94
Boot disk, 271
Borland:
  cheap software, 230
  customer support, 280
  free on-line time from, 218
Boston Computer Society, 77
Box drawing characters, 202
Boyan 3D, 220
Bps, 105
Bricklin, Dan, 112
Browse utility, 56, 224
Buerg, Vern, 224, 237
Bug, software, 92
Bulletin boards, 18–19, 50, 216, 235
  fees, 51
  free, 218–19
  merchants', 51
Bus, 102, 103, 129–30
Byte, 87

C

Cables, for boards, 103
Cache, 130
CAD, 34
Calendar software, 48
Call, to program, 94
Cards, 102
  installing, 103
Carpal tunnel syndrome, 70
CD Rom, 162
Central processing unit, 85–87 (*see also*
  Processor)
CGA, 143, 144
Character mode, 33
Cheap word processors, 187
Children and computer literacy, 7
Chin, Wayne, 237
Chips, 96
Chips and Technologies BIOS, 137
CHKDSK, 265
Classes, 181
Clock, 129
Clones, 122–25 (*see also* PC clone)
  Macintosh, 125
  in mail order ads, 173
  quirks of, 123
College computer courses, 75

Color graphics standards, 143
Color laser printers, 157
Color printers, 155
COM file extension, 100
COM1, 273
Command driven interface, 191
Comments, 201
Commercial software, and viruses, 240
Commodore, 76, 121
Communications, computer, 12–13, 18–19, 215–21
  (*see also* On-line information services)
Communications software, 50–52, 219–21
Compaq, 113, 123
Compatibility, 125
  and BIOS, 137
Components, 84
Compressed files, 237
CompuServe, 12, 18, 52, 235, 238, 268, 280, 281
  billing, 217
  fax, 162
  free sign-on paks for, 218
  phone number, 216
  recommendations, 178–179
  software for, 220–21
  writers on, 61, 217
Computer (*see also* AT; Clones; IBM PC; Macintosh;
  PC; Software; XT)
  addiction, 62
  attitudes toward, 58–61
  backup, why needed, 283–85
  basic concepts, 84–107
  basic function of, 84
  best, 119–20
  books, 73–74
  breakdowns, 256
  bureaucracy, 60
  buying, 128–48
  chips, 96
  communications, 215–21
  configuring, 128–48
  cost, 2, 15, 120
  dead on arrival, 180–82
  disks, 96–99
  education resources, 72–78
  file, 99–102
  file directory, 101
  fire drill, 290–91
  hands-on courses, 74–76
  hardware families, 120–21
  health concerns, 68–71
  information, how stored, 87
  jargon, 82–83
  justification for buying, 4–44
  magazines, 240–41
  memory, 135–37
  moving, 99
  NeXT, 126–27
  operating system, 93–96
  paper, 165
  port, 102
  portable, 163
  press, 173–75
  price, 104
  program, 89
  rebooting, 261
  replacing books, 67

revising with, 64
salespeople, 169
selling out by using, 59
slots, 102
stores, 168–72
time needed to master, 68
as tool, 1
upgrading, 103
usage as a game, 62
use by children, 7–8
used, 167
viruses, 238–40
warranties, 171
when to buy, 117
at work, 78
Computer archetype, 81
Computer furniture, 164
Computer games, 8, 94
Computer program (*see* Program; Software)
Computer science, 80
Computer Shopper, 77
Conferencing, on-line, 220
CONFIG.SYS, 280
Configuration, for beginners, 121
Consultants, computer, 176–77, 178, 212
Contact Plus, 212
Context-sensitive help, 190
Context switching software, 226
Continuous form paper, 154
Control codes, 104
Control file, 100, 250
  missing, 264
  overlaid, 266–67
Copy, 192
Copyediting, 11
Copying files, 247
Copy II Mac, 224
Corefast, 286
Corrections, 66
Courses, for computer beginners, 75
CP/M, 94, 112
Cps, 153
CPU (*see* Central processing unit; Processor)
Creativity:
  computer as an aid to, 19–22
  decreased by technology, 67–68
Cricket Draw, 34
Crosstalk, 219
Cursor control, 199–200, 249
Customer support, calling, 279–81
Customizing software, 250–51
Cut and paste, 48–49, 214
Cut sheets, 153

D

Daisy wheel printers, 151
Data, destruction of, 283–85
Database:
  for businesses, 41–42
  cost of using, 13
  indexes for random information, 43
  listed by name, 41
  on-line, 12–13

phone number, 212
random, 43–44, 207–12
selecting, 212–13
special purpose, 43–44, 212
structured, 40–41, 212–13
and unstructured information, 42
Data entry, 14
dBase, 41, 205, 212
DEC, 76
Defaults, 247
Default value, 93
Delete function, 192
Delivery date, 172
Dell Computer, 173
DELPHI, 12, 52, 216
  writer's conference, 217
Demos, 170–71
Department stores, 172
Desk accessory, 47, 136
Desktop Express, 221
Desktop publishing, 52–54, 221–22
  and ATEX, 200–201
  complexity of, 15
  drawbacks for the amateur, 53
  history, 116
  monitors, 143
  print shop as alternative, 54
  software, listed by name, 53
  and speedy processors, 134–35
Desktop utilities, 47–49, 213–15
Desqview, 226
Diagnostic disk, 277
DIALOG, 12
Dictionary, adding words to, 251
DIP switches, 275
Directory, 101, 248, 269
Directory path, 102
Discounting, 232
Disk access, and speed, 130
Disk controller, 141
Disk drive, 97, (*see also* Diskette; Diskette drive; Disks)
  buying, 138–42
  light, 97–98
  noise, 271
Diskette, 96–99
  capacity, 100
  cost of, 138
  distribution, 247
  errors, 270–71
  formatting, 98
  how data is stored, 97
  limitations of, 140
  Macintosh, 138
  proper insertion of, 270
  protective envelope, 97
  read-only, 270
  sizes of, 138–39
  sleeve, 97
  unreadable, 276
Diskette drive:
  broken, 277
  waiting for diskette, 260
DiskFit, 286
Disk full error, 267
Disk Optimizer, 223

Disk platter, 97
Disks, 96–99
  how used, 138
  selection of, 138–42
Disk sharing, 139
DiskTop, 47
DisplayWrite, 20
Distribution diskette, 247
Distributors, shareware, 234
Document, word processing, 192
Do-it-yourself hardware, 146
DOS, 94, 122
  batch files, 95
  history, 112
  memory limitations, 137
  memory requirements, 135
DOS shell, 222–23
Dot matrix printers, 151–56
  cost, 153
  fonts, 152–53
Dow Jones, 12
Downloadable fonts, 155
Draft mode, 153
Drawing software, listed by name, 34
Drawing with computers, 20
Driver, printer, 104
Duang Jan, 203

E

Ease-of-use word processors, 30
Editor (software), 214, 224
EDLIN, 224
Education, 74–76
EGA, 143
8086, 130
8088, 129–30
  cost of systems, 133
  and multitasking, 133
Electronic mail, 217
Electronic submissions, 200–201
Electronic text, difficulty of browsing, 66
Electronic typewriters as printers, 151
Employment agency bulletin boards, 51
Emulation:
  printers, 104
  software, 126
Envelopes, printing on, 154
Epson, 268
  FX 80, 158
  LQ-2500, 158
  LX-800, 152
  printers, 104
Equations, 203
Erased files, restoring, 223–24
Erasing, difficulty of, 64
Ergonomics, 70
Error messages, 246, 264–66
Errors (*see also* Help; Troubleshooting strategies)
  boot disk, 271
  disk full, 267
  file missing, 264–65
  getting help with, 279–81

modem, 273–74
  numbered, 276
  parity check, 275
  printer, 273
  printing, 269
  program not found, 269
  read only file, 270
  software, 246
Excel, 45
EXE, 100
Expanded memory, 214
Extended memory, 214
External modem, 105, 160
Eyestrain, 69, 144

F

Failure, of hard disk drives, 98
Fanzines, 16
Fastback, 286
Fax, via on-line services, 217
Fax cards, 161
Features, common to all word processors, 192–94
FGREP, 49, 211, 265
FIDOnet, 18, 52, 178, 219
Figures, 197
File, 99–102
  defined, 100
  directory, 101
  lost, 264–66
  messed up, 262–63
  name, 100
  program files list, 248
  read only, 270
  saving, 262, 289
File copy backup, 286–87
File Express, 212
File extension, 100
File finder software, 225
FileMaker Plus, 41
Filename, 100
File recovery software, 223–24,
File transfer protocol, 219
File transfers, on-line, 217
Finances, managing on computer, 6
Findit, 225
Findswell, 225
FISHNET forum, 242
Flashback, 286
Floating references, 29, 197
Floppy disk, (*see* Diskette)
Floppy disk drive, 138–39
Flowcharting software, 34
Flow of ideas, arranging with outliner, 38
FLUSHOT, 240
Font cartridges, 155
Font control features, 204
Fonts:
  dot matrix, 152–53
  inkjet printer, 156
  laser, 158
Footnotes, 29, 197
Ford, Nelson, 235
Foreground, 133

Formatting, 98
    of document, 194
    high level, 141
    low level, 141, 278
FORTRAN, 13
Forum (CompuServe) 238, 242, 268, 281 (see also
        CompuServe)
FoxBase, 41
Freelance, 33
Fritter, 67
Fritterware, 20
FullWrite Professional, 30
Function key driven interface, 191
Function keys, 145
Furniture, 164–65

G

Games, video standards, 144
Gamma Productions, Inc., 203
GEnie, 12, 52, 216, 217, 221, 238
Glare, 144
GOfer, 209, 265
Grammar checkers, 32, 196, 215
Grammatik III, 32, 215
Grandview, 36, 40, 208, 210
Graphical interface, 115, 206
Graphics:
    disk space requirements, 140
    and mouse, 161
    software, 33–35
    and speedy processor, 134
Graphics card, 143
Graphics formats, 33
Graphics libraries, 33
Graphics mode, 33
Greek, 16, 30, 31, 203
Guide, 39, 209

H

Haas, Peter, 231
Halftones, and scanner, 35
Hard disk, 97–99 (see also Disk drive; Disks)
    capacity, 100
    card based, 278
    cleaning up, 267
    controller, 141
    directory, 101
    disappearing, 277
    external, 142
    failure, 278
    how data is stored, 97
    parking heads, 99
    problems caused by power supply, 279
    reasons for buying, 139–40
    sales contract, 171
    selecting, 138–42
    sizes, 140
    speed, 140
    utilization, 140
    warranties, 171

Hard disk utility, 226
Hardware, 84
    broken appearing, 269–75
    great laws of, 116–19
    history, 110–16
Hardware buying principles, 116–19
Hardware components, table, 86
Hardware Envy, 118
Hardware problems, 180–82
Harvard Graphics, 33
Head crash, 99
    recovery software, 224
Headers and footers, 194
Headstart, 223
Health problems
    CRT workers, 68–70
    eye problems, 69
    listed, 69
    miscarriages, 70
    mouse-induced, 161
Hebrew, 16, 30
Help
    hardware problems, 279
    on-line, 178-79
    shareware, 238
    software problems, 279–81
    users groups, 178
Help screens, for word processor, 189
Hercules, software to run CGA on, 226
Hercules compatible graphics, 143
Hercules In-Color Card, 144
Hewlett-Packard Laserjet, 104, 158
Hexadecimal number system, 88
HFS Backup, 286
HGCIBM, 226
High density diskettes, 138
Homebase, 47, 213
Hopper, Grace, 92
Hung system, 260–62
Hypertext, 38,
    links, 39

I

IBM, 284
    as market leader, 177
    and PC software, 114
    reasons for buying, 122–23
IBM AT, 123, 129, 130, 136, 138
    diskette drives, 138
    disk speed, 130
IBM compatible computer (see Clones)
IBM mainframe communications, 220
IBMNET forum, 238, 268
IBMNEW forum, 238
IBM PC (see also AT; Clones; PC; PS2; XT)
    BIOS, 137
    design of, 113
    history, 111–13
    speed, 129
IBMSW forum, 281
Illegal software, 232–33
Illustrations, 14–15, 33
Image copy backup, 285–86

Imagewriter LQ, 155
Imagewriter II, 155
Index generation features, 201–02
Information, real nature of, 87
InfoTrac, 241
Inkjet printers, 156–57
Input, 84
Installing software, 247–49, 268–69
Instant Recall, 43, 210, 211
Instruction byte, 89
Integrated software, 29, 45
Internal modem, 105, 160
Interrupts, 274
Intuitive design, 208
IQUEST database, 12, 52
IRQ-1, 274
IZE, 43, 210

J

Jargon, 82–83
Jobs, Steven, 111, 126
Junk mail, 17, 29, 205

K

K, 96
Kaiser Permanente CRT study, 70
Kermit, 219
Keyboard, 85, 145–46
    problems with, 274
Keyboard modification software, 226
Keystroke recording, 204

L

Laptops, 163
Laser printer, 34, 52, 157–58, 204
Laserwriter, 157
Leading Edge, 29, 171, 268, 274
Lecture aids, 17
Letrhead, 35
Letterhead, 35, 154
Libraries, laptop noise in, 163
Library (software), 241
Lighting, and eyestrain, 69
Line drawing features, 202
Line drawings, and scanners, 35
LIST, 224
List prices, software, 229
LITFORUM forum, 242
Logic, 89–93, 256
Loops, programming, 90
Lotus Agenda, 40, 210
Lotus Express, 221
Lotus Metro, 47, 213
Lotus 1-2-3, 45, 100, 205
Low level formatting, 141
LQ mode, 154

M

MacCalc, 45
Mace Utilities, 224
Machine language, 25
Macintosh, 121
    backup software, 286
    boards for, 148
    communications software, 221
    courses, 76
    desk accessory memory requirements, 136
    and desktop accessories, 47
    diskette drives for, 139
    diskettes, 138
    drawing software for, 34
    enthusiasts, 124
    file finders, 225
    GEnie and, 238
    grammar checker, 215
    and graphics, 33
    hard disk, 142
    history, 115–16
    hypertext, 39
    keyboards, 145
    lack of clones, 125
    MAUG forums, 238, 268
    memory, 136
    memory requirements, 135
    modems for, 160
    monitors, 144
    mouse for, 161
    MultiFinder, 133
    multitasking, 132
    operating system, 94
    outlining word processor, 203
    printers, 155–56
    reasons for buying, 124–25
    recovery software, 224
    and shareware, 185
    slots, 103, 148
    software for MCI Mail, 221
    spreadsheets, 45
    success in corporate world, 116
    word processors, 30
    word processors, cheap, 187
Macintosh Interface, 115
Macintosh Plus, 130, 136, 144, 145, 148, 243
Macintosh SE, 102, 129, 130, 136, 139, 144, 145, 148
Macintosh II, 103, 129, 132
MacPaint, 34
MacProof, 215
Macro, 204, 226
MacUser, 28, 173, 240
MacWorld, 173, 236, 240
MacWrite, 30
Magazine Index, 175, 241
Magazines, 240–41
Magic words, 81
Mail, electronic, 217
Mail merge, 205
Mail order, 141, 172–73
    safety tips, 231–32
Mainframe, compared to PC, 114
Mainframe computers, 14–15
Manes, Stephen, 20
Manuals, software, 245–46, 253

Manuscript production, 9–10
Map making software, 34
Margins, 194
Mass market and software, 230
MAUG forum, 238, 268
MaxThink, 36, 39
MCGA, 143
MCI Mail, 162, 221
Meg, 96
Memory, 87–89, 95–96, 135–37
Memory chips:
  bad, 276
  history, 111
Memory resident software, 210, 214–15, 269 (see
    also TSR)
Menus, 28, 161, 190–91
MHz, 129
Microchannel bus, 103
Microperf paper, 165
Microsoft, 112
Microsoft Excel, 45
Microsoft Windows, 116, 133, 243
Microsoft Word, 29, 30, 54, 144, 187, 221
Microsoft Write, 187
MIDI, 19
MIDI board, 146–47, 179, 274
MIDI synthesizers, 102
MindWrite, 36, 187
MindWrite Express, 203
MockPackage+, 47, 213
Modem, 104–5, 159–60
  benefits of, 160
  and communications software, 50
  external, 105
  internal, 105
  and phone dialer software, 48
  problems with, 272, 273–74
  sales contract for, 171
  software for, 219
Monitor, 104, 142–45 (see also Screen)
  analog, 143
  broken, 279
  color, 142
  cost, 142
  and eyestrain, 69
  monochrome, 142
  problems with, 272–73
  TTL, 143
More, 36, 209
Motherboard, 85, 102
Motorola chips, 132
Mouse, 39, 79, 102, 161
Move, 192
Moving bar menu, 191
MTBF (Mean Time Between Failures), 98
MultiFinder, 133, 136
MultiMate, 29, 190, 224, 263
MultiPlan, 45
Multitasking, 132–34
Music, 19

N

Navigator, 220

Newsletters, 16
New technology, problems with, 117–18
New users SIG, 177
NeXT computer, 126–27
9-pin printers, 152
NLQ mode, 152
Non-Roman alphabets, 16, 203
Norton Commander, 223
Norton Utilities, 224
Norton Utilities Advanced Edition, 226
Nota Bene, 30, 192, 197, 203, 232
Notepad, 43, 212, 213
  and desktop software, 48
NuBus, 103
Numeric key pad, 145

O

Obsolescence, 117
On-line, printer, 261
On-line information services, 18, 52 (see also
    BIX; CompuServ; DELPHI; GEnie)
  billing for, 217–18
  choosing, 215–17
  forums, 242
  getting help on, 178–79
  how to join, 218
  problems with, 272–3
Operating system, 93–95
  and directories, 101
  and diskette drive, 98
  file names, 100
  and software packages, 243
Optical disks, 162
Oracle, 133
OS/2, 133, 135
Outline, example of, 38
Outliners:
  eliminating need for drafts, 65
  function illustrated, 36–38
  with graphics capability, 209
  included with word processor, 203
  listed, 36
  selecting, 207–12
  use of, 11–12
Output, 84

P

Page numbering, 194
Paper, 66, 154, 165–66
Paperchase, 12, 52
Paradox, 41, 212
Parameter, 93
Park program for hard drives, 99
Path, directory, 102
Patriquin, Norm, 265, 287
PC, 121, 122
  ANSI.SYS driver, 272
  ARC programs, 237
  backup software, 286
  batch files, 95

PC (*cont'd.*)
  communications software, 221
  context switching, 226–27
  copy command for backup, 288
  courses, 76
  cursor control conventions, 199–200
  disk drives, 138–42
  file finders, 225
  filenames, 100
  finding lost files on, 265
  grammar checker, 215
  graphics programs, 33
  help resources on-line, 238
  history, 111–15
  keyboards, 145
  line drawing characters, 202
  memory, 96, 135–37, 214
  models, 123
  modems for, 160
  monitors, 143–44
  mouse, 161
  multitasking, 132–34
  operating systems for, 94
  ports, 102, 273–74
  printer control codes, 104
  processor, 129–34
  reasons for buying, 124–25
  recovery software, 223–24
  shareware, 185, 210–12
  shareware forum help, 281
  slots, 148
  software for MCI Mail, 221
  spreadsheets, 45
  word processors, 28, 29, 33, 187
PC-Calc +, 45–46
PC clone, 113–14
  BIOS, 137–38
PC compatibles, problems with software, 268
PC Computing, 173
PC Connection, 231
PC-Deskteam, 47, 213
PC-File, 212–13, 238
  as aid in creating index, 202
PC-Fullback, 286
PC-Hypertext, 211
PC Magazine, 28, 30, 31, 118, 158, 173, 206, 236, 240
PC-MOS, 94
PCopy, 287
PC-Outline, 36, 200, 208, 211, 236
PC Paintbrush Plus, 34
PC-Stylist, 215
PC Tools Deluxe, 213, 223, 286
PC World, 173
PC-Write, 29, 187, 238, 281
PC XT, 123, 243 (*see also* XT)
Peas buying program, 91
Personal Computing, 173, 240
Personal Information Managers, 39–40, 207–12
PFS: Professional Write, 29
Phoenix BIOS, 137
Phone dialers, 213
Phone line, 273
Phone number database, 212
Phone numbers and desktop software, 48
Phone outlet, 165

Photography, and scanners, 35
Pie chart, 33
PIM (*see* Personal Information Managers)
Pixel Paint, 34
Pop-up software, 47 (*see also* Memory resident software)
Port, 102
Portable computers, 162–63
Postscript, 204
Power loss, 96
Power supply, problems with, 279
Presentation Manager, 116
Press, computer, 173–75
Preview mode, monitors, 144
Printer, 102, 104, 149–59
  availability of, 15
  carriage size, 155
  color, 34, 157
  color dot matrix, 155
  controls, 155
  cost, 157
  daisy wheel, 151
  dot matrix, 151–56
  durability, 154
  and envelopes, 154
  fonts, 155
  and graphics, 34
  and illustrations, 14
  inkjet, 156–57
  laser, 52, 157–58
  9-pin, 152
  noise, 159
  and paper feeds, 154
  problems with, 273
  psychological effects of, 150
  ribbons, 158, 273
  special paper, 159
  speed, 153
  24-pin, 154
  waiting for, 261
  wasting paper, 66
Printer cable, 159
Printer covers, 164
Printer driver, 104, 269
  for inkjet printer, 156
Printer emulation, 104, 159
Print spooler, 56
Problem solving, keeping log, 249
Processing, 85
Processor, 85
  relationship with software, 88
  selecting, 129–35
  speed, 129–32
Procomm, 219
Prodigy, 52, 216
Production cycle, 10–11
Product listing, 26
Program, 89–93
  defined, 24–25
  loops, 90
  parameter, 93
  sample, 91
  switches, 90
Program diskettes, 25–26
Programmers:
  as artists, 106

and computer addiction, 63
as priesthood, 59
recommending hardware, 176
Programming, 63
Programming logic, 89–93
Programs, and main memory, 96
Promoting your work, 17
    word processor features for, 204
Proportional spacing, 153
Psearch, 49, 211, 265
PS/2
    diskette drives, 138, 113, 123
Psychological effects of typestyles, 150
Public domain software, 21
Public (Software) Library, 235, 287
Publishers, standards for illustrations, 15
Pull-down menu, 191

Q

Q&A Word, 30
Quattro, 45
Qubecalc, 45
Quicksoft, 281

R

Radiation, from monitors, 69
RAM (Random Access Memory), 85 (see also
    Memory)
RAM disk, 132, 135–36
Random information database, 210
Random information managers, 43, 207–13
RBase, 41, 212
RBBS, 52
READ.ME files, 237, 248, 268
Read/write head, 97, 99
Reboot, soft, 261
Recommendations, 109
Redlining, 201
Red Ryder, 220
Reflist, 43
Reformatting hard disk, 223
Registering shareware, 233
Registering software, 253
Registration number, and customer support,
    280
Requirements, for software, 242–43
Reset button, 261
Resolution, 142
Reviewers, 109, 119
Reviews, software, 236, 241
Revision, hazards of, 64
Ribbons, printer, 158, 273,
    for 24-pin printers, 155
Rice, Ann, 65
Rifkin, Jeremy, 59
Rightwriter, 32
Root directory, 101
Rotating backups, 289–90
Rumpelstiltskin, 62
Russian, 16, 30

S

Salespeople, 169
Save, and diskettes, 98
Saving file, 262, 289
Scanners, 35–36, 102, 162
Screen, 85 (see also Monitor)
    difficulty of reading, 66–67
    displaying junk, 266–67
    and eyestrain, 69
    problems with, 272–73
Script language, 219
SCSI port, 102, 142
Search and Replace, 192
Secretaries, 249
Self-publishing, 15–16
Sensible Grammar, 215
Service, importance of, 180–82
Shafer, Dan, 28
Shareware, 21, 184–86, 233–40, 253
    backup software, 287
    communications programs, 50, 220–21
    desktop utilities, 47, 213
    DOS shell, 223
    file finders, 225
    getting help with, 238, 281
    grammar checker, 215
    installing, 236–37
    outliner, 211
    random information database, 209, 210–13
    reviewed in magazines, 236
    rules, 234–35
    sources for, 235–36
    spreadsheets, 45
    text searchers, 49
    users group as source, 241
    utilities, 56
    and viruses, 239–40
    word processors, 187
Shareware distributors, 235, 241–42
Shell, DOS, 222–23
Shells, 55
SideKick, 47, 213, 214
SIGs, 76
60020, 132
60030, 132
Sleeve, of diskette, 97
Slides, for presentation graphics, 34
Slots, 102–3, 147–48
Soft reboot, 261
Software (see also Program; Shareware)
    for backup, 286–87
    bug, 92
    commercial sources of, 229–33
    compatibility with system, 242–43
    copying, as crime, 232–33
    customer support for, 279–81
    defined, 89
    errors, 246
    errors that look like hardware failure, 269–75
    expenses of supporting, 230
    getting help with, 279–81
    installing, 247–49
    interaction with hardware, 88
    list price, 229
    new programs that won't work, 267–69

Software (*cont'd.*)
  package, contents, 25–26
  parameter, 93
  psychological effect of failure of, 256
  registration, 253
  strategy for buying, 183–87
  support for, 228–29
  upgrades, 254
  as work of art, 105–7
Software Carousel, 226
Sorting, as function of PIM, 40
Speed, 129–32
  and desktop publishing, 134–35
  and disk activity, 130
  software requiring, 132
  and word processing, 131
Speed-up software, causing disk problems,
  271
Spell checker, 25, 27, 194
  adding words to dictionary, 251
  for writer, 196–97
Spreadsheet, 44–47
  function of, 45–46
  history, 112
  listed by name, 45
  problems with, 46
Sprint, 30–31, 187, 218, 221, 230
  and desktop publishing, 54
  floating references, 197
  low price of, 187
Starter set software, 186
Statistics, 13
Storage devices, 95–99
Stores, 168–72
  support issues, 181–82
Stuck, what to do when, 260
Style analysers, 32, 215
Style sheets, 205
Subdirectory, 101
SuperPaint, 34
Support, customer, 279–81
Surge protectors, 164
  problems with, 279
Switches, in programming, 90
Symantec Utilities, 224
Sysop, 51
System commands, 95

T

Table of contents, generating, 202
Tandy, 29
Tandy 1000, 223
  special boards for, 148
TAPCIS, 220–21, 238
Taxes, and spreadsheet, 44–46
Teaching software, 18
Telenet, 217
Telephone, 48, 165, 212, 213, 273
Telephone charges for on–line access, 217–18
Terminal emulation, 220
Text management, 210
Text searchers, 49–50
Thesaurus, 25, 197

ThinkTank, 36
Thoughtware, 40, 121
3BY5, 211
386 chip, 123–24, 133
386 SX chip, 130
Time/Life Books, 30
Toner cartridges, 157
Tool, definition, 24
Tools to get and share info, *table*, 50
Tools to manage the computer, *table*, 55
Tools to organize information, *table*, 41
Tools to organize thoughts, *table*, 36
Tools to organize yourself, *table*, 47
Tools to produce and format manuscript,
  table, 27
Tools to produce publications, 52–54
Top Desk, 47
Tornado Notes, 43
Trackball, 161
Track on disk, 97
Tractor feed, 154
Trade shows, 241
Transmission speed, 105
Tree structured directory, 101
Troubleshooting strategies, 257–79
TSR, 47, 133 (*see also* Memory resident
  software)
  and memory requirements, 136
  removing, 275
TTL monitors, 143
Turbo XT, 123
Tutorial, using, 249
Tutorial mode, 190
Tutorials, 28
24-pin printer, 154
  ribbons for, 155 286, 130, 133, 134
TYMNET, 217
Typing, 68
Typing skills, 78

U

Undelete utility, 223–24
Undo, in word processor, 262
Unerase, 266
Unerase utility, 223–24
Uninterruptible power supply, 164
UNIX, 76, 94
  and NeXT, 126
Upgrades, 254
USA Today, 70
Used computers, 167
Users groups, 76–78, 235, 241
  and bulletin boards, 51, 77
  and free on-line offers, 218
  function of, 77
  and hardware modifications, 147
  how to locate, 77
  shareware, 241
  software libraries, 77
  as source for recommendations, 177–78
Utilities, 54–57, 222–27
  drawbacks of, 56–57
  part of operating system, 95

V

Vendex, 29
Ventura Publisher, 53, 221
VGA, 143
Video card, 143
Video standards, 143–44
Views of data, 210
Viruses, 238–40
VISICALC, 112
Vision problems, and monitors, 144
Visually impaired, software for, 226
VP Planner, 45

W

Waiting, benefits of, 117
Wait state, 129
Warranties, 171
WHEREIS, 225, 265
Wide carriage printers, 155
Windows (Microsoft), 133
WordPerfect, 29, 30, 187, 221
  customer toll free support, 280
  and desktop publishing, 54
  on Macintosh, 30
  monitors for, 144
Word processing:
  and mouse, 161
  and PC history, 112
  and processor speed, 131
Word processing machines, 10
Word processor, 16
  bad ones still useful, 188
  best sellers, 29
  changing, 188
  cheap, 187
  cost, 187
  customizing, 250–51
  disks, 25–26
  features, 28–29, 189–206, 193 (*table*)
  and file names, 100
  fixing ruined document in, 262
  as fritterware, 21
  history, 26–27
  learning to use, 249–53
  listed by name, 29–31
  manual, 245–46
  memory requirements, 135–36
  monitor display, 142
  preview mode, 35
  and printers, 104

saving file in, 289
selection of, 186–206
solving problems with, 260–69
troubleshooting strategies, 257–69
Word processor accessories, 31–32
Wordstar, 29, 199
Wozniak, Steve, 111
WriteNow, 30, 187
Write protect tab, 271
Writers:
  attitudes toward computers, 58–60
  benefits of modem for, 160
  changed by computer use, 63–68
  computer costs and, 120
  computers for, 121, 128–48
  database needs of, 42, 212–13
  exchanging information on CIS, 61
  hardware needed by, 129–48
  on-line writer's conferences, 217
  portable computers for, 163
  printers suited for, 149–159
  reasons for using computers, 9–22
  software buying strategies, 183–86
  word processor features for, 195–201
  word processors for, 30
Writer's block and computers, 20–21
Writer's conferences on-line, 217
Writer's Digest, 65
Writer's Market, 151
Writer's Workshop, 43
Writing, history of, 60
Writing style, and computer use, 63–65
Wry-neck, 69
WYSIWYG, 31, 143

X

XMODEM, 219
XT, 130, 133, 136, 138, 141, 148
  diskette sizes, 138
  history, 112
  installing boards for, 147
  memory, 136
  slots, 148
Xywrite III Plus, 30, 187, 192, 206

Z

ZyINDEX, 49, 209